Chinese I

Contents

Acknowledgments

This book originated from a panel on "New Chinese Ecocinema and Ethics of Environmental Imagination" that we organized for the annual convention of the Association for Asian Studies in Boston, March 2007. However, the conceptualization of the details and the final materialization of the project as a whole result from the cooperation of many individuals and span distant geographies: from the niches of eco-habitats of northern California, through the immense reach of Australasia, to the spaces of cosmopolitan Hong Kong. The trans-Pacific and trans-Oceanic nature of this book has been particularly helpful in broadening the scope of our vision. As co-editors, we thank all the contributors for taking time out of their busy schedules to join us in this collaborative work. We are especially grateful to the publishers of Hong Kong University Press: Colin Day and Michael Duckworth, and to our project editor Dawn Lau. Their interest, support, and professionalism are very much appreciated. We have also learned a great deal from two rounds of constructive reviews of the book manuscript by anonymous reviewers of Hong Kong University Press.

Sheldon H. Lu would like to dedicate this book to his son, Michael, born in the productive Year of Ox, the same year as the book's publication date. Michael will plough the field and harvest the fruits of labor in due time.

Jiayan Mi would like to thank the Committee on the Support of Scholarly Activity at The College of New Jersey for the award of 2008–2009 SOSA, and the dean of Culture and Society, who offered him a mini-research grant for revising and editing the manuscript. He also would like to dedicate this book to his daughter Coco Mi, a little green guard whose buzzwords are: turn off the lights/ save the Earth.

An early version of Chapter 3 by Nick Kaldis appeared as "National Development and Individual Trauma in *Wushan yunyu* (*In Expectation*)," in *The China Review* Vol. 4, No. 2 (Fall 2004): 165–191. An early version of Chapter 8 by Ban Wang appeared as "Documentary as Haunting of the Real: The Logic of Capital in *Blind Shaft*," in *Asian Cinema* Vol. 16, No. 1 (Spring/Summer 2005): 4–15. Both essays have been thoroughly revised and rewritten for this anthology.

Sheldon H. Lu
Jiayan Mi

Contributors

Chia-ju Chang is assistant professor of Chinese at Brooklyn College, New York. She received her Ph.D. in comparative literature from Rutgers University. Her research interests include ecocriticism, ecofeminism, animal studies, Zen philosophy, and post-Mao Chinese cinema. She is currently working on developing Zenist concepts of "dangxia" (this very moment) and the interconnectedness between the human and the nonhuman as an alternative mode for ethics of care and egalitarianism. She was recently elected to the Executive Council of ASLE (Association for the Study of Literature and Environment) for the term of 2009–2011.

Mary Farquhar is professor at Griffith University, president of the Chinese Studies Association of Australia (2005–2007), and director of the China Law Network in Australia. She specializes in China studies and is also qualified in law. Her publications include *Children's Literature in China: From Lu Xun to Mao Zedong* (1999), which won the annual International Children's Literature Association Award in 1999. Her most recent work is on Chinese cinemas with Chris Berry, *China Onscreen: Cinema and Nation* (2006), currently being translated into Chinese. She has won multiple Australian Research Council Discovery grants, the most recent being on Chinese martial arts movies and Australian technology (2007–2009).

Andrew Hageman is a doctoral candidate in the English Department at the University of California, Davis. His research focuses on intersections of technology, ecology, and ideology in late twentieth-century literature, cinema, and critical theory. He has published an ecocritical essay on David Lynch's *Mulholland Drive* in *Scope*.

Donghui He is assistant professor of modern languages and literature at Whitman College.

Nick Kaldis is associate professor of Chinese cinema, language, and literature at Binghamton University (SUNY). He has published essays on modern Chinese literature, contemporary Chinese film (from Taiwan, Hong Kong, and the PRC), and numerous translations. His manuscript on Lu Xun's *Yecao* is currently under submission, and he is co-editing a collection of nature writing essays by Taiwanese author Liu Kexiang.

Xiaoping Lin is associate professor of Asian art and cinema at Queens College, City University of New York. He has published extensively on contemporary Chinese visual arts and films in *Third Text* and other art journals. His new book is entitled *Children of Coca Cola and Marx: Chinese Avant-Garde Art and Independent Cinema*.

Xinmin Liu currently teaches in the East Asian Languages and Literature Department at the University of Pittsburgh. He received his Ph.D. in comparative literature at Yale in 1997 and has since taught courses on Chinese language, literature, and culture at Trinity, Wesleyan University, and Yale. His teaching and research are chiefly on ethical and philosophical implications in realms of selfhood, sociality, and progress. Author of many published journal articles, he has given numerous lectures at academic and professional meetings. He has recently completed a book manuscript with the title *Guideposts to Self Realization: Evolution, Sociality and Ethics in Modern China*, and is currently working on a book project on themes intersecting ecocriticism, ethics, and cultural histories in contemporary China.

Sheldon H. Lu is professor of comparative literature at the University of California, Davis. He is the author of *From Historicity to Fictionality: The Chinese Poetics of Narrative* (1994; Korean edition 2001); *China, Transnational Visuality, Global Postmodernity* (2001); *Culture, Mirror-Image, Poetics* (in Chinese, 2002); *Chinese Modernity and Global Biopolitics: Studies in Literature and Visual Culture* (2007); editor of *Transnational Chinese Cinemas: Identity, Nationhood, Gender* (1997), and co-editor of *Chinese-Language Film: Historiography, Poetics, Politics* (2005).

Jiayan Mi is a tenured assistant professor of literature, film and critical theory in the departments of English and Modern Languages and Literature at the College of New Jersey. He is the author of *Self-Fashioning and Reflexive Modernity in Modern Chinese Poetry, 1919–1949* (2004). He is currently completing a book project, tentatively titled *Heteroscapes: Topography and Contested Navigations in Modern Chinese Literature and Film*. He has published articles in both Chinese and English on comparative literature, visual and cinematic culture, globalization and cultural consumption, and East-West postcolonial and gender politics.

Jing Nie received her Master's degree in film studies from the School of Film at Ohio University, and her Ph.D. in comparative literature from the University of California, Davis. She is working on a book manuscript: *Beijing in the Shadow of Globalization: Production of Spatial Poetics in Chinese Film, Literature, Drama.*

Jerome Silbergeld is the P. Y. and Kinmay W. Tang Professor of Chinese Art History and director of the Tang Center for East Asian Art at Princeton University. He teaches and publishes in the areas of Chinese painting history, both traditional and contemporary, Chinese cinema and photography, and Chinese architecture and gardens. He is the author of more than fifty articles and book chapters, as well as seven books and three edited volumes, including *Chinese Painting Style* (1982), *Contradictions: Artistic Life, the Socialist State, and the Chinese Painter Li Huasheng* (1993), *China into Film* (1999), *Hitchcock with a Chinese Face* (2004), and a book on director Jiang Wen's two films entitled *Body in Question* (2008).

Chris Tong is a Ph.D. student in comparative literature at the University of California, Davis. He co-founded the Research Cluster on Space and Spatiality at the UC Davis Humanities Institute, where he had served as a graduate student researcher. He received his Bachelor's degree from Stanford University.

Ban Wang is William Haas Professor of Chinese Studies in the Departments of Asian Languages and Comparative Literature at Stanford University. His major publications include *The Sublime Figure of History: Aesthetics and Politics in Twentieth-Century China* (1997) and *Illuminations from the Past* (2004). He has been a recipient of research fellowships from the National Endowment for the Humanities and the Institute for Advanced Study at Princeton. He taught at Beijing Foreign Studies University, SUNY-Stony Brook, Harvard University, and Rutgers University. His current project is tentatively entitled *China and the World: Geopolitics, Aesthetics, and Cosmopolitanism.*

Hongbing Zhang is an assistant professor in the Department of English and Foreign Languages at Fayetteville State University, North Carolina. He is currently completing a book manuscript on travel, space, and cultural transformations in China from the 1860s to 1910s. He received his Ph.D. in East Asian Studies at the University of Chicago.

Introduction

Cinema, Ecology, Modernity

Sheldon H. Lu

If there were water
And no rock
If there were rock
And also water
And water
A spring
A pool among the rock
If there were the sound of water only
Not the cicada
And dry grass singing
But sound of water over a rock
Where the hermit-thrush sings in the pine trees
Drip drop drip drop drop drop drop
But there is no water

T. S. Eliot, *The Waste Land*

Following the economic boom in the post-Mao-Deng and late socialist era, China is now facing unprecedented environmental crises. Although Chinese cinema has given consistent attention to the grave ecological deterioration in this part of the planet, scholarly study of ecological consciousness in Chinese films has been largely neglected. In order to respond to an urgent issue as well as to fill a critical gap, this volume raises the concept of "Chinese ecocinema" as a new critical paradigm in Chinese film studies. The purpose of this volume is to investigate how Chinese films engage environmental and ecological issues in the active re-imagination of locale, place, and space.

China's ecological woes make up a long list: massive earthquakes; epidemics of SARS and bird flu; periodic sandstorms; air, water, and soil pollution; desertification; flooding and drought; deforestation; the loss of land to urban sprawl; and numerous coalmine accidents. China, like the rest of the world, is now facing the age of global warming as well, a worldwide phenomenon to which China itself has become a major contributor. The temperature in Chinese cities has risen steadily over the years. As icebergs thin and melt away in the North Pole, so do the glaciers of the Himalayas and the Tibetan Plateau. Ice from the Himalayas is the source of water for China's mightiest arteries — Yangtze River and Yellow River.

Our present project partakes of a broad emergent critical tradition known as ecocriticism. However, existing ecocriticism is predominantly centered on the model of literature. An influential anthology of ecocriticism states that "ecocriticism is the study of the relationship between literature and the physical environment."[1] Moreover, ecocriticism is mutually imbricated with the study of biopower or biopolitics, namely, the study of the production and reproduction of life, the relationship between the human body and the ecosystem, and the controlling and administering of the human body in modern capitalist and socialist regimes.[2] For us, ecocriticism should not be limited to literature but include other art forms and media. However, studies of films from an ecocritical point of view are few and patchy. Film criticism ought to be a major constituent of ecocriticism. In the simplest terms, ecocinema is cinema with an ecological consciousness. It articulates the relationship of human beings to the physical environment, earth, nature, and animals from a biocentric, non-anthropocentric point of view. In the final analysis, ecocinema pertains to nothing less than life itself. Last but not least, the study of Chinese ecocinema specifically should be placed squarely within the specific intellectual and socio-historical Chinese contexts that may be different from Euro-American settings in significant ways.[3]

This collective project focuses on the cinematic traditions of Greater China: mainland China, Taiwan, and Hong Kong. Though the historical range of the book is from the 1980s to the present, we do not mean to suggest that there is no ecocinema prior to the 1980s in the region of the world that has been called, perhaps problematically, "Greater China." It is a matter of choice for us to concentrate on the cinema since the 1980s because this period marks the beginning of a new phase of a state-sponsored modernization campaign that has resulted in ecological problems on an unprecedented scale. As readers will see, the book gives more coverage to films made in mainland China; this has to do with the fact that the magnitude and severity of the ecological problems of the mainland are mind-boggling and unparalleled elsewhere. It is no surprise that so many contemporary Chinese films embody a sense of ecological crisis.

First of all, Chinese ecocinema is a critical grid, an interpretive strategy. It offers film viewers and scholars a new perspective in the examination of Chinese film culture. Second, ecocinema is a description of a conscious film practice among numerous Chinese film artists. What we describe in this volume are mostly individual, independent film initiatives that often stand in opposition to the prevalent cultural climate at the time. Given the enormity of China's ecological challenges, China's ecocinematic imagination is necessarily historically situated. Such a cinema can be nothing but a direct reflection on and response to urgent social, historical, cultural, and environmental issues.

Chinese ecocinema traverses feature films as well as documentaries. It partakes of both the New Chinese Cinema and the New Chinese Documentary. As we establish the genealogy of Chinese ecocinema in the following sections, we see that a profound ecological consciousness has been rooted in the very beginning of the New Chinese Cinema since the early 1980s.[4] Hence, ecocinema has been a vital constituent of the New Chinese Cinema. Furthermore, it has also been part and parcel of what is known as the New Chinese Documentary (*Zhongguo xin jilupian*) that emerged from the late 1980s.[5] The purported pursuit of realism lies at the heart of this documentary trend, where the candid camera eye looks at neglected, suppressed aspects of life and marginal social groups. A concern with the environment has been a main preoccupation of such a documentary impulse.

Epistemes of Nature and Humanity

Ancient Chinese cosmology and ethics are largely centered on the notions of the "unity of Heaven and humanity" (*tianren heyi* 天人合一) and "spiritual correspondence between Heaven and humanity" (*tianren ganying* 天人感應).[6] This was the dominant, although not the only, tradition. Even at times of violent ruptures involving war and dynastic change, a "mandate of heaven" (*tianming* 天命) was required to authorize the overthrow of the existing human order.

Socialist China under Mao Zedong registered the most radical break from the traditional Chinese belief in a harmonious social and natural order. Mao's revolutionary theory is a style of thought that stresses "contradiction" and "struggle" in human society as well as between humanity and nature. Throughout the Mao era (1949–1976) in Chinese history, the theory and practice of class struggle was promulgated in a heavy-handed manner. Class struggle was thought to be the key to revolution and socialist nation-building. Mao's idea of voluntarism (*zhuguan nengdong xing* 主觀能動性, literally "subjective initiative"), namely the belief in the infinite capacity of the human will to change adverse physical environment, commands an extreme anthropocentric attitude toward nature. The philosophy of struggle implies human beings' inevitable conflict with and eventual triumph over nature. Humanity must emerge as the master of nature. To leapfrog into modernity, subjective initiative could inspire and empower backward, disadvantaged China to catch up with the advanced capitalist West as well as allow Mao himself to overtake the Soviet Union as the new leader of the world communist movement. In the frenzy of the catch-up game during the Great Leap Forward period (1958), a most egregious expression of such voluntarism is seen in a slogan that was sanctioned by none other than Mao himself: "the field's yield goes as high as human courage goes" (*ren you duoda dan, di you duogao chan* 人有多大膽，地有多高產). This callous ignorance of the laws of nature would ultimately lead to an agricultural disaster and a nationwide famine.

In the early and mid-1970s, Mao and his followers rewrote Chinese history as a "history of the struggle between Confucianism and Legalism" (*ru fa douzheng shi* 儒法鬥爭史). They excavated sources of traditional Chinese thought to legitimate their conception. Mao's voluntarism was corroborated by such notions as "humanity's determined triumph over nature" (*ren ding sheng tian* 人定勝天) and "subjugate the course of Heaven and appropriate it [for human ends]" (*zhi tianming er yongzhi* 制天命而用之), which were interpreted as a major strand of thought of the Confucian philosopher Xunzi 荀子 (340–245 B.C.), who was miraculously portrayed as a Legalist (*fajia* 法家) in Mao's rereading of Chinese intellectual history.[7] A sublime jingoism of the state propaganda machine targeting the peasants is "fight Heaven, struggle with the earth, and win a high yield" (*zhantian doudi duogaochan* 戰天鬥地奪高產). In Mao-style socialist agriculture, land must be made arable as much as possible. Virgin soil is turned into wheat fields, mountains are reshaped into tiered rice paddy, wilderness is burned and converted to farmland, and natural lakes are turned into fish ponds. This resulted in a fundamental disequilibrium of the ecosystem.

In the post-Mao era, the Chinese Communist Party officially declared the end of class struggle and took economic development as the central task of the country. This state-sponsored developmentalism aimed at modernization that is measured by substantial annual increase in GDP. In the single-minded pursuit of high economic growth rate, natural environment and human habitat were steadily deteriorating year by year. In such a primitive industrialization process, toxic industrial waste was directly dumped into rivers. As China was earning the title of the "factory of the world," a large part of the country was in fact becoming a global dumpster and wasteland.

Deng Xiaoping's Reforms and Openness (*gaige kaifang*) was marked by a profound apoliticism and economism. Deng did not seek to inspire the Chinese by propagating ever newer slogans and theories; he discouraged open discussions on issues of ideology. Although there is such a thing as "Deng Xiaoping Theory" (*Deng Xiaoping lilun*) in the parlance of the Chinese Communist Party, Deng's theory boiled down to a few straightforward aphorisms. One of his most well-known phrases is "development is the imperative" (*fazhan shi ying daoli* 發展是硬道理). In a way, Deng reversed Mao's voluntarism and redirected the country's attention to the building of the economic base. As a consequence, economic development was often achieved at the expense of nature and ecology. In the least, the ecosystem was neglected so long as a high rate of economic growth was achieved.

At the beginning of the twenty-first century, the Chinese leadership headed by Hu Jintao promoted the slogan of "harmonious society" (*hexie shehui* 和諧社會). This is a corrective reaction to social and environmental problems that resulted from decades of neoliberalist development. As David Harvey points out, Deng's China constitutes a unique version of "neoliberalism with Chinese characteristics."[8] The unchecked neoliberalist market economy is a powerful engine for economic growth as well as a tool for ecological degradation. In the face of glaring economic disparity, social inequality, and ecological destruction, the current leadership calls for "harmony" with nature and within society. The idea of "green GDP" is proposed as a counterbalance to the previous reckless pursuit of one-sided economic growth.

The New Chinese Ecocinema

In the context of the post-Mao New Chinese Cinema, it appears evident that the rethinking of Chinese modernity has been intricately tied to a heightened awareness of the ecosystem. China's belated modernity has often been expressed as water pathology. Such examples are plenty. *Yellow Earth* (1984), a foundational text of the New Cinema and the Fifth Generation, should be taken as a classic example of the New Chinese Ecocinema. Barren land, water shortage, and inert earth are signs of an ill ecological system, and as such the symptoms of a dying way of life. This yellow land, a metonymy for China, is in need of fresh water and new energy for rejuvenation and rebirth.

The film is also an anguished meditation on the possibility of revolutionary "subjective initiative" to effect change to inert nature and unenlightened masses. The story is about an Eighth Route Army soldier's visit to a backward village on the banks of the Yellow River in northern Shaanxi Province. His duty is to collect folksongs and then transform them into revolutionary songs as a way to raise peasants' consciousness. However, this tale of enlightenment leaves the viewer with an ambiguous ending, if not outright pessimism. The girl Cuiqiao, one of the enlightened few, drowns in the Yellow River as she attempts to cross it to join the revolution. There is a severe drought at the end of the film, but the peasants still stubbornly believe in the power of the "dragon-king of the sea" to save the parched land. It is uncertain if the communist soldier would ever succeed in awakening the masses and transforming nature.

The film *Old Well* (1987), directed by Wu Tianming, nicknamed the "godfather" of the Fifth Generation, with Zhang Yimou as the lead actor, also takes on the central theme of water shortage. The wells in the village are drying up. The source of life disappears. Digging and finding a new well becomes an allegory of the replenishment and renewal of the old village, and by extension, China itself.

The construction of modern China involves not only the rejection of dusty backward yellow earth, but at the same time the projection of a blue imagination. This is the message of the influential television series *River Elegy* (*Heshang*, 1988–1989), which urges the Chinese to bid farewell to the backwater of China's river culture and to openly embrace the ocean. China's old hydraulic system of rivers and canals has less to offer to the needs of a modernizing society. Modernity is fantasized as a blue ocean. Oceanic modernity implies two things: political liberty and neoliberalist market economy. As we have seen, Deng's rule stifled political liberty and crushed the student democracy movement in Tiananmen Square in 1989. But Deng's China accelerated the entry to the blue ocean, namely, a global neoliberalist market economy buttressed by international trade.

However different they might seem in certain respects, voluntarism and developmentalism both treat nature as a standing reserve for human appropriation. This instrumental rationality finds its greatest expression in the building of the countless dams and reservoirs along China's rivers. These man-made structures alter the natural course of flow of the rivers and destroy the original ecological system. Residents, factories, and cities all rush in to use and expropriate China's tired and overstretched water resources. The most controversial of all is the Three Gorges Dam project. Intended to control flooding and generate electricity, the construction of the dam has caused the destruction of numerous homes along the river, inundated historical and archeological sites, and disturbed the original equilibrium of the ecosystem. Jia Zhangke's feature film *Still Life* (2006) and his documentary *Dong* (2006) direct the viewer's attention to the plight of the people along the river in the aftermath of the building of the dam. The taming of Yangtze River is a forceful manifestation of humanity's attempt to conquer nature.

China's youthful fantasy about leaving pre-modern earth behind and leaping into oceanic modernity comes to a moment of critical self-reflection in the late 1990s and the early twenty-first century. The negative psychological and social side effects of lopsided developmentalism have been acutely felt by residents of China. Films such as *Shower* (1999) take on *Yellow Earth* and reverse the trope of water from pathology to a spiritual healing power. The fantasy of blue oceanic modernity (represented by the coastal city of Shenzhen) is found to be inadequate. The traditional bathhouse is portrayed as a source of harmony and a safe enclave against the onslaught of overhasty modernization and commercialization. The demolition of the bathhouse to provide space for the building of a shopping center at the end of the film laments the disappearance of a mode of dwelling.

While the water imagery in *Shower* derives from the ancient city of Beijing, Lou Ye's critically acclaimed *Suzhou River* (2000) takes the viewer to an unsightly site at the edge of Shanghai, which has been positioned as the shining showcase of China's modernization since the 1990s. The film focuses on the underbelly of Chinese society and unfolds a mysterious tale of murder, love, double identity, and confusion along the muddy Suzhou River. A glimpse of a fairytale-like Nordic blonde mermaid on the filthy bank of Suzhou River promises to magically re-enchant the ugly modern world. However, in reality, the mermaid is nothing but a show girl in a seedy nightclub where she dresses up as a mermaid, wears a blonde wig, and swims in a water tank to entertain guests.

Environmental destruction and urban demolition have surfaced as important themes in Chinese cinema, literature, and arts in the 1990s and the early twenty-first century. Indeed, the whole nation is often blind to the ecosystem as it is rebuilding in a reckless rush to globalization and modernization. Because of the unprecedented scale of modernization-cum-destruction, an ethical imperative and a bioethics have come to the fore in Chinese cinema. One sees screen images of pristine organic communities and tranquil pre-modern ways of life remote from the noisy streets of urban centers. There is a sense of nostalgia for pre-modern, pre-capitalist modes of living. Furthermore, a renewed spirituality is found in cinematic discourse. A whole range of ecological themes has surfaced in feature films as well as documentaries. The return to (Buddhist) holistic thinking, the non-anthropocentric treatment of animals, the caring for mentally challenged people and physically disabled citizens, and the establishment of "green sovereignty" are some of the manifestations of a new biocentric approach to nature, humanity, and modernity.

There are noticeably several prominent themes and subjects in Chinese ecocinema. The following categories of ecocinema are preliminary, and by no means exclusive and exhaustive. Sometimes several themes or subjects overlap, and can be interrelated and co-present in the same film.

1) How the lives of ordinary people are affected by the destruction of nature and environmental degradation in the relentless processes of revolution, modernization, and industrialization. Such films include *Yellow Earth*, *Old Well*, *Suzhou River*, *The Marriage of Tuya* (*Tuya de hunshi*, Wang Quan'an, 2007), and *Still Life* (Jia Zhangke, 2006).

2) The effects of urban planning, demolition, and relocation on the lives of ordinary residents. The fate of migrants in the city. The films *Shower*, *The World* (Jia Zhangke, 2004), and *Lost in Beijing* (*Pingguo*, Li Yu, 2007) address such themes.

3) The lives and struggles of people with physical or mental disabilities. Good examples include *Beautiful Mama* (*Piaoliang mama*, Sun Zhou, 2001), a story of the relationship between a courageous mother (portrayed by Gong Li) and her mentally handicapped son; Zhang Yimou's *Happy Times* (*Xingfu shiguang*, 2000) is a comedy featuring a young blind masseuse (portrayed by Dong Jie); *The World of Zhouzhou* (*Zhouzhou de shijie*, Zhang Yiqing, 1998) is a documentary about a mentally challenged kid who aspires to be a musician/conductor; Shi Runjiu's documentary *Anding Hospital* (*Anding yiyuan*, 2002) focuses on the relationship between a doctor and her patients in a mental hospital in Beijing; *Shower* is in part a film about love for a mentally challenged character, Erming, the younger brother.

4) The relationship between humans and animals. Examples include *Cala, My Dog* (*Kala shi tiao gou*, Lu Xuechang, 2004); *Kekexili: Mountain Patrol* (*Kekexili*, Lu Chuan, 2005) on the subject of anti-poaching in Tibet and Qinghai; Zhang Yiqing's documentary *Ying and Bai* (*Ying yu Bai*, 1999), a story about a panda and his female trainer Ying and how they have lived together for many years.

5) Projection and description of an organic communal mode of life distinct from the daily routines of civilized city folks. Such stories are usually about China's ethnic minorities and are set in remote geographic areas. *Mongolian Ping Pong* (*Menggu pingpong*, aka *Green Grassland* [*Lü caodi*], Ning Hao, 2004) relates the story of children in the primitive grassland of pre-industrial Inner Mongolia. Tian Zhuangzhuang's documentary *Delamu* (2004) tells the story of ethnic minorities in a mountainous region. *Postmen in the Mountains* (*Nashan naren nagou*, Huo Jianqi, 1999) describes communal life and the relationship between human beings as well as between humans and animals in the mountains. Even Feng Xiaogang's commercial blockbuster *The World without Thief* (*Tianxia wuzei*, 2005) does not forget to pay lip service to pre-industrial Tibet as a spiritual pure land free of greed and crime. Sun Zengtian's documentaries *The Last Mountain God* (*Zuihou de shanshen*, 1992) and *Reindeer, Oh Reindeer* (*Shenlu*, 1997) track the customs and beliefs of ethnic minorities, who were formerly communities of hunters in the thick forests of the Greater Xing'anling mountains in Northeast China. Their way of life is disappearing in a modernizing world.

6) A return to religious, holistic thinking and practice and the difficulty of doing so in a commercialized society. Examples include Ning Hao's film *Incense* (*Xianghuo*, 2003) and *The Silent Holy Stones* (*Jingjing de mani shi*, 2006) by Tibetan filmmaker Wanma Caidan.

Space, Locale, Landscape

The New Chinese Cinema in the early and mid-1980s is very much built on a re-imagination of the locale. There is a re-orientation toward the rural, primitive landscape as a way of distancing from the hackneyed, corrupt, and sterile habits of urban culture. The projected landscape in the New Chinese Cinema is disorienting for the familiar conventional film viewer steeped in the tradition of socialist realism. It seems as if the spectator could only begin to glimpse at the truth by virtue of remoteness to the urban centers of (Han) civilization. In *Yellow Earth*, nature — vast skies and endless mountains in the fashion of a Chinese landscape painting — invites viewers to properly rethink something as familiar as the yellow earth under their feet. The defamiliarization and refamiliarization of natural landscape is an unnatural re-educational process in the awakening of a new cultural, environmental consciousness. The same can be said about Chen Kaige's *King of Children* (*Haizi wang*, 1987), a ponderous film that reflects on the possibility of unlearning entrenched doctrines and old habits and relearning things directly from the source — nature. In Zhang Yimou's debut film *Red Sorghum* (*Hong gaoliang*, 1988), it takes a wild uninhibited encounter between the sexes (grandpa and grandma) in a fertile green sorghum field to rejuvenate the vital primitive spirit of the Chinese people to fight on and live. The rural, the primitive, and the foreign are equally important in the films of another giant from the Fifth Generation of filmmakers, Tian Zhuangzhuang. In Tian's earliest films *On the Hunting Ground* (*Liechang zhasa*, 1985) and *Horse Thief* (*Daoma zei*, 1985), the defamiliarization of and consequent insight into the nature of Chinese culture and history must be obtained through a detour — by way of traveling to the non-Han ethnic minority territories of the Mongolian grassland and Tibetan plateau. In his documentary *Delamu*, Tian continues his exploration of the life of the Chinese ethnic minority. The memorable film *Sacrificed Youth* (*Qingchun ji*, 1985) by the Fourth Generation woman director Zhang Nuanxin is also an educational film, telling the story of how urban youths live among ethnic minorities in a far-away corner of China and how they unlearn the stifling habits accumulated in the city life of the Han.

Landscape, a term that is usually associated with natural scenery, has accrued a new dimension of meaning during China's process of industrialization. Indeed, *Manufactured Landscapes* (2006) is the name of a documentary by Canadian film director Jennifer Baichwal and photographer Edward Burtynsky. The film follows Burtynsky to China as his camera captures the immense industrial man-made, "manufactured" landscapes. These are huge awe-inspiring factories, mines, shipyards, and dams created by the Chinese as they march on the path to industrialization and rightfully earn the title of the "Factory of the World." The sheer physical size of such industrial sites exceeds ordinary human imagination in such a way that no anamorphic lens is wide enough to scan their totality. These man-made physical structures have perpetually changed the face of the planet and the living environment of humanity. Such mammoth manufactured landscapes literally surpass the reach of human vision and the scope of imagination, and constitute a veritable new sublime, a "sweatshop sublime."[9] The people who work in these factories and sweatshops receive a minimal wage as they churn out billions of shoes and toys, and countless commodities for the consumption of the entire world population. Critics, artists, and cultural workers find their tools utterly inadequate to map out this monstrous totality, let alone effect change to the vast chain of mechanisms of production in the capitalist modern world.

As tens of millions of exploited workers toil for a meager wage in China's numerous sweatshops, especially along the coastline and the southern province of Guangdong, the emergent middle and upper class, the *nouveau riche*, move out of urban centers to theme villas newly built in the outskirts. They live a bourgeois lifestyle in simulated English towns, French villas, and Dutch villages. These theme villas are European-style homes catering to the taste of the upcoming Chinese bourgeoisie who have grown rich in what is officially called a "socialist market economy." One particular theme park, World Park (*Shijie gongyuan*), is the very subject and setting of Jia Zhangke's film *The World*, a film that has received extensive commentary by at least three contributors in this volume. The plight of those earthbound migrant workers in the park is a jarring satire of China's collective fantasy of upward mobility in a globalized world.

In preparation for the Olympic Games, urban construction and destruction proceeded on an unprecedented scale with breakneck speed. Beijing's cityscape underwent another round of facelift. The Big Egg (National Opera), the Bird Nest (Olympic Stadium), the Big Shorts (new China Central Television Tower), the new terminal of the Beijing International Airport, all designed by famous Western architects, were erected as symbols of China's globalization and its joining the rest of the world. While such monumentalization of space continues, the commercialization of space also proceeds unabated. Old buildings, hutongs, and neighborhoods are torn down to make room for the construction of shopping malls (*shangchang*), commercial districts (*shangye qu*), commercial streets (*shangye jie*), pedestrian streets or plazas (*buxing jie*). For instance, renovated Nanjing Road in Shanghai, Wangfujing in Beijing, and Fuzimiao in Nanjing are well-known examples of such shopper-friendly, touristy "commercial pedestrian streets."

The monumentalization of space in the early twenty-first century is at the same time the globalization of space, projecting an image of China's openness to the outside world. This is unlike the monumentalization of national space in the Mao era, of which the most famous case is the completion of "ten great buildings" (*shida jianzhu*) in Beijing in 1959 to commemorate the tenth anniversary of the founding of the People's Republic of China. Those buildings — Great Hall of People, Museum of Chinese History, Beijing Train Station, Agriculture Exhibition Hall, and so on — are monuments of socialist modernity and markers of Chinese national solidarity.

From the 1990s to the twenty-first century, massive waves of urban demolition and destruction have radically and irreversibly changed traditional Chinese cityscape. Consequently, the representation of urban space has also become more prominent in Chinese cinema. Beijing's signature traditional courtyard, "*sihe yuan*," formerly populated by the vast majority of residents of the city, is now a luxury home that only the most deep-pocketed can afford to own. Ordinary residents had been driven out of their old, dilapidated, cramped courtyards for the sake of the beautification of Beijing in expectation for the Olympic Games. Shi Runjiu's documentary *Zhang's Stir-Fried Tripe and Old Ji's Family* (*Baodu Zhang he Lao Ji jia*, 2006) is such a tale about the imminent demolition of their homes as part of the city's campaign to clean up for the Games. The two families are located in the scenic Shichahai and Qianhai area. They are told to relocate to other parts of Beijing so that this place can be turned into a beautiful lawn. The Zhang family restaurant is a hundred-year-old family establishment, well liked and frequented by customers in the area. Its special dish of stir-fried tripe is now a rare recipe. The dish will disappear with the demolition (*chai*) and relocation (*qian*) of the restaurant as dictated by the municipal planners. Over against the public, official, state-sponsored, gigantic projects of urban development, Shi's documentary lens lingers on the life dramas of ordinary citizens in small private spaces. For generations these residents have lived in their old courtyards, which they call "home." They now face an uncertain future as they need to move out from an intimate place to an impersonal space. The film narrative follows the characters' fears, discussions, and negotiations about where to build their future home and how to conduct business in an unfamiliar new location.

Organization of the Volume

Environmental consciousness in contemporary Chinese cinema spawns a full range of topics and issues. For the sake of convenience and clarity, we group the chapters in the present collection into four main areas: 1) hydro-politics: water, river, and national trauma; 2) eco-aesthetics, nature, and manufactured landscape; 3) urban space in production and disappearance; 4) bioethics, non-anthropocentrism, green sovereignty.

The authors of this first section tackle the central trope of the river in the cinematic configurations of China's environmental crises. Jiayan Mi probes the pathology of Chinese rivers in the New Chinese Cinema, or in his own terminology, "ecoggedon." Sheldon H. Lu writes about a group of films that are set against the background of the construction of Three Gorges Dam and the impending flooding of the area. Nick Kaldis zeroes in on a single film, *Wushan yunyu* (*In Expectation*, literally *Rain Clouds over Wu Mountain*). All these chapters question the project of Chinese modernity as domination over nature. Andrew Hageman chooses a much smaller river, Suzhou River on the outskirts of Shanghai, and entertains a possible posthumanist perspective in Lou Ye's use of camera angles and narrative points of view in the film *Suzhou River*.

The second part of the book deals with spatial aesthetics, the representation of nature, and the manufacture of "natural landscape" in Chinese cinema. Mary Farquhar describes the creation of "idea-images" (*yijing*) in Zhang Yimou's martial arts film *Hero*. Digitalized landscape in accordance with traditional Chinese aesthetics has added a unique charm to Zhang's orientalist tale. The manufactured pristine, primordial "sinascapes" evoke in fact rather culturally specific impressions of the world of ancient China.[10] Jerome Silbergeld focuses on one particular film by Jia Zhangke, by now the world-famous *World* (*Shijie*, 2004). The film title refers to World Park, a theme park in Beijing that is a simulacrum of landmarks from around the world. The park offers those Chinese, who do not have the means to travel around the world, a vicarious opportunity to trot the globe in what is ironically called the present "age of globalization." Silbergeld teases out the ironies of the film and contemporary Chinese society at large, and at the same time eruditely points out previous examples of the replication of architecture in China's long imperial history. Hongbing Zhang's piece confronts the ugliness of environmental ruins in the films of Jia Zhangke. He analyzes Jia's film aesthetics where human beings are often dwarfed by the enormous background within each picture framework. Diminutive human figures portrayed in long shots are utterly impotent to change and reverse the destruction and ruins surrounding them.

The chapters in the third part of the book zero in on urban space. Ban Wang queries the primitive accumulation of capital and the extraction of raw material from nature in the murder tale *Blind Shaft*. He also focuses on the cityscape of ruins in the Northeast (*Dongbei*), the former industrial heartland and present rust belt of socialist China, in the documentary *West of the Tracks*. Jing Nie seizes on the favorite locale of filmic representation — the capital city of Beijing — to examine urban malaise and alienation resulted from modernization. She analyzes such films as *Cell Phone* (Feng Xiaogang), *Shower* (Zhang Yang), *Beijing Bicycle* (Wang Xiaoshuai), and again the perennially fascinating *The World* (Jia Zhangke). Altogether these films offer a mirage of urban space and cityscape under construction or in the process of disappearance in postsocialist China: simulated, created, demolished, or torn down. Chris Tong focuses on reconfigurations of urban space, not of socialist China, but of capitalist Hong Kong from across the border. The city is still in the process of what Ackbar Abbas calls "disappearance" even after its unification with China. He analyzes several relevant films by Fruit Chan in order to navigate the changing urban space of Hong Kong.

The fourth part of the book is concerned with the emergent bioethics in the age of global environmental crises. Xinmin Liu takes up what seems to be the most difficult yet important question of ecocriticism, i.e., the ethical imperative behind cinematic imaging/imagination. Liu scrutinizes the films of Huo Jianqi among other directors, addressing the themes of community-building, humanity's relationship with nature, and the mode of human dwelling, which are of paramount significance in ecocinema. Xiaoping Lin analyzes Ning Hao's film *Incense*, a heavy yet humorous film about the adventures of a Buddhist monk who tries to preserve his temple and etch out a living for himself in a modernizing secular world that has no use for religion. Similarly, Donghui He focuses her study on the efforts of "reconstructing God-fearing communities" in contemporary films about Tibet by Tibetan and Han Chinese directors. Chia-ju Chang's chapter is an ecofeminist study of the relationship between humans and animals in Chinese and Taiwanese literature and film. All these chapters look at films that search for forms of spirituality in an age that has more faith in commodity-fetish.

Planet Earth

As the temperature of the planet steadily rises, the relationship between visual spectacles and environmental politics also heats up on a global scale. Former American Vice President Al Gore won an Oscar for his documentary *An Inconvenient Truth* at the Academy Awards in 2007. Moreover, he was awarded a Nobel Prize for Peace in 2007. Although he lost the presidential election to George Bush, Jr., he is the clear winner on the environmental front. As China was preparing to seize its moment of international recognition in preparation for the 2008 Olympic Games in Beijing, the world's attention was turned to the polluted air and sky of Beijing. By some estimate, China has surpassed the United States as the biggest emitter of carbon dioxide in the world. Many Chinese cities are on the list of the most polluted cities in the world. Such an unbearable environmental crisis is a wake-up call to Chinese citizens as well as to all people in the world. Ultimately, the degradation of nature is not limited to any particular nation-state at this moment, but is truly a world-historical problem.

Must nature and humanity stand in an antithetical relationship to each other in the global march toward progress and prosperity? If modernity is inevitably predicated on the reduction of the planet to heaps of ruins, Walter Benjamin's messianic forebodings ring particularly true. As Benjamin famously states in his essay "Theses on the Philosophy of History," the angel of history looks back to the past and sees a pile of wreckage and debris, and historical progress cannot be sundered from barbarism and destruction.[11] T. W. Adorno further develops this strain of thought and elaborates on the notion of "natural history" (*Naturgeschichte*). The subtle co-extension and equal importance of the two terms "nature" (*Natur*) and "history" (*Geschichte*) in the original German are lost in the English translation. The question is how one can grasp nature as historical and history as natural in all their transitoriness. "The starting point here is that history, as it lies before us, presents itself as thoroughly discontinuous, not only in that it contains disparate circumstances and facts, but also because it contains structural disparities."[12] Human history thus consists of fragments, discontinuities, disjunctures, and ruins. In contrast to original nature, human history has transformed, in the words of Georg Lukács, into a "second nature," which is an alienated world of convention, reification, rationality, technology, and industrialization. The work of art ought to play a special role in the resurrection of the petrified, degenerate, anthropocentric world. In a dialectical leap of thought, Adorno explains the function of "signification," or what we might call "cultural expression," in regard to nature and humanity in the following manner:

> The basic quality of the transience of the earthly signifies nothing
> but just such a relationship between nature and history: all being or
> everything existing is to be grasped as the interweaving of historical

and natural being. As transience all original-history is absolutely present. It is present in the form of "signification." "Signification" means that the elements of nature and history are not fused with each other, rather they break apart and interweave at the same time in such a fashion that the natural appears as a sign for history and history, where it seems to be most historical, appears as a sign for nature.[13]

"Signification," in the form of allegory for Benjamin, or film art in our case, is that which might overcome the division between nature and history. This is the humanization of nature and the naturalization of humanity toward an organic synthesis of the two. Film art is, in an appropriately Benjaminian-Bazinian fashion, nothing less than the redemption of physical reality. The work of art thus re-awakens nature after it has been subjugated to domination and devastation in the Enlightenment-modernization process. In its highest aspiration, ecocinema purports to redeem the fallen world of ruins and eco-catastrophes and re-enchant the imperiled planet.

Filmmakers, like all cultural workers, have a stake in the kind of world they wish to live in or imagine about. Cultural critics share this responsibility of building and envisioning a better future. The ethical imperative for humanity at the present historical juncture ought to be a turn to the planet. In regard to this new critical orientation, Masao Miyoshi writes the most daring words:

Literature and literary studies now have one basis and goal: to nurture our common bonds to the planet — to replace the imaginaries of exclusionist familialism, communitarianism, nationhood, ethnic culture, regionalism, "globalization," or even humanism, with the ideal of planetarianism. Once we accept this planet-based totality, we might for once agree in humility to devise a way to share with all the rest our only true public space and resources.[14]

I would add one caveat to Miyoshi's exposition of "planetarianism" — that is to broaden his range of "literature and literary studies" to include film and film studies, as well as all other cultural expressions and the studies thereof.

Part I.

Hydro-Politics: Water, River, and National Trauma

Framing Ambient *Unheimlich*:
Ecoggedon, Ecological Unconscious, and Water Pathology in New Chinese Cinema

Jiayan Mi[1]

This is a ditch of desperate dead water,
Where wind can blow but raise no ripples.
Best just to throw in more scraps of copper and iron,
Might as well pour in your leftovers of cold porridge.

This is a stretch of hopeless dead water,
Which is certainly not where beauty resides,
Best just to give it up for ugliness to cultivate,
And see what kind of world he can turn it into.

Wen Yiduo, "Dead Water," 1925[2]

The above epigraph is taken from the well-known poem "Dead Water" (*Sishui*), written in 1925 by Wen Yiduo, a precursor of modern Chinese poetry, just after he had returned from his studies in America to a China torn by civil war. In this poem Wen expresses poignantly his anger, despair, and hopelessness over China's poverty, corruption, misery, and chaos. Obviously "a ditch of dead water" stands for a China in which the poet can find neither hope for the Chinese people nor a sense of beauty in China's natural environment, because the "water" that nurtures and sustains China is "dead."

So, in a very radical and perhaps anti-ecological manner the poet calls on his people to dump more wastes and pollutants ("scraps of copper and iron" and "leftovers" of food) into the stretch of water so that its "ecosystem" (its social and political system) will deteriorate even more rapidly and, as the poet anticipates, a new and different world will be born out of its ruins. Although Wen's wish to destroy a hopeless world is "unecological," his approach is not literal but metaphorical, sarcastic, and even surrealistic. In contrast, what is happening to the water resources in the contemporary world is by no means rhetorical or fictitious but indeed a bleak reality of "dead water."

Global and China's Water Crisis

Water, a fundamental source of life, is now facing an unprecedented crisis that is threatening massive catastrophes to all life on earth. Given the increasingly grave situation, it may be that the world will end not by nuclear bombs but by water — its scarcity (drought), its excess (flood), its toxicity (pollution), or other cataclysms (hydrological dams). A report entitled "Water for People, Water for Life," issued by the World Water Assessment Program (WWAP) in 2003, states that "by 2020, the average water supply per person worldwide is expected to shrink by one third compared to now" and as a result, "25,000 people will die daily from hunger with an estimated 815 million people suffering from malnutrition."[3]

Another report, entitled "Beyond Scarcity: Power, Poverty and the Global Water Crisis," issued by the United Nations Development Programme (UNDP) gives additional startling facts about the global water crisis. According to this report, "some 1.1 billion people in the developing world do not have access to a minimal amount of clean water ... Some 2.6 billion people — half the developing world's population — do not have access to basic sanitation."[4] Due to this deprivation in water and sanitation, some 1.8 million children die each year from diarrhea. The causes of this crisis, the report states, can be traced to poverty, inequality, and unequal power relationships as well as flawed water management policies.

As a result of global warming and climate change, some parts of the world have suffered devastating flooding, thunderstorms, and water-borne natural disasters such as Hurricane Katrina, the 2004 Indian Ocean tsunami, and El Nino, which have inspired Hollywood water-themed films such as *Waterworld*, *A. I.*, and *The Day after Tomorrow*, as well as Al Gore's documentary *An Inconvenient Truth*.

The water crisis has affected China most severely. According to Ma Jun's report in his groundbreaking book *China's Water Crisis*,[5] China faces water shortages, water pollution, and a deterioration in water quality: four hundred out of six hundred cities are facing water shortages to varying degrees, including thirty of the thirty-two largest cities. Rampant dumping of toxic discharges and harmful chemicals into the water has polluted 70 percent of the rivers and made them "run black";[6] as a result, 700 million people drink contaminated water every day. Ninety percent of the shallow aquifers under cities have also been polluted. Some 300 million peasants cannot drink safe and clean water. China already has the world's worst cessation of river flows. The World Bank has warned that if the current unsustainable situation is not changed, then by 2020 China will suffer the worst consequences of water scarcity: some 30 million people will become environmental refugees.

Water as a Nodal Point of Ecological Sensibility

A "nodal point" (*point de caption*), according to Lacan, is a "quilting point" in the signifying process, a point that stitches, or constructs the meaning of the world: "the *point de caption* is rather the word which, *as a word*, on the level of the signifier itself, unifies a given field, constitutes its identity."[7] Water as a nodal point can address the overarching issues that inform New Chinese Ecocinema.

Perhaps the most intense engagement New Chinese Cinema undertakes, beyond the socio-political aspects, is with the impact of the environment on the difficult formation of Chinese identity. The films are informed by an acute epistemological critique of the myopic ideology of modernization responsible for environmental degradation and ecological damage, resulting in a grave condition I call "ambient *unheimlich*" — displacement, anomie, estrangement, dysfunctionality, malaise, and homelessness. Central to this ecocentric cinema is the foregrounding of water as a vital trope for symptom, trauma, and/or pathogenesis that registers ecological awareness of unchecked environmental catastrophe (ecoggedon).

Instead of treating water as a mere representation of its physical status (its absence/drought and its excess/flood), in this chapter I will address it as a *verb*, inquiring into its function as an ecological practice, a dynamic semiotic that mediates the formation of a complex network of political, social, and cultural identities. The chapter will further examine the polysemic figure of water as a poignant articulation of cultural malaise, environmental dysfunctionality, and psychological anxiety emblematical of post-Mao mainland China and post-Miracle Taiwan. The chapter finally argues that beneath these seemingly ecodystopian films lies New Chinese Ecocinema's utopianism of messianic redemption and elevated humanism. By focusing on water as a site of contested signification, this chapter examines cultural, psychological, and political pathology in certain important mainland Chinese and Taiwanese films. I suggest that water as a symptom will offer new perspectives on ambient habitat and viral politics.

Directors in the Chinese New Wave from its inception have demonstrated their acute sensibility regarding China's water crisis: Chen Kaige's *Yellow Earth* not only inaugurates Chinese New Wave filmmaking but, more significantly, ushers in Chinese ecocinema. Films that engage water as a site of ecological imagination can be clustered into three groups, each addressing a crucial aspect of China's water-borne crisis:[8]

1. Shortage/scarcity/drought in Chen Kaige's *Yellow Earth* (*Huang tudi*, 1984), Wu Tianming's *Old Well* (*Laojing*, 1986), and Tsai Mingliang's *The Wayward Cloud* (*Tianbian yi duo yun*, 2005);

2. Toxification in Lou Ye's *Suzhou River* (*Suzhou he*, 2000), Tsai Mingliang's *The River* (*Heliu*, 1997), and *The Hole* (*Dong*, 1998);

3. Colonization/disruption of water in Zhang Ming's *Clouds over Wushan* (*Wushan yunyu*, 1996) and Jia Zhangke's *Still Life* (*Sanxia haoren*, 2006).

Technically speaking it is not difficult to identify the causes of the water crisis: water shortages are caused by deforestation, soil erosion, desertification, overgrazing, over-use of water, land reclamation, and interrupted river flow. Toxification is caused by the discharge of industrial, municipal, and human untreated waste water; pollution spill and garbage dumps; and colonization of water by the construction of giant dams, causing in turn the forced relocation of millions of people, loss of regional biodiversity, and disruption of aquatic ecosystems.

However, China's water crisis is not simply a physical issue, but also reflects a pathological way of articulating identity and modernity in the form of loss, anxiety, trauma, and ecodespair. To understand this water-obsessed pathology, we introduce Freud's conception of "*das Unheimliche*" or "the uncanny" (1919) as a kind of theoretical kernel for ecological imagination and engagement.

The Spectrality of Heimlich-Unheimlich

According to Freud, the German word *unheimlich* is etymologically associated with its opposite term *heimlich*, thus suggesting a paradoxical ambivalence. On the one hand, *heimlich* means something familiar, intimate, native, homely, comfortable, friendly, secure, and domestic; on the other hand, it also means something ghostly, secret, foreign, unfamiliar, gruesome, mystic, uncanny, homeless, hostile, and dangerous. Thus the term *heimlich* ultimately coincides with its opposite, *unheimlich*: "What is *heimlich* thus comes to be *unheimlich*."[9] This paradox implies that the uncanny is familiar and strange, comfortable and dangerous, domestic and foreign, known and inaccessible.

For Freud, the most strange, eerie, and frightening is not that which is far away from our experience and feelings (the exotic, foreign, the utterly new and alien) but that which is close to home: the private and the familiar that has been rendered foreign through repression and distortion, but then returns. Freud writes, "[F]or this uncanny is in reality nothing new or foreign, but something familiar and old-established in the mind that has been estranged only by the process of repression ... In this case, too, the *unheimlich* is what was once *heimlich*, home-like, familiar; the prefix 'un' is the token of repression."[10] In other words, the *unheimlich/heimlich* pairing constitutes a psychic ambivalence, an uncanny Otherness within the self.

Water as a Cipher of the *Unheimlich*/Unhomely

To begin with, water, the source of life, is the most familiar, native, and homely element for human beings; it is associated with feelings of being at home. But when water becomes scarce or polluted, it suddenly becomes defamiliarized, denatured, or demonic, posing gruesome threats to the world and making life homeless, exilic, unhomely, and uncanny. The sense of an imminent end to water creates a ghostly pairing of *déjà vu* — the feeling of "strangely familiar" and perpetual alienation, leading to the experience of being a stranger or an Other within the self.[11] This spectrality of *heimlich/unheimlich* — the sense of being estranged from the home and becoming unhomely — constitutes the kernel of water pathology in the New Chinese ecological unconsciousness.

In Chen Kaige's *Yellow Earth*, due to water scarcity and drought, the Loess Plateau, once the home of Chinese civilization, becomes a wasteland devoid of any vegetation, and utterly uninhabitable. The vast, barren, and demonic landscape with which the film opens eliminates any possibility of salvation, including the revolutionary promises of Gu Qing, a self-proclaimed "savior" whose return at the end of the film is so elusive and ghostly. Most significant to the water pathology is the death of Cui Qiao in the Yellow River and her uncanny return as holy water contained in a jar that haunts the rain prayer ceremony at the end of the film. The ending of her life in the muddy river signifies a wretched state of ecological breakdown. In *Old Well*, the search for water by digging wells has obsessed multiple generations. The emptiness of the dry wells has become so uncanny that it gives rise to a dream narrative that sustains the villagers for generations (Figure 1.1). Although the dream of finding water is fulfilled at the end of the film, such closure is more illusionary because the water that Sun Wangquan helps find in a deep well by using hydraulic technology is not sustainable and will dry up one day.[12]

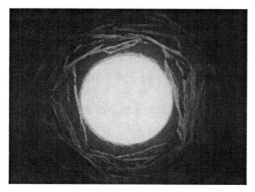

Figure 1.1   *Old Well*. This extreme low-angle shot of the empty well at the opening of the film exactly creates an uncanny Other that haunts the water-seeking villagers.

In *Suzhou River* Lou Ye tackles deepening toxification and its victimage caused by global capitalism, industrialism, and consumerism. The film opens with the anonymous videographer-narrator's obsessive tour around the bustling Suzhou River, which is portrayed as "Shanghai's dirtiest river," associated with pollution, misery, crime, disease, poverty, debris, decay, prostitution, and suicide. Suzhou River, as an ecologically dangerous backwater of Shanghai, reflects the director's toxic anxiety and consciousness in engaging his critique of the myth of the "Shanghai Miracle," as exemplified in the phallic landmark, the Oriental Pearl Tower. Literally, the innocent Mudan, who jumps into the river to commit suicide, is killed by the toxic pollutants dumped by both industrial factories and residents around the banks; symbolically, she is transmuted into a mermaid, an "invasive species" imported from the West, as she emerges from the river incarnated as the blonde mermaid performer Meimei, held captive in a water tank for show business. The double of Mudan/Meimei, who haunts both Mada and the narrator, speaks of China's post-socialist schizophrenic pathology of dislocation and ecological malaise in an era of massive uprooting of space and habitat.[13]

Tsai Mingliang's *The River* also presents a critical view of how water pathologizes the human body and creates an unhomely space for humanity in the dystopian environment of cosmopolitan but uncanny Taipei. The film begins with Xiao Kang first encountering a female friend on a two-way escalator in front of a big department store, and then cuts to a film team shooting a scene of a male corpse in the filthy Tamsui River. The female director (cameo role for Hong Kong director Ann Hui) keeps complaining that "the dummy doesn't look real." After much pulling up and down, dumping and splashing, the limbs of the corpse are broken: its feet have sunk and its right arm is torn apart. This dismemberment of the dummy in the dirty, black, and muddy Tamsui water foreshadows Xiao Kang's fate in the film. During the lunch break the director meets Xiao Kang and turns to him for help in impersonating a drowned corpse in the water ("Can you swim? How about floating?"). Xiao Kang initially expresses his concern about the quality of the water ("The water is so filthy down here"), while the director attempts to assure him ("We'll clean you up when you hit the shore. Clean you up fast, real fast"). Finally, she entices him to do it for the fun of acting in a film.

During shooting the director urges Xiao Kang to go "easy and relax." In Tsai's signature style of a static long take we see Xiao Kang wading into the river and mimicking the corpse by floating face down in the water (Figure 1.2). The director yelps that "He is much better than the fake body." In the next scene we see Xiao Kang washing himself in the bathroom of a hotel: looking in the mirror, he brushes his teeth and uses the same brush to clean his legs, hands, chest, even massaging his left nipple. After washing, he sits with his back to the camera in front of the bed drinking water while we see his bare upper body reflected in the mirror; the two table lamps on his right side are also reflected on the TV screen on his left side (in a *mise-en-scène* of doubling and apparition). While drinking a glass of water, he smells his left hand, his armpit, and then his right hand — then removes the towel and steps into the bathroom for another shower with his naked upper body reflected in the mirror again. His female acquaintance comes into his room and they have sex (both bodies are reflected in the mirror).

Figure 1.2   *The River*. Xiao Kang "dies" better than the dummy in the filthy Tamsui River.

The next scene cuts to Xiao Kang wearing sunglasses (unlike in the opening scene) and riding his motorbike on the highway back home. He starts to shake his head uneasily and uses his right hand (the hand which dropped off the dummy) to touch the right side of his neck. He passes his father as if they are strangers. Only when his father hears a crash does he turn back to see his son fall from his motorcycle onto the ground, debilitated by a neck pain. Throughout the rest of the film his parents shuttle him around the city to seek all sorts of treatment (Eastern and Western medicine, and religious and shamanistic exorcism) to cure his inexplicable neck ailment. But in Tsai's ecological unconscious, Xiao Kang's disease is incurable.

Tsai is obsessed with water and all of his films are waterlogged or soaked in one way or another. What does such ubiquity of water signify for Tsai? In many interviews Tsai has claimed that water simply stands for love: "I always regard the characters in my films as plants which are short of water, which are almost on the point of dying from lack of water. Actually, water for me is love; that is what they lack. What I'm trying to show is very symbolic: it's their need for love."[14] Water can only be the index of "love" when it is a benign source of life. However, when water is polluted to the point of toxicity, it is no longer a source of love but love's negation, a kind of "non-water." A "non-water" element is the prefix "un" in the word of the "*unheimlich*," which means, for Freud, "the token of repression";[15] for Bhabha, "the unhomely moment."[16]

When Xiao Kang impersonates a corpse in the toxic Tamsui River, he is literally enacting death. That is why the director praises him by saying that he dies much better than death itself. In other words, Xiao Kang is not acting the role of the dead body; rather, he has to be dead himself so that the sense of death looks "real." It is through his "death" that the viscerally mutilated corpse has become re-animated — "the return of the dead." Thus Xiao Kang is symbolically the walking dead: derealized, living nowhere, and "unhomely." That is why he cannot keep himself from repeatedly crashing his motorbike; that is why his neck pain cannot be diagnosed and successfully healed or exorcised. However, it is exactly this unnameable neck pain (as the cipher of the "*un*") which frequently attacks and hurts him, keeps him alive and drives him around the city in search of a therapeutic "love" as his own family suffers pathogenic flooding and complete dissolution. This is indeed a kind of "perverse salvation"[17] that characterizes Tsai's eco-unconscious and viral politics.[18]

The Spectropoetics of *Yanmo*/Inundation

Water is even more traumatized and denaturalized in both Zhang Ming's and Jia Zhangke's films about the ecosystem and habitat devastation that the world's largest hydropower project — the Three Gorges Water Dam — has brought to the reservoir area and to the entire Yangtze River watershed. The two films can be treated as sequential in terms of the order in which their events take place. *Wushan yunyu* depicts the official commencement of construction of the dam in 1994 (as can be seen from the opening ceremony and speech presided over by Premier Li Peng on a fuzzy black-and-white TV in Mai Qiang's Signal House); the film's alternative title, *In Expectation* (*Zai qidai zhong*), indicates what may lie ahead. *Sanxia haoren* reveals what the area looks like as the water level rises 175 meters when the dam is completed and filled with water in 2009; hence the film's English title *Still Life* captures more graphically what remains in "this post-disaster landscape,"[19] as petrified fragments or lifeless objects displayed as testimonial evidence of what has bygone (Figure 1.3).

Three words in Chinese — *yan* 淹 (inundation), *chai* 拆 (demolition), and *qian* 遷 (relocation) — can be configured as heightened signifiers to articulate the ecocidal condition revealed by these two films. As a result of the rise of the water level to 175 meters upon the completion of the dam in 2009 (the film repeatedly reveals the sign "water level 175 meters" painted on the rocky cliff close to Mai Qiang's signal tower and on the city stone wall and high buildings in Wushan city), all visible things including houses, farmlands, natural scenery, and historical sites will be submerged under water. Thus, before the flood arrives all the buildings in the

Figure 1.3   *Still Life.* This spectral crack, which ironically looks like a hollowed phallic symbol, mirrors the irreversible psychological trauma of the displaced relocatees.

entire area are slated for demolition, to be reconstructed elsewhere. The ringmaker, Old Huang, refuses to fix his old house because "it's going to be flooded," as he replies to an inquiry posed by Old Mo in *Wushan yunyu*; in *Sanxia haoren*, we see half-nude workers muscularly hammering away at high buildings and pounding them into rubbles. As a result of the imminent flooding and demolition, over 1.3 million people in the reservoir area are forced to abandon their homes and livelihoods in order to be relocated and resettled elsewhere. The Three Gorges Dam has created "the largest resettlement operation in modern China: social and political discontent could have explosive consequences."[20]

On the surface, the process of "yan-chai-qian" indicates a logic of sequentiality and a narrative of causality, a linear movement of the *raison d'être* of an action. However, what actually occurs is the most brutal and radical experience of the *unheimlich* (loss, disappearance, estrangement, trauma, and the unhomely) in the threnody of "yan-chai-qian."[21] The "*un*" is both omnipresent and omnipotent in that it not only marks the boundary of destruction of the ecosystem, biodiversity, and massive uprooting of people in the reservoir area, but also gives rise to an uncanny space of haunting, apparition, and doubling — the return of the dead, which I call spectropoetics. That is, what is submerged under water will surreptitiously resurface above water; what is demolished physically will be psychologically reassembled, albeit in fragments and with the scars of injuries; and those who have moved away will be recalled to themselves by the shock of *déjà vu*.[22]

Moments of being *unheimlich* loom large in the two films, and are powerfully conveyed through the mise-en-scène. For instance, the sign "water level 175 meters" painted along the Three Gorges area and in the city of Wushan signifies far more than the words themselves. It not only indicates the water level that will inundate the whole city, hence standing for the ultimate completion of the gigantic water dam, but it also cryptically shows the termination day for the city, an eschatological death drive toward the demise of the *heimat*, the home. It is an uncanny sign that is psychologically animated, like a ghost, haunting the daily life of the people living on the eve of the deluge. Therefore, "175 meters" is the "post" or "afterlife" that retroactively determines and prefabricates the "living" moments, creating disturbing symptoms of paranoia and schizophrenia among the people of Wushan (such as Old Mo's accusation of Mai Qiang's alleged rape of Chen Qing, and the hallucinations occurring to both Chen Qing and Mai Qiang, a point to be discussed later). On the one hand, this mathematical sign of the highest water level literally commemorates China's engineering dream and political ambition to "conquer nature" (*rending shengtian* 人定勝天) by mobilizing national and global capital to build the world's largest dam purportedly for regulating flooding from the upstream reaches, generating electricity to ease the energy demand, and improving navigation; on the other hand, this diabolical sign evokes a self-mortifying sense of subjectivity, acting and hanging at a vantage point like a Lacanian *objet petit a*, a mis-identified fantasy object of lack in which the subject's libidinal desire cannot be gratified but is instead desublimated as an exilic "Other" from Mother Earth.[23]

Even more ironic about this "175 meters" inundation level is the over-hyped tourist fever of "Farewell to the Three Gorges" (*Gaobie Sanxia re*). Since construction began in 1993, both the national media and the travel agencies along the Yangtze River have cashed in on the "water level 175 meters" as a hot selling spot to promote tourism, claiming that the majestic Three Gorges scenery will be gone forever after its completion and urging the whole nation to rush in to the Yangtze River to get a last glimpse of the Three Gorges. Many large luxurious cruise ships carry visitors on the waters of the Three Gorges. Those five-star cruise ships bear Western/British royal or Chinese imperial names such as "Queen Victoria," "Princess Anne," "Princess Jeannie," "Princess Sisi," "Catherine," "Empress," "Viking Century," "President," "Emperor," "King of the East," to list just a few examples, making tourists feel as if they are traveling on the Thames or the Hudson. Such estrangement has rendered the Three Gorges into a site of exotic spectacle for consumerism, and sadly, has turned the local residents into "noble savages" on display to satiate the curiosity of tourists.

Do the visitors have any awareness of the impending eco-disaster that will destroy the entire city of Wushan (and its neighbor city Fengjie), or of the suffering of the local people who are forced to abandon their homes for resettlement? The answer is obviously negative. In the early sequence of the film when Lili, a street girl who is brought to the Signal House by Ma Bing to entertain Mai Qiang, is swimming in the river in the evening, she glances at a brightly lit ship cruising past. Excitedly, she waves, shouting loudly at the moving ship: "Hey, where are you going? I'm here. Where are you going, big ship? Did you hear me?" Although she yells loudly and repeatedly (at least five times), her voice merely flows over the vast empty expanse of water, echoes in the misty valley, and dissolves in the distant darkness as the camera pans to the still water from left to right. Surrounded by darkness and enshrouded in the valley, the well-lit ship moves like a ghost boat on the ominous waterways. The question "Where are you going?" is actually the cry of Lili's own inner predicament about her future. Later, when a group of tourists is reading the sign painted on the city wall of Wushan — "This city will be gone and flooded. The water level will rise to 175 meters" — Chen Qing, a hotel receptionist, urges them to move along telling them that "it [the flooding] has nothing to do with you." This sarcastic line shows the local resident's resentment at the indifference and apathy of the public to the plight of the displaced.

The double victimization of the local people from governmental hegemony and fanatic consumerism in the Three Gorges reservoir area is best expressed in the two scenes featuring both Mai Qiang's and Chen Qing's abnormal ways of killing fish. In one early scene in the Signal House, when the television is broadcasting the opening ceremony of the Three Gorges Project and the speech given by Premier Li Peng, without evincing any interest in this news, deadpan Mai Qiang starts to practice his calligraphy and to prepare dinner for his visitors, Ma Bing and Lili. He alternately holds up two live fish from an orange plastic bucket and finally picks one. First, he stuns the fish with a blow to the head (a close-up shot of the fish, the whack, and the hand), then, he stares impassively at the camera, and finally, he slits the fish open. He walks out of the room with blood spattered on his hands, then returns to kill another fish. While Ma Bing and Lili flirt, the camera cuts to a close-up of the two dead fish lying on the chopping board bleeding, their stomachs slit open and their intestines in the bowls (Figure 1.4). In a parallel scene in the second half of the film, Chen Qing repeats exactly the same process in killing two fish in her apartment in the city of Wushan.

Figure 1.4   *Clouds over Wushan.* The poor victims of the ecocide.

Why does director Zhang Ming focus so long and so vividly on the visual details of killing not only one but two fish and by two people, a man and a woman, in different places? Some significant messages must be encoded in this episode. On the surface, as fish are often associated with sex and fertility, these parallel scenes establish "a symbolic link" between Mai Qiang and Chen Qing.[24] Likewise, as man belongs to *yang* and woman to *yin*, the fish may stand for *yang* and *yin*. In Chinese cosmology, the yang-yin duality constitutes the "Qi," a primal force that operates the harmony of the universe. So, allegorically, the director may suggest that the killing of the two fish foreshadows an ominous future fate of Wushan: that is, the destruction of both the fertility that sustains the people and the harmony of the universe. This reading will ring ecologically true when the Three Gorges Dam is completed — 1.3 million people will be forced to relocate; biodiversity and rare species such as the Yangtze River dolphin, the Chinese sturgeon, and the Yangtze alligator will face extinction; the water in the reservoir will be contaminated by billions of tons of industrial wastewater, sewage, and chemical pollutants, turning the reservoir into "a huge, stagnant, stinking pond";[25] and catastrophes such as earthquakes, landslides, mud-rock flow, sand silt, and soil erosion will occur. In this sense, the first fish that is killed may be seen to stand for the residents in the reservoir area, who are powerless and subalternized, subject to victimization and exploitation; the second slaughtered fish may be seen to represent the irreversible damage of nature and the whole ecosystem of the Three Gorges. The killing of the fish also suggests the disruption of the Qi that governs the harmony between human beings and nature, hence projecting a doomed future for the Three Gorges. It is through such elusive use of the cinematic mise-en-scène of the fish that Zhang expresses his critique of environmental politics.

The Hydro-Politics of *Yunyu*/Clouds and Rain

Another parallel structure is inscribed in *Wushan yunyu*, which is crucial to show the ecological imagination of the film and the director's ecological engagement through his rewriting of the events. The title of the film is polysemic with literary, cultural, and mythological allusions. First, the word "*Wu*" in Chinese stands for witches, sorcerers, and shamans; witchcraft is "*Wushu*." Thus Mountain Wu or Witches' Mountain is where witches reside and exercise their black art to create magical things (such as conjuring up clouds and rain). Could this literal association indicate that the use of technology to build the world's largest hydroelectric dam resembles a kind of modern witchcraft, producing the magic of electricity, flood control, and improved navigation? Geographically, Wushan, a county located in the Three Gorges, somewhere between the Qutang Gorge and the Wu Gorge (Witches' Gorge), has two thousand years of history replete with cultural relics such as the famous "Wushan Man," the fossil of one of the earliest human beings in the area, about two million years ago. The Wushan area will be entirely submerged after the dam's completion.

More important, Mountain Wu is mythologically associated with the Goddess of Yaoji, the twenty-third most beautiful daughter of the Queen of the Western Heaven, who, with her eleven fairy sisters, descended from their celestial Yaochi palace to Mountain Wu in order to help the flood-taming hero Great Yu defeat the twelve vicious dragons who had congested the Yangtze River, causing flooding and disasters everywhere in the area. Together the goddesses and the hero dredged the watercourse and let the flood flow into the East China Sea (another political reference and ecological satire against the current construction of the dam). After overcoming the flood, Yaoji and her sisters remained on earth. Sitting on the mist-shrouded peaks of Mountain Wu, she directed passing ships (like Mai Qiang), protected people from danger, summoned wind and rain for mankind, and planted precious herbs for medication. She remained on earth so long that she forgot heaven and finally transformed herself into a spectacular peak, the famed Goddess Peak (Shennu Feng). Her eleven sisters also turned into peaks of lesser grandeur. Together with the Goddess Peak, they are now known as the Twelve Peaks of Mountain Wu.

The film's title, *Yunyu* (Clouds and Rain) has become a poetic metaphor for sexual intercourse or eroticism in Chinese culture, deriving from the poet Song Yu's (c. 290–238 B.C.) political-erotic "The Rhapsody on Gaotang" (Gao Tang Fu), "the first extended description of mountain landscape in Chinese literary history."[26] This prose poem creates a pastoral mythic world in which vast streams, fish, strange animals, flowering trees, blossoming flowers, birds, and supernatural spirits dwell together harmoniously on Mountain Wu. Most interestingly, the poem tells of King Xiang of Chu's dream of a romantic encounter with a lady of rare beauty from Mountain Wu when the King and Song Yu are visiting the Great Mash of Yunmen. After enjoying an orgy with the Goddess ("the clouds of sexual pleasure never cease"), the King asks her identity. The lady replies, "My home is on the southern side of the Witches' Hill, where from its rounded summit a sudden chasm falls. At dawn I am the morning cloud [*zhaoyun*]; at dusk the evening rain. So dawn by dawn and dusk by dusk, I dwell beneath the Southern Crest."[27] Upon waking, the King finds her gone. To remember her, the King orders a shrine built on "the Temple of the Morning Clouds."

The film's two characters, Mai Qiang and Chen Qing, are in many ways mysteriously connected. In addition to the mirror scene of fish killing, in the early sequence in the Signal House Mai Qiang tells Ma Bing and Lili that he "dreams of someone" (*wo mengjian yi geren*). In the police office, when police officer Wu Gang interrogates Mai Qiang about why he picks Chen Qing to sleep with, Mai Qiang stammers, "I felt … I felt … I felt … the moment I saw her, I immediately … I felt I had seen her before." The camera cuts to Chen Qing's apartment at night: lost in thought, she asks her son whether someone is calling her name (the second time to raise this question). But her son's answer is negative (*meiyou*). Another allusion is the name of the hotel where Chen Qing is working as a receptionist: "Xianke

Lai" literally means "Welcoming Celestial Guests."[28] Obviously the director tries to parody the ancient romantic encounter in this film. The rewriting of this mythic text into a contemporary context is not intended to provoke nostalgia of a pastoral good time as in Western nature and environmental literature,[29] but to debunk its aura through an ironical twist. If the King's fleeting sexual encounter with the alluring Goddess from Mountain Wu is romantic, intimate, and blissful, then Mai Qiang's sexual relationship with Chen Qing is full of violence, fear, pain, and indignity. Old Mo's accusation that Mai Qiang has raped Chen Qing is also ironic, since firstly, he could not provide any evidence to prove his case; secondly, Chen Qing herself has denied the accusation; and finally, it is actually Old Mo himself who has used his power as hotel manager to "rape" her.

Moreover, by introducing the notion of rape (*qiangjian*) into the film, the director is undoubtedly not only reversing the ancient myth of romantic passion, but also launching his critique of ecological politics. The brutal construction of an ecologically damaging dam, which has given nature an incurable wound, is a rape of the ecosystem. If Chen Qing is a contemporary Yaoji, she is a goddess violently stripped of her power by modern progress. One closing scene of the film shows her standing on the balcony, anxiety and fear etched on her face as she looks at the Yangtze River dotted with diminutive cruise ships, while thunder cracks in the misty, distant mountains. If Chen Qing is a contemporary lady of Eros who has the magic power to make "clouds and rain," then her sexual power is paralyzed by the dam's violent blocking of the flow of "yin" energy and its destructive inundation of her celestial dwelling "Xiankelai." Can this project, which brings about "ecoggedon," be seen as a kind of progress? This is exactly the question most ironically posed by the police officer Wu Gang. After hearing Ma Bing teasing Mai Qiang saying he "is making progress" by finally having sex with a woman, Wu Gang angrily shouts back at Ma Bing, "Is rape a kind of progress?" To reiterate this phrase in the context of our discussion, we ask: Is the violent destruction of the ecosystem and the "rape" of Mother Earth a type of progress? This is the fundamental question director Zhang Ming tries to ask through the narrative reversal and ironization of the ancient myth in the film.

The Topography of Ecological (Dis)location

The post-Mao New Chinese Cinema is often criticized for becoming "ethnographical" or "auto-ethnographical,"[30] by voluntarily packaging China's ethnic spectacles through strategical cancellation, recreation, and even distortion of her cultural "authenticity" in order to win Western critics' recognition and to satiate Western audience's Orientalist fantasies of an exotic China. The magical ingredients which showcase China as both the subject and the object of a morbid gaze are, as in Zhang

Yingjin's catalogue, "primitive landscape and its sheer visual beauty (including savage rivers, mountains, forests, deserts); repressed sexuality and its eruption in transgressive moments of eroticism (read "heroism"); gender performance and sexual exhibition (including homosexuality, transvestism, adultery, incest) as seen in exotic operas, rituals, or other types of rural custom; and a mythical or cyclical time frame in which the protagonist's fate is predestined."[31] Though this critique does accurately describe some aspects of Chinese film, it also falls into the trap of conceptual universalization and theoretical abstraction without focusing on the ecological situatedness prevalent in the New Chinese Cinema.

Rather than unfairly categorizing all New Chinese films as "ethnographical," I would argue that water-themed films are essentially topographical in that they are place-oriented, focusing on a specific region, locality, space, and community. They represent a kind of Jamesonian "cognitive mapping" of China's ecological and environmental *topoi* (place and places), a cinematographical navigation of how identity is ecologically mediated not only by a (dis)connectedness between one's primary places but also by the tentacular radiations of the places from each other.[32] The Chinese filmmakers' ecological imagination powerfully captures the places that define China's topographical identity: the Loess Plateau, Taihang Mountain, the Three Gorges, the urbanscapes of Shanghai and Taipei; it also charts China's major watersheds: those of the Yellow, Fen, Yangtze, Suzhou, and Tamsui Rivers. In other words, these places are not invented to be consumed as visual feast; they are situated places with not only geographical authenticity but also ecological deterioration — places mostly unpleasing to the eyes of the audience: drought and poverty in *Yellow Earth* and *Old Well*; pollution and filth in *Suzhou River* and *The River*; decay and displacement in *Clouds and Rain over Wushan*, *The Hole*, and *Still Life*. This cinematic topography, which focuses on the emotive and affective bond between people and their environments,[33] connects death by drowning (literally or symbolically) with ecological breakdown — Cui Qiao's death in the Yellow River, Qiao Ying's sexual fulfillment with Wangquan at the bottom of a collapsed well, Xiaokang's acting role as a corpse in the Tamsui River, Mudan's death in the Suzhou River, Chen Qing's "rape" case and the death of the gangster in the Yangtze River, and even Sanming's and Shen Hong's separation from their respective spouses; hence, these films become more thanatographical statements about death, suffering, mourning, and survival.

Cinematic topography not only maps the symptoms caused by ecological dislocation but also identifies the fundamental causes of ecological devastation. Take the Loess Plateau (*Huangtu Gaoyuan*) in *Yellow Earth* as an example. This plateau covers 640,000 square kilometers in the upper and middle reaches of the Yellow River and stretches over parts of seven Chinese provinces. It was the cradle of Chinese civilization, but it has become "China's sorrow" due to its ecological degradation. Research has pointed out that the Loess Plateau is formed both by natural factors such as climate warming and aridification, sandy soil texture, erosion-prone land surfaces, strong and frequent winds, and also, primarily, by anthropogenic causes including deforestation, overgrazing, overcultivation, misuse of water resources, and destruction of vegetation.[34] Particularly, as a result of massive deforestation and destruction of vegetation, soil erosion is "devastating on the Loess Plateau on the middle stretch of the Yellow River, which is about 70% eroded."[35] Ecological destruction brings about poverty and suffering for the people living in the region of "yellow earth," as the film reveals to us. One of the most effective methods of rehabilitating this damaged ecosystem is reforestation, returning vegetation to the regions (coupled with bans on tree cuttings, planting on steep slopes, unrestricted grazing and with sustainable water management). In *Yellow Earth*, a mysterious, solitary, wild pear tree standing at the crest of the hill holds the key to the "greening" of the barren yellow earth and bespeaks Chen Kaige's ecological sensibility.

Much has been written and said about several spectacular scenes such as the yellow earth, the Yellow River, the waist-drum dancing and the rain prayer ceremony in *Yellow Earth*, but few have touched on this "solitary wild pear tree." The reason why this lonely pear tree is ignored may be caused by the fact that it always appears on screen elusive, peripheral, diminutive, and distant upon the hilltop (Figure 1.5).

Figure 1.5   *Yellow Earth*. This mysterious and elusive pear tree stands lonely on the vanishing horizon of the Loess Plateau.

Careless viewers may never have noticed its existence at all because its on-screen time is so fleeting; the tree often appears as a one-second establishing shot in the film. However, this simple plant, no matter how unspectacular it looks, carries a significant ecological message for both Chen Kaige and his groundbreaking debut film. This tree is not a cinematic prop but a living tree that Chen encountered when he traveled to the Loess Plateau with Zhang Yimou and He Qun looking for locations for the film. "On a winter's day," as Chen later recalls, "the earth is bare, transmitting an expansive feeling. It seems barren but warm inside. Gradually, we made out an almost bare birch-leaf pear tree perched like a pavilion at the top of a distant slope. Silent and lonely, its outline on the exposed winter wilderness seemed to affirm existence of life."[36] In *Yellow Earth*, this tree has a high frequency of on-screen appearances: it appears altogether seven times. At the beginning of the film, after seven dissolves superimposing man with the wide-angle pans of the vast barren Loess Plateau, Gu Qing, a cultural worker from the Eighth Route Army, appears mid-screen. On hearing a *xintianyou* ballad in the distance, he turns his head to the left and sees the following:

> (#16 shots BE) The hillcrest is bleak and bare. There is no sign of human habitation except for a white path winding up against the brown earth and disappearing over the crest. A solitary wild pear tree stands at the top.[37]

> (#18 shots BE) The solitary wild pear tree on the crest.

> (#20 shots BE) The wild pear tree stands in silence on the crest, stripped to its last leaves.
> (Later in the film the following shots of the tree are provided:)

> (#322 shots BE. After hearing the news about Gu Qing's departure next day and knowing of her impending marriage) ... A lonely wild pear tree stands at the crest.

> (#390 shots BE. Cui Qiao seeing off Gu Qing and singing) Gu is walking toward to the tree in the distance.

> (#391 LS. After singing "A tree can't take root if planted on a dry stone") Cui Qiao sees the pear tree standing at the crest in the distance.

> (#416 BE. After Cui Qiao's wedding procession, her father leans against the door) On the hillcrest, the wild pear tree, bare of all its leaves, stands in silence.

As Jerome Silbergeld asks about a water jar, another minor "esoteric image" in the same film, "Why would the film-makers put so much into so little? Or better put, how can they get so much from what seems, at first, to be so little? ... How does such a 'simple,' momentary image, more painterly tableau than a cinematic montage, not only encapsulate their subtle message but also express the very nature of their cinematic artistry?"[38] This tree, although there is no single close-up shot, is an intensely charged signifier that, I suggest, possesses the same significance as the water jar in decoding the ecological unconscious of the film.

The tree appears at each crucial moment in the film. The opening three BE shots establish the spatial relationships between Gu Qing and the setting of the yellow earth. But this spatial identity is also very subjective and uncertain since it is from Gu Qing's personal point of view as he is searching for the source of the singing voice.

The next three shots of the tree show the relationship between Gu Qing and Cui Qiao, and its disturbing change from emotional attachment to desperate separation. The last shot of the tree after Cui Qiao's forced marriage suggests the imminent death of both Cui Qiao and the yellow earth since the tree has been stripped of its leaves, even though it is still early spring.[39] Furthermore, tree imagery also appears in the wreaths of green leaves wrapped around the peasants' heads when they hold a rain prayer ceremony at the end of the film.

Simply put, this lonely wild pear tree stands for Gu Qing, whose arrival in the village seems to embody hope, to deliver messianic promises, and finally to bring changes to the debilitating status quo for the villagers, particularly for the adolescent Cui Qiao. That Gu Qing himself is the pear tree can be literally deciphered from his name: "Gu 顧" in Chinese means "oversee, attend to, take care of, pay attention to"; while "qing 青" stands for "green" or "youth." Thus the name connotes "to oversee or care for the green/youth." Who is "the green/youth"? It is Cui Qiao, as "cui 翠" in Chinese also means "green." So it is the young girl whom Gu Qing should care for and attend to. Most significantly, both Gu Qing and Cui Qiao are mysteriously bound, like *yang* and *yin*, an inseparable duality because "qing" and "cui" form the compound term "qingcui 青翠," which also means "green" (or better, "fresh or flourishing green") in Chinese. Their transcendent fusion into "qingcui" can be understood from another light. As Jerome Silbergeld points out, "The earth is female in relation to sky and mother to man, but earth is male in relation to water."[40] On the one hand, the growth and survival of the phallic tree, which is Gu Qing, have to depend on the support of the fertile earth, which is embodied by young Cui Qiao; their separation foreshadows the tragedy — the death of Cui Qiao and the quick withering of the pear tree in early spring. On the other hand, the prosperity of the yellow earth has to be nurtured by the water, as embodied by the water bearer Cui Qiao. But with her death in the Yellow River, drought begins and life on the arid Loess Plateau is no longer sustainable. Therefore, "the mating of Cuiqiao to Gu Qing is a sublimated wedding of dreams,"[41] yet this dream of "qingcui" or "flourishing green" on the bleak yellow earth may reflect the new generation filmmaker's ecological unconscious desire for a "greener China."[42]

From Optical Unconscious to Ecological Unconscious

It is due to the supercapability of photographic representation of the camera compared to the naked eye (the camera's exceptional powers of enlargement, close-ups, slow movement, and split-second exposure) that Walter Benjamin coined the metaphor of the "optical unconscious" ([*das*] *Optisch-Unbewusste*) in his 1931 essay "A Small History of Photography." For Benjamin, the human eye's ability to penetrate social reality is limited because "we have no idea at all what happens during the fraction of a second when a person *steps out*." Yet photography, "with its devices of slow motion and enlargement, reveals the secret. It is through photography that we first discover the existence of this optical unconscious, just as we discover the instinctual unconscious through psychoanalysis"; photography "reveals in this material the physiognomic aspects of visual worlds [*Bildwelten*, image worlds] which dwell in the smallest things, meaningful yet covert enough to find a hiding place in waking dreams."[43] In his 1936 "Artwork" essay, Benjamin further elaborates on the photographic technology, the *camera obscura*, as optical unconscious:

> With the close-up, space expands; with slow motion, movement is extended. The enlargement of a snapshot does not simply render more precise what in any case was visible, though unclear: it reveals entirely new structural formations of the subject. ... It is evidently a different nature that speaks to the camera than that which speaks to the naked eye; different above all because it substitutes, for a space interwoven with human consciousness, another space, an unconsciously permeated space. ... Here the camera intervenes with the resources of its lowerings and liftings, its interruptions and isolations, its extensions and accelerations, its enlargements and reductions. The camera introduces us to unconscious optics as does psychoanalysis to the unconscious impulses.[44]

More significantly, with the concept of the optical unconscious, Benjamin attributes a sense of historicity to photographic representation of the camera, a difference between technology and magic reformulated as "a thoroughly historical variable."[45] Within this historicized optical unconscious, the individual experience of modern life is transformed into a collective constellation of dream, memory, fantasy, utopian wishing, and messianic redemptive promise. It is at the level of the optical unconscious that the beholder is urged to seek "the tiny spark of contingency, of the Here and Now," and thus to find "the inconspicuous spot" where a forgotten future might be rediscovered. As Benjamin says, "[For] it is another nature that speaks to the camera than to the eye: other in the sense that a space informed by human consciousness gives way to a space informed by the unconscious."[46] Here, Benjamin endows these new mimetic techniques of camera with a new capacity to reconstruct the experience that had been shattered by the new visual representational apparatuses. In this light, photography and film can serve to heal potential by rescuing the capacity for the audience to restructure a new spatio-temporary order — that is, their own collective unconscious past.

The question of how this redemptive empowerment granted to the new optical reproduction can serve to reintegrate distorted experience brings us back to Benjamin's ocular metaphorics. In the "Photography" essay and "Artwork" essay, he makes two analogies: the association of the dispassionate lens of the camera with the eye of the psychoanalyst, and the camera with the surgeon's knife. In the former, the camera's super-mimetic technical capabilities can penetrate and explore the "unconsciously permeated space," just like the psychoanalyst's analysis of the patient's unconscious world. The visible but unseen visual data grasped by the camera can be similar to the Freudian parapraxes of slips of the tongue. Thus, for Benjamin, the camera, by focusing on the hidden details of familiar objects and extending our vision to unknown realms, can bring out therapeutic and emancipatory elements to the audience, who can thus be empowered and awakened from the dream world of phantasmagoric mass culture.

In the latter analogy, the truth of comparing the cameraman to the surgeon lies in the fact that both operatively penetrate into the tissues of reality, which consist of "multiple fragments," in order to "assemble [them] under a new law."[47] According to Benjamin, film montage plays the synthetic function that reintegrates modern experience distorted by the alienated capitalist industrialization.[48]

The visuality in New Chinese cinema precisely reflects the significance of Benjamin's "optical unconscious" through its heightened camera work to penetrate "the unconsciously permeated space" of Chinese ecological and environmental conditions, in a strong documentary and direct cinematography. This *cinéma-vérité* creates powerful vignettes of authentic "images of ecology"[49] — from the alien yellow earth to the demonic Yellow River, from the repressive Taihang Mountain to the dismembered Three Gorges, from the disoriented Suzhou River to the carcinogenic Tamsui River — provoking acute consciousness of the shocking truth of China's grave ecological reality. Though these ecological images are presented and manifested in a fractured and dispersed perspective, they present critical snapshots of a traumatized yet enabling "ecological unconscious" of dreams and yearnings for a green and clean world — the greenism in *Yellow Earth* and a clean-up river which "would be clear and full of fish," as the narrator wishes at the end of *Suzhou River*.

For Lawrence Buell, the ecological unconscious — which he calls "environmental unconscious," through absorption of Fredric Jameson's "political unconscious," Tuan's "topophilia," Theodore Roszak's "ecological unconscious," and Mitchell Thomashow's "the ecological identity" — can provide "the power of imagination" that enables environmental sensitivity to make visible aspects of psycho-perceptual reality and disjointed ambience which are hitherto invisible.[50] The ecological unconscious gives rise to an anti-establishment art practice that engages with the dominant environmental logic; it reveals the shocking and awakening aura of emotive processes in images charged with historical potency. In a word, the ecological unconscious reconnects us to the intimate and familiar *heimat*, namely, the world of water which is clean, ample, and safe — *shanqing shuixiu* 山青水秀 (green hills and clear waters).

From Yellow Screen to Green Screen

Yellow Earth shocks the world by the creation of a defamiliarized, "alien, remote and other-worldly" landscape with its luminous yellowish color.[51] If "yellow screen" signals an ecologically deteriorating earth caused by anthropocentric abuse of the ecosystem and unsustainable use of natural resources, then "green screen" not only represents ecocentrism, sustainability, biodiversity, and bioregionalism, but also film's environmental and ecological activism in engaging with ecological injustice, ecological panopticism,[52] and speciesism. "Green screen" celebrates "watershed consciousness" and promotes "toxic consciousness," two fundamental perceptions that empower contemporary environmental and ecological movement.

"Watershed consciousness," which has become "the most popular defining gestalt in contemporary bioregionalism,"[53] advocates a place-based ecological understanding of the interconnectedness between the biotic community and its abiotic environment. It embraces a transregional vision of a resourceful earth. As a heightened form of home awareness, it involves grassroots "ecosocial" participation in protecting and conserving land, soil, vegetation, and water resources. As we have seen in these films, China's watershed is suffering its worst crisis in the post-Mao era of economic boom. As Hu Kanping and Yu Xiaogang have observed:

> China's river basins are in crisis — suffering from water shortages, severe pollution, and water ecosystems threatened by ill-conceived dam and other construction projects. These threats to river basin health in China are caused not only by rapid economic growth, but also due to fragmented and disputing government bureaucracies and limited avenues for public participation to pressure for better environmental law enforcement. China's lack of sustainable management of river basins not only endangers the health of water ecosystems, but also threatens the country's socioeconomic development and environmental protection.[54]

Green watershed calls for more public participation, individual responsibility, and sustainable governance of the river basins in China. Independent documentary filmmaker and environmental activist Hu Jia's *The Silent Nu River* (*Chenmo de Nujiang*) is one of the engaged participations. In this docu-film, Hu Jia interviews local people along the Nu River about the ongoing dam project, thus lending a strong voice to the local community to express their grassroots resistance against ecological injustice.

"Toxic consciousness" makes us alert to the limits of natural resources and the dangers of both chemical and man-made pollutions. Nature should not be seen as a "standing reserve" only to serve the development of human beings. Natural resources, which are "virtually used up," will not be sustainable, so their plentitude is just a kind of illusion. "Toxic consciousness" can offer "insight into a culture's shifting relation to nature and to the environment at a time when the imminence of ecological collapse was, and is, part of the public mind and of individual imaginations."[55]

Water as Catharsis

In the final scene of Dai Sijie's *Balzac and The Little Chinese Seamstress* (2002), when the violinist Ma returns to China from France after many years to look for his alluring "goddess" Little Seamstress who had initiated his adventure of romantic passions, he is watching a news video about the flooding of the Three Gorges area. The water evokes Ma's fantasy, opening up the secret door into a pre-inundated pristine world in which he is passionately playing his violin and his friend Luo is reading Balzac's novel for Little Seamstress. The underwater world sutures the gap of a disrupted time so that Ma is able to dream of his mesmerizing reunion with his "goddess" in his youth under the flood water. This finale is so enchanting that one feels that life in the submerged world is more real and joyful than the world above the water. Indeed the underwater world is a treasury replete with both personal and collective history and memory, always providing rejuvenative and therapeutic power for those who are ecologically displaced and *unheimlich*. The return to the water is a kind of return of the repressed, a recuperative journey into the primordial ecosystem in which the rebirth of life is made possible.

In Bruce Sterling's classic cyberpunk novel *Schismatrix*, in order to get samples of life from their new abyssal ecology Europa, Abelard Lindsay and Vera Constantine return to the earth, which is abandoned due to environmental exhaustion, from the Outer Orbital Colony. They travel down to the ocean world and discover that "the water of life gushed from the depths of the valley."[56] They later design "an aquatic Posthuman,"[57] an angelic new life without intestines, sins, jealousy, or the desire to struggle for power so as not to be able to consume natural resources or pollute the planet. The new angelic being, whose "nerve-packed stripes housed a new aquatic sense that could feel the water's trembling, like touch at a distance," is "self-sufficient, drawing life, warmth, everything from the water."[58] This utopian aquatic posthuman life who communicates not through conventional human speech but through glowing (like the water) foretells Lindsay's final transformation into a bodiless new life by a transcendental, omniscient "Presence," that is, the ultimate apotheosis of water as theology of life.

2

Gorgeous Three Gorges at Last Sight:
Cinematic Remembrance and
the Dialectic of Modernization

Sheldon H. Lu

It is not that what is past casts its light on what is present, or what is present its light on what is past; rather, image is that wherein what has been comes together in a flash with the now to form a constellation. In other words, image is dialectics at a standstill.

— Walter Benjamin, *Arcades Project*[1]

Toward the end of the film *Balzac and the Little Chinese Seamstress* (*Balzac et Petite Tailleuse*, *Xiao caifeng* 巴爾扎克與小裁縫, dir. Dai Sijie 戴思傑, 2002), Little Seamstress decides to leave her home village and go to the city, to face an unknown future. Her lover Luo Ming asks who has changed her. She answers: "Balzac." Despite Honoré de Balzac's antimodern inclinations and his nostalgia for the past, to the Chinese readers who were lucky enough to have access to his books, he represented the Other of the backward, enclosed, repressed life in the last years of the Mao era. The novels of this Western writer embody enlightenment, modernity, and civilization. The works of Balzac and other European writers were secretly read in the Chinese "dark age" of cultural deprivation, or what is officially called the "Cultural Revolution."

Figure 2.1   Dai Sijie (born 1954).

This chapter is a selective analysis of several films: *Balzac and the Little Chinese Seamstress*, *In Expectation* (*Wushan yunyu*, 1996, dir. Zhang Ming), and *Still Life* (*Sanxia haoren*, 2006, dir. Jia Zhangke). What is common in all these films is the pending submergence of life under water upon completion of the Three Gorges Dam Project. Villages, towns, cities, and historic relics will all be wiped out in the relentless flood of modernization. Together, these films glimpse at the last moment of life before the disappearance and burial of memory, life, and history. The Three Gorges Dam has greatly impacted the inhabitants along the Yangtze River and has caused massive internal migration of population within China. The figure of the Chinese migrant is the logical result of the modernization agenda. These films bear testimony to the collective consequence of China's decision to flood traces of its own history and memory.

Balzac and the Little Chinese Seamstress is a Sino-French co-production based on Dai Sijie's novel and is directed by Dai Sijie. Set in a remote village in Sichuan Province in the early 1970s, the film unfolds the story of Luo Ming (Chen Kun) and Ma Jianling (Liu Ye), two Chinese "re-education youths" (*zhishi qingnian* 知識青年, or *zhiqing* 知青) from the city with "reactionary" family backgrounds, and their encounter with a local peasant girl, Little Seamstress (Zhou Xun). This is a time when Western "bourgeois" thought and books were banned in the ultra-leftist political climate of China. By chance these youths discover books of Western literature that were hidden by another "sent-down" youth, Four Eyes (Wang Hongwei). They secretly read these translated masterpieces of nineteenth-century European literature by such authors as Stendhal, Flaubert, Dostoevsky, and Kipling. Among the European classics they read are Stendhal's *Le Rouge et le Noir* (*Red and Black*), Gustav Flaubert's *Madame Bovary*, and Dostoevsky's *Crime and Punishment*. But Little Seamstress's favorite author is Balzac, and her favorite book is Balzac's *Ursule Mirouët* (*Ursula*). She becomes enamored of the dress of French ladies as seen in the book illustrations, and even tries on a bra so as to enhance her body's sensuality. The young people's taste of the forbidden fruits of knowledge soon leads to forbidden love. Luo and Little Seamstress fall in love and, as a result, Little Seamstress becomes pregnant and has to go through an abortion, which is illegal at the time for unmarried women. Thus, Western literature serves as the catalyst for the awakening of self-consciousness in an era of profound political and intellectual oppression. Little Seamstress decides to change her life by leaving the primitive hometown Phoenix Village. She has learned from Balzac that "a woman's beauty is a priceless treasure." With nothing else in her possession except a youthful body, she embarks on a physical journey to a brave new unknown future.

With all the humor, comedy, and fascinating local color, the film is nevertheless an apparent criticism of the stifling atmosphere of a particular historical era of Chinese socialism. The legacy of Balzac and other towering European writers is conveniently appropriated by the director as a vital source of humanism for which

Figure 2.2   Little Seamstress (Zhou Xun) and Luo in *Balzac and the Little Chinese Seamstress*.

Figure 2.3   Little Seamstress (Zhou Xun), Luo, and Ma in *Balzac and the Little Chinese Seamstress*.

the Chinese people thirst. Balzac has been lionized as one of the greatest writers of nineteenth-century realism by a long list of literary critics and social theorists, including the influential Karl Marx. But Balzac's political stance and artistic style cannot be simply characterized as belonging to a straightforward progressive humanist agenda. The eminent Marxist Hungarian theorist Georg Lukács attempts a dialectical understanding of the contradictions as well as strengths of nineteenth-century European writers. Balzac's heart is with the old French nobility, but he sets out to describe the process of its decline and death in France's historical evolution toward capitalism. In Lukács's words, "The destruction of the nobility — Balzac's ideological and political starting point — was only one aspect of this total process, and however biased Balzac may have been in favor of the nobility, he saw quite clearly the inevitability of its extinction, nor did he fail to see the internal decadence, the moral deterioration of the nobility in the course of this process."[2] Thus, there appears to be a contradiction between Balzac's regressive *Weltanschauung* (worldview) and progressive literary style (aesthetics). Lukács highlights the novelist's methodological innovation — realism, despite Balzac's eschewed understanding of social classes and his personal sympathies with certain social groups.

Balzac's political stance as well as the complex issue of artistic representation in nineteenth-century Europe are certainly not the concern of the Chinese youth trapped in a primitive corner of Sichuan Province in Dai Sijie's film. For those who have been denied of knowledge, anything Western that they can grab is intrinsically different, interesting, enlightening, and liberating. However, the one-sided linear humanist discourse of enlightenment reaches a moment of critical, dialectical self-reflection toward the end of the film. The consequences of modernity come under question. Time cuts to two decades later, the 1990s. This is the historical moment when a capitalist-style market economy is fully legitimized in China. The country has subscribed to an economic open-door policy and a developmentalist logic as formulated by Deng Xiaoping, whom Mao Zedong once denounced as a "capitalist roader" (*zouzi pai* 走資派). China is in the process of incorporating itself into the order of global capitalism.[3] The former "re-education youths" are now middle-aged men in Shanghai and France respectively. Luo is a well-established professor of dentistry in Shanghai, whereas Ma has been a successful violinist in France. Ma has lived in France for many years and has performed with the Lyon Symphony Orchestra. One day Ma watches a French TV report about the construction of the Three Georges Dam and the imminent destruction of the village in Sichuan where he and Luo lived. This prompts him to take a trip to the old mountain village and search for the unforgettable village girl, Little Seamstress. Filled with nostalgia for the past, he especially buys a bottle of French perfume to bring to Little Seamstress. At his arrival in Phoenix Village, Little Seamstress is nowhere to be found. The villagers will soon relocate as the whole place will go under water. They prepare sacrifices to the village and their ancestors by making and floating paper boats in water. Ma also swims amidst the paper boats. Twenty years ago he came of age at this place. His revisit is homage to the disappearing past as well as mourning for lost youth.

These two old friends Luo and Ma reunite in Shanghai. Postcard-like images of Shanghai's Bund and Pudong betoken another face of China — the showcase of economic prosperity as a result of China's Reforms and Openness (*gaige kaifang*). The neon signs and glitzy images of cosmopolitan Shanghai toward the end of the film form a sharp contrast to the primitive mountainous village, which is the predominant setting in the early part of film. The old friends reminisce about their youth in the early 1970s, the years they spent together as "re-education youths" in a village in Sichuan. They watch a video that Luo shot during his tour of the region. The footage includes the old, nearly toothless village chief who was such a powerful authority in the old days. In fear of him, Ma, who brought a violin with him to the village, renamed Mozart's *Concerto for Violin in G* with the absurd and yet felicitous title *Mozart Thinks of Chairman Mao*. They dreamed about returning to the city and leaving this backward place in the early 1970s. However, as the whole area will be inundated by the construction of the Three Gorges Dam, they now cast an elegiac, nostalgic look at the fast disappearing past.

During their reunion, Luo confesses that he went to Shenzhen to look for Little Seamstress, but without success. He was told that Little Seamstress had gone to Hong Kong. As we know, the trafficking of young women from the mainland in Shenzhen and Hong Kong is a widespread phenomenon and has become a subject of representation in Chinese and Hong Kong cinema. Chinese film viewers know that Zhou Xun, the actress playing Little Seamstress, portrays a mainland prostitute in Fruit Chan's film *Hollywood Hong Kong* (*Xianggang youge Helihuo* 香港有個荷裏活, 2003), which is part of Chan's "Prostitution Trilogy." Another film in this series is the famous *Durian Durian* (*Liulian piaopiao* 榴槤飄飄, 2001), which describes the life of a Chinese girl Xiaoyan (Qin Hailu) from the Northeast (*Dongbei*) living in Hong Kong as a prostitute. Zhou Xun has also portrayed other memorable female characters as migrant workers. She is a housemaid in Wang Xiaoshuai (王小帥)'s *Beijing Bicycle* (十七歲的單車, 2000), a woman from the countryside who puts on the clothes of her boss in her absence and mimics the ways of city women. Her identity is revealed to outside observers only when she is hit and wounded by the bicycle delivery boy Gui, another peasant who works in Beijing and looks at the manners of city folks from the outside with envy. Zhou Xun is also the actress in Luo Ye (婁燁)'s *Suzhou River* (*Suzhou he* 蘇州河, 2000), where she acts in the double role of the Mermaid, a female performer in a seedy bar in the Suzhou River area, and Mudan, the kidnapped daughter of an illegal vodka dealer. In all these films and roles, what is revealed is a huge population of migrant workers who have left their rural home to search for work in the cities.

In the final shots of *Balzac and the Little Chinese Seamstress*, the whole village is submerged under water, along with Little Seamstress's sewing machine, while the soundtrack plays the beautiful notes of Mozart's *Concerto in G for Violin*. The film produces an overpowering sense of mourning for and remembrance of things past.

As a coming-of-age story in part, this film reminds the viewer of another film — *Sacrificed Youth* (*Qingchun ji* 青春祭, 1985) directed by Zhang Nuanxin. That film is also about city youths who are sent to the countryside during the Cultural Revolution. It is in a village that these young people mature and discover their sense

Figure 2.4   Zhou Xun acts as a mainland prostitute in Hong Kong in Fruit Chan's *Hollywood Hong Kong*.

Figure 2.5   Zhou Xun portrays a rural girl working as a housemaid for a rich Beijing family in *Beijing Bicycle*.

Figure 2.6   Xiaoyan (Qin Hailu), a mainland Chinese prostitute working in Hong Kong, in Fruit Chan's *Durian Durian*.

Figure 2.7   Zhou Xun acts as an entertainer, Mermaid, in Lou Ye's *Suzhou River*.

of self and sexuality. The village years are their "rite of passage." As the Cultural Revolution ends, these "re-education youths" leave the village and return to the city. At the end of the film, the narrative voice states that the village has been destroyed in a landslide. Their past has been physically erased from the planet, but the memory of their youth persists.

Figure 2.8 *Sacrificed Youth* (Qingchun ji).

The idea of constructing a dam in the Three Gorges area originated in the 1950s. The dam, once completed, would generate energy, better control floods, and facilitate transportation along the river, it was believed. It was none other than the Great Leader himself who envisioned the building of such a dam in his famous poem "Swimming" (Youyong), published in 1956. The following is the second stanza of the poem where Mao indulges in a fantasy of the future:

風檣動，龜蛇靜，起宏圖。一橋飛架南北，天塹變通途。更立西江石壁，截斷巫山雲雨，高峽出平湖。神女應無恙，當今世界殊。

Sails move with wind,
Tortoise and Snake are still,
Great plans are afoot:
A bridge will fly to span the north and south,
Turning a deep chasm into a thoroughfare;
Walls of stone will stand upstream to the west
To hold back Wushan's clouds and rain
Till a smooth lake rises in the narrow gorges.
The mountain goddess if she is still there
Will marvel at a world so changed.

Figure 2.9   Mao's calligraphy of his own poem "Swimming."

"Walls of stone will stand upstream to the west/ To hold back Wushan's clouds and rain/ Till a smooth lake rises in the narrow gorges." 更立西江石壁，截斷巫山雲雨，高峽出平湖. These lines are Mao's poetic rendering of the future reservoir and dam at the Three Gorges. The construction of the Wuhan Yangtze Bridge was underway at the time. Hence, in the poet's imagination, "A bridge will fly to span the north and south/ Turning a deep chasm into a thoroughfare" 一橋飛架南北，天塹變通途. Mao was engrossed in his "grand plans" 宏圖 to transform China's landscape. The belief that human beings can change and conquer nature is a main feature of the Maoist ideology. "Voluntarism," human volition, or the will, can alter the natural course of things. Mao's exuberant poetic imagination of the future is matched only by his own calligraphy. With elements of the wild cursory style (*caoshu* 草書), the poem, as copied in Mao's staple calligraphy, conveys the vectors and lines of the poet's extravagant mind.

Interestingly enough, the Three Gorges Dam was never initiated in Mao's lifetime. In the end, Mao did not approve of the project. As a native of what was the ancient Chu state 楚國, Mao was well aware of the poetry and cultural legacy of this area. A more faithful translation of the second last line should read: "The mountain goddess should be well" 神女應無恙. This reveals what we would nowadays call an "ecological consciousness." The figure of the "mountain goddess" (*shennü*) reaches back to the ancient lyric poetry of the Chu state (*Chu ci* 楚辭), the writings of the great masters Qu Yuan 屈原 and Song Yu 宋玉. Modernization would not only cause the eradication of the region's infrastructure but would also disturb the spiritual heritage of China's past. In Mao's own words, the dam would "cut through Wushan's clouds and rain" 截斷巫山雲雨. Yet, Mao hoped that the mountain goddess would not be perturbed by a grandiose modernization project. His romantic longing for the future is qualified by a concern for the past cultural heritage.

The area along the upper Yangtze River, the ancient Chu Kingdom, or part of what is present Hunan-Hubei-Sichuan, is known for its mysterious, exotic cultural tradition. Its shamanism is different from the culture of the Central Plains (Zhongyuan). From the exalted poetic world of Qu Yuan and Song Yu to the folklore of ordinary people, Yangtze culture appears to be an enchanted dreamy world inhabited by mountain goddesses and mysterious spirits. In Song Yu's "Gaotang Rhapsody" (Gaotang fu 高唐賦), the mountain goddess appears in the dream of the King of Chu and says, "In the morning I am a floating cloud, in the evening I am a passing rain" (旦為朝雲，暮為行雨). The poem by Mao, a modern descendant of the ancient Chu State, clearly alludes to and inherits this cultural legacy of the Yangtze River. (Suffice to recall that Mao presented a set of *Chu ci* [*Poetry of the Chu*] to Japanese Prime Minister Kakuei Tanaka 田中角荣 during the latter's 1972 visit to China as the two countries were normalizing their diplomatic relationship).

In the current rush to hasten modernization, Chinese engineers hope to transform, tame, and conquer nature. This is indeed the flip side of modernization and enlightenment. As defined in plain words by Max Horkheimer and Theodor Adorno in their book *Dialectic of Enlightenment*, "Enlightenment's program was the disenchantment of the world. It wanted to dispel myths, to overcome fantasy with knowledge."[4] Socialist modernity then, is to dispel superstition, old myths, and feudal traditions. Hence, modernization itself has become a mythology and a grand metanarrative in modern China.

What the Three Gorges project would entail, with its steel, cement, cranes, and bulldozers, is precisely the disenchantment of millennial-old traditional culture along the Yangtze River. The lingering, mysterious, shamanistic (wu 巫) culture in the Wu Gorge (Wuxia 巫峽) or Wu Mountain (Wushan 巫山) will be conquered and replaced by the modern, post-Enlightenment rationality of science and technology. It is all the more extraordinary to find a moment of hesitation and doubt in the utopian thinking of the Great Leader-Helmsman-Poet regarding the Three Gorges project. He envisions the cutting of "clouds and rain" into halves while hoping that in doing so the mountain goddess will not be affected. The grand mythology of socialist modernity and the local myth of Wushan clouds and rain seem to co-exist in the poetic imagination. The Chinese dialectic of enlightenment is, for a moment, frozen and suspended in the poem. The tension embedded in the ambition to create "a smooth reservoir/lake" amid the chasm of the Three Gorges comes to a standstill. Mao hesitated, and did not take this step in his lifetime.

It is the Soviet-trained hydraulic engineer, China's Premier, Li Peng 李鵬, who wished to accomplish the great feat that Mao himself did not dare to do. As a native of Sichuan, Li also wanted to do something for the people of his fellow province. Amid voices of opposition, including that of Mao's former secretary Li Rui 李銳, Li Peng went ahead with the plan and initiated the controversial Three Gorges Dam project.

Rainclouds over Wushan (*Wushan yunyu* 巫山雲雨), also commonly translated as *In Expectation*, is the very title of a film (1996) by a young Chinese director who graduated from the Beijing Film Academy, Zhang Ming 章明. The story is also set against the background of the pending flooding of a town along the Yangtze River due to the construction of the Three Gorges Dam. In the town itself, signs are posted that the water level would rise to 175 meters. The whole town will be submerged under water once the hydraulic project is completed. People must disperse and move to higher ground. Chinese tourists from faraway places come to the town in order to see the Three Gorges before they disappear from the map.

The sexual connotation of the title is brought into full play in the film. The film's plot centers on Mai Qiang, a signal operator along the Yangtze River waterway, and his sexual encounter with a single mother, Chen Qing. Mai Qiang is a solitary, quiet, introverted character living and working all by himself at a signal station that directs traffic on the Yangtze River. His buddy Ma Bing wants to change his lifestyle and one day brings along with him a shady young woman, Lili, during a visit. Although Mai Qiang refuses to have sex with Lili even after Ma Bing sets them up, Mai Qiang's sexual desire is aroused by Lili nevertheless. After the departure of Ma Bing and Lili, Mai Qiang cannot contain his desire anymore and roams the nearby town. He meets Chen Qing, a single mother, sleeps with her, and leaves money with her at the end of their sexual liaison. Chen Qing works at a hotel and has had an ongoing affair with the head of the hotel, Lao Mo. Lao Mo is jealous of Chen Qing's relationship with the newcomer Mai Qing, and reports a case of "rape" to a young local police officer, Xiao Wu, or Wu Gang. Xiao Wu investigates and interrogates the people who might be involved — Mai Qiang, Chen Qing, and Ma Bing. Chen Qing does not admit that she was raped by Mai Qiang. Mai Qiang is thus left free. At the end the film, he revisits Chen Qing, for a possible long-term relationship.

Figure 2.10 Mai Qiang and Lili in *In Expectation* (Wushan yunyu).

Throughout the film, there is a very thin line between law and crime, between prostitution and intimacy, between the law-enforcing police and the civilians. The police officer Xiao Wu, an all-too-human figure, is busy with the preparation of his marriage. His personal interest is piqued when Ma Bing tells Xiao Wu that he can help him buy a refrigerator at a cheaper price even as he, Ma Bing, is being interrogated by the police officer for a possible complicity in crime. In fact, Lao Mo, head of the state-owned hotel, could be accused of having committed a criminal act himself when he falsely informs the police of an alleged rape. After their sexual act, Mai Qiang gives money to Chen Qing, who accepts it. The amount of money is excessively larger than the usual fee for a prostitute. It is not clear if this constitutes an act of prostitution or an act of generosity to help a struggling single mother. The entangled relationships between Ma Bing, Lili, and Mai Qiang are also unclear. Is Lili a friend of Ma Bing's? Or is she hired by Mai Bing as a prostitute for his friend, Mai Qiang? Moral boundaries are blurred throughout the film. What one notices are the daily necessities and acts of contingency in the ordinary lives of citizens along the Yangtze River.

Early on in the film, there is a scene when Mai Qiang's TV is turned on in his signal station. The TV broadcasts the news of the opening ceremony of the Three Gorges Dam project, with the presence of Premier Li Peng and other high-ranking Chinese leaders. In the second half of the film when the scene of action moves from the isolated signal station to the hustle and bustle of life in the town, "doomsday" looms larger and larger. At the back of the mind of each resident is the thought that the town will be eventually flooded and destroyed by the Three Gorges Dam. This ominous prospect affects every aspect of their life and future plans. The grand project that is supposed to help the local residents will eventually uproot them from their habitual place of living. Is this boon or bane?

The film that most directly tackles the issue of the Three Gorges Dam is Jia Zhangke (賈樟柯)'s *Still Life* (*Sanxia haoren* 三峽好人), which won the Golden Lion Award at the 2006 Venice Film Festival. The setting of the film is the two-thousand-year-old town Fengjie 奉節, near the Three Gorges, on the Yangtze River. Predictably, the town is being gradually erased as the completion of the dam nears. Two characters from Shanxi Province come to Fengjie to look for their long-separated loved ones. A coalminer, Sanming (Han Sanming), looks for his wife, whereas a nurse, Shen Hong (Zhao Tao), hopes to find her husband. When Sanming arrives and tries to locate the old address of his wife, he is informed that the old place is already flooded and under water. While waiting for a reunion with his wife, he lands a temporary job as a demolition worker. The daily task of the demolition team is to chip away and tear down the remaining buildings of Fengjie. What the viewer sees by following Jia's characteristic slow horizontal pan is an endless landscape of rubble, ruins, and destruction against the background of the natural beauty of the Three Gorges. The immense magnitude of this state-engineered physical destruction is beyond imagination and amounts to what might be called the "ugly sublime." As one critic puts it, "It is precisely the spectacular ugliness of the physical devastation of the urban environment around the Three Gorges that captures the camera's gaze: an anti-still life that monumentalizes destruction, giving it an awful, sublime grandeur normally reserved for scenes of natural beauty."[5]

The unfathomable magnitude and magnificence of the Three Gorges, especially Wu Gorge, have been long celebrated in Chinese literature and culture. This sense is captured in the memorable lines of the Tang poet Yuan Zhen: 曾經滄海難為水，除卻巫山不是雲 "Having experienced the sea, it is difficult to be impressed by ordinary water/ No cloud appears appealing after the Wu mountain." The unparalleled natural beauty is only matched by an equally unparalleled degree of destruction. The Three Gorges Dam boasts of being the largest dam in the world: so it is potentially a great man-made ecological hazard as well as the human destruction of nature and culture.

Figure 2.11   Jia Zhangke, *Still Life* (Sanxia haoren).

As Sanming and Shen Hong navigate the bureaucracy and local customs in search for their respective spouses, the viewer gets to see other ugly side effects of the dam project, namely, the social aspects. Corruption, theft of public assets by the local Relocation Office, insufficient compensation for dislocated residents, and the omnipresence of gangsters are the order of the day. The film reveals these abhorrent problems with a candid camera that is unusual for a Chinese filmmaker who must struggle with strict film censorship in the People's Republic of China.

While trying to find her husband, Shen Hong runs into Dongming (Wang Hongwei), a former colleague of hers and her husband's, just when he is working on an archeological site, a tomb from the Western Han Dynasty.[6] This brief passing detail is nevertheless a significant allusion to the brute fact that precious historical relics will be swept away and buried by the Three Gorges Dam. Tourists from all over the country come here to catch one last glimpse of the Three Gorges. On a cruise ship leaving Fengjie for Shanghai, the tour guide broadcasts the beauty and historical importance of the area to the tourists. She recites a famous poem by Li Bai (Li Po) that all Chinese school children learn: "Departing from Baidi City in the Morning" 早發白帝城：

> In the morning I bade farewell to Baidi amidst colorful clouds,
> And crossing a thousand li I returned to Jiangling in a single day.
> While gibbons on the riverbanks cried endlessly,
> My light boat already passed by myriad mountains.

> 朝辭白帝彩雲間，千里江陵一日還。兩岸猿聲啼不住，輕舟已
> 過萬重山。

Baidi Cheng (literally, City of the White Emperor 白帝城) is famous to readers of Tang poetry and lovers of *The Romance of Three Kingdoms* 三國演義 (*Sanguo yanyi*). It was the place where Liu Bei, emperor of the State of Shu 蜀, entrusted his toddler son/would-be orphan (*tuogu* 托孤) to the tutelage and care of his loyal minister Zhuge Liang before his death. The city has been ingrained in the Chinese consciousness as the locale of an exemplary eternal tale about the relationship between a loving sovereign and a loyal minister. The detriment that the Three Gorges Dam brings to this legendary ancient city is to flood it and surround it by water until it becomes little more than a tiny island.

One of the most vivid and charismatic characters in the film is perhaps none other than the gangster Mark (Xiaomage 小馬哥), a Chow Yun-fat fan. He strikes up a friendship with Sanming and transforms from an exhorter of his money to his protector. In one scene, Sanming and Mark are eating and drinking together. Mark indulges in a facetious yet earnest nostalgia for the past (*huaijiu* 懷舊) in a Chow Yun-fat-esque manner, reminiscent of Chow's stellar performances of heroic gangsters in *A Better Tomorrow* (*Yingxiong bense* 英雄本色) and *The Killer* (*Diexue shuangxiong* 喋血雙雄): "We do not fit in contemporary society. We are too nostalgic for the past." "There are no good people left in Fengjie anymore."

Throughout the film, there is a jarring juxtaposition between beautiful natural landscapes and ugly man-made ruins. As the camera pans horizontally, the stunning scenery of the Three Gorges unfurls like the scroll of a classical Chinese landscape painting, *shanshui hua* 山水畫 (literally "pictures of mountains and rivers"). All that stands in sharp contrast to unsightly human-induced destruction. As the viewer follows the meanderings of the characters, the word "chai" 拆 (demolition, tearing down) is on walls and buildings marked for demolition. Indeed, demolition has been the present physical reality of the Chinese nation as well as the trauma of individual citizens.[7] Mammoth state-sponsored modernization plans often disregard the feelings and needs of individual residents.

A companion work to *Still Life* is Jia Zhangke's documentary *Dong*, which also won major European awards for documentary film. The feature and the documentary were shot in Fengjie at the same time. "Dong" refers to the protagonist of the film, Liu Xiaodong, an artist who comes down to the Three Gorges from Beijing to paint.[8] The first half of the film is set in Fengjie, where Liu hires a dozen demolition workers as his male models for painting. The second half of the film moves to Bangkok, Thailand, where Liu hires a dozen Thai prostitutes as models, again for his paintings. What the two halves of the documentary have in common is the concern with the fate of human beings against anonymous social forces beyond their control. Both groups, Chinese or Thai, are reduced to the state of homelessness. They are migrants in search of job and dignity. In the first part, there is a segment where Liu Xiaodong visits a family and consoles the mother and young daughter whose father died in a work-related accident. The girl will never see her father again. The human toll of the Three Gorges project is clearly felt in the tragic life of local people. Once in a while, the protagonist-narrator Liu Xiaodong speaks directly to the camera about a general, unnamable "great sadness" (*da bei*) as an artist and an observer of society. Yet he is also interested in life, vital forces, and the human body as subjects of his painting. He admires the bodies and muscles of the young worker-models and wants to capture them on canvas.

Liu Xiaodong visited and painted at the Three Gorges several times. One of his paintings, *New Immigrants of the Three Gorges* (*Sanxia xin yimin*) is a gigantic oil painting that is ten meters wide and three meters high. The private collector of this painting auctioned it off at the Poly Autumn Art Fair in Beijing in November 2006, and sold it at the price of 22 million yuan (about 3 million US dollars). The buyer was a female entrepreneur, Zhang Lan, a tycoon in the Chinese food industry. The exorbitant price of Liu Xiaodong's painting is an index of the public's concern with the Three Gorges and the plight of the dislocated locals.

Figure 2.12 Liu Xiaodong, *New Immigrants of Three Gorges* (Sanxia xin yimin).

Figure 2.13 *New Immigrants of Three Gorges*, detail.

At an art exhibition in Chongqing in February 2007, a Chinese-style "brush-and-ink" (*shuimo hua* 水墨畫) painting, *People's Dwellings at the Three Gorges*, completed in 1995 by famed veteran Chinese painter Wu Guanzhong 吳冠中, was estimated to be worth at least five million yuan.[9] The painting is an elegant, stylized rendering of houses in traditional local architecture. The beauty of the homes is a far cry from the rubble and ruins that we see in Jia Zhangke's film. Wu Guanzhong's earlier oil painting, *Ten Thousand Li of the Yangtze River* (*Changjiang wanli tu*), was auctioned at the price of 37,950,000 yuan in 2006. Apparently, the capture and re-presentation of a place that will soon be disfigured or wiped out completely have made Wu's artworks so precious. His paintings are a nostalgic last look at a vanishing present.

Figure 2.14 Wu Guanzhong's painting, *People's Dwellings at Three Gorges* (Sanxia minju tu).

All these films and visual images revolving around the building of the Three Gorges Dam bear testimony to the ruthless physical eradication of cities, towns, villages, and communities. This is the result of reckless modernization under the reign of instrumental rationality that treats nature as a "standing reserve" awaiting human appropriation. The moving images of the cinema speak to a model of enlightenment and a vision of modernization that have become increasingly problematic in the age of global warming, or global environmental challenge.

3

Submerged Ecology and Depth Psychology in *Wushan yunyu*:
Aesthetic Insight into National Development

Nick Kaldis*

[A]nxiety at the looming threat of becoming truly disenfranchised in the most profound sense of the word — of losing ownership over one's body, of becoming alienated from oneself.

—Larissa Heinrich[1]

The Three Gorges Dam project continues to generate debate among scholars, journalists, government officials, environmentalists, developers, and others. The magnitude of the project staggers the imagination: at a cost of over 20 billion dollars, it will be the largest and most expensive dam ever known;[2] several million people will be forcibly relocated by the 1,983-meter-wide, 185-meter-high dam; water levels between Wuhan and Chongqing will rise more than 500 feet, submerging "13 cities, 140 towns, 955 business enterprises, 1,352 villages, and 115,000 acres of prime agricultural land," as well as countless archeological sites, historical, and artistic treasures (Berkman 1998: 31).[3] Engineering, archeological, political, environmental, and other such studies and statistics concerning the project abound, but to date, one of the few artistic treatments of the project's impact on the local environment and its residents is director Zhang Ming's *Wushan yunyu* (Wu Mountain Clouds and Rain; aka *In Expectation*).[4] But what does an artistic treatment of such a subject offer that other modes of understanding cannot?

This film demonstrates that artistic — in this case cinematic — representation is an indispensable way of understanding the profound psychological impact of large-scale development on the local citizenry, and of exploring both the conscious and unconscious consequences of ecological and human habitat devastation on the

---

* A different version of this essay appeared as "National Development and Individual Trauma in *Wushan yunyu* (In Expectation)," *The China Review* Vol. 4, No. 2 (Fall 2004): 165–191.

individual psyche. For no amount of statistical and historical research is capable of registering the influence of development on the individual psyche, yet this may be the site where development makes its deepest inroads. Nonetheless, the effect of external events on the psyche, profound though it may be, leaves few visible traces. Works of the imagination, especially imagistic fictional texts, engage experience at this level, and exemplify a way of "knowing" the world that cannot be reduced to other ways of knowing (e.g., scientific and "objective" historical data). As Michael Eigen puts it: "In art, life looks at itself, takes itself apart and pieces itself together in ways it cannot do in literal living. One reason art feels more real than life is its nascent ability to extract in concentrated form experiential nuclei that slip away in living."[5]

This chapter proceeds from the conviction that cinematic works can contribute to our understanding of larger social and cultural phenomena such as the massive ecological and social costs of state-sanctioned development.[6] The following close reading of the film *Wushan yunyu* instantiates an interpretive framework for explicating how artistic thinking grasps the complex effects of massive ecological disruption — the building of the Three Gorges Dam — on landscape, communities, and the outer and inner worlds of individuals. It might be expected that a film critical of the Three Gorges project would be realist or documentary in form, delivering a fairly explicit political statement. However, a political critique is only implicit in *Wushan yunyu*. Zhang Ming instead eschews the familiar cinematic techniques and narrative styles that might bolster such a critical perspective in favor of a powerfully imaginative, imagistic, and ambiguous approach to his subject matter. While these aspects of *Wushan yunyu*'s style make it resistant to easy paraphrase and interpretation, a close reading reveals a consistent pattern in the film's cinematic grammar: simply put, against the backdrop of the Three Gorges project the film juxtaposes issues of conflicted sexual desire. More precisely, the film is an exploration into the relationship between the destruction of the local ecosystem and the psychosexual conflicts of residents being displaced by that destruction, and almost all of the film's events arise out of this overarching structural relationship between national development and individual sexuality.[7]

The film is radical for its sustained adherence to this suggestive, imagistic style, what I define below as paratactic cinematics. It is doubly radical, this chapter argues, in its uncompromising attempt to explore repressed and disavowed sexual conflicts in contemporary Chinese society, and in linking disruptions in human desire and sexuality to the destruction of the environment and communities.

In sum, the goals of this chapter are: 1) to place the insights of aesthetic cognition alongside other forms of knowing, such as sociological, economic, historical (including cinematic/literary-historical), etc.; 2) to demonstrate a type of hermeneutics that proceeds *from* careful attention to the artistic knowing embodied in the cinematic text *to* larger contextual issues, ecological and otherwise;

3) specifically, to delineate the ways in which *Wushan yunyu* imagines and examines the psyches of individuals who are forcibly undergoing a traumatic experience of environmental destruction on a massive, historically unprecedented and highly disorienting scale. Under such conditions, the film shows, the psyche is traumatized in specific ways. It becomes alienated from its own environment, experience, and desire, resulting in a confusion of real and imagined relations to other people. The film conveys this disorienting condition by means of recurring cinematic devices, events, and motifs which add complexity and ambiguity to the viewer's already tenuous understanding of these seemingly "ordinary people"[8] and their affairs. All of this takes place against the politically charged backdrop of the Three Gorges Project, to which we turn first.

The Three Gorges Backdrop: Development as Inundation

> As we selected scenes for the film, its style was already gradually coming into focus, for choice implies design. In Wushan we found chaotic collections of angular buildings with no discernible reason for existing, and row upon row of blank walls. These extremely inharmonious and rootless artifacts struck the eye, waiting to be interpreted through motion pictures. ... [T]he boring blank walls stimulated our imagination, enabling us to achieve a certain visual effect.[9]
>
> — Zhang Ming

Among the most prominent features of *Wushan yunyu* are the recurring references to the Three Gorges Project. The first is, of course, the film's title, which is an ironic commentary on the way the project resurrects certain discredited CCP revolutionary myths of socialist domination over the elements.[10] Mao Zedong was very enthusiastic about the idea of such a great dam, and in 1956 wrote a poem which contains the lines: "A bridge will fly to span the north and south/ Turning a deep chasm into a thoroughfare/ Walls of stone will stand upstream to the west/ To hold back *Wushan's clouds and rain*/ Till a smooth lake rises in the narrow gorges/ The mountain goddess if she is still there/ Will marvel at a world so changed" (my emphasis).[11] The idea of such an unprecedented, gargantuan undertaking as the Three Gorges Dam, with its ties to the heady utopian atmosphere of the 1950s,[12] was somewhat of an anachronism by the 1990s when revolutionary discourse had lost much of its legitimacy and inspirational power. But the reality of the Three Gorges Project is a stark reminder that grandiose CCP propaganda is not a bygone relic of the (mythical) past, nor is it necessarily divorced from reality. Contrary to official discourse, the film suggests that the byproduct of this reality is precisely what discredited the former ideology in the first place — a dystopic rather than utopian cause-and-effect relationship between the state's modernization efforts and the lives of its citizens. In other words, the representation of the Three Gorges Project in the film contests through image the state's representation of the project in ideological narratives of development and modernization.[13]

Zhang Ming has been cautious about directly relating the imagery of the Three Gorges Project in the film to the main characters' sexual confusion, dysphoria, and apathy, probably so as to sidestep politically sensitive implications. In one notable statement, for instance, Zhang ambiguously likens man's contemporary existence to living in a "great void," in which one witnesses "those monotonous repetitive actions and characters wandering like ghosts."[14] Perhaps the closest he comes to explicitly highlighting the connection between the dam and the characters' psychological problems is in the following statement: "In the time of peace and prosperity in which we live, many peoples' emotional desires cannot be satisfied. Our film is concerned with this fundamental aspect of existence."[15]

It is left to the viewer to discern and explain precisely how the film, within its chosen setting of the Three Gorges backdrop, addresses this relationship between the current era of "peace and prosperity" and its concomitant emotional desires. Formulating such conclusions necessitates a careful reading and analysis of the numerous recurring elements in the film.

Paratactic Cinematics

> Our initial security and confidence in some unified narrative to come has been dispelled without return by the interventions of experimental film: we are no longer necessarily in reliable hands, things may never cohere.
>
> —Frederic Jameson[16]

> This film invariably forces one to change one's viewing habits because it thoroughly eliminates all theatrical motivations, giving you neither the means nor the need to speculate as to further plot developments; it simply incites you to interpret and intuit what has taken place.
>
> —Wang Xinyu[17]

In style, *Wushan yunyu* departs significantly from the conventions of continuity editing, although an evident — if not familiar — chronology is discernible. The most notable features of the film's structure are instead numerous scenes with recurring events and motifs, which conjure up inexplicable connections between characters and events, endowing the film with a mysterious, ambiguously symbolic quality that resists chronological narrative explanation and easy paraphrase.

The film employs a type of cinematic parataxis, a "method of 'presenting' materials, side-by-side, without commenting definitively on their relation to one another."[18] This strategy, as Wang Xinyu has so aptly noted, forces viewers to draw from their own imaginations, engaging their desires in the process of making sense of the events and relationships in the story.[19] Detailed scrutiny of these repeated events and motifs allows one to induce the relations between them and formulate the larger insights embodied in the film's visual poetics.

The first (and most deceptive) of the film's recurring structural devices are intertitles introducing the main characters. Upon each character's initial appearance, there is a cut to a black background with white lettering briefly introducing that character. For instance, "Mai Qiang, 30 years old, signal operator at Jiushizi. Ma Bing arrives in the afternoon, bringing Lili." These documentary-like informational screens, so clearly addressed to the audience, position viewers as omniscient observers of the characters and events. They imply that we are privy to truths and facts pronounced from an extra-diegetic vantage point, providing us with an impartiality and distance from which to view and judge the characters, actions, and events of the story. The assumption is short-lived; in truth, the intertitles actually impart to the viewer a false sense of objective mastery over the screen images. For instance, following the intertitle introducing him, there is a shot of Mai Qiang painting,[20] then a brief, extreme close-up of a pair of binoculars, which Mai Qiang picks up to scan the river. Cut to a matching shot of what we believe to be our shared point of view with Mai, a river vista as seen through his binoculars (including a green mountain in the background and a large tourist boat meandering up the muddy river), conveying a sense of objective visual mastery of this river landscape. However, while we are gazing through the binoculars, ostensibly together *with* Mai Qiang, he suddenly enters the shot from bottom screen left, hauling two buckets of water, and pausing to stare at some men painting the future waterline on a boulder (Figure 3.1).[21] This editing device causes the audience's point of view to abruptly shift from an initial omniscient vantage point (intertitle followed by shot of Mai Qiang) to a subjective one within the diegetic (point-of-view shot, looking through the binoculars, with Mai Qiang), to one of utter disorientation. As the narrative progresses, it becomes evident that viewers are experiencing the disconcertment of Mai, Chen, and other characters. Images of the natural environment he inhabits and observes, into which we have been momentarily sutured, are fraught with ambiguity and insubstantiality. None of it has permanence, yet the mind is unable to fathom the paradoxical imminent disappearance of this river landscape beneath itself, as indicated by the signs painted on rocks and walls surrounding Mai, marking the future level of the reservoir. Environmental critique and cinematic technique are here inseparable: we can no more envision this ecological reality than we can grasp the image of Mai appearing in the distance of his own subjective point-of-view shot.

Figure 3.1   Mai Qiang hauling water up from the river, observing markers indicating the future water level.

Numerous aspects of the film's style contribute to this disorienting effect. Among the most prevalent is the deluding direct cinema or documentary feel of many scenes. Intertitles, long takes, hand-held shots, available lighting, simultaneous sound, and infrequent use of a musical score[22] all impart an air of realism to the events being filmed.[23] But the camera refuses to collaborate with the audience in creating a familiar version of on-screen reality, withholding the visual and cognitive omniscience upon which the factual documentation and understanding of events rely. Nor does any character act as a viewer surrogate to provide an intra-diegetic position and gaze of understanding and clarity. Nothing confirms a larger "truth" or master narrative that ties events and protagonists together, contextualizing them within a familiar cinematic version of reality.[24] Wang Xinyu, in describing these defamiliarizing effects of watching the film, concludes that *Wushan yunyu* imparts such a novel viewing experience that it might be considered a "new experiential" (*xin tiyan*) or "new sensibility" (*xin ganjüe*) film.[25] The recurring images and events throughout the film force viewers to "interpret and intuit" what they see and experience on the screen, rather than treating them as passive recipients of information conveyed through familiar imagery and narrative schemes, and pointing to commonplace conclusions. This interpretive process leads to unique insights concerning the relationship between the ecological devastation precipitated by national development and individual psychological trauma.

In addition to the paratactic links implied between images and events in *Wushan yunyu*, one cannot overlook the similar behavior and surroundings of Mai Qiang and Chen Qing, which directly foreground the importance of visuality and visual dynamics to an understanding of the film. Both protagonists are associated with signs, symbols, and visuality, yet neither is able to make sense of his/her environment or communicate with others in a satisfactory manner. Additionally, they both seem to dream while awake, and have trouble distinguishing between inner and outer perceptions and voices. From the opening of the film, Mai Qiang is associated with signs, symbols, and visuality in general: his residence and occupation are in and of themselves loci of signification; he frequently stares silently at things, such as the previously mentioned sign indicating the future water level of the reservoir; there are close-ups of his binoculars and television; he dreams that he "saw a certain person"; he is a painter.

Intra- and extra-diegetic connections between Mai Qiang the painter and Zhang Ming the cinematic artist (who studied painting in college) in one particular sequence aptly demonstrate the keen insight of aesthetic cognition, and can be interpreted as a commentary on the Three Gorges Project. Early in the film, Mai Qiang, who paints in his spare time (grinding and mixing his ink and painting with a traditional *maobi*), degrades his own creative visual expressions when he throws some of his landscape paintings to his friend Ma Bing, who is out of toilet paper. Ma Bing refuses to use them, not on account of his aesthetic sensibilities, but because he believes these paintings are good enough to sell for profit in Beijing. The sequence brilliantly allegorizes connections between development, degradation of the ecosystem, consumerism, artistic creativity, and viewer interaction with the visual arts. The landscape artist, whose environment (both the source of his livelihood and the inspiration and subject matter for his art) and way of life are being destroyed by development, debases his work by reducing it to an item whose value is merely in its physical use. Yet even as he cavalierly treats his creative work as toilet paper, to be covered with filth and discarded, his materialistic friend sees it only for its exchange value, something convertible to a more coveted currency. In this environment, the values of creativity and aesthetic appreciation have disappeared entirely. The image of landscape painting, the highest creative achievement of traditional Chinese visual artistic expression, is here literally and metaphorically soiled as a result of the surrounding ecological destruction and the crass materialist mindset of the citizen-consumer and dilettante that the ideology of non-sustainable development produces. This scene also allegorizes the Three Gorges Dam's ecological impact on the Yangtze River and the Wushan region: the reservoir will swell the river and immerse the landscape of Wushan in silt and filth in exchange for electric currency.[26]

Other than those already mentioned, many other scenes and sequences associate Mai Qiang with visuality and visual dynamics and link his character to that of Chen Qing, via their participation in analogous scopic behaviors. This prominent foregrounding of visual signs and symbols firmly establishes a primary process visual logic from the outset of the film. Parataxis, repetition, contiguity, and metonymy are among the major modes of primary process thinking, also referred to as the "logic" of the unconscious.[27] These are the modes of cognition to which the viewer must accede in order to understand and interpret *Wushan yunyu*.

This is emphatically stressed through a filmic envelope formed by the opening and closing sequences of the film, which almost identically parallel one another. In both scenes, one of the red and white signal arrows that determine the direction of riverboat traffic is being hoisted up a flagpole by a silent Mai Qiang. It is not spoken dialogue or written language, but signs and symbols that are being used to convey meaning within the diegetic.[28] These are signals directed at the viewer, indicating that visual imagery and symbolism convey the film's insights more than dialogue or any narrative aspects of the diegetic. There is, however, no explicit key to interpreting the events and images, only their paratactic recurrence and the background against which they are presented. This forces the viewer to engage, and to some degree, reproduce the primary process logic of the film during the act/art of interpretation.

The female protagonist Chen Qing is in many ways Mai Qiang's counterpart or soul mate, and is likewise closely associated with visual symbols. Consequently, her initial appearance takes place in a sequence that directly parallels the opening shots of Mai Qiang at work. Like Mai Qiang, she first appears raising a sign directed at (the same?) boats on the river, advertising her hotel to disembarking tourists (Figure 3.2). The intertitle introducing her is misleading: after briefly describing her job as a tourist guide it states that she is "preparing for her second wedding" (*zhengzai zhunbei ta di'er ci hunyin*). However, her new fiancé and the wedding will never be shown; instead her sexual relationship to Lao Mo and Mai Qiang will be foregrounded.[29] In another parallel, she walks upward from the river's edge and soon passes a sign indicating the future water level of the reservoir. Chen Qing is even given to hallucinating people and voices, just as Mai Qiang sees someone in his dreams. At one point, she looks up to see a strangely anachronous figure, a man dressed in Daoist-type garb, staring at her from just outside the hotel doorway. She quickly lowers her head in embarrassment for a moment; when she looks up again, he has disappeared. In a later scene, while preparing fish, she imagines a voice calling her name.

Figure 3.2   Chen Qing advertising her hotel to disembarking tourists.

It is tempting to view Chen Qing allegorically as representing the witches, succubi, and shamanesses associated with this region since ancient times. Indeed, her hallucinations might indicate that she traverses both the natural (conscious) and supernatural (unconscious) worlds. However, it is Mai Qiang whose apparent simultaneous physical presence in two different places at once lies at the heart of the story's mysterious events (most significantly, a sexual encounter that may or may not have occurred), linking him to incubi and sorcerers. For instance, the mysterious (Daoist?) figure hallucinated by Chen Qing resembles Mai Qiang (and is played by the same actor, Zhang Xianmin), and this apparition is accompanied by the sound of thunder. Again, conventional/traditional associations and expectations — gendered and mythic — are subverted by the film's style, leaving the audience to "interpret and intuit" its paratactic sign system.

Fish, which have a long history in Chinese symbolism and mythology, are at the center of one of the film's eeriest recurring motifs.[30] In separate scenes, both Mai Qiang and Chen Qing are shown reaching into a reddish bucket of water and selecting a fish for dinner. They alternately handle the two live fish, finally reselecting the first. Both characters stun the fish with a cleaver whack to the head, then momentarily stare blankly ahead, as if they themselves stunned, suddenly aware of something, or hearing imaginary voices. Finally, each slits the fish open. Through these mirrored actions, it is implied that the two are somehow connected in a mysterious way that defies space, time, and explanation.[31] Additionally, both Mai Qiang and Chen Qing are repeatedly associated with water, that traditional symbol of flowing, changeable, yin/female energy, and contemporary ominous symbol of developmental doom and ecological devastation for this region.

Engaging the film's oblique mythical imagery and correlations via an ecocritical perspective reveals another of the film's key insights, concerning the supernatural world's dependence on the existence and preservation of the natural environment. Natural landscapes and phenomena are indispensable to Chinese mythology, and many of its important characters and events are embodied in the natural phenomena of the Three Gorges region in and around the vicinity of Wushan, among other places (the sexually charged mythology of the area is discussed in the following section). Through belief systems such as mythology and legend, a culture is able to project, engage, and sustain its collective psyche. They act as the repository of a people's repressed desires, conflicts, and other emotional dramas that are essential to but cannot be acted out or given adequate space in most social contexts and man-made environments. *Wushan yunyu* brilliantly reveals that, when epic-scale modern technological and engineering "marvels" destroy and usurp the awe-inspiring natural spaces integral to a culture's mythology — a key component of its collective unconscious — then the psyches of individual citizens can become profoundly distressed.[32]

Recurring scenes and images as well as characterization thoroughly establish the centrality of visual dynamics to the structure of the film, and these dynamics dislocate the familiar rational perceptual and cognitive frameworks upon which viewers normally rely. The preceding exploration has argued that, to grasp the significance of the film's insights, the viewer's experience must be one of both recognition and giving in to the logic of primary process thinking and paratactic cinematics that undergird *Wushan yunyu*'s images and narrative structure. This visual grammar ambiguously correlates two main structural themes — the large-scale ecological devastation of Three Gorges Project (discussed previously) and the troubled psyches of individuals who are being traumatized by this obliteration of their social and natural habitats. Under such conditions, they experience detachment, disorientation, anomie, and dysphoria, and are alienated from their surroundings, from other people, and from their own experiences. For the protagonists Mai Qiang and Chen Qing, this takes the form of a confusion of real and imagined sexual relations with other people.

The Cinematic Imagination of Conflicted Sexual Identity

> Nature provides ... signifiers, and these signifiers organize human relations in a creative way, providing them with structures and shaping them.
>
> —Jacques Lacan[33]

> What I have called its meaning ... [lies] ... in the problem of the indeterminacy itself and that of assessing the nature of an external force that does something to you, but which, by virtue of the fact that its power transcends your own and cannot be matched, by definition also transcends your capacity to understand it or to conceptualize — better still, to represent — it.
>
> —Frederic Jameson[34]

Wushan yunyu's "cinematic imagination of a sexual identity"[35] begins with the title, which is replete with ancient literary and sexual allusions. Prior to the investigation of the alleged rape that dominates approximately half of the film, sexual issues are already foregrounded and central to the story and its location. To begin with, the film's literary title alludes to the ancient poet Song Yu's erotically charged "Gao Tang Fu."[36] This ancient prose poem associates Wushan with a succubus that visits men in their dreams, then leaves them forlorn when they wake up and find her gone.[37] The poem and the setting of the film draw upon the area's rich mythological tradition: the town of Wushan lies at a point below the Qutang Gorge, near the end of a wide stretch of the Yangtze, just before entrance to the twenty-five-mile Wuxia, "Witches Gorge," the middle and "most foreboding" of the famous Three Gorges.[38] Wushan is also adjacent to the point where the Daining River empties into the Yangtze. The entire area has long been associated with witches (the "Wu" in *Wushan* can stand for witches, sorcerers, shamans), the gorge itself perhaps getting its name from a myth that tells of a goddess (now represented by a rock formation on Goddess Peak (*shennü feng*) and her eleven sisters, who "came to earth to help Great Yü the flood-tamer drain the Chinese earth and make it habitable for ordinary humans and how the eleven sisters became the eleven peaks of Witches Gorge, and how she herself remained in petrified but otherwise human form as a sentinel on the twelfth peak, to help rivermen safely through this still-dangerous passage."[39]

The multiple ancient allusions in the title thus set the tone for the film's sexually charged fatalistic and dystopic atmosphere of conflicted desire.[40] Like the mirage of a mythical leviathan about to materialize, the future dam and reservoir portend the imminent erasure of their world looming unseen over the spaces where the characters reside, eat, meet, shop, work, sleep, and make love. Against this backdrop of an unseen but inexorable spectacular and destructive developmental process, the director singles out and explores the analogously less tangible psychosexual conflicts engendered by such living conditions.

Mai Qiang's alienated sexuality is first explored in the scene where he is selecting a fish for his dinner (the fish represents a symbolic link between Mai and his alleged rape victim Chen Qing, who will later be seen selecting and preparing fish in exactly the same manner). Lili, with whom Mai Qiang will have an ambiguous sexual relationship, appears while Mai is preparing the fish.[41] Mai, his hands covered with fish blood and entrails, discovers Lili, a total stranger, in a short skirt, dancing alone in his office. He stares vacantly, bewildered or mesmerized by her inexplicable appearance and overt sexual posturing. All of their interactions will be awkward and ambiguous.

As with most of the characters in the film, viewers are not given much insight into Lili's personality, desire, and motives, and must surmise the precise (sexual) relationship between Lili and the men with whom she associates. One critic, for example, calls her "a young prostitute,"[42] while another labels her "Ma's bored g.f. [girlfriend]."[43] Lili appears to be on autopilot — she performs the role of a sexpot with aplomb, but it is as if there is little more to her identity, nothing behind her performance, just the shell of an artificial character. She expresses few emotions aside from a childlike impulsiveness, frequent boredom, and contrived sensuality, all performed for the gaze of Mai Qiang and Ma Bing.

Ma Bing is himself somewhat of an enigma, a man who may or may not have just gotten out of prison. He has obvious difficulty distinguishing sexuality from aggression. He pushes Lili about, slaps her head while talking to Mai Qiang, drags her into the bedroom for sex, and even tries to force Mai to have sex with her. Conversely, Ma shows far more respect and tenderness toward Mai, addressing the latter as his "teacher" (*shifu*). In a scene with homoerotic overtones, he even willingly hugs and kisses Mai, according to the rules of a card game, and then refuses to continue playing, sarcastically quipping that he might "fall in love" with Mai Qiang.[44]

To return to Mai Qiang, he seems utterly incapable of the rape with which he will eventually be charged. He looks on silently, but uncomfortably, almost contemptuously, as Ma Bing orders or shoves Lili around. He feels extremely awkward and unnerved when he has the opportunity to have sex with Lili, choosing instead to make conversation, and later drapes his shirt over her after she impetuously strips down to her underwear and takes a dip in the river. The following morning, he apparently lies that he had sex with her so that Ma Bing will have to give her some money (as the result of a bet, a friendly deal, or of her being a prostitute).

As for the widow, Chen Qing, her first scene of intimacy with another character brings to light a sexual conflict with her boss. Since she is arranging her (second) marriage, she now tries to end this relationship with Lao Mo, the manager of the hotel where she works. Lao Mo is shocked and upset, but he agrees, then asks if they can still have sex that day. Chen Qing shrugs him off in disgust, but says "wait a minute" (*deng yixia*) as Lao Mo is going out the door. The camera cuts to a tourist boat on the muddy river, leaving the outcome in question, while paratactically linking this scene to the earlier point-of-view shot through Mai Qiang's binoculars. Chen Qing, like Mai Qiang, seems to have no capacity for pleasure, sexual or otherwise, and appears to be oblivious to her own apathy. Even while declaring the end of her relationship with Lao Mo, she expresses a paradoxical mix of contempt for and submission to his sexual advances. For both Chen and Mai, a confused and detached relationship to one's own sexuality is implicitly connected to living in an environment that will shortly be deluged by government-sanctioned development.

There is also an erotic connection linking Mai Qiang, Chen Qing, and Chen's son. In this, the film's most overtly erotic scene, the little boy, Liang Er, is at his kitchen table painting with brush and black ink, as Mai Qiang was shown doing earlier. Liang Er's attention is diverted by his mother who begins bathing behind a semi-transparent curtain in the same room. The boy stops painting and stares at his mother in Oedipal fascination as she washes then briefly fondles her breast. This scene, as with many others in the film, explores a character's sexuality through images and association with looking — here, a child's scopophilia — and is somewhat disturbing in its portrayal of the mother's potentially incestuous exhibitionism, as she fondles herself in front of her own young child. Perhaps a sense of being an innocent abused by the men in her life (namely Lao Mo, who is her boss, and Mai Qiang, who may have raped her) has compelled her to unconsciously seduce her own son in order to reverse (displace) the loss of power she experiences in those other sexual relationships, in which she is uniformly portrayed as numb, passive, and emotionally detached in her sexuality. In disavowing her own experience of being instrumentalized and objectified, she reenacts the drama, this time taking control of the dynamic by assuming (a sublimated sense of) agency. Like the Three Gorges reservoir and the surfeit of male desire and power that engulfs her, Chen Qing here floods the mother-child relationship with her own conflicted sexual desire. The interpretation of this and other scenes in the film relies not on dialogue but on images that remain discursively untethered from any narrative structure or continuity editing. Interpretation here must comply with the film's paratactic cinematics and primary process thinking, as in the above analyses of recurring motifs and events, character behaviors and associations, mythical references, etc.

Following the scene of Liang Er gazing at his naked mother, the mysterious central sexual episode of the film occurs. It is a tryst, a rape, or a fabricated accusation of rape, for the actual event is never revealed to the other characters or to the viewer. That something actually has happened seems likely. When interrogated at the police station, Mai Qiang admits that he went to "Xiankelai" hotel for a "private affair" (*sishi*) with a woman, and calmly says: "I slept with her (*wo gen ta shuijiao le*) and then left all my money on the table." When officer Wu Gang asks Mai Qiang why he chose Chen Qing, Mai falters over the words, "I felt ... I felt ... I felt ... the moment I saw her, I immediately ... I felt I had seen her before."

Mai's fatalistic, hallucinatory attitude towards his own sexuality is paralleled with Chen Qing's mystification of her own desire. Only moments after the interrogation scene, Chen is shown sitting in her home. She suddenly looks off into space, and asks her son, "Did you hear someone calling Mommy's name?" In a comparable scene near the end of the film, Mai also appears to hallucinate or sense that he is being beckoned. Mai Qiang and Ma Bing are sitting on the veranda of the signal house after Mai Qiang has been released for lack of evidence. Ma informs him that Chen Qing is "not getting on well," that the rape scandal ruined her impending wedding and she's alone again, raising her child. He concludes that "it's a real shame." After pausing a moment, Mai Qiang tells Ma Bing to stay and run things while, fully clothed, he slowly walks into the river, then swims towards the city. Cut to the hotel lobby, where Mai Qiang enters, dripping wet. Chen Qing leaves the front desk and briskly walks to her upstairs apartment. Mai Qiang follows, stripping off his soaked shirt. She stops outside her apartment door, and turns to face him, crying. She slaps his face, then repeatedly slaps his bare chest with both hands, as he awkwardly tries to pull her close. Both of these protagonists, who are embedded in a schematic of visual signs and references to visuality, appear to live in a world of psychological and interpersonal confusion. The film's narrative, likewise, hovers around a sexual relation between the two but refuses to move beyond ambiguous imagistic associations. Concerning what previously transpired between Chen and Mai, the audience — and most of the characters — remains baffled.

The film presents viewers with a frustrating conglomeration of implications and inferences. The backdrop against which this assemblage is framed is a man-made, as-of-yet nonexistent place that, even in its invisibility, dominates over and nullifies the characters' environment. They struggle unsuccessfully to maintain reliable cognitive maps[45] of this world and its symbol systems, slipping into a confused realm of part objects where the tangible and the fantasized mutually interact, free of the normally more rigid and reliable borders. Within this milieu, individuals pursue sexual relations through unrecognized, disavowed, or (unconsciously) fantasized sexual desire.

A psychoanalytic-semiotic framework helps us probe the depths of this film's pessimistic exploration of the psyche and ecological devastation. The characters in *Wushan yunyu* are surrounded by the signs of a developmental project that portends the inevitable submersion of their city and surrounding natural environment. In this context where visual perception and sign systems are paramount, visuality and signification nonetheless fail to confer meaning, thereby undermining the subject's ability to establish an identity within its environment[46] (like the dam and reservoir, the sexual crisis that disrupts this community has no visual analogue; it is unrepresented/unrepresentable, remaining ambiguously vague but pregnant with significance). Even if they could manage to fix themselves within this novel sign system, it would provide them with but an illusory moment of stable identity, only to be put under erasure by the rising dam waters. Such a situation constitutes an artistic amendment or supplement to the well-known post-structuralist/Lacanian formulations of the subject's place in the system of signifiers and signifieds.

In Lacan's formulation, the conflicts of the pre-linguistic (mirror stage) and linguistic (Oedipal) processes, through the various repressions they precipitate, inaugurate subjectivity in a self traumatically (yet unconsciously) divided from itself, initiating the (conscious) subject/ego into the symbolic order of language and sign systems, the mortar of society.[47] In this system, identity, "the *moi*, the ego, of modern man," is an imaginary construct of the signifying systems — social (symbolic) discourses — that "envelop man in a network so total ... so total that they give the words that will make him faithful or renegade," determine his destiny and his acts, and will follow him to the grave.[48] The symbolic and imaginary orders provide conscious identities that prop up and sustain our false sense (misrecognition) of self and Other in modern "scientific civilization."[49] Lacan describes the process by which a subject living under the aura of modernization, through the "delusional" nature of language, "forget[s] his own existence and his death [i.e., his divided self and repressed unconscious] ... misconstrue[s] (*méconnaître*) the particular meaning of his life in false communication":

> Communication can be validly established for him in the common task of science and in the posts that it commands in our universal civilization; this communication will be effective within the enormous objectification constituted by that science, and it will enable him to forget [the split and alienated nature of] his subjectivity. He will make an effective contribution to the common task in his daily work and will be able to furnish his leisure time with all the pleasures of a profuse culture.[50]

In Lacan's formulation, all social subjects are necessarily split and alienated subjects, created via both scopic (mirror stage) and symbolic (linguistic) processes. Thus, if there is any possibility of resistance, transcendence, or transformative social practice, it depends on our prior subjectivization within the socio-symbolic order, i.e., the prior establishment of a social identity. Once an identity within the social world has been secured, only then is the stepping (partially) outside the symbolic order and perceiving one's immersion in this delusional state possible. Lacan does not envision this possibility as a moment of enlightenment and freedom from ideological fetters, with the subject becoming fully aware of and overcoming the split and alienated nature of his identity. Instead, this event is associated with "the advent in the subject of that little reality that his desire sustains in him with respect to the symbolic conflicts and imaginary fixations," which comes to the surface in the "intersubjective experience[s] where this desire makes itself recognized."[51]

The subjects (characters) in *Wushan yunyu*, however, cannot establish a fixed identity in the social order, let alone go on to recognize or direct the tiny remnant — "little reality" — of the psyche's reality that manifests itself in intersubjective desire. In other words, without the stability of even a "delusional" system of "false communication," without a symbolic order that grounds false/imaginary constructs of self in a recognizable social network of symbols and consensual validations with other false selves (i.e., split and alienated subjects), without this discursive delusion, a desiring subject cannot even begin to grasp that bit of reality which reveals the subject/self as accomplice to its own conflicts and fixations. Agency and opposition to that order are thereby rendered moot. The film's characters react to these conditions by projecting their desire into a realm of confused, vague fantasy, hallucinations, disembodied voices, or dream visions.

Conclusions

The social and political ramifications of this psychological state of affairs are as follows: The politically mandated destruction of the environment, residential communities, and economic livelihoods, on a massive and incomprehensibly disorienting scale, performed in the name of a discredited state ideology, gives birth to a potentially devastating phenomenon — the disturbance of subjectivity at the unconscious level, of one's relationship to one's own body and psyche, and to the minds and bodies of others. Oppositional consciousness vis-à-vis the status quo and (non-mandated) social change are thereby rendered obsolete. If, as *Wushan yunyu* demonstrates, the disorienting nature of technological development can reach into the depths of one's psycho-sexual identity and create confusion there, then there is little possibility of success in other types of social relations, namely forming bonds with others in the spirit of shared political action or resistance. In *Wushan yunyu*'s "representation of ... psychic masochistic malaise, we see an irreversible situation testifying to the end of individuality and the impossibility of collective opposition to the status quo."[52]

This foreboding pessimism is embedded in the structure of the film. There is no narrative closure and catharsis, no gesture towards the promise of less disruptive and more locally engaged, ecologically friendly, and sustainable developmental policies. Instead, the traumatizing exigencies of national development are shown to be woven into the very fabric of everyday life, creating irresolvable intra- and interpersonal conflicts, anomie, sexual dysphoria, dislocation, loss, etc. The film seems determined to infect viewers with the disorientation, anomie, and dysphoria suffered by its characters. Primary process logic and paratactic cinematics help to project the characters' confusion and disorientation onto the viewing audience. *Wushan yunyu* is thus an exemplary instantiation of both aesthetic cognition and ecocinematic criticism. This chapter demonstrates how a work of art can make original and complex contributions toward our understanding of the conflicted state of human agency under conditions of ecological devastation in China today.

Cynical as this aesthetic vision may be, *Wushan yunyu* presents us with an instance of Nietzschean "pessimism of strength," as it constitutes, through images, an aesthetic but thoroughly activist political intervention into the contemporary Dengist and post-Dengist political discourse of economic development and prosperity, of "socialism with Chinese characteristics."[53] It articulates the connections between existential environmental conditions and desire, between state-dictated ecological destruction and psychosexual identity. This is a likely reason for the banning of this film in China. It links the arrogant championing of man's domination over nature and the faith in "symbol[s] of uncontrolled development"[54] to a sense of confusion, detachment, and dysphoria experienced by citizens as a result of development.

Consequently, one could argue that this film be read as an allegory of any nation experiencing rapid, large-scale development, in which the government-propagated ideology of the unquestionable good of economic "progress" and "modernization" is shown to be the cause of irreversible ecological damage and the obliteration of historically-rich local communities, bringing alienation, rupture, and confusion to the inner and outer worlds of the very citizens whose lives it is ostensibly improving. In other words, in films such as *Wushan yunyu*, cinematic explorations of social phenomena in contemporary China can instantiate "alternative perceptual epistemologies" that contribute to a more general, globalizing critique of modernity.[55]

4

Floating Consciousness:
The Cinematic Confluence of Ecological Aesthetics in *Suzhou River*

Andrew Hageman

"How does media work, then?"
"Look out the window. Not toward the Bund — check out Yan'an Road."

—Neal Stephenson, *The Diamond Age*[1]

The Theoretical Headwaters of Ecocinema

The astonishing critical and commercial success of Al Gore's *An Inconvenient Truth* (2006) has revealed to an unprecedented degree the potential power of uniting cinema and ecological thought. In addition to boosting popular environmental awareness and activism globally, this film has helped open a significant space for ecocinema studies: the critical analysis of the intersections where cinema and ecology meet. While the field of ecological criticism (ecocriticism) has been growing since the 1980s, the scope of these studies has heretofore focused primarily on literature.[2] But, in the wake of *An Inconvenient Truth*, the scope is widening, so that the central ecocritical questions concerning how human beings perceive, conceptualize, and represent the world we live in are now being applied to films as well.[3] Through close analyses of cinema (fiction films and documentaries) as well as literature and other cultural texts, we can begin to perceive the various ideological frameworks (historical, economic, national, etc.) that shape the ways we can and cannot think about ecology. This work is crucial to understanding the details of the urgent ecological crises we face today and how literary and cinematic texts substantially inform our capacities to confront them.

To conduct such ecological criticism demands a widening of our analytical aperture. By widening the aperture, the diegetic environments that are conventionally assigned the passive role of backdrop are brought prominently into view. The objective here is not, however, to invert an anthropocentric focus and thereby fetishize the environment to the exclusion of human-centered narratives. Rather, a wider aperture increases the depth of field so as to enable us to consider how our narratives inevitably unfold within the ecological structures of the world we inhabit. Our ability as critics to shift into this mode is especially compelling when a film is explicitly about the environment. A Chinese cinema example is *Kekexili* (2004), which directly confronts the spectator with the landscapes of Tibet and the eco-heroes fighting to save the endangered antelope of this region. Similarly, *Manufactured Landscapes* (2006), while not Chinese-directed or -produced, requires the spectator to look directly at the horrors that late-capitalist high-technology production, consumption, and disposal unleash upon the Chinese people, land, and waterways. In a slightly less explicit way, ecological critique is also a logical approach to Chinese films like *Yellow Earth* (1984) or *Postmen in the Mountains* (1999), where the protagonists and their stories appear explicitly interconnected with their local landscapes and ecosystems.

Less obvious objects for ecocritique are Chinese films set in burgeoning metropolises like Beijing, Shenzhen, or Shanghai. And yet, urban ecologies and their cinematic representations demand analysis no less than their wilderness or agrarian counterparts. For example, Shanghai is one of China's most powerful economic engines: it is a hub of production and consumption, a magnet for China's floating population of migrant laborers, and a global port through which goods and information flow in vast quantities. As such, actions that take place in Shanghai reverberate throughout the nation's economic, ecological, and ideological structures. We cannot fully grasp the significance of wildlife poaching in Tibet or the toxic devastation of rural waterways through e-waste without understanding the relationships of these people, animals, and places to urban centers like Shanghai. Moreover, Shanghai's complex cityscape of rapidly disappearing *shikumen* (石庫門) or "stone cave houses," widely dispersed colonial architecture like that of the Bund and along Suzhou River Road, and its proliferation of mediatronic monoliths like the Citigroup Tower and Aurora Plaza that illuminate Pudong, create a potent metropolitan ambience that each day approaches (if not surpasses) Ridley Scott's futuristic vision of L.A. in *Blade Runner* (1982) (Figures 4.1 and 4.2).

To incorporate the urban sprawl environments of a global city like Shanghai into the catalog of literary and cinematic settings that demand ecological study is, however, only part of the reason this chapter focuses on Lou Ye's *Suzhou River* (2000). Not only does this film add urban environmental content to the scope of ecocinema studies, but it also offers a highly productive opportunity for theorizing the ecocritical import of cinema form. This is especially true because *Suzhou River* diverges formally in a number of ways from other films directed by Lou Ye's Sixth Generation contemporaries. While Sixth Generation Chinese cinema has become almost synonymous with a digital, hand-held aesthetic, the majority of these films

Figure 4.1   The illuminated architecture of the Bund at night.

Figure 4.2   The Pudong skyline, featuring the Oriental Pearl TV Tower, the Jin Mao Tower, and the mediatronic Aurora Plaza and Citigroup Tower.

employ the aesthetic as a heavy-handed didactic means of exposing contemporary social issues — think Jia Zhangke's *Xiao Wu*, *Platform*, and *Unknown Pleasures*.

Unlike this appeal to stark realism, Lou Ye exploits this gritty cinema aesthetic in *Suzhou River* to explore the ways people formally synthesize the fragmented experience of life in contemporary Shanghai into a coherent narrative in order to survive in this dynamic and often volatile urban environment. Rather than representing social issues as something that can be conveyed through seemingly direct documentation, the combination of the hand-held aesthetic with erratic editing techniques such as rapid-succession jump cuts mixed with fast zooms and pans as well as non-linear narration in *Suzhou River* makes the spectator constantly aware that the film is about more than just the plot line. It is also about how our minds and the world we inhabit are formal systems that are complex and inextricably coupled with each other.

In this way, *Suzhou River* draws attention to the relationship between its content, formal aesthetics, and the experience of circulating within the city's integrated systems of social, economic, architectural, and waterway flows. Another way of articulating such an exploration of the systems and structures that constitute life in contemporary Shanghai is to think of the film as an attempt to perceive and represent the ecology of the city. This chapter, by attending to form and content from an ecocritical perspective, illuminates the ways *Suzhou River* aesthetically informs the spectators' conceptualizations of this urban environment. Of special interest are the ways its formal divergences push against the ideological horizons of how we can think about ecology today. After all, if critical analysis of films can reveal the ideological blind spots built into our constructions of nation, gender, race, and class, surely this work can do the same for our ideas about ecology.

The Flotsam of Fantasy: Objects of Disgust

Identifying the ecological relevance of *Suzhou River* begins at the content level with the first visual images of the film. In this initial montage, the camera pans and zooms around the surface of the film's heavily polluted namesake waterway, drawing our attention to various bits of floating garbage. In a direct way, this seems to invite an ecological approach to analyzing the film, but this invitation is far more complicated than a simple reflex response to seeing pollution on screen. When the videographer/narrator's voice-over accompaniment declares that, "There's a century worth of stories here, and rubbish, which makes it the filthiest river," he connects the filthy condition of the river to the narratives about to unfold in the primary diegesis of the film.[4] As such, the narrator introduces the spectator to the river simultaneously as a natural waterway that bears the unseemly marks of its use and abuse and as a metaphor for narrative.

The river's status as a metaphor is complicated though. On the one hand, the river is a figure of the objective narratives of all the other people we observe with and through the videographer/narrator when looking at the river. On the other hand, however, the river represents the floating narratives the protagonist invents about himself and his relationship to others. This deceptive complexity is contained in his suggestion, "If you watch it long enough, the river will show you everything. It will show you people working. It will show you friendship, families, love, and loneliness as well." At first glance, these lines seem to point to the objective lives of others: the object of the videographer's gaze. But his statement takes on a different significance if we interpret "loneliness" as a self-reflexive statement on the part of the videographer. Applying "loneliness" to him suggests that he is also a Shanghai inhabitant who, like the barge workers and people walking along the river, is being observed, even now, as he floats down the river filming others. Like them, he is grappling with a sense of isolated disconnection rather than interconnection, and this feeling of disconnection is what drives his filmic attempt to re/create connections — to re/create an urban ecology. As such, the Suzhou River is an ecological figure, not only because it embodies literal pollution, but because it serves as an aesthetic narrative means for exploring the material interconnectedness of people with each other and their environs.[5]

This introductory configuration of the river as narrative metaphor also ascribes to it a striking element of danger. In the lines quoted above, the narrator implies that not just the flotsam of Styrofoam cups and plastic bags count as pollutants, but the narratives he documents and manufactures are also impurities that threaten to be absorbed by those who traffic in them. In other words, the stories we produce and consume resemble the material commodities we produce and consume. Both can be sources of enjoyment, but excessive participation in the fantasies that sustain our love stories and our culture of conspicuous and ceaseless consumption can lead to serious consequences. We create, even co-create, narrative fantasies as a defense mechanism that enables us to persist in this late capitalist world of ceaseless production and consumption. Yet uncritical enjoyment of these fantasies is precisely what prevents us from accepting the deterioration our global economic condition visits upon the environment, including ourselves.

All of this reveals the sophisticated ecological tone this early sequence establishes in *Suzhou River*. Indeed, other scholars have attended to this opening passage of the film: for example, Gary Xu's eloquent reading of this sequence as framing the film as a "history of ruins, of urban decay" that represents Shanghai as "a natural wonder, which irreversibly proceeds to death instead of cyclical regeneration," or Linda Chiu-han Lai's sophisticated description of this scene presaging what she calls the characters' "psycho-geography" of Shanghai (80; 220–24).[6] These are both invaluable interpretations, but it is imperative to note that the uncanny power of this sequence is in fact largely due to its dialectical resonance with the brief part of the film that precedes it. Just over one minute of the film prior to the river sequence consists of a completely black screen accompanied by voice-over dialogue. The man and woman speaking to each other are hidden, as is the context of their dialogue. As a result, these mysterious words floating into our purview on the dark media stream are an audio equivalent of the rubbish we see atop the Suzhou River in the subsequent visual sequence. Like the rubbish, the voices suddenly materialize to address us, originating in the dark and inaccessible abyss of a remote "elsewhere." Someone else deposited these things into the liquid and media streams passing before our eyes and ears, and soon enough this floating debris will pass beyond our immediately perceptible milieu and into yet another abyssal "elsewhere." The dialectical interplay of this double opening frame exemplifies how *Suzhou River* is a film that not only evokes certain ecological matters, but does so through aesthetic means that are themselves ecological.

To put this complex assertion another way, the appearances and disappearances of debris are indeed matters that are central to thinking about ecology. Part of what makes ecology so difficult to think about, and why it is therefore difficult for us to make ecologically sound changes in the physical world, is our ideological inability to perceive ourselves as already and always inscribed within ecological structures. It is much easier to see the garbage floating along, to bemoan the ignorance of the others who put it there, and then proceed to lament what it is likely to do to those who live where that garbage will eventually end up. But *Suzhou River* does not afford this aesthetic illusion of critical distance and remove — neither from the literal pollution nor from the narratives unfolding on the screen. Because this sequence is shot from the perspective of the narrator as he floats on a boat down the Suzhou River, the garbage does not pass out of sight. Rather, we keep pace with it and thus cannot escape its presence.

Augmenting the power of this sustained look at the garbage is the parallax view this perspective engenders. While the voice-over codes the sequence as subjective, the bobbing focalization from the river's surface aligns the camera with the objective point of view of the flotsam pollutants. The result is a parallax of oscillating subjectivity and objectivity that gives us the uncanny impression that we are simultaneously viewing Shanghai from the perspective of the videographer and being shown how this environment looks from the perspective of a bobbing bit of rubbish. This experience of seeing ourselves from the point of view of the environment that we usually think of as the object we perceive by looking outward is the unsettling feeling of the gaze of ecology leveling on us: it is a frightening realization that plastics and toxins are not produced and flushed elsewhere out of our lives, but that they are unrelentingly present. Now, like Lacan feeling the returned gaze of the sardine can riding the waves, the spectator begins to perceive the position he/she occupies in the world from a different perspective.[7] This synthesis of alternating points of view illuminates the structures of ecology that were heretofore formally and ideologically hidden, and as a result the notion of "environment" is replaced with that of "ecology." Similarly, the floating populations of laborers in Shanghai, as well as its petty bourgeoisie, are not simply "others" to pity or detest through narration. Their voices are speaking out to us from the darkness on the other side of the barriers we maintain through fantasy to keep the unseemly if not poisonous realities of our world at bay.

In this way, the initial black screen voice-over and river-shot sequence synthesize form and content to suggest that *Suzhou River* is a film about the objects we create and expel, the people we rely upon yet despise, and the fantasies that sustain this condition of life. Lou Ye has spoken explicitly about the significance of this audio-visual synthesis in the landmark Chinese cinema anthology co-edited by Cheng Qingsong and Huang Ou, *My Camera Doesn't Lie*:

> Everything you see in movies is fictional ... I think this dirtiness is not dirtiness in the conventional sense. It is reality. It's a reality that my camera can record. People walking along the bank, on the bridge. ... This is the real representation of real life. ... The beginning of the film is like the beginning of an essay; I hope this narrative sentence can precisely communicate my real impression of *Suzhou River*. My camera doesn't lie. (265)

The phrase, "My camera doesn't lie," which belongs both to Lou Ye and the videographer of *Suzhou River*, reveals crucial challenges presented by the aesthetic position his film takes. While this phrase is symptomatically repeated by a wide range of Chinese cinema scholarship, relatively little has actually been published specifically on its crucial role in *Suzhou River*.[8]

For example, in her essay "The Amateur's Lightning Rod," Yiman Wang refers to Lou Ye's "My camera doesn't lie" statement as "this generation's virtual 'declaration of independence' insofar as it emphasizes an *oppositional* agency derived from a subjective amateur perspective (*my* camera) and a unique truth claim (*not* lying)" (23). Wang's analytical observation of Sixth Generation directors' aesthetic approach to realism is extremely insightful, but let us also consider Lou Ye's phrase in the specific context of *Suzhou River*, especially as this film diverges in an unsettling way from the predominant aesthetic senses of realism among films by his counterparts and even his own other films. The documentary-style realism of films by Jia Zhangke, Li Yang, or Zhang Yuan, for example, presumes positions of critical distance that do not self-reflexively engage the film's and filmmaker's participation within the very society it sets out to critique by capturing and representing images of it. Contrary to this aesthetic, *Suzhou River* draws attention to itself as a text that is self-reflexively immersed in the same polluted waters and social milieu of the post-socialist Shanghai/China that it represents. While other films document their characters from an outside position of observation, *Suzhou River* fuses together the external observations of others with internal focalizations of the videographer's own fantasies and desires.

What makes this fusion unsettling is how Lou Ye omits and/or uses ambiguous cinematic cues that resist distinctly coding scenes as either external observation or internal fantasy. It is useful here to compare this ambiguous rendering of "documentary realism" in *Suzhou River* with another problematic documentary of a China-in-flux, Michelangelo Antonioni's *Chung-Kuo Cina* (1972). Like *Suzhou River*, Antonioni's film began as a documentary project officially sanctioned by the powers controlling media production in China.[9] Furthermore, both films were later denounced by these same powers for diverging from their original documentary parameters: Antonioni's film for providing what the Chinese powers deemed a subjective vision of life in Shanghai, Beijing, and other locations rather than providing objective depictions of the achievements of "New China" and the Great Proletarian Cultural Revolution the officials had believed would comprise *Chung-Kuo Cina*; and Lou Ye's film for going outside the closely controlled confines of China's film production system.

Suggestively, the official consternation over both films had less to do with the content "documented" than about their relationships with subjectivity. The ideological process of collectivization vital to Mao's Communist China and the Cultural Revolution in particular would be enabled by an absence of liberal humanist subjectivity — but Antonioni's film formally suggested subjectivity and individualism. Ironically, the very same absence of subjectivity that fostered Mao's China has greatly enabled labor exploitation in today's transnational capitalist China, and this is what *Suzhou River* reveals through its formal experimentation with handheld camera aesthetics, gritty realism, and ambiguous subjectivities. In this way, the flotsam of voices and rubbish materializing before us then disappearing as *Suzhou River* opens, comprises a critical aesthetic dam that disrupts conventional ideological flows and thereby exposes key formal ambiguities in the creation and representation of subjectivity in cinema, so we can modify the ways we diagnose our position as subjects existing in the ecology of the present moment.

Cognitive Cine-Mapping: An Ecological Aesthetic

The opening sequences discussed above frame *Suzhou River* as a technologically-mediated exploration of Shanghai's complex ecology. In the body of the film that follows, we wander the city with and through the videographer/narrator, trying to discern the nature of the social and spatial networks that course through Shanghai and its residents. This impulse to circulate through the city to investigate the lines and nodes of its networks is further enhanced by key formal elements of the film. Non-linear narrative techniques, ambiguously connected diegetic layers of experience and imagination, and confusing doublings of characters and cityscapes collectively invite speculations on the nature of the pattern that links every piece of the film together. And yet, Lou Ye renders these elements ultimately irreducible. The same cinematic moments that initially provoke exploration of the city and its residents foreclose the very prospect of arriving at any conclusive resolutions, and the film refuses to confirm or disconfirm whatever patterns one constructs. This formal aspect of *Suzhou River*'s fabric creates an aesthetic mode this chapter calls "cognitive cine-mapping."

"Cognitive cine-mapping" is a modification of Fredric Jameson's "cognitive mapping" concept in his landmark "Postmodernism" essay and its numerous reiterations. In the essay, Jameson claims that new aesthetic forms of cognitive mapping are required so that "We may again begin to grasp our positioning as individual and collective subjects and regain a capacity to act and struggle which is at present neutralized by our spatial as well as our social confusion" (92). Our spatial and social confusion, according to Jameson, goes hand in hand with new environments such as sprawling global cities where capital, people, resources, and styles flow in ever increasing volumes and speeds. When such places — and few cities exemplify the Jamesonian postmodernist cityscape better than turn-of-the-twenty-first-century Shanghai — surpass our capacity to map them, they also defy our aesthetic capacities for representing them. Any attempt to represent the experience of being in Shanghai, or any other contemporary Chinese metropolis for that matter, requires new aesthetic forms.

In *Suzhou River*, Lou Ye creates this new aesthetic form of cognitive cine-mapping. In part, he does this by departing significantly from other Sixth Generation urban films like *Beijing Bicycle*, with their distinct visual and narrative juxtapositions of clearly delineated wealthy and poor urban populations. Instead of a binary vision of a gleaming city surface and greasy underworld in diametric opposition, à la Fritz Lang's *Metropolis* (1927), Lou Ye's cognitive cine-mapping represents Shanghai dialectically as a network of co-evolving systems within systems that are too numerous and complex to grasp or represent fully. While the experience of living in Shanghai is incompletely represented by this dialectical form, this aesthetic approach is critically productive, especially when considered from an ecological perspective. Think of a spider that cannot survey its entire web, yet survives by building cognitive maps based on the vibrations that flow to it along intersecting strands. *Suzhou River* works through similarly ecological cognitive cine-mapping aesthetics. In place of modernist anxieties or postmodernist schizo-celebrations, the film represents the contradictions at the core of any attempt to represent the totality of Shanghai as anything other than an ultimately irreducible confluence of systems.

One of the most significant modes of cognitive cine-mapping in *Suzhou River* occurs in the interconnected diversity of cityscapes and doublings of characters. In both cases, the doubles do not pose as oppositional or negative others. Rather, each exists as an antinomy rather than intersecting diametrically with the others. The primary example of this is Lou Ye's sophisticated use of images that have come to stand in for modern Shanghai — in particular from the 1990s onward. The colonial architecture of the Bund signifies Shanghai's salad days of the 1920s — already enmeshed in networks of global capital and migratory flows. Across the river, the new Pudong skyline mirrors the Bund, but as a distorted reflection of global capital manifested in glass and steel skyscrapers rather than bulky yet ornate stone buildings. Suggestively, Shanghai is increasingly conflated, inside China and out, with only the Pudong version of itself. But it is imperative not to be drawn into such a strictly postmodernist picture. Indeed, the various towers designed by the John Portman architectural firm that have shaped Shanghai's skyline and will continue to do so into the future make the Bonaventura Hotel of Jameson's "Postmodernism" essay blandly pedestrian. Yet, in juxtaposition with the Bund, the gleaming surfaces and unfathomable heights of the new utopian vision rising on the Pudong skyline can never fully displace the city's history.[10]

This multifaceted skyline is extremely relevant to *Suzhou River* because the film almost completely suppresses the shiny new figures of the Shanghai cityscape. The Oriental Pearl TV Tower is one of the very few skyscrapers to appear in the film. In place of this architecture of new promise, *Suzhou River* portrays the relative non-places of Shanghai comprised of concrete apartment blocks and defunct industrial factories and warehouses bordering the river. Gary Xu articulates this clearly when he notes, "The new skyscrapers and the new TV Tower fade into the background; placed in visual prominence are the garbage and the dilapidated buildings" (80). Bolstering Xu's point with sustained ecocritical attention to this cityscape representation reveals there is something more happening here than just a shift in focus. At a glance, Lou Ye's foregrounding of the non-places of Shanghai seems to participate in a dualistic strategy of exposing the ugly realities of life that support the city's superficial glamour. However, because the urban glamour is so remarkably repressed, the effect of focusing on these non-places is more complicated than strictly oppositional interpretations. By absenting the most well known visual aspect of the city's landscape, the film evokes a disturbing and uncanny feeling that something massive has been repressed but is lingering just outside the frame, from where it threatens, at any moment, to return.

It is vital to note, however, that no aspect of the Shanghai cityscape is completely suppressed. Recent historical films set in 1920s/30s Shanghai, like Ang Lee's *Lust, Caution* (2007), James Ivory's *The White Countess* (2005), and Lou Ye's own *Purple Butterfly* (2003), render a very different effect wih their complete elision of contemporary Shanghai through consistently high-angle camerawork and/or studio lot shooting. While the complete erasure of contemporary elements of the city in these films produces fantasies of nostalgic return that arouse varying degrees of historicity, the peripheral, near-absent presence of the skyscrapers in *Suzhou River* depicts contemporary Shanghai as a place where the historical vector of the city's ecology becomes visible only through an anamorphic gaze.

In a sense, the effect in *Suzhou River* is akin to the experience of walking (or boating, in the case of the film) through Shanghai: even as one's gaze remains mostly at the level of human movement, one can feel the enormous presence of the skyscrapers looming overhead. Paradoxically then, the larger forces shaping the ecology of the city — the symbols of global capital erected through floating population labor — are even more hauntingly present when just barely visible. Contributing to this sensation at a lower level of the city skyline are the shots of the colonial-style apartment building across the street from the videographer's home. These buildings allude to the semi-colonial history of Shanghai, and of China, and the contradictions this status has wrought. As with the mostly suppressed skyscrapers, Lou Ye institutes a subtle approach to focalizing these symbols of 1920s/30s Shanghai. Inserting a few select shots of Shanghai's modern skyscrapers and historical colonial housing, rather than a didactic plethora of either or both, lends a dissonant quality to the film's cognitive cine-mapping that demands active interpretation of the place being re/created on screen.

Lou Ye's minimalist approach works to emphasize the importance of the rare intrusions of Shanghai's towers upon the architectural environment of the film's Shanghai. As such, the one sequence in *Suzhou River* that devotes significant screen space to these towers represents a deep structural inconsistency that interrupts but also unifies both Shanghai as a city and the film itself as narrative. This sequence offers strangely partial shots of the Oriental Pearl TV Tower. And this irruption into the predominantly flat environment of the film is further enhanced by its coincidence with one of the most fraught moments of the love stories in *Suzhou River*. The Pearl is displayed through a combination of objective shots and the subjective focalizations of Mada and/or Mudan. During the previous night, Mada found Mudan working in a convenience store on the outskirts of the city. They apparently stayed up all night and are now watching the sunrise over Pudong, with the Pearl claiming a large part of this vision as it nearly fills the screen. In the narrative context of their romance, the sunrise seems to signify the hope of rejuvenating their once lost love. Simultaneously, the Pearl signifies the promise that Shanghai, and China with and through it, will rise to global economic and cultural prominence. As such, personal and national narratives of life in turn-of-the-twenty-first-century Shanghai converge in the synthesized ecological figuration of the sunrise and the Pearl Tower.

Figure 4.3   Mada and Mudan watch the sunrise, evoking feelings of a new beginning.

Figure 4.4 Ideological anxiety and illusion converge in the appended view of this concrete and glass symbol of China's newest utopian future.

And yet, as the plot almost instantly reveals, this image of the characters and the tower is both ideological and illusory. When the Pearl was completed in 1995, it was the tallest structure in Pudong (and one of the tallest towers in Asia), and it represented the revised utopian future of Deng Xiaoping's China, recently reformed and reinserted into the network of global capital and trade. In other words, the Pearl is an architectural attempt to reconcile China's communist principles with its venture into the world market: it is a manifestation of socialism with Chinese characteristics (具有中國特色的社會主義).[11] The symbolic ideological role it serves is underscored by an apparent need to preserve the illusion of its prominence, as the Jin Mao Tower and the Shanghai World Financial Center among others erected recently in Pudong have vastly surpassed the Pearl's height. When you stand on the Bund, the Pearl Tower still appears to dominate the skyline, and there are numerous urban legends speculating that the municipal and/or national officials insisted that the map of towers to be built in Pudong was designed to maintain this optical illusion.[12] As Alan Balfour already put it in 2002, "The Oriental Pearl seems quite lost in this new company, already a relic of past dreams and past symbols" (112). The anxiety surrounding this maintained (perhaps enforced) illusion is even reflected in the foyer sculpture of the Shanghai Urban Planning Exhibition Center (Fig. 4.5), which depicts the Pearl hyperbolically towering far above all the other landmark buildings of Shanghai.

When the Pearl appears in *Suzhou River*, it evokes the promise of the future it symbolizes at the level of content yet forecloses this fantasy through form. The tight framing of the shot effectively castrates the tower. By showing only an appended view of the tower's base, Lou Ye formally reveals the ideological anxiety and illusion that converge in this concrete and glass symbol of China's newest utopian future. This interpretation diverges somewhat from Jerome Silbergeld's insightful reading of this sequence. While Silbergeld also discusses the Pearl as a figure of fantasy and future dreams, he emphasizes the relationship of this sequence to

Figure 4.5   A sculpture in the Shanghai Urban Planning Exhibition Center depicts the Pearl hyperbolically towering above the other landmark buildings of Shanghai.

Hitchcock's *Vertigo* as "a neo-Buddhist icon substituted for a Christian one," which exemplifies a cultural hybridity different from a Western response that sees the "sexual potency of this upright image" (29). By contrast, the emphasis here is on the tightly framed shots that cut off the tower's phallic symbolism. Indeed, this interpretation requires the same initial symbolism of potency Silbergeld mentions, but it proceeds to focus on the subtle formal deflation of the symbol. Furthermore, without ignoring the crucial importance of the film's evocations of cultural hybridity, the emphasis in this chapter is on the ecological aesthetic created by synthesizing representations of place with the stories of those who inhabit this urban ecology. Lou Ye does this by paralleling the visual image of the partially shorn tower with the long-awaited romantic interlude between Mudan and Mada. The shot of Mudan with her head on Mada's shoulder as they watch the sunrise evokes similar feelings of a new beginning for their romance. And yet, the tight framing of this shot mimics the shot of the Pearl Tower. This connection increases when, in an instant, the illusion of romance is shattered by the very next scene, in which the police collect the videographer from his apartment to identify Mada's dead body that, along with Mudan's corpse, has just been dragged from the river. This juxtaposition of the deflated Pearl Tower and the people who cannot survive their participation in the illusory romances of its ideological promises of bright futures on the horizon suggests that the ecology of contemporary Shanghai is unsustainable.

Cognitive cine-mapping in *Suzhou River* is thus a sophisticated form of deconstructing the components of this urban environment that conventionally serve as metonyms for Shanghai, and at the same time, China. Lou Ye's aesthetic approach to this is especially noteworthy because his film does not deconstruct cityscape metonyms as if to reveal an alternative yet equally reified "real" Shanghai. Rather, the perspective of Shanghai assembled in *Suzhou River* maps out the totality of the city as a network of interlocking ideological systems materially manifested. The cognitive cine-mapping of *Suzhou River* fuses form and content to demonstrate that we can only inhabit Shanghai — inside the film and out — as subjects enmeshed in an ultimately irreducible urban ecology of concrete ideology and ideological concrete.

Tarrying with the Flotsam: Riding out Our Fantasies

The demise of the reunited lovers returns us to the ecological elements of the opening sequences. Mada, Mudan, and the motorcycle have all become inert objects whose presence in the Suzhou River pollutes the water. Suggestively, the motorcycle — the critical vehicle that drives the film's multiple narratives — is granted extended screen time with a shot of a crane removing its defunct body from the river. This unexpected lingering over the motorcycle underscores the strange connection of people, commodities, and narratives in *Suzhou River*. And, like the flotsam captured by the videographer, these objects cannot simply be ignored. The film unrelentingly refuses to let them float away. In fact, it insists that we look at them multiple times and through multiple subject positions.

Most striking among these focalizations of the dead is Meimei's. Upon hearing the news from the narrator that Mada and Mudan are dead, she immediately rushes from her houseboat apartment to see the corpses for herself. As Meimei nears the bodies laid out under a tarp on the street, loud discordant sounds disrupt the diegetic-only sounds of the rain. The volume and discordance intensify to a painful pitch when Meimei looks down at their bodies (especially at Mudan) then back at us — the videographer, the camera, and the spectator. In place of the disaffected expression she has worn through nearly the entire film, Meimei's face is now contorted with an expression of absolute horror. And her uncharacteristic expression is underscored through a kind of double repetition. Not only does Meimei turn around twice in this sequence to face the camera, but in the second instance, as she goes in for a closer look at the corpses, the editing replays her turn so we see this single action twice (Figure 4.6). What these audio and visual techniques focus our attention on is the terror-stricken visage of someone facing the dissipation of the psychological borders that separate our fantasies from reality. In this moment, Meimei and the spectator are jolted from the comfort of consuming the characters and commodities of narratives from a distance, and it becomes clear that we are somehow embedded within this system of narrative production and consumption.

Figure 4.6   Meimei displays a look of terror when confronting the psychological borders separating fantasy from reality.

What demands attention here are the divergent responses of Meimei and the videographer to the traumatic intrusion of the real upon their fantasies precipitated by the sight of Mada and Mudan's corpses. Meimei, in the face of her lost fantasies, seems to repress the horrific moment of recognizing a semblance of her own subjectivity in the "Other" of Mudan's dead body. She denies the horror by clinging to her fantasy of romance, as indicated clearly by the note she leaves for the videographer pinned to her boathouse wall. Invoking the videographer's promise to find her — this promise was the very first audio object that floated into our milieu from the dark abyss beyond the opening frame of the film — reveals Meimei's desperate desire to keep the story Mada and Mudan represent alive in spite of their demise. That Meimei leaves her familiar places in Shanghai signals, however, a realization that such illusions of romance cannot be sustained in Shanghai. At least they are not sustainable in Shanghai as configured by her current cognitive map of the city. Although it would be possible to interpret Meimei's leaving as demonstrating her positive qualities of optimism, strong will, and commitment to reality in contrast to the narrator's pessimism, weak will, and preference for images and imagination, this chapter argues, on the contrary, that her departure is in fact a regressive response to the trauma of Mudan and Mada's deaths. From the perspective of an ecocritical-ideological interpretation, the case of Meimei's leaving reveals that the desire to maintain the impossible fantasy swerves too far away from the material conditions of Shanghai. To flee is the only option left to her if she wishes to preserve her romantic fantasies despite having seen what they can do to people in this urban ecology.

The videographer, on the other hand and contrary to his promise, remains in his familiar Shanghai territories. Not only does he explicitly say that he is going to break his promise by not going after Meimei, but the film visually confirms this as it concludes with a sequence of shots that appear to resume his initial journey from west to east along the Suzhou River. He has now advanced to a point near the confluence of the Suzhou and Huangpu Rivers where they merge before eventually emptying into the sea. In contrast to Meimei's response, the videographer chooses to ride out the Shanghai fantasy to its end — to see what the fantasy yields when he fully faces and embraces it rather than unconsciously re-investing in it.

The nature of this fantasy, when ridden out to its eventual end, is radical inconsistency. And it is crucial to note that this radical inconsistency is revealed by a return in the voice-over narration to figures of ecological imagery that reflect the correspondent opening sequence. Near the end of the film, the videographer says, "And then the sun will come out and the river would be clear." Here he is evoking the imagery of better living in a clean environment in an apparent contrast to the pollution in the opening frame. But the ecological fantasy of resolution contained in this moment is undermined by the disjunction of visual imagery contradicting his promise of clarity. The aesthetic affect of hand-held, long-take shots that has predominated throughout the film is startlingly replaced by a composite editing that superimposes several images of the last bridge before the Suzhou and Huangpu Rivers come together. While one of the bridges remains in its horizontal position, the others are pivoting and hesitating in states of flux between horizontal and 90-degree verticality, all of which formally renders Shanghai a place in which inconsistent visions and representations intersect but do not simply dissolve into a single unified view. This visual dissonance is intensified by what the narrator says to follow up this speculation of the rivers becoming pure. The English-subtitled version follows through with the fantasy of a clean Suzhou River with the words "… and full of fish. I could run after her like Mardar."[13] However, the spoken Chinese makes no mention of Mada, or fish for that matter. Instead, the videographer says, "I'm not lying; you'll see." While the inter-linguistic disjuncture is itself suggestive, the content of the English subtitles is a production matter that would not underwrite significant claims. That said, whether the narrator has continued with the clean river imagery or proceeded directly to tell the spectator he is not lying, his articulation contradicts the blurry turn the visual aspect of the film is taking. In other words, the return to ecological expression as a means of characterizing the form and contents of the film is far more unsettling than its initial appeal makes it seem. What does become clear in this aesthetic inconsistency is that the desire to see the world in ecological ways contains an inherent contradiction within its very ideological structure that prevents us from satisfying this desire.

Following this composite inconsistency, the videographer's point of view slumps in one of the last visual shots of the film: in a black screen voice-over, he says, "So, I'll just take another drink and close my eyes, waiting for the next story to start." This "waiting for the next story to start" is a highly ambiguous conclusion. It could be a new start when he opens his eyes again after merely closing them for some time; it could be a new story starting after he regains consciousness or within

Figure 4.7　The blurry composite image of Pudong that creates dissonance with the narrator's verbal promise in this moment of clarity on the horizon.

the creative space of the unconscious, as the last camera movement suggests he might have fainted or collapsed; or, because the narrative of Mada's and Mudan's story identified the bootleg Buffalo Grass vodka — the brand that the narrator is drinking in mass quantities during this last river sequence — as one of the culpable elements in the couple's deaths — perhaps the narrator will start a new story on the other side of suicide. Each of these possibilities for "the next story to start" is left open due to the ambiguous frames of the film that arrive from and depart into mysterious abyssal "elsewheres." Moreover, as the Chinese character 蘇 in 蘇州河 is also the root of 蘇醒 (to regain consciousness) and of 蘇生 (to come back to life), the film's title and its namesake river bear the linguistic trace of shifting and returning levels of consciousness, not limited to those available within the scope of a single lifetime.

There is something ecological about this multi-layered ambiguity of audio and visual content and form. The film does not offer any escape from the dark, polluted realities of contemporary Shanghai. Nor does it offer the relief of entering a new fantasy — the direction Meimei takes when she effectively disappears from the film and the videographer's world. Instead, *Suzhou River* compels us to tarry in the murky world of our own late capitalist creation. We are forced to float with the discarded filth in a manner that makes possible alternative diagnoses of the ecology of the present moment, painful as the process and its results may be. As the darker implications of the ambiguities within 蘇 suggest, such tarrying with the negative flotsam might well prove to be a fatal encounter with the real. Yet, the prospect of another story starting makes this dangerous aesthetic one of eventual, though not immediate, hope. Before the next story can start, we must first fully ride out the fantasies that comprise contemporary Shanghai — the ultimately destructive fantasies that permeate the city's ecology, from its residents and rebar to the polluted currents of the Suzhou River.

Bathing in the Eco-Ideological Delta

But where does this aesthetic of indefinitely prolonged hesitation in *Suzhou River* leave us? The idea of tarrying with the flotsam of late capitalist production, distribution, and consumption is not only painful, but it likely seems a counterintuitive aesthetic to endorse at this historical moment. After all, we are immersed daily in multiple media reminding us of the many environmental crisis points we are approaching and those we have already passed. The logical reflex to this input, it would seem, is to spring immediately into action. Although there is indeed a certain logic to this reflex, immediate (in the temporal and Hegelian senses of the word) action will likely rehearse the same ideology that has facilitated the wanton ecological degradation in the first place. If the experience of our increasing awareness of ecological crises is disorienting in a similar way to Jameson's description of postmodern disorientation, as this chapter has argued, then immediate reactions conditioned by a perception of present conditions as unrestrained speed and confusion are just as likely to spin the wheels of capital yet faster as they are to initiate revolutionary thought and action on ecological matters. An alternative, therefore, is to work with aesthetic representations that decelerate narrative and experiential flows and thereby facilitate the re-coordination of the position(s) we occupy within this disoriented epoch of ecological crisis.[14]

Lou Ye's *Suzhou River* creates this kind of aesthetic eddy that reveals something of the ideological constructs that shape our notions of interconnectedness with fellow human beings and the material environment. This film opens a space for diagnosing the ideological structures of its present moment because the narrative forms and content of the film resist the tempting desire to ignore or, increasingly, to distance ourselves from those aspects of the contemporary world that disgust and/or embarrass us. To presume a distance enables the displacement of culpability onto someone else, and just such a narrative is currently being assembled in the United States to render China a foreign arch-villain responsible for rising ecological crises.[15] Furthermore, this distance lets us imagine that the Styrofoam cups and the nameless laborers we see floating along the river in the opening sequence will simply disappear if we drop them into currents flowing away. But *Suzhou River* does not liquidate these painful objects from sight. By keeping pace with the rubbish and migrant laborers, and by focalizing the world and the spectator from their points of view, the film abrades the comfortable and conventional illusion that these focalized subjects are nothing more than insignificant objects in circulation. As a result, *Suzhou River* complicates our desire to cast off objectionable objects, offering instead intimate explorations of these elements of the world we are creating — elements certain to return (likely with a vengeance!) no matter how assiduously we try to repress them.

This critical hesitation is complemented dialectically with the film's cognitive cine-mapping aesthetics. As this chapter has shown through analysis of the suppression and provocatively minimal presences of modern and colonial Shanghai cityscapes, *Suzhou River* depicts struggles with disorientation in contemporary Shanghai. And, because Shanghai is a nexus of national and global networks of capital, information, and populations, this metropolitan disorientation is local, national, transnational, and global at the same time. Since the late 1970s, but especially since the 1990s, Shanghai and China have been coming to terms with the processes of transitioning from the communist project and its various iterations of collectivity into new forms of interconnectedness as participants in the networks of global capitalism. Instead of accentuating the apparent disjuncture between communism and capitalism of this transition, the cognitive cine-mapping in *Suzhou River* figures this interstitial period as a shift between two divergent modes of living and theorizing deep structures of interconnectedness.

More specifically, the film represents Shanghai through a complex network of dialectical tensions among the cityscapes of different eras and the futures these have portended as well as the ambiguous character subjectivities and narratives. This aesthetic communicates the challenges and urgencies inherent in the reorientation work required to map the ecology of Shanghai within our current ideological frameworks, but it also presents a formal means for advancing this work. In this way, *Suzhou River* operates through an aesthetic form of visual networks linking media-technologies, people, and places. This aesthetic form is strikingly similar to the one in the epigraph of this essay from Neal Stephenson's *The Diamond Age* — a 1995 novel set in a science fiction far-future Shanghai that the city already resembles today.[16] Only, now the question has become one of ecocinema: How does the intersection of cinema, ecology, and ideology work? The answer: watch *Suzhou River*.

Part II.

Eco-Aesthetics, Heteroscape, and Manufactured Landscape

5

The Idea-Image:
Conceptualizing Landscape in Recent Martial Arts Movies

Mary Farquhar*

[This land of] rivers and mountains is so enchanting
That countless heroes compete
To bow in homage.

—Mao Zedong, "Snow," 1936

In the famous birch forest scene in the martial arts film *Hero* (*Yingxiong*, Zhang Yimou, 2002), two women warriors dressed in red fight among golden autumn leaves. Moon says that she will kill Flying Snow to avenge the death of her warrior master. She leaps high above the forest and dives with drawn sword towards Flying Snow, who summons the wind and a storm of swirling leaves to blow her away. Flying Snow kills Moon and the forest turns blood red. In this scene, the birch forest is more than mere setting. The forest leaves become weapons, foiling Moon's sword-strike and allowing Flying Snow's deadly sword thrust. Like the warriors themselves, the landscape is both beautiful and violent. It decides life and death. *Hero* is set during the Warring States period in the third century B.C., where stunning landscapes display the marvelous realm of China that warriors have been fighting over ever since.

Hero has become one of China's most controversial films because of its supposed glorification of the ruthless Emperor of Qin as a hero. In spite of its contentious narrative, almost all commentators applaud the visual beauty of the film, shot by virtuoso cinematographer Chris Doyle. This beauty includes its landscapes. Shelley Kraicer, for example, calls the birch forest sequence "an ecstasy of swordplay ... [and] one of the most beautiful scenes ever recorded on film."[1] Jia Leilei calls such

*   This essay was partly supported by a Visiting Research Fellowship to work on film and landscape in 2005 at the Humanities Research Centre of the Australian National University.

martial arts worlds a "realm of marvels": a realm of swirling autumn leaves, killer butterflies, and tree monsters; a place where "mountains fall, earth rips asunder, and gigantic waves of water crash into heaven."[2] However, there is as yet no in-depth study of the role of landscape in Chinese film, let alone martial arts film.

This chapter presents a new way of looking at landscapes in twenty-first-century martial arts blockbusters, primarily through a discussion of landscapes in *Hero*. I propose a conceptual framework that highlights the role of landscape in film, including "martial arts in the age of digital reproduction."[3] I argue in the first section of this chapter that martial arts landscapes are both art and artifice, visualized by the filmmakers and realized through film technologies. These technologies now include digitization, which George Miller has called the most important contribution to filmmaking since the advent of sound.[4]

The second section details the conceptual framework for analyzing cinematic landscapes. The concept at the core of this framework is the "idea-image," a centuries-old Chinese way of conceiving, creating, and responding to landscape in traditional Chinese painting. I suggest that this framework, currently sporadically applied to Chinese cinema, is the basis for conceptualizing landscape in martial arts film in which setting and mood are as important as narrative and action. The idea-image is applicable to a particular frame, separate scenes, or the total work. Certainly, the framework foregrounds landscape, often relegated to the background in film studies.

The third and most substantial section applies the concept of the idea-image to *Hero*'s landscapes. I discuss, in turn, the concept of *tianxia* ("all [land] under heaven") at the heart of the film, the use of color to both structure the film and convey a mood, and the film's transformation of locations into landscapes through digitization. I argue that these digital landscapes add a new dimension to martial arts' imaginary "realm of marvels." In a sense, this cinematic enhancement of nature is Chinese ecocinema. It takes us directly to Roger C. Anderson's original and tongue-in-cheek proposal in 1966 for "ecocinema" as "a plan for preserving nature." His plan is preservation through movies that technologically improve, refine, and replicate the natural world (including sights, sounds, and even smells) so that ecocinema becomes "an art form vastly superior to nature itself." Nature lovers can then ignore pollution, environmental degradation, sand, dust, mosquitoes, and song sparrows with laryngitis, never needing to give "a genuine dickey-bird a second glance."[5]

However, Chinese nature lovers did not ignore actual environmental pollution, ironically caused by filmmaking on location. In the Postscript, I turn to images of the land as real rather than ideal, linking land, landscape, location, and the law through recent environmental debates. In these debates, location-as-environment and landscape-as-cultural-memory in films such as *Hero* are reconstrued as heritage. The marvelous manipulation of background plates of locations in the virtual world contrasts with the alleged degradation of heritage sites by filmmakers in the real world. The proposed Chinese plan for preserving nature is, however, environmental law, not (eco)cinema.

Martial Arts Landscapes and Digital Art

The position in this chapter is that cinematic landscapes are not real, whereas film locations may be. Locations were carefully selected and transformed into on-screen landscapes in such films as Ang Lee's *Crouching Tiger Hidden Dragon* (*Wohu canglong*, 2000) and Zhang Yimou's *Hero* and *House of Flying Daggers* (*Shimian maifu*, 2004). These cinematic landscapes also have a particular emotional significance to the filmmakers.

Ang Lee sought the most exotic locations within China for his Oscar-winning *Crouching Tiger*. The film was billed as featuring superstars of the Chinese cinema in "an epic love story and a thrilling action drama set against the breathtaking landscapes of ancient China, filmed entirely on location" in the People's Republic of China.[6] Zhang sought similarly remote locations for *Hero*, ranging from Mongolian forests in the northwest to heritage lakes in the southwest. Half of *Daggers* was shot in Ukraine. Thus, location (even Ukraine)=mainland China=ancient China=breathtaking landscapes within the film. By implication, these locations exist in some form today. The art and artifice of the on-screen image are concealed in the propaganda just as they are concealed in the seamless production values of these films.

Crouching Tiger set a new standard for transnational martial arts films. Technology introduced breathtaking possibilities for the moving image. The film's director of photography, Peter Pau, talks of the time-consuming postproduction of *Crouching Tiger*'s bamboo fight scene at Hong Kong's Asia Cine Digital, conceived as a modern version of King Hu's famous bamboo forest fight in *A Touch of Zen* (*Xianü*, 1970). Pau wrote, "I supervised 300 wire removals, sky replacement, and the coloring of the entire bamboo sequence on the computer," a difficult task exacerbated by "thousands of bamboo leaves moving in the background."[7] The result is a balletic, swaying, almost dreamlike fight, which Stephen Teo calls "the most elegaic tribute to Hu that has yet been conceived so far."[8] This sequence relies on the bamboo for its mood and its invocation of the work of a past master.

Zhang Yimou also used computer graphics for *Hero* and *Daggers*, primarily accomplished at Animal Logic's digital film bureau in Australia. Both films are renowned for the breathtaking splendor of their on-screen landscapes. In both, Animal Logic team members helped provide this splendor by digitally transforming background plates of different locations in various ways. Sometimes they added to the plates, sometimes they subtracted from them. They added computer-generated

(CG) leaves, movement, and color washes to the Mongolian birch forest plates in *Hero* to produce a gold-red scene of wondrous beauty. They added CG flowers to a background plate of a field almost bare of flowers in *Daggers* to create a combat scene set in a pastoral paradise. "We flowered up the flower field," said Anna Hildebrand, a company representative.[9] Conversely, they digitally deleted an entire village that scarred an actual mountain slope in *Daggers*, so that the hero's horseback ride on a winding road seems to happen within a virgin forest. This is Anderson's ecocinema, where human pollution is literally expunged from the frame with a digital flick of the finger. The myth, magic, and marvel of landscape sequences in *Crouching Tiger*, *Hero*, and *Daggers* are therefore digital illusions, seamlessly edited so the viewer cannot tell that the images on screen have been altered. Because they are set in the past, these two films present an idea-image of China's bygone, seductive, and pristine landscapes as heritage: they are a poetics of space in which setting is not only crucial but often the pivot on which a work revolves.[10] In *Hero*, these landscapes are called *tianxia* ("all land under heaven"), a long-held notion of the land, and a political concept of territorial unity. These two ideas merge through *Hero*'s story of political and military contest held over two thousand years ago to unite China into a single empire. *Dagger*'s story similarly begins as a political contest in the Tang Dynasty but soon collapses into a love story. The contest involves combat, the heart of the martial arts movie. Hence, the landscapes in both films are "locations to (literally) die for."[11]

However, as we have shown, location does not *equal* landscape. Simon Schama points out in *Landscape and Memory* that "it is our *shaping perception* that makes the difference between raw matter and landscape" (my emphasis). The landscape tradition, he continues, signifies a heritage: a "shared culture … built from a rich deposit of myths, memories, and obsessions" that "shows just how much we have to lose" in the planet's environmental degradation.[12] Landscape is therefore an art that transcends location, transmitting cultural myths, memories, and emotion beyond everyday experience.

Landscape or setting in the martial arts world is part of China's "realm of marvels." Like the concept of *tianxia*, this world is not realistic although it refers to actual historical events in *Hero*. In literature and film, the martial arts realm is a romanticized outlaw space in China, where heroes and heroines fight for justice. This space is called the *jianghu*. It is peopled by wandering knights or warriors who fight according to codes of chivalry. *Wuxia* means the "knight errant" or "martial chivalry," which gives martial arts film its Chinese name: *wuxiapian*, "films of *wuxia*." The space of the *wuxia* is the *jianghu*, originally referring to hermit dwellings, then to a shady outlaw world, and finally to the entire imaginary martial arts realm.[13] The importance of landscape in imagining this world is found in the term for *jianghu* itself: *jiang* means "rivers" and *hu* means "lakes" and, by extension, covers China, if not the entire world.

Thus, for example, Ang Lee wrote that *Crouching Tiger* is an enchantment, a dream of China. His scriptwriter James Schamus describes the immensity of this dream through its locations.

> This film was shot in almost every corner of China, including the Gobi Desert and the Taklamakan Plateau, north of Tibet, near the Kyrgyzstan border. We were based for a time in Urumchi, where all the street signs are in Chinese and Arabic. Then all the way down to the bamboo forest in Anji and north to Cheng De, where the famous summer palace is ... So it is really bringing together almost every conceivable idea you could have of China.[14]

The dream is not realistic. As outlined in the Postscript, the dream relies on real locations, enhanced and exploited on-screen. In *Crouching Tiger* and its martial arts successors, the locations come together as an idea of China itself that no longer exists and an imaginary *jianghu*. Indeed, *Crouching Tiger* relates to Lee's boyhood fantasies: "It's a history ... It's a dream ... Gone with the wind.[15]

Sword fighting martial arts movies such as *Crouching Tiger*, *Hero*, and *Daggers* are therefore produced outside the realistic conventions of filmmaking. They are often set in the past and project images of a bygone China. Ang Lee's image of China in *Crouching Tiger* is a dream in the guise of personal and cultural memory. Zhang Yimou's image of China as *tianxia* is a gorgeous tapestry of ancient landscapes awaiting conquest. How do we conceptualize these cinematic landscapes wrought by digital technologies, when they are so essential to a particular film and belong, in turn, to an immense and evolving cultural imaginary called the *jianghu*?

The Idea-Image and Martial Arts Landscapes

The idea-image is an aesthetic concept which can bring together various aspects of martial arts on-screen landscapes. Jia Leilei states that most Chinese scholarship on this genre looks at theme, style, and director, and not at setting.[16] However, Chinese aesthetics has well-developed theories that conceptualize the landscape as art and image and may be applied to film. The key concept is called *yi* or *yijing*: the "idea-image." Bai Xiaojun traces its usage back to the Eastern Han Dynasty (25–220 A.D.). In subsequent centuries, the term was extended, reinterpreted, and theorized at length in different areas of the arts and by many of the best known art philosophers in Chinese history. Bai claims:

> In Chinese painting theory, the idea-image [*yi* or *yijing*] is the most fundamental and most important aesthetic category. It belongs to the spheres of aesthetic consciousness and appreciation. It is a concept that both artist and audience call on to capture their dynamic response

> in terms of thought and feeling. The process of creating and realizing
> the idea-image in art is also a process whereby a certain scene in the
> external world calls forth a certain subjective image and informs the
> creative act.[17]

As the concept includes the realization of the "idea" as an "image," I have translated it as "idea-image." The power of the concept lies in an acknowledgment that neither the cinematic nor painterly image is real. It is an idea-image that is not only rendered visible on-screen and improved by digital technologies: the image also carries an introspective aura, an emotional register, and a cultural heritage. It reveals a landscape of the heart and mind.

Zhang Yimou and others have used the concept of the idea-image to talk about the highly technological medium of film, whether realist or martial arts fantasy. Zhang's use of the term is similar to Simon Schama's "shaping perception," which transforms locations into landscape painting, but Zhang's interpretation always has human inhabitants in the picture. In an interview with Zhang in the 1990s, he told me that most of his films, including the groundbreaking film for which he was cinematographer, *Yellow Earth* (*Huang tudi*, dir. Chen Kaige, 1984), "wrote an idea-image" (*xieyi*). *Xie* means to write; *yi* means an idea or an idea-image, which Zhang said, precedes filmmaking.[18] In saying this, Zhang makes two points. The first is that he links his film art to the centuries-old tradition of Chinese landscape painting in which depicting an idea-image (*xieyi*) is the highest form of art in contrast to merely reproducing likeness or "realism" (*xieshi*, "writing the appearance"). The second point is that Zhang is referring to a filmmaking practice where the idea comes *before* filming, again as in the case of *Yellow Earth*. I have elsewhere described this process, which involves intense emotion, reflective visualization, and an understanding of the relationship between land and people to be realized on-screen or on canvas. Mark Cousins speaks more generally of Zhang's films:

> [He] has talked about the way Chinese painting has affected his work.
> His shots are often very wide. Space and landscape weigh as heavily
> within the frame as the human elements.[19]

For Zhang Yimou, landscape or setting is also part of the martial arts world. This world is not realistic although it refers to actual historical events in *Hero*. Jia Leilei adopts the idea-image in landscape terms more generally to discuss classic martial arts combat scenes, including bamboo forest fights, flying over roofs, climbing walls, and soaring over water. He writes that such scenes — variously performed in many martial arts films including *Crouching Tiger*, *Hero*, and *Daggers* — delineate the idea-image (*yijing*) that informs the mythic martial arts world.[20]

The idea-image is therefore an aesthetic concept that actively incorporates setting in Chinese film. This is at odds with a common perception in moving image theory where, for example, James E. Cutting claims that backdrop is "vista space" and the "typically narrative content of vista space in film is nil." He contrasts vista space (beyond 30 meters for a pedestrian) to action space (1.5 to 30 meters) and personal space (within 1.5 meters) in the real world, which in film collapses into just one (action space).[22] The concept of the idea-image is therefore a significant difference between Western and Chinese ways of perceiving setting or vista within film scenes and, indeed, a difference that pervades Eastern and Western culture, according to Chinese film scholar Ran Ruxue.[22]

Neither Zhang nor Jia systematizes this language into a coherent poetics of cinema, perhaps because most Chinese reader-scholars readily understand it. Nevertheless, like Jia, Zhang sees audiences' lasting impressions of *Hero* as color and image in, for example, the lake or forest scenes. He emphasizes feeling and mood (*qingjing*) linked to landscape. He and the filmmaking team consider symbolic color-coding as not only new to the martial arts genre but also essential to *Hero*'s idea-image (*yijing*), lyricism (*shiyi*), and emotion (*gan*).[23] Zhang storyboarded *Hero* as a way of directly conveying his ideas to the special effects teams. However, according to the Animal Logic team, he did not intellectualize the film during shooting but talked of emotion and color. These aspects of the film will be discussed in more detail in the next section. The point is that emotion and color are embedded in their understanding of the film's idea-image.

In aesthetic theory, the idea-image encompasses emotion through the related concept of "the realm of the heart" (*xinjing*). This realm refers to the feeling and mood that are not only embodied in a work but also inform the nature of the idea-image itself. Bai Xiaojun quotes the contemporary artist-scholar Liu Haisu: "An artist's thought and feelings, or in other words his realm of the heart, is realized through a work's idea-image" (*yijing*).[24] For Jia Leilei, the idea-image in the martial arts world is saturated with emotion and, indeed, violence. It is not a harmonious painterly world. Instead, it relies on human conflict that is resolved through combat. Jia suggests that film audiences are held spellbound by the martial arts spectacles before them. He sees their response to "visual marvels" (*shijue qiguan*) on the screen becoming "marvels of the heart and mind" (*xinlide qiguan*). Such marvels, he writes, take the martial arts film beyond realism to a "realm of sensual marvels" (*qiyide shi ting wangguo*).[25] This is precisely the critical response to *Hero* that Chen Mo calls a "visual ballet," a "sensual feast."[26]

In film analysis, the idea-image facilitates an emphasis on landscape and setting as well as characterization, narrative, and style. It describes a creative process from a work's conception to its reception. It operates in contemporary Chinese filmmaking and film criticism as one way of looking at the cinematic image as well as a finished film.[27] In the following section, I apply the concept more systematically to *Hero*.

The Idea-Image of *Hero*

This section applies the idea-image to three aspects of *Hero*. The first is a discussion of *tianxia*, or "all land under heaven," as *Hero*'s central idea-image. Within this context, the second aspect is the role of color and setting to structure the narrative and to display the land on-screen. Finally, the idea-image is related in detail to the digital transformation of particular locations and sets into breathtaking images of China's landscapes. The discussion includes specific stills and interview material from the post-production team at Animal Logic.

Hero's "All land under heaven"

Just as *Crouching Tiger* projects every possible idea of China, *Hero* invokes a vision of a united China as its central idea-image. The King of Qin fights to unite China, which is described as *tianxia*, literally "all [land] under heaven." *Tianxia* is translated benignly as "our land" in the international release (2004). It actually means the entire country of China, the Chinese empire, and extends to cover the whole world. *Hero* invokes all these meanings, including a map of the Warring States (475–221 B.C.), which the King plans to unite into the first Chinese empire through military conquest. These plans trigger the film's plot: assassination attempts by martial arts warriors from the state of Zhao. But the King is also clear that *tianxia* refers to territories awaiting further conquest beyond the borders of these states.

In terms of both narrative and image, *tianxia*, as a united empire, begins the film with a brief historical statement on the King's achievement in conquering the Warring States and becoming China's First Emperor (221–207 B.C.). The plot tells of the ultimately unsuccessful assassination attempts on the King as historical fact through fictional warrior-assassins: Nameless, Broken Sword, Sky, and Flying Snow (the only female warrior). In the end, the male warriors submit to the King because his vision of unification in the characters *tianxia* will supposedly bring peace to the people. The idea of *tianxia* also ends the film, with images of the Great Wall as the monument that marks the reach of Qin's power and thence serves as the architectural symbol of imperial unity and power. Landscape is therefore not simply a tableau, vista, panorama, or cultural memory. It expresses power as a manifestation of human law, control, and conquest. Historically, its siren power impels heroism. As Mao Zedong wrote in his 1936 poem, "Snow" (Xue), China's landscapes are so enchanting that emperors and "countless heroes" over the ages have fought to possess it.[28] The Qin emperor is first of these heroes on Mao's list.

In history and in *Hero*, then, the King achieves his vision. Nevertheless, the narrative surrounding *tianxia* as a metaphor for unity and peace in the film has aroused considerable debate and even revulsion, especially as the Qin emperor's historical reputation over two millennia is of brutality and repression. Wang You's opinion of *Hero* is typical:

> While *Hero* superficially talks about *tianxia*, it is the Qin emperor's *tianxia*, an evil scoundrel surnamed Qin who wants to seize *tianxia* and make all the people in the world his slaves. The Qin emperor is a character like Hitler and *Hero* not only sings his praises but also lets ordinary people die to realize his personal ambition. How can audiences support a film like this?[29]

However, Chinese audiences *did* flock to see *Hero*, which earned more at the box office than any other film before in a century of Chinese cinema.[30] Other commentators, both Chinese and Western, refer to the film as a much more ambivalent and visually splendid work. Robert K. Eng claims that the film deconstructs "the limits of honor, the concept at the heart of *wuxia* [the martial arts hero], imperialism, and nationalism," and the ending sounds a note of mourning, not triumph.[31] Jia-xuan Zhang agrees, claiming that the final shot of the Great Wall moves from sunlight to shadow: "the glory of the united empire is accompanied by a feeling of darkness."[32] These comments show how Chinese and Western analyses of *Hero* may dramatically diverge or fail to deal with ambiguities when they discount imagery and setting. For Zhang Yimou, color-coding is central to *Hero*'s idea-image, and so any analysis of *tianxia* must take account of color.

Color-coding "All land under heaven"

Tianxia as imagery rather than narrative in *Hero* has been widely applauded. Color is crucial, both structurally and visually. Tan Dun, the musical director, said that we should even *hear* color in the film's musical score.[33] Visually, dark palace scenes and multicolored flashbacks structure the narrative and come together at the beginning and end of the film.

In the beginning a lowly Qin magistrate, Nameless, is summoned to the King's palace to recount his defeat of the King's assassins. He is dressed in black as he sits in a black carriage, escorted by black-uniformed Qin soldiers on horseback through bleached desert sands. They gallop to the King's black palace, a vast set at the Hengdian Studio complex near Hangzhou. Nameless is overwhelmed by the palace architecture and by the soldiers in the large forecourt. When he eventually meets the King in his throne room, Nameless is shot small and low while the King is shown high and distant in the frame.

The following narrative alternates between the throne room, as Nameless tells his stories, and outside flashbacks that tell three different versions of the alleged killing of the King's enemies. The flashbacks are in vibrant colors: a bleached desert, a red calligraphy school, a golden forest, and a blue-green lake. The last version is supposedly the real story of Nameless's attempt to assassinate the King by moving ever closer as he tells his stories, so as to be able to kill the King with a "strike within ten paces" (*shibu yisha*). The King invites Nameless to kill him with his own sword but Nameless submits instead to Broken Sword and the King's vision of eventual peace and unity, mystically embodied in a calligraphic rendering of the character for "sword" in red, and in the notion of *tianxia*. Thus, *tianxia* as an imperial geobody also embodies aspects of Chinese culture through scenes that link the sword with calligraphy, chess, and *qin* music. The final shots bring palace and land, inside and outside, together. They alternate between multiple shots of Nameless's execution and funeral in the dark palace and of white, desert scenes for the deaths of Broken Sword and Flying Snow. White signifies "truth" for Zhang Yimou and "death" in China's traditional color symbolism.

Hero's primary color is black, the dynastic color of Qin and of power. Zhang has said that he always wanted to shoot a black palace because no one had done it on film or television.[34] Jia Leilei calls *Hero* a "black martial arts film." Zhang, he writes, replaces the mythic martial arts world — the *jianghu* — with a historical setting. In so doing, he displaces the heroic spirit of the martial arts hero onto the only living hero in the end, the historical Qin emperor in his black palace, surrounded by his black army who invade the colored spaces of their enemy like locusts, unleashing a hail of black arrows with their war cry, "Feng." Black dominates more than the color imagery. For Jia, the film's "black history" is still fiction, but it is a legend very much of this world (one meaning of *tianxia*) rather than the telling of a mythic martial arts story of the imaginary *jianghu* or even *tianxia*, which incorporates all worlds. However, this analysis neglects the role of other colors in the total work even though Jia writes that such flashbacks as the birch forest and lake scenes have already become classics of the martial arts canon.[35]

For Zhang Yimou, as we said, color carries emotion and mood as well as narrative structure. This signature style was evident in his early work as a cinematographer and his earliest directorial works: *Red Sorghum* (*Hong gaoliang*, 1987), *Judou* (*Judou*, 1989), and *Raise the Red Lantern* (*Da hongdenglong gaogao gua*, 1990). He said that in *Hero*, "red symbolizes passion and jealousy, blue love, white truth and green youth."[36] The colored flashbacks in gold-red, blue-green, and white act as narrative, symbol, and emotional counterpoint to the black of Qin. The flashbacks rely on a careful selection of locations, apparently never before seen on-screen: the bleached-white sands of the Dunhuang region in the northwest, the gold-red forests in Inner Mongolia, and the pristine blue-green lakes at Jiuzhaigou in the southwest. Besides careful selection, these locations were also cleaned up during and after filming. Aspects of "pestiferous nature" that dogged the filmmakers — leaf loss, rain, flies, sandstorms, and wind — were avoided by choosing the time or season for shooting various sequences.[37] Main or background plates of these locations were then digitally transformed to create dream flashbacks of the magical visions of live action.

Digital transformations of "All land under heaven"

Hero was the first film in which Zhang Yimou used computer graphics and he feels the less, the better.[38] But, as we show in the following discussion, digitization is crucial to the spectacle, whether it be action, setting, or color.

To achieve a sense of the King of Qin's overwhelming power, for example, Animal Logic digitally increased the numbers of soldiers in the opening "black" palace sequence during post-production. The main or background plate was a long shot of the palace, with Nameless walking to the entrance steps through several rows of soldiers. The post-production process involved many shots of the same rows of soldiers in different positions across the courtyard. These shots were digitally combined to create a final image of thousands of soldiers in the courtyard, flanking Nameless as a small, lone figure walking towards the palace steps. Soldiers fill either side of the frame. Thus, vista space surrounds action space to magnify the awesome sense of Qin power.

Nameless's execution is another example of the difference between a background plate, filmed at the huge palace set at Hengdian, and a final shot (Figures 5.1a and 5.1b). The background plate shows Nameless standing back-on in silhouette facing the soldier-executioners across the courtyard.

Figure 5.1a Background plate of Nameless's execution in the palace forecourt. Visual effects by Animal Logic. Copyright EDKO Film.

Figure 5.1b Final shot of Nameless's execution in the palace forecourt. Visual effects by Animal Logic. Copyright EDKO Film.

The dark energy of the King's power to execute according to the law is entirely absent in the background plate. This is added during post-production by a cloud of black, CG arrows flying toward Nameless in the final plate. Shown as a point-of-view shot, they appear to fly at both him and the viewer in an image of great power. Vista space comes alive with dark and deadly action into the very personal space of Nameless. In the following shot, Nameless's bodiless shape is shown surrounded by arrows against the palace wall. These arrows are real arrows, stuck into the dark wall to outline his silhouette. His funeral follows.

In the film, Animal Logic transformed the remote location scenes into colored flashbacks in two ways. In the first, action was filmed *in situ* and then digitally enhanced. The brief for the birch forest fight in Inner Mongolia, for example, was to create a mood of ominous enchantment (Figures 5.2a, 5.2b, and 5.2c).

Figure 5.2a Background plate of the Mongolian birch forest. Visual effects by Animal Logic. Copyright EDKO Film.

The setting, colors, and editing were crucial to both the shooting and the final effect.

> "I had a guy over there specifically to keep an eye on the leaves," says Zhang [Yimou, the director]. "He made videotapes of their progress as they turned from green to yellow. I'd call every day. 'What do they look like?' 'Too green. Still too green.'" As soon as half the leaves were golden, the crew rushed north. Says Zhang: "We used three or four cameras simultaneously at different angles. And the leaves had to be perfectly yellow. We even implemented a leaf classification system. Special-class leaves could be blown [using industrial fans] in the actors' faces, first-class in front of them, second-class behind them and third-class were scattered on the ground." A mat gathered leaves as they fell so the crew could collect, clean, and classify them, then gently send them drifting back down again.[39]

The combat was filmed with the actors Maggie Cheung (Flying Snow), Zhang Ziyi (Moon), and stuntmen dressed in red (Figure 5.2b).

Figure 5.2b Wire-fu in the birch forest. Visual effects by Animal Logic. Copyright EDKO Film.

The twirling, flying, dancing combat moves were achieved through wire-fu, long established in the genre, with the wires and the cranes that held them erased from the background plates and the action speeded up during editing. The problems for the visual effects team were, first, that the background trees were almost bare by the end of one week's shooting (Figure 5.2a) and, second, that the leaves had to be transformed into a whirlwind that Flying Snow summons to fend off Moon's fantastical dive from high in the frame. The visual effects team used the real tree trunks in the background plate and created CG leaves in a special animation program to simulate both real leaves and a magical wind (Figure 5.2c).

Figure 5.2c Final shot: CG leaves swirl in the birch forest fight scene. Visual effects by Animal Logic. Copyright EDKO Film.

At Moon's death, stillness replaces frenetic action. A CG droplet of blood falls from sword to earth and in a long shot the forest is digitally transformed from gold to deep russet to all red, the color of passion, jealousy, and revenge. The scene ends with a close-up of Flying Snow, dressed in red in a blood-red frame, followed by a long shot of Moon slain on a carpet of red leaves.

Animal Logic's second way of working was against a green scene stage (in Hengdian), which was pulled to delete the green during editing, and composited against the background plate of the setting. One example is the shots of Nameless riding in red, alone, in a vast desert. The action was actually shot on gravelly earth against a chromo-green scene backdrop. The animators pulled a key against the green to isolate the character. They then digitally inserted a backdrop of real desert mountains, which were transformed through color change and cloud speed, to suggest that Nameless was galloping across a desert: a red dot against a vast sky and land.

A further example is the famous blue-green lake scene. Zhang Yimou's brief to the visual effects team was to create a mood of mourning and serenity for Flying Snow's alleged death. Part of the brief was to be as photo-real as possible even though the scene is make-believe in terms of the story. To enhance a sense of stillness, the sequence was filmed beside the pristine Jiuzhaigou lakes during the only two hours in the morning when the lake surface was mirror-like. As in the birch forest sequence, the lake changed over the shooting period. At the beginning it was gorgeously colorful in yellow, green, gold, and red (Figure 5.3a) but at the end the mountains were wrapped in snow. The background plate therefore becomes a template for the finished sequence in which blue, the color of love, is predominant.

Figure 5.3a   Background plate of the lake at Jiuzhaigou. Visual effects by Animal Logic. Copyright EDKO Film.

Like the birch forest sequence, some action was wire-fu work beside the lake. Other action shots, later composited onto the background plate (Figure 5.3c), were filmed against a chromo-green backdrop at the Hengdian studio complex (Figure 5.3b).

Figure 5.3b   Action shot against a chromo-green backdrop. Visual effects by Animal Logic. Copyright EDKO Film.

Figure 5.3c   Final lake action shot. Visual effects by Animal Logic. Copyright EDKO Film.

Finally, drops of water were added using computer graphics. A key frame of one droplet (composed of hundreds of tiny water particles) was produced by animation followed by lighting and rendering into droplets. The layers were then composited together in a seamless process.

The palace scenes are dark and menacing; the birch forest sequence is lush and wondrous; the lake scene is gorgeous and serene. Such sequences exemplify both Zhang Yimou's work as an auteur since the 1980s and the sensual spectacle of the martial arts genre. In speculating on *Hero*'s lasting reception, Zhang refers to the combination of setting, color, and action:

> If someone says "*Hero*" in a few years, you'll remember color, such as the sea of golden leaves in which two ladies dressed in red are dancing in the air. You'll remember a lake, still as a mirror, where two men convey their sorrow through their swords like birds flying on the water, like dragonflies.[40]

The above examples of Animal Logic's work, in the context of both Zhang's idea-image of the film and his "color" brief to the visual effects team, clearly link location, color, and action into the finished frames. Landscape is an active element of an enchanting *tianxia*, the magical martial arts world. It projects diverse spaces in which different heroes fight for political power. Indeed, the Chinese title, *Yingxiong*, is ambiguous and can be translated as either *Hero* or *Heroes*. To see the black King of Qin as the only hero of this film is to ignore the film's diverse landscapes and its many heroes that come together through the concept of *tianxia*: an idea, a land, its history, its philosophy, and its peoples. Indeed, the land itself is heroic.

Conclusion

The idea-image is one way of looking at the active role of landscape in films such as *Hero* — of *tianxia*, its color-coded structure, and its technological transformations of location into the martial arts' "realm of marvels." While the conceptual framework needs further elaboration in terms of cinematic landscapes more generally, it brings landscape into the picture in terms of the filmmakers' conception of their work, the filmmaking process, and audience response. But the idea-image is about landscape, not the land. It is retrospective memory, virtually created, that binds a land and peoples into a very modern version of the nation.

As Mao Zedong suggests in "Snow," we cannot separate the landscape from its people and politics: an idea-image of great power that elicits passion. As Ang Lee and Zhang Yimou show in *Crouching Tiger* and *Hero* respectively, we cannot separate the martial arts landscape from cultural memory: idea-images of the *jianghu* that encode deep desire. Mao, Lee, and Zhang display the exotic spaces of China as emotion-laden spectacle-enchantments. They aestheticize the land in poetry and on film as idea-images that now circulate globally. Despite the complexity of the concept of the idea-image and its myriad forms, it is nevertheless exactly that: an image of an idea. As images, the ideas of the land in these poetic and cinematic examples are defining perceptions of China that are applauded by audiences worldwide. But audience responses include the land as well as the landscape. The flipside of landscape as an idea-image is actual images of a land damaged by location shooting.

The Postscript outlines public and policy responses to damaged locations behind cinematic landscapes, which are reinterpreted as heritage sites — the eulogized space of real China.

Postscript: Location, Landscape, and the Law

As stated, the position in this chapter is that cinematic landscapes are not real, whereas film locations may be. Landscape's role both *inside* Chinese film-as-text and *outside* film-as-cultural-memory-and-heritage is neglected in scholarly literature on martial arts films. Simon Schama claims that landscape is our "shaping perception" of the land. *Hero*'s landscapes are shaped by Zhang Yimou's idea-image of *tianxia* as a gorgeous spectacle that triggers a struggle for control over millennia. This Postscript moves from the idea-image as a way of understanding on-screen landscapes to intersections of landscape, law, and cinema off-screen. The focus is on a struggle outside the frame: an environmental struggle over film locations in China. The economic exploitation of scenic sites in film is publicly reinterpreted as environmental exploitation, even degradation. Clearly, spectacular idea-images of the landscape on film fuel the struggle for their preservation. For Gaston Bachelard, landscape images are "the space we love, [to be] lived in ... with all the partiality of the imagination."[41] Once the space becomes "loved" and "lived in," then combat follows according to the conventions of the martial arts genre. After all, combat, not contemplation, is the whole point of these movies. Thus, as indicated earlier in this chapter, the King maps the immediate territories to be conquered. Mapping in the film includes control through the military and the laws of Qin, which require the death of enemy heroes. Outside individual films, martial arts landscape imagery lives on cumulatively as a Chinese territory which is worth fighting *for*, rather than *over*, and which must be preserved.

In creating the imaginary landscapes of China, martial arts films such as *Hero* have recently triggered a regulatory protection regime. As Jet Li observes, most people cannot get to *Hero*'s remote locations.[42] It is therefore the tourist, conservation, and on-screen images that identify, map, and enrich the landscape as beloved memories, often far more pristine than the actual locations themselves. When set alongside images of China's environmental crises today, they impel an ecological consciousness that demands government protection for natural reserves and scenic spots. In this context, landscape has taken on a life of its own. It has become heritage.

As a purveyor of heritage locations, *Hero* is indirectly implicated in the environmental protection debate. The debate has two dimensions. First, in 2006, blockbuster filmmakers were accused of damaging the very environment they were celebrating on-screen. Second, the debate highlighted the inadequacy of China's environmental protection regime, leading to the release of new regulations on March 1, 2007. According to the regulation:

> Some big-budget films and artistic performances these years are over-obsessed with economic returns, and have greatly damaged the natural environment. Thus film shooting and artistic performances in natural reserves, scenic spots and sites of historical interest must be strictly restricted.[43]

The controversy erupted in China around Chen Kaige and his team, who allegedly destroyed and littered parts of China's Shangri-la in Yunnan Province, when shooting China's most expensive (martial arts) production to date, *The Promise* (*Wu ji*, 2006). *Crouching Tiger* began the fad for such martial arts blockbusters with exotic film locations, of which *Hero* is by far the best-known successor. Local newspapers report that neither Ang Lee nor Zhang Yimou gained permission to shoot their films in remote areas, although the report made no claims of environmental harm. In fact, officials in remote areas encouraged such filming because it earned fees and promoted tourism. The debate began in May 2006, when China's vice minister of construction criticized Chen in a public forum, for abandoning a reinforced concrete structure beside the famous Blue Sky Pond (*Bigu Tianchi*) in Yunnan and "destroying the natural surroundings." Other damages included a road and the destruction of dozens of square meters of azaelea bushes. The filmmakers, who claim they had a contract with the local administration, allegedly also harmed trees in Beijing's Yuanmingyuan gardens. Strong criticism followed in the media and Chen was fined 90,000 yuan in 2006 for damage to the Blue Sky Pond area.[44]

The Chen scandal extended to other films and other cultural performances. The media debate included newspapers, websites, television commentary, and eyesore pictures of damage across all three media. Claims of damage in the Jiuzhaigou national park — world heritage site, host of the Third World Natural Heritage Conference in 2007, and one of *Hero*'s locations — have been made against the filmmakers of *Condor Hero* (*Shendiao xia lü*). Administrators of Jiuzhaigou and other heritage areas have since rejected filming requests, pledging environmental protection over economic exploitation.[45] The controversy has also spread from film to cultural performances and from remote to urban areas. Zhang Yimou is criticized in this regard for having despoiled sites for outdoor performances in Yangshuo, Lijiang, and Hangzhou's famous West Lake. In this new environment, Zhang signed an environmental protection agreement with the management of a scenic spot in Sichuan to film his latest martial arts melodrama, *Curse of the Golden Flower* (aka *The City of Golden Armour*, *Mancheng jindai huangjin jia*, 2006).[46]

A systemic problem that has emerged in the environmental debate is that the laws are inadequate and enforcement is fragmented. Protection is shared among the State Forestry Administration, the State Environmental Protection Agency (SEPA), and the Ministry of Construction. SEPA, for example, has no legal basis to require pre-filming environmental impact assessments. The relevant administrative regulations that are applicable to *The Promise*'s concrete structure beside the lake come under the Ministry of Construction. A *China Daily* article called for regulatory integration across state and local organizations to create an effective environmental protection regime. The March 1, 2007 regulations on filmmaking and environmental protection (jointly issued by SEPA, the State Administration of Cultural Heritage, and the Ministries of Construction and Culture) have begun this integration and signal further policy shifts. Infringement will attract heavier penalties, up from Chen's 90,000 yuan fine to a minimum of 500,000 yuan and a maximum of 1,000,000 yuan.[47] Zhou Shengxian, minister of SEPA, said that a comprehensive legislative framework on environmental protection will be released in the next decade so as to revise China's *Environmental Protection Law*, promulgated in 1989 when economic exploitation of the environment was uppermost.

This debate highlights the importance of film location and landscape in twenty-first-century China's perception of its environment — and plans to preserve it. Ironically, Chen Kaige was nominated for a "green hero" award for protecting the environment in 2006. Not surprisingly, he did not win. However as one voter said, "We know he can't get the award but are still nominating him, for the issue of environmental protection wouldn't have had so much attention without him."[48] From the cinematic display of heavenly landscapes in the diegetic past, China's policymakers and public now insist that the land is heritage, to be protected for the future. SEPA Minister Zhou said, "The implementation of environmental policies will [now] be as forceful as steel, not as weak as tofu."[49]

6

Façades:
The New Beijing and the Unsettled Ecology of Jia Zhangke's *The World*

Jerome Silbergeld

For many, the cute nine-year-old Lin Miaoke, who lip-synched to the lovely voice of seven-year-old Yang Peiyi (Figure 6.1), encapsulated the story of the Beijing Olympics ceremonies. Instigated by a member of the Communist Party Politburo in the name of "national interest" to project a "flawless image" of the nation on opening night, according to the event's music designer Chen Qigang, this unacknowledged teamwork of young talent was cited immediately afterward by the opening ceremony's organizer Zhang Yimou as the high point of the event, saying he was "moved" by it "from the bottom of my heart."[1] For others, it encapsulated something else: the gap between surface and substance, the distance between reality and fantasy, the contrast between what the Chinese government wanted the world to see and what it did not want to show, between present realities and futuristic dreams, between Chinese collectivity and Western ideals of individuality, between some Chinese and other Chinese. The question of façades was raised again and again, for example, by the stuffing of empty seats at Olympics venues with identically uniformed, collectively rehearsed, colorfully choreographed Chinese "fans";[2] by a flag-bearing procession featuring children of China's fifty-five ethnic minorities who turned out to be performers in an all-Han children's arts troupe;[3] by child Chinese gymnasts of uncertain age;[4] and by the creation of specially designated protest zones meant to demonstrate the government's commitment to free expression made to the International Olympic Committee in 2001.[5] With the Olympics already conspicuously en route, director Jia Zhangke set his 2004 cinematic allegory *The World* (*Shijie*) in the fantasyland of Beijing's biggest theme park in order to explore this same set of themes.[6]

 The World begins with its main female character, Zhao Tao, wandering through a backstage crowd of fellow theme park workers, shouting repeatedly, "Does anyone have a Band-Aid? Does anyone have a Band-Aid?" more than fifteen times, before she finally gets one (Figure 6.2). Although "wounded," she is all smiles and friends with everyone. The film ends with Zhao Tao lying dead, along with her boyfriend,

Figure 6.1   Singer Yang Peiyi (left) and the face of Lin Miaoke (right). From *New York Times*, August 12, 2008, A1.

asphyxiated by the gas from a stove in a co-worker's apartment, while the building manager (the image of a towering factory smokestack belching gas flames into the Beijing sky behind him) assures the other workers, "I told them so many times to be cautious ... they never paid attention." ("Yes, yes," the workers respond, not free to say anything else.) What happens in between is all low-drama, less important for its narrative than for the situation it describes: romance in cramped quarters and romantic betrayals, petty theft of hearts and hope, petty corruption, one obligatory industrial accident. For those with no privacy and no power, for whom a breach of etiquette or open dispute with management would mean expulsion, conflicts are conducted with a smile and wounds are delivered in small increments.

Figure 6.2   *The World* (Shijie, dir. Jia Zhangke, 2004). "Does anyone have a Band-Aid?" World Park performer Zhao Tao, performed by actress Zhao Tao.

Set in Beijing's World Park,[7] bedecked with Pyramids and Sphinx, Stonehenge and Acropolis, St. Peter's and Taj Mahal, a Leaning Tower, the Tower of London, an Eiffel Tower ("Our own Eiffel Tower," the recorded park welcome boasts; only 108 meters tall as opposed to the 300 meters that Paris has to offer, but big nonetheless), New York's Twin Towers ("The Twin Towers were bombed on September 11," notes one of the staff, " … we still have them"), and much more, none of this architecture is diminished in the visitors' imagination by its miniaturization. The film follows in petty detail the working lives of those who staff this entertainment center, poor workers drawn to the city from impoverished rural families, catering to an urban, middle-class clientele with time on their hands for leisure. The ever-gracious Zhao Tao befriends an itinerant Russian performer (her only uncompromised relationship, perhaps because the two speak to each other mostly in their native language, which the other does not understand), a mother of two young children back home, who eventually descends from park work into sex work with well-liquored, sexually aggressive park customers; one suspects that the management encourages this in catering to their clientele (website advertisements of the World Park are frequently combined with ads like "Single Chinese girls: Chinese girls and women searching for serious relation"), and Tao herself has to cope with unwanted propositions (Figure 6.3).

Figure 6.3 *The World.* Hallway in the performance world: Zhao Tao about to be propositioned.

The clientele and the staff live in wholly different worlds (Figure 6.4). At one point, Tao and a recently arrived construction worker watch a jet plane up in the sky. "Tao," he asks simply, "who flies on those planes?" "Who knows?" she replies. "I don't know anybody who has ever been on a plane." She has been on a plane herself, but it is a park exhibit, retired from its travels, a fake where her boyfriend Taisheng challenges how far she will "go" sexually and then challenges her sincerity. The toll on those separated from their spouses, the burden of living without private space, is transparent. *The World* does not exaggerate; it operates through understatement and analogy rather than melodrama; not angst or dread but just a lonely resignation. There is no blood at the end, yet clearly a Band-Aid could not cover the social wounds that ooze freely throughout the length of the film. While asking around for a Band-Aid, at the opening of the film, Tao inquires of some card players, "Who's losing?" to which the reply is, "We all are."

Figure 6.4 *The World.* Hallway in the performer's backstage world.

"Give us a day and we'll give you the world" (*Nin gei wo yi tian, wo gei nin yi shijie*) reads the neon logo at the park entrance; but it is mainly a world for customers who lack the means or the permit to go forth and see the real world, while for those who work there it is more like a prison sentence. And for the film-going audience, it *is* the world — at least, it is the larger world of modern China that is depicted or signified here. It is a world to which modernity has come with a rush, a rush facilitated by its own belatedness on the one hand and by China's own sudden and unexpected mastery of modern economics on the other. It is a rush and a resistance at the same time, in which the temptations of Western culture are both embraced and held at arm's length, in which shallow visions of the West are given the appearance of depth in the form of solid substitutes, and in which fantasy replaces what was once known as reality. The theme of replication is thickly deposited in this *World*: performers making up their faces gaze into mirrors which usually reflect just surfaces but sometimes reveal the truth; the park audience watches films of the park's replicas, two steps removed from the original architecture while some in the audience take their own videos of the film, a third step removed; segments of animation, using cheap, cell-phone style graphics, periodically interrupt the film and blur the boundaries of reality and fantasy; World Park performer Zhao Tao is played by actress Zhao Tao, her boyfriend Taisheng by actor Chen Taisheng. Between the mirror and the original image, things are not always identical: "I see the world without ever leaving Beijing," says Tao, but a moment later she is amazed to see a *real* passport acquired by her former boyfriend. Behind Tao's back, Taisheng takes up an affair with a flashy entrepreneur who produces cheap knock-offs of Western brand name fashions. The rare appearance of an "outsider," a poor garbage-picker who briefly stops and turns to the camera, is timed to coincide with the framing of director Jia Zhangke's credit line (Figure 6.5); after all, Jia himself is picking metaphorical garbage while appropriating for his film *The World* all of the props that the World Park has to offer.

Imitation of the West takes the form of ersatz theme parks — in Beijing, The World's cross-town rival, Happy Valley amusement park features its own six

Figure 6.5 *The World*. The two worlds: a garbage picker stands in for director Jia Zhangke.

"worlds": the Lost Maya, the Aegean Harbor, Shangri-La, the Ant Kingdom, Firth ("ecological") Forest, and Atlantis, all constructed on a once densely occupied *hutong* site from which the residents were forcibly relocated. At Princeton, film major and world-class diver Kent De Mond was hired for a summer's work at Happy Valley in 2006, the summer that building was completed and the park finally opened. The upshot was a sophisticated documentary film, *Atlantis*, which De Mond produced for his senior thesis project. At Happy Valley's seventy-five acres in southeast Beijing, just outside the fourth ring road, De Mond joined an international team doing stunt dives from platforms at 30 feet, 150 feet, and 230 feet into a 24-foot wide pool, landing from the high board at some sixty miles an hour (Figure 6.6). "The place," he says in his narration, "was targeted to young middle income earners who made between 350 and 400 U.S. dollars a month, and every day visitors would line up for over three hours to ride the park's biggest attractions. When Happy Valley opened, I was blown away by the elements of foreign culture, or at least imagined foreign culture, that were incorporated into the park."

Figure 6.6 *Atlantis* (dir. Kent De Mond, 2007). Divers.

Before opening day, De Mond recorded the construction of the iron mountain representing Atlantis, rising from the twenty-acre pond in the center of the park (Figure 6.7), built by rural migrants, homeless, sleeping where they worked, and paid 50 yuan per month. "It seems that no attention is paid to worker's safety," he says. "Welders often work without face shields, and others are suspended hundreds of feet above the ground without any sort of harnessing. The scaffolding seemed jerry-rigged, and the wooden planks are not securely fastened to their supports. Cement is often mixed by hand. Besides the respiratory problems caused by the cement dust, only small amounts of concrete can be made at a time. Many structures must be poured in sections, creating seams in the concrete which allows water to seep in and weaken the structure. While many of the workers wore hard hats, there were just as many who didn't."

Figure 6.7   *Atlantis*. The iron mountain.

"Everything that could possibly go wrong with our show did go wrong," says film narrator De Mond. So was it any surprise that on the day before the scheduled grand opening, which the mayor of Beijing and the minister of culture were to attend, a massive crack appeared down the middle of this man-made mountain, which was sinking, reminiscent perhaps of Atlantis itself, crumbling and ready to sink into the sea? The landfill on which Atlantis was built was settling, like the ground beneath Shanghai's Pudong district, which is sinking under the weight of new high-rise buildings at the rate of 1.5 centimeters per year, and like Pudong, it was both sinking and tilting, threatening to rip the mountain's internal propane gas lines wide open and explode. Asked what he thought about the situation, the show's American producer says, "I like it. Because it's a first. Who would ever *think* that your set would actually *drop*?" But, subjected to the kind of high risk and negligence that the Chinese worker frequently faces, a Ukranian woman diver says, "If I get out of this place alive, then I will be very happy."

As an exercise in understatement, *The World* avoids the expressive anger of films like Zhang Yimou's *Judou* (1991) and *Raise the Red Lantern* (1991) and returns instead to the subtlety of films like *Yellow Earth* (dir. Chen Kaige, 1984), *Horse Thief* (dir. Tian Zhuangzhuang, 1985), and *King of the Children* (dir. Chen Kaige, 1987). It obliges the viewer to make his or her own judgments, and what you take away from it depends a lot on what you bring to it, yet there is not much question about what those judgments are supposed to be. It probes beneath Beijing's image-conscious façade, much as *New York Times* reporter Nicholas Kristof did during the Olympics when he personally set out to test the system after Beijing's Public Security Bureau set aside three designated protest areas. The interviewer was interviewed, asked what he intended to protest and why he thought any protest was needed, told that he would need to provide the names and identity numbers of anyone who showed up at his protest and that anyone who accompanied him would have to be interviewed first, and given nearly an hour's instructions on rules to follow in a session thoroughly videographed by police. Afterwards, he asked whether carefully following the instructions given would assure the granting of his application, to which he received the reply in no uncertain terms, "How can we tell? That would prejudice the process."[8] Wang Wei, vice president of the Beijing Olympics Organizing Committee, commented, "We think you really do not understand China's reality. China has its own version and way of exercising our democracy."[9] Jia Zhangke's other films, especially his recent celluloid strip of natural ecology in *Still Life* (2006) and *Dong* (2006), one fictional and the other documentary but the two inseparably intertwined, suggest an intended reading of *The World*'s workplace ecology that has little sympathy with Beijing's new reality, its façades, its tortured definitions, and its reckless abandonment of authenticity. But must we agree? The heart, or at least my heart, agrees, but there are winners and losers in China's great gamble and the head recognizes complexities and questions that are more than academic.

In the later part of the 1980s, there was a popular song which went, "Visit Xi'an to see the China of 2,000 years; visit Beijing to see the China of 500 years; visit Shanghai to see the China of 100 years; visit Guangzhou to see the China of 10 years …" That has all changed. Now all over China, Western form has emerged with a "suddenness" that is not greatly diminished by the fact that the current building boom has been going on for nearly three decades.[10] In old cities, up pop newly constructed cities that make New York and Paris look like creaky senior citizens of urban modernity; topped off in Beijing by Western-designed civic architecture like Rem Koolhaas's CCTV headquarters, Paul Andreu's Grand National Theater ("The Egg"), and in Shanghai the Grand Theater in People's Square designed by Jean-Marie Charpentier. More recently, outside of these metropolitan centers, surrounding Beijing and Shanghai and Guangzhou and Shenzhen, up from what were recently productive agricultural fields spring newly planned, thematically designed suburbs, conceived of by city mayors, and designed by European architects in styles that are not simply importations in space of "what's going on" today in Europe but transplantations in time as well of what was once going on long ago. An entire quaint British village with half-timber structures, shop signs written in English, restaurants and pubs serving English food and with a mini-cathedral that is closed to religious services but frequented for wedding photographs, and policemen costumed as red-jacketed fur-trimmed bobbies walking the streets, joins eight other Euro-American-themed villages ringing the city of Shanghai, meant to accommodate a population of 25,000–40,000 each — Swedish rustic, German Bauhaus (designed by the son of Nazi-architect Albert Speer, who also designed Beijing's Olympic green), and others (conspicuously absent are Japanese and Russian models) — all of which, as permanent features, make *The World*'s make-believe-for-a-day experience seem quite understated. Private ventures like Zhang Yuchen's Château Maisons-Laffitte outside of Beijing complete the picture, right down to the forcible evictions. (Figure 6.8) [11]

Figure 6.8   Zhang Yuchen outside of his Château Maisons-Laffitte, Beijing. From New York Times online, December 25, 2004, http://www.nytimes.com/2004/12/25/ international/asia/25china.html?_r=1&scp=1&sq=zhang%20yuchen&st=cse& oref=slogin.

There is a price to be paid for this, only part of which is the electively relinquished sense of reality. From the fields that once grew crops, now comes no food (China, a huge grain exporter in 1990, is a net importer today). Those who recently tilled this land, now suddenly dispossessed by land seizures, join a labor pool prepared to work far away from their families, under unregulated and sometimes wretched conditions, for little pay. "People are one thing China doesn't lack," one of *The World*'s managers acknowledges, referring to the tens of millions of unemployed Chinese citizens, so workers possess no leverage. There being no privately owned land in China, local and sub-local party cadres authorized to control its disposition are a necessary component of every land-use decision enacted. The lining of pockets with ill-gotten money now transforms many of the party's functionaries from yesterday's zealous ideologues into today's models of self-aggrandizement, including wheeler-dealers like the former mayors Chen Xitong in Beijing and Chen Liangyu in Shanghai, now serving sixteen- and eighteen-year jail terms, respectively.[12] A landed project as large as the World Park, 115 acres which opened in 1993 and now accommodate more than 1.5 million visitors annually, absorbed and consolidated a huge number of private landholdings and could not have come into being without the engagement of numerous high-level local officials.

Workplace ecology is inseparable from natural ecology. There is no need here to repeat what has been so well documented elsewhere,[13] but the immediate outlook for China's ecological welfare is grim. China's ecological predicament, from a tainted environment to tainted food products, is said to have become the foremost topic of Chinese coverage by the Western news media. Any number of ecological crises resulting from China's urban boom could be readily named, for example, the drying up of Lake Poyang due to uncontrolled dredging of its sandy lakebed for use in concrete to build China's high-rise buildings and the dams needed to supply their electricity. On average, one huge boatload of sand passes from the lake into the Yangzi River waterway every thirty seconds. Until recently the largest freshwater lake in East Asia, with 37,000 square kilometers of surface area, Poyang now lacks both the water and the food to sustain the millions of waterfowl which have historically used it as their wintering-over site for migrations from faraway Mongolia, Manchuria, Korea, and Japan, and the lake is now reduced in the dry season to less than 500 square kilometers. Photographer-book artist Michael Cherney (known in China as Qiu Mai) has commemorated this man-made tragedy in a handscroll elegy entitled *Twilight Cranes* (2007) (Figure 6.9).[14] As Chinese ecology comes to the fore in reality, and in scholarly literature like Elizabeth Economy's *The River Runs Black*, Thomas Campanella's *The Concrete Dragon*, and Andrew Mertha's *China's Water Warriors*, it will do so increasingly in film and art as well.[15] Beijing-based photographers Hai Bo, Zhang Dali, and Yin Xiuzhen, Beijing's Liu Xiaodong, New York–based painter Ji Yunfei, and American artist Maya Lin are among the many

Figure 6.9   Michael Cherney (Qiu Mai). *Twilight Cranes*, 2007. Photographic handscroll, detail. Collection of the artist.

major artists turning their attention, and ours, in this direction.[16] Zhang Hongtu has recently produced a series of oil paintings (Figure 6.10) based on Ma Yuan's (ca. 1190–ca. 1225) famous *Water Album*, about which he writes:

> In today's *shan shui*, today's water is dirty, today's air is polluted. Today's mountains are too covered with polluted air to even see. I don't want to make propaganda, but I want to catch the artist's love of *shan shui*, to share the artist's hopes and his hopeless feelings about what has happened to the environment in China. I tried to envision how the ancient Chinese *shan shui* painting masters would face today's mountains and water. For example, if Ma Yuan were to stand before today's rivers and lakes, fouled by chemical toxins and industrial waste, would he still be able to paint his twelve-part *Water Album*?[17]

Figure 6.10   Zhang Hongtu. *Re-make of Ma Yuan's Water Album #1 (780 Years Later)*, 2008. Oil on canvas, 127 x 183 cm. Collection of the artist.

So, *The World* comes to us in a timely fashion. Its architectural structures, the ecology of its workplace, its Band-Aids, and faulty heaters all stand thematically for conditions far larger than those shown here in microcosm. ("It still hasn't snowed this winter," Zhao observes in a nod to global warming, her last words in the film. "Strange," replies her supervisor, as Zhao proceeds to an on-stage performance with fake snow. When she is dead, *then* it snows.) But what if the film's overall take on unbridled modernization/Westernization is itself largely a Westernized or modernized perspective? What if the undisputed bad news about China's workplace and natural ecologies is not really all that new or revolutionary and instead part of an uninterrupted, slowly devolving pattern? And what if there is another way, a Chinese way, of looking at this? Might this film read differently in another place, at another time? *Yellow Earth*, Chen Kaige's much-revered film of 1984 (Figure

Figure 6.11 *Yellow Earth* (Huang tu di, dir. Chen Kaige, 1984). Cadre Gu Qing arrives at the peasant wedding banquet.

6.11), a prime example of the Chinese *xungen* root-seeking movement, attempted to suggest why, some three decades after "Liberation," China had changed so little and still so closely resembled the autocratic culture of its own past. *Yellow Earth* portrayed the efforts of a Communist Party song-gatherer to win hearts and minds in an impoverished northern Shaanxi community, resulting in a frustrating stand-off between his promise of a quick and easy revolution and the peasants' intractable traditionalism.[18] At the time, and even more so after the Tiananmen incident five years later, *Yellow Earth* seemed profoundly on-target as a metaphor of China's changelessness. But, by the turn of the millennium a few short years later, China *had* changed and *Yellow Earth* (its artistic reputation still largely intact) could be viewed as a poor predictor, short-sighted and out of date (although its conclusions seem not so wrong if applied more narrowly to party intransigence and the still-growing divide between rural and urban China). The cinematic characters who staff the theme park, ethnic Chinese impersonating Japanese geisha, Korean and Indians, ancient Egyptian and black African dancers, are mostly rural immigrants working for such low wages that they can hardly afford to return home (when talking to friends, how little they earn is a "trade secret"). But will *The World* appear any more accurate than *Yellow Earth* does if, in another fifteen or twenty-five years, rural China is pulled up by its bootstraps, workplace conditions improve accordingly, and the sacrifices of its economically deprived youth succeed in launching all of China onto the economic fast-track and liberalizing its politics?

What the Chinese world will look like in twenty-five years is anybody's guess. But for the historian, it is worth noting the precedents which mitigate against viewing *The World*'s replica-reality as historically unique, which question not so much its significance as the nature of its significance and cast a distinctively Chinese light on the importation of "World" culture into the Central Kingdom. In the late third century B.C., en route to making himself the First Emperor, Ying Zheng conquered the remaining rival kingdoms one by one, and as he did so, he replicated their local rulers' palaces along the banks of the Wei River, in the suburbs outside his capital city in Xianyang. The Han royal historian Sima Qian wrote of this:

> Rich and powerful families from all over the empire, 120,000 families, were moved to Xianyang. ... Whenever Qin would wipe out one of the feudal states, it would make replicas of its halls and palaces and reconstruct them on the slope north of Xianyang, facing south over the Wei. From Yongmen east to the Jing and Wei rivers, mansions, elevated walks, and fenced pavilions succeeded one another, all filled with beautiful women and bells and drums that Qin had taken from the feudal rulers.[19]

Presumably, architects were sent to make drawings of these *in situ*; perhaps these replicas were made in reduced scale; and given the diversity of the regional kingdoms before Shihuangdi's efforts at unification, the varieties of architecture that stretched along the northern river banks might well have seemed as strange, exotic, and fascinating to the Xianyang locals of that time as the World Park's simulacra do to Beijing's residents today. Shihuangdi was a uniter, not a divider: he took the written languages of the various kingdoms — as incomprehensibly localized then as "Chinese" spoken dialects have remained throughout the many centuries since his time — and from them forged a single, unified character set; and he single-mindedly and ruthlessly pursued the goal of unification in government procedures, philosophical writing, weights and measures, transport vehicles, and roadways. Shihuangdi's architectural reconstructions, therefore, ought not to be seen as an exercise in diversification and need to be understood to the contrary.

Other parallels to *The World*'s replication of world famous places can be found in the royal hunting parks from the late Zhou, Qin, and Han: zoological and botanical gardens, stocked with all the fauna and flora that could be acquired from within the kingdom or from beyond by means of tribute, they were, equally, geological parks with simulated landscapes not only from the whole known world within China and beyond its borders but also from the imagined distant realms of the immortals, and exotic, often fanciful architecture was an essential ingredient of their world geography. Those parks have long since vanished but are recorded in flamboyant terms in the literature, particularly the *fu*-form poetry, of the day. We might well ask about the ecological effects of bringing into being those massive compilations of other sites, with all their wild beasts and strange fruits, and about the lives of those who constructed and staffed those worlds. These go unmentioned in the poetry of Sima Xiangru (179–114 B.C.), Yang Xiong (53 B.C.–18 A.D.), and the other accounts of the day, so expansive yet so limited, which serve today as textual simulacra of those ancient material simulations.[20] Happy Valley amusement park's Atlantis, supposedly the largest man-made mountain in Asia, makes one think back to the Genyue Garden of Northern Song emperor Huizong, both in its grandeur and in its sudden demise.[21] Other royal replications might include: the Han emperor Wudi's building of a simulacra Kunming Lake in his imperial park in 120 B.C. in anticipation of his assault on the lakeside capital of the Dian kingdom (modern-day Yunnan Province), and given his successful military conquest there in 107 B.C., Chinese emperors right down to the last of them maintained garden lakes with that name; the European-style palaces at the Beijing Summer Palace in the Yuanmingyuan, in the style of the palaces of Versailles, constructed during the reign of the Qianlong emperor according to the designs of Jesuits Giuseppe Castiglione and Michel Benoist;[22] the Putuo Zhongcheng Temple built under Qianlong, completed in 1771 at the northern Summer Palace in Chengde as a near replica of the Potala in Tibet;[23] and, more loosely, Mao Zedong's Beijing architecture of the 1950s, culminating during the Great Leap Forward in 1959 with the "Ten Great Projects," including the Great Hall of the People, the Museums of History and the Revolution, and the National Museum of Chinese Art, "borrowing his enemies arrows" in the form of Stalinist style (with Chinese characteristics) in a symbolic effort to seize leadership of the international Communist movement.[24] Today, the Northern Song period Pagoda of the Six Harmonies in Hangzhou is accompanied by a hillside full of replica pagodas from around the whole country.

The geological and architectural features of most of those parks and palaces were miniaturized, and that miniaturization could readily have been justified in the terms by which the first (and arguably most important) Chinese treatise on painted landscapes, Zong Bing's (373–443) *Preface on Painting Mountains and Water*, rationalized his substitution of brushwork for the real thing as lacking nothing *in effect*:

> We should be troubled only by that lack of skill which comes from
> a failure to render diminution convincingly. ... Then, a picture well
> executed will also correspond with visual experience and be in accord
> with the mind. That correspondence will stir the spirit, and when the
> spirit soars, truth will be achieved. And though one should return
> again and again to the wilderness and seek out the lonely cliffs, what
> more could be added to this? The divine spirit is infinite [literally,
> "without delimitation"]; yet it dwells in forms and inspires likeness,
> and this truth enters into forms and signs. And when one can truly
> depict this, he has exhausted the possibilities of his subject.[25]

The principle here is the same that underlies the many forms of simulation and miniaturization found throughout the traditional Chinese arts, from painting to scholar's rocks, from gardens to tray plantings: the simulated *is* the real thing. Neither is the painted landscape nor the "real" landscape the original, for the "original" itself is the immaterial, not-yet-realized *xiang* — the ur-image, the unformed form, the original pattern or template located in the Dao — from which all realized material examples derive. In contrast with essential Euro-American philosophical traditions, reality is ever-evolving from instant to instant in a self-generating system, with no beginning, no end, and no Supreme Creator; there is no dichotomy between material and spiritual.[26] With this notion of ontology developed in theory and driven deep into the collective Chinese psyche, notions of originality and simulation differ significantly from their Western counterparts. Copywork and forgery scarcely bear the same kind of stigma in China as they do in Europe. In painting, one of the canonical standards for judgment was whether a work was well grounded in the diligent copywork of earlier masters.[27] Of copywork in painting, Wen Fong has written:

> The ability to create a perfect forgery ... was a matter of virtuosity and pride. The legal or ethical problems of an "honest business transaction" never entered into the picture. As a matter of fact, it was precisely for very good reasons of ethics and even better ones of tact, that the owner of a forgery was usually protected, as far as possible, from knowing the truth. ... If someone is gullible enough to buy as well as derive pleasure from forgeries, why spoil the poor man's illusions?[28]

As in conjuring, voodoo, and Chinese alchemy, the role of replication, miniaturization, and substitution are tied to the achievement of mastery, the accumulation of power, and for individual, clan or dynasty especially, the attainment of longevity. The Qin emperor Shihuangdi, the Han emperor Wudi, the Qing emperor Qianlong all had the same thing in mind when constructing their parks and that thing is, in a word, control.

So, when we come back to Jia Zhangke's world, we also return to the question of how to understand this world of imitation pyramids, towers, and bridges, and likewise, the world of urban high-rise and the wee British villages now going up as new suburbs for China's emergent upper class. Are these a mark of the decline and bankruptcy of traditional Chinese culture, a preference for the patently fake and performative, or only a moment of appropriation, of strengthening and cultural expansion before the process of Sinification sets in, a sequence seen many times before in Chinese history? Like Chen Kaige's *Yellow Earth*, will this someday be seen as fine cinema but a poor predictor of things to come? Like any good narrative, Jia's tale implies more than it makes explicit. It remains ambiguous whether Zhao Tao, this sweetest and most innocent of *The World*'s characters, overcome by betrayals and disillusionment, commits suicide, or if she is the victim of a faulty technology, due to a careless building superintendent who says he cautioned her about gas leaks, as if a warning alone would discharge his responsibility. But betrayal and irresponsibility, false hopes and harsh realities blend seamlessly and unambiguously into the larger reality of China's headlong rush to modernize and capitalize as fast as possible, at whatever price, into the question of just how high the cost of this might be, and into the certainty that the fate of China's ecology and that of its people are ultimately one and the same.

Ruins and Grassroots:
Jia Zhangke's Cinematic Discontents in the Age of Globalization

Hongbing Zhang[*]

Produced at a time when China was being swept deeper and deeper into the currents of globalization, Jia Zhangke's films can be viewed today almost as an impossible effort to arrest that flow, as at once a cinematic reconstruction, a comment, and an intervention toward that very historical process. They can be taken simultaneously as important and active participants of the ongoing debates on the process of globalization in China today. Recent Chinese theories and comments on globalization are as ideologically different as one could imagine, but we can still stake out, with the audacity of theorization and historicizing at the outset, the problematic underlying their polemics and arguments as something of a shared discursive ground — globalization is a continuation of the historical process of modernization, but its historical emergence has also brought something fundamentally different with it. While modernization has long been understood in China essentially as a temporal movement in which China will be improved from its old tradition to the universalized ideal of a new tomorrow, now globalization is broadly perceived as a spatial movement in which the improvement of China means its integration into the current dominant world system of market, commodity, capital, and culture. But, as much as how the spatial movement functions as a continuation of the temporal movement — e.g., culturally, the former as a disenchantment with the latter? — needs further theoretical exploration as well as historical reflection, this shared view of globalization as integration-cum-modernization also has to deal with some new

* An earlier version of this chapter was presented in the panel "New Chinese Ecocinema and Ethics of Environmental Imagination" at the 59th Annual Meeting of the Association for Asian Studies, Boston, March 22–25, 2007. I would like to thank all the panelists, discussants, and audience at the conference, and I am particularly grateful to Sheldon H. Lu and Jiayan Mi for their comments, advice, and support at various moments in the evolution of the ideas presented in this chapter.

challenges: What and how to integrate, what to be left behind, who has the power to integrate what and whom, and how to define the relationship between the integrated and disintegrated?[1]

These questions and their various possible answers have no doubt informed Jia's films, especially his recent films like *Unknown Pleasures* (*Ren xiaoyao*, 2002), *The World* (*Shijie*, 2004), and *Still Life* (*Sanxia haoren*, 2006), but he approaches the issue of globalization through a particular lens of ecological consciousness and a unique cinematic use of the spatial relationship between the character and the mise-en-scène and, by an extension beyond the optical illusions of the cinematic world, of that between man and environment. As viewers, we see that he frequently puts various types of ruins in the setting and focuses his camera largely on those people who have been discovered and characterized in China today as *cao gen* or "grassroots." This cinematic maneuvering sends out a strong ideological message, however, and it directs our attention to the edges of globalization as a historical monster and to the margins of China as a miracle of globalization, where the lines between the integrated and disintegrated are drawn in a most visible and yet complicated way. On the screen, the unique presentation of the relationship — essentially of a cognate nature marked by a sense of being the disintegrated — between the grassroots character and the ruinous mise-en-scène has shown for us, in a seemingly de-sentimentalizing manner, Jia's sentiments of discontent toward globalization. They are similar to the sentiment that recognizes the historical inevitability of globalization in the world today, on the one hand, and is intensely dissatisfied with some of the failures of its historical promises for the Chinese people on the other. In such a sentiment, the presentation on the filmic screen also distinguishes Jia's effort to explore the so-called "*yuan shengtai*" or the "original eco-state of life" beyond the glamour of globalization from many other efforts and appropriations that have been increasingly commercialized as a cultural fashion of nostalgia in China today.

Globalization and Cinematic Flatness

What has made Jia's films stand out in today's Chinese cinema as something different from other Sixth Generation, Fifth Generation, entertainment, and government-sanctioned so-called "leitmotif" movies, appears to be the frequent production of a cinematic flatness on the screen, whereby we see that major characters in the films are controlled and restrained by the mise-en-scène and, in turn, the socio-historical reality it represents. As subject, they seem to enter the filmic frame only to be subjected to the enormous objectifying power of the camera lens and thus rendered not much distinct from the surroundings, as if they were immediately sucked and swallowed up — though not yet completely — by the material and social environment. The cinematic space would appear thereby to lose much of the human dimension as depth to it. So, we see — against the sea of bicycles and the crowd in *Xiao Shan Going Home* (*Xiao Shan huijia*, 1993), the ramshackle streets in *Xiao Wu* (1997), the old brick walls and the yellow earth littered with ashes from coal mines in *Platform* (*Zhantai*, 2000), the dilapidated and desolate bus stop and train station in *Unknown Pleasures*, the scaled-down landmarks and forests of construction steel cables in *The World*, the endless debris from demolished houses and destroyed buildings and the silent currents of a gigantic river in *Still Life* — how the major characters look particularly weak, small, inconsequential, and insignificant, dwarfed by these enlarged mise-en-scènes and struggling futilely under their weight. This imbalanced spatial relationship between the character and the mise-en-scène in these films has offered us, for sure, something of a new Bakhtinian chronotope that registers a changed sense of historical time and space experienced by the Chinese at the present moment.[2] It also suggests something of a cinematic strategy, taking shape in the convoluted discursive shift from modernization to globalization.

On Jia's cinematic screen, the relative smallness and seeming insignificance of his characters against a vast material and social background would nevertheless always produce a defamiliarizing effect among the viewers who have been accustomed to seeing Chinese films with melodramatic narratives and enlarged characters. In the revolutionary realist films, whose stylistics and ideologies dominated much of the second half of twentieth-century Chinese cinema and persist today in many of the government-sponsored "leitmotif" films, we often see that the major positive characters, representing a progressive collectivity as the future of history, would always act in a melodramatic way and stand out heroically in front against those negative characters — usually counter-revolutionary forces and reactionary elements — in the background or off-screen. Their heroic images would thereby be rendered large against the physical, material, and social environments. The socialist realist movies made in the early 1980s to address the scars and wounds from the Cultural Revolution and the problems of the just-started social and economic reforms would replace the imposing heroes and heroines representing a revolutionary collectivity with an individual who was usually equipped with a universalized humanity or unwavering political will, but they inherited, nevertheless, the tradition of producing larger-than-life human subjects that dwarfed their immediate material and social environment on the screen. With their actions, thoughts, and feelings presented often in an inflated mode to the viewers, these figures became the primary voice of social criticism, political reflection, and cultural enlightenment as well as being a most recognizable site of psychological identification and emotional discharge. In the radically changed cultural and social context since the early 1990s, where we see increasing commercialization and transnational interpenetration on a global scale, Chinese film directors from the Fifth Generation, the government-sponsored and other entertainment movie camps would continue to generate and meet the demand of the audience — shaped by the aesthetics and ideologies of earlier Chinese movies and recently imported Hollywood movies — for an inflated subjectivity in their films. Against the overshadowed and squeezed mise-en-scène of the material and social environments, enlarged images of human subject would continue to appear on the screen, either as a figuration of some deep-seated aspiration for human dignity, national identity, or philosophical transcendence; as the rebellious face of human desire against those naturalized patriarchal structures; as a visual metaphor for the melancholy feeling over some helpless and hopeless socio-political failure; as a representative of certain morally correct force; or as a fantastic idol of love and passion in their undisguised commodity-forms.[3]

It is significant for us to observe that, in these films, the spatial tensions and conflicts between the character and the mise-en-scène (whether the latter serves as an immediate resistance and restraint or an ultimate manifestation and reification of the former's subjectivity) occupy only a secondary place after the dramatized relationships between the characters. They are, for sure, still a necessary and significant component of what constitutes the melodramatic plot and cinematic depth. In the meantime, the enlarged images of human subjects and the dramatized struggles among them reflect, in a truly dramatic manner, the various movements, campaigns, and ideologies of voluntarism that have appeared in all sorts of forms in modern Chinese history. The imperial gesture of the characters toward the dwarfed mise-en-scène reminds us, especially in those revolutionary and socialist realist films and some of the Fifth Generation films, of the discourse of "civilization versus savage wilderness."[4] The discourse is undoubtedly a core component of the grand narrative of modernization and modernity that has encouraged the Chinese to reform and change or to transcend their living environment, whether the latter is social, political, material, or natural. In the light of this narrative, the present environment is viewed then, primarily, as the remainder and reminder of the past that needs to be improved or even overcome on the way to a better life located in the future. The social totality, if any, represented successfully in these movies, is accomplished therefore not so much through the mise-en-scène or the spatial context as through the human characters, the dramatic relations between them, and their aggressive acts towards the environment. The highlighted subjectivity on the screen serves essentially as an agency of historical change and, in that regard, also prefigures the future of the society. Here the chronotope of space-time dynamic is constructed, more than anything else, around time, history, and the human agency of historical change.

From this Chinese cinematic tradition, Jia's films have emerged as a departure, with almost a stylistic reversal on the screen, of the spatial relationship between the character and the mise-en-scène. In his movies, medium and long shots are frequently used to keep characters away from the foreground, zooming them out into the broad and distant background, sometimes so far away that they even become indistinguishable from their surroundings. Being part of the mise-en-scène within the frame, the objects and extras in the otherwise unoccupied foreground would sometimes block the major characters of the films from the viewers. Yet simultaneously, they would always give, together with the mise-en-scène on other sides of the frame, a strong sense of cinematic embeddedness and geographical locatedness to the characters, who would otherwise appear to break away from their immediate material and social background, as in those earlier movies of enlarged subjectivity and conspicuous voluntarism. Now framed by the mise-en-scène on the four sides, the characters' images in Jia's films are smaller, and their struggles and tensions among themselves and against the material and social environment — the primary contents of the narrative plot — are thereby rendered visually more contained and less visible and dramatic.

The diminishing of subjectivity as such would definitely expand the purview of mise-en-scène or spatial context on the screen of Jia's films. On the other hand, the use of long take — the other feature of his cinematic style — to shoot some distanced and seemingly uneventful scenes would turn the historical time, which often appears on the screen as if coming to a standstill and thus becoming a becoming-space of time or a "time-image," virtually into a narrative space rather than a narrative time that would otherwise manifest itself on the screen in what Gilles Deleuze calls "movement-image."[5] In the meantime, the idiosyncratic use of the soundtrack, especially of pop songs, and those of TV programs not only reinforces the general mood and theme of Jia's movies, but the audio and video intertextualities also greatly expand the cinematic space, as if to deliberately break through the boundary and distinction between the cinematic screen and the real world, while also serving to suggest the historicity of that very space.

The historical validity and authenticity of Jia's cinematic style — an essentially global style that is said to be a product less of the local post-socialist realism in China than of the aestheticized realism popular on the current international art film market[6] — has to be sought nevertheless in the historical time and space experienced by the Chinese in the age of globalization. And the ideological emissions of his style also have to be examined accordingly by reassembling and inserting them back into the changed historical space so as to stake out their historical content and determine their historical function. The cinematic flatness produced by Jia's filming style, especially the small character and shrinking subjectivity — taken here as part of an overall semiotic reconstruction and cinematic interpretation of the historical reality — has registered his own perception of present Chinese life as a much reduced and thereby more inconsequential human existence in the torrents of globalization. In the meantime, it has also demonstrated his commitment, arguably with the same intensity if not more than that for the people, to the social and material conditions in China today. Yet a critical analysis of the environment's semiotic contents — especially the architectural ruins — and of the grassroots people struggling in the staged space is expected to move us beyond the cinematic stylistics to a horizon of the ongoing historical process of globalization, from which Jia's cinematic style has emerged as at once a consequence and an imaginary solution.

The Disappearance of Nature

In Jia's films, the enlarged spatial context on the screen, gained at the cost of human subjectivity, has to be distinguished from the natural landscape of the pre-industrial age, and his environmental consciousness has to be differentiated from the consciousness of nature. The distinction would lead us, then, to situating Jia's movies right in the cultural politics in contemporary Chinese cinema of relating nature and naturalized agrarian life to the ongoing historical process of modernization and globalization.[7] In Chinese cinema since the 1980s, nature or naturalized agrarian life has long been represented on the screen as an objectified target of historical struggles for change in such films as *The Legend of Tianyun Mountain* (*Tianyun shan chuanqi*, dir. Xie Jin, 1980) and *Yellow Earth* (*Huang tudi*, dir. Chen Kaige, 1984), where, as an absolute Other of history, the remote mountain and yellow earth are also used as an ultimate ahistorical template to launch historical reflections on the calamities of the Cultural Revolution and the failure of the communist liberation movement and rhetoric. Or, we see, in the form of naturalized agrarian landscape in the ethnic minority area, nature is ceded from historical changes as a utopian enclave in *Sacrifice of Youth* (*Qingchun ji*, dir. Zhang Nuanxin, 1985) for the cultivation and promotion of a humanist and feminist consciousness. And in the appearance of the vast field of red sorghum, it is idealized in *Red Sorghum* (*Hong gaoliang*, dir. Zhang Yimou, 1987) as the final and ultimate reserve of some primitive passion of the individual and the nation that is staged on the screen to explode against the invading Japanese. Or, in the image of green mountains, it is represented in *Postman in the Mountain* (*Nashan naren nagou*, dir. Huo Jianqi, 1999) to redeem in the much commercialized and alienated Chinese life some disappearing ethic of labor that is based upon the notion of a harmonious relationship between man and nature, and which is seen on the screen to be successfully passed over from father to son.

Parting company, both ideologically and aesthetically, with these cinematic practices, Jia's cinematic discourse implies, as we will see, a denial within itself — a denial of nature and naturalized landscape as an ultimate outside and exteriority or as a transcendental utopian enclave of history in his cinematic discourse of modernization and globalization. In what is presented largely as an urbanized space in his movies, we see an increasing marginalization and disappearance of nature and naturalized agrarian life or, to be more exact, a trajectory where nature and naturalized agrarian life, if any, are represented on the screen — often in a dystopian fashion — to be part of the ongoing historical process of modernization and globalization.

Of Jia Zhangke's films, perhaps *Platform* and *Still Life* provide us with a better view of the disappearing nature or the naturalized agrarian life than *Unknown Pleasures*, *The World*, or *Xiao Wu*, which offer only fleeting glimpses on the edge of their frames. Set in the small town of Fenyang in Shanxi Province, *Platform* allows us to follow the young performers of a newly privatized theater troupe into a rural China, whose yellow color, grayish houses, and numbing dreariness would remotely remind us of the landscape in *Yellow Earth*. The cold and expansive rural and natural environment might momentarily offer some fresh air to the young people whose life within the old walls of the town has become more and more monotonous and boring against the influences of change from coastal China. But essentially it plays the same role, as the urbanized space does in the town, of a depressing and recalcitrant material and social environment for the young people's pulsating aspirations for a change. Yet, unlike the claustrophobic pre-industrial landscape in *Yellow Earth* that naturalizes the patriarchal structure and simultaneously asserts itself as a limit to the historical change the communist enlightenment project is supposed to bring but fails to do so, the landscape in the rural China of *Platform* is deeply penetrated and transformed by modern historical changes. Indeed, the coalmines operated beneath the farming land or in the dreary hills surrounding the village where the young performers stay, and the railroad passing through the barren and wild mountains, all suggest that the rural landscape is being gradually industrialized and thus has lost much of its power to naturalize beyond history. Furthermore, the villagers' silent courage to risk their lives working in the coalmine for money instead of continuing to farm their land, and the young performers boisterously running after the passing train in the mountains which illuminates contrastively the depressing harshness of the rural existence and landscape, also signal its fast disappearance in the ongoing national drive for modernization (see Figure 7.1).

Figure 7.1   Young performers pursuing the passing train in the mountains in *Platform*.

On the other hand, following the two characters that come to the city of Fengjie to look for their spouses in *Still Life*, we are to see on the screen a different type of natural landscape in the Three Gorges. The foggy green of the trees on the steep mountains and the greenish waters of the river running at their foot constitute the natural landscape, whose ideal natural beauty is presented however to be preserved or reproduced now primarily on the ten-yuan bill of the Chinese currency as the demolition laborers have noticed, and in the poetic lines from ancient China that the modern tourist industry appropriates as a selling point of nostalgia to appeal to its customers. Subjected to the changes brought about by the Three Gorges Dam project that is part of China's global search for energy to sustain its booming economy, the natural landscape is presented here as elegiacally disappearing. Yet unlike that in *Platform* whose disappearance might signal all the more the need for the unquestioned and seemingly unquestionable modernization drive, its disappearance here, due directly to the surging and swallowing waters frequently measured out in metrics on the screen, is presented as a visual question to the very drive for energy. While the appearance of the cold and gray natural environment in *Platform* is viewed largely as depressing and tough for the inhabitants, it is the disappearance of the warm and green landscape that is seen here as a threat to the everyday life of the inhabitants.

It is apparent for us to see that the two types of nature or natural landscape are cinematic products of two different discourses — the discourse of modernity in *Platform* where the ideal proper of modernity and the national modernization drive are left essentially unquestioned and not criticized, and the discourse of globalization in *Still Life* where a critical consciousness is also presented conspicuously for China's modernization drive and its global ambition for economic power in the world. While Jia's differentiated use of the two discourses in his movies merit further clarification in the below, for now we can see that the two types of natural landscape's shared marginalization and disappearance — their subjection to historical change and reduction in narrative time and space — are managed on the screen not only to reflect a continuous historical process in contemporary China where nature is experienced indeed as something fast disappearing at the approach of drastic historical changes. They are presented on the screen also to indicate, on Jia's part, a persistent cinematic preoccupation with the human world of here and now, thereby refusing to give nature in his cinematic discourse the utopian space of being an outside, an exteriority, or an enclave of history. In this sense, the persistent use of the various types of nature or natural landscape in the films is purported by Jia only to register, beyond the visual and ideological illusions, the different social, political, and ideological divisions and struggles in the production of space where, à la Henri Lefebvre, the "differential spaces" on the screen can always be traced back to the "contradictions of space" generated in the historical process of modernization and globalization that China is undergoing at present.[8]

Ruins and Public Space

For Jia, the filmmaker of the so-called "urban generation,"[9] the human world of here and now refers primarily to public space in a contemporary Chinese urban setting. This space takes all kinds of physical form in his films — street scenes of traffic, crowds and stores, city walls, video room, train station, bus and ship, park, construction site, factories, and so on. It is a physical, material, and social space that seems to have endless fluidity and openness, where people see and hide, meet and escape, where legitimate business and illegal activities mix up, where social responsibilities take shape, and private desires are incarnated. It is also a space undergoing incessant changes and transformations, where new things rise to coexist, co-opt, and compete with the old ones, and sometimes simply replace them, though always leaving behind some irreplaceable and indestructible remains and residues as if deliberately to demarcate the limit and historicity of the new arrivals.

On the screen of Jia's films, the dialectical "Other" of the public space — the intimate and private space of a home — is squeezed to its minimum. This is not just because, as an interior space of human dwelling, it suffers the most from the cinematic shrinking of subjectivity. It is also because its supposed or expected occupants, whom the filming camera is anchored to frequently identify with or follow, are arranged to be on constant move in the open, either physically running away from home in the hope of securing a better life elsewhere, or being financially too poor to afford it at all, or still searching for it with hope and anxiety, or simply witnessing helplessly its destruction and transformation into a homeless and deserted public space with indefinite rubble and ruins.

Of all the rich signs and symbols populating the public space of Jia's films that a preliminary semiotic survey would list, two signs stand out that could be of structural significance to the space: the police and architectural ruins. By watching all his movies from the earliest *Xiao Shan Going Home* to the recent *Still Life*, we are able to detect a cinematic trajectory where the police decrease and the ruins increase, and the 2002 film *Unknown Pleasures* becomes something of a turning point in these semiotic movements. Indeed, in *Unknown Pleasures* and the movies before it (including *Xiao Shan Going Home*, *Xiao Wu*, and *Platform*), the police make a visible presence on the screen as a managing and regulating force of the space, directing traffic, catching and disciplining thieves, educating disobedient lovers, arresting bank robbers and other criminals, and safeguarding the various reforms and changes launched and promoted by the state in its modernization drive.[10] But its omnipresent power in the public space is marginalized almost to an invisibility and replaced on the screen in the later films of *The World* and *Still Life* largely by non-government security guards, whose power is now greatly reduced and limited to some local institutions and private companies.[11] In the meantime, architectural fragments and ruins, which only make a fleeting appearance in the frames of the earlier movies, now have a prominent presence in *Unknown Pleasures* and culminate as a dominant sign in the public space of *The World* and *Still Life*.

What this semiotic change on the screen registers is in fact the director's changed perception toward the ongoing historical process whose significant events Jia explicitly refers to in *Unknown Pleasures* — Beijing's successful bid for the 2008 Olympics and China's joining of the WTO. These two events are incorporated in the film to indicate unmistakably a new stage in China's historical integration into the world system and the penetration of globalizing forces into China. And the way they are introduced to us on the screen — the TV news of the Olympics coming through the eyes and ears of the two disaffected and jobless adolescents who in their street wanderings and pursuits of girls do not care about what is going on in the nation and the world, and the WTO information through the mouth of a schoolgirl talking to one of the disaffected adolescents — also suggests Jia's view of the historical process as already a pervasive influence in Chinese daily life. Likewise, the removal from the screen of the police, the otherwise most visible apparatus of the nation-state in everyday life, is also part of the filmmaker's semiotic reconstruction and cinematic interpretation of the changing role of the state in the new age, a role now making its effect felt not so much through administrative measures and public display as through economic control and market regulation. This is indeed a new cinematic move, quite different from Jia's previous configuration of the state power in the image of police disciplining and mobilizing the public in the national modernization drive. In the new discursive reconstruction and interpretation, the power of nation-state is now represented on the screen, if not to be outright weakened and erased, at least to be transformed from a spectacle in the public space to an invisible presence (and yet still intensely felt) therein, so much so that it could make room for some new types of spatial connectedness and difference between the character and mise-en-scène, between man and environment, to emerge in the filming frame.

The ruins that grow incrementally on the screen of Jia's recent films can be viewed as another part and aspect of his semiotic reconstruction and cinematic interpretation of the same historical process of integration-cum-modernization. But the ruins here ought to be seen more in terms of their present or spatial value than in the modernist terms of "age value" or historical value as they have been customarily seen in the Western art history of ruins and in much of the modern Chinese visual culture of ruins. Also, they should be no longer viewed in a nationalist light, as are the ruins in the Yuanmingyuan, which are interpreted as a "memorial to national shame in the pre-Revolutionary era."[12] Indeed, many contemporary Chinese artists and filmmakers have used demolitions and ruins in their works to register "the transformation of a new sensory economy" and concomitantly to "enter into an uneasy, asymmetrical, and contradictory relationship with the teleologies of modernization, developmentalism, globalization, and social progress,"[13] but many of them still use ruins in terms of their age or historical value, viewing demolition sites as "timekeepers of urban history," as "the spatial repositories of personal and collective memory in effigy," and as scars and traumas.[14] By contrast, in Jia's films, the ruins, which have been generalized symbolically as "the ruins of post-Mao China,"[15] appear in the movies' public spaces, whether used as certain ambient elements or as structural points, but always to be viewed as leftovers, sticking-out elements that are not assimilated and integrated, spatial differences that demand a different type of spatial connectedness from those present and seen on the screen, and around — and because of — which a certain degree of spatial uniformity might be able to be achieved in the public space. So, the ruins on Jia's screen, sometimes with the aid of audio and video intertextualities, never fail to direct the viewers' attention back to that at once abstract and historical process of globalization, simultaneously always releasing some added ideological emission or message, the content of which depends on the specific semiotic combinations he put them into on the screen.

It is not surprising, then, to see that in the film *Unknown Pleasures*, set in the inland city of Datong, ruins start to spread in public space, while globalization, as a worldwide historical process, is indicated on the screen. But, in the movie, the piles of debris from demolished houses on the street through which Zhao Qiaoqiao, the image girl for a liquor company, walks in her chic outfit, appear to be not much different visually from the surrounding houses and street scene, which all look gray and shabby (see Figure 7.2). Nor is the long stretch of wasteland across which Xiao Ji, the adolescent with a crush on Qiaoqiao, has difficulty riding his motorcycle, much different from the dusty bus stop on one side and the gray and bleak brick apartment buildings from the 1950s and 1960s on the other side.[16] Likewise, the waste and garbage left on the construction site of a highway and around the makeshift stage on which Qiaoqiao is seen dancing to promote the liquor, look little different from the surrounding lands and houses, except for the brand new highway and the decorated stage. The toned-down difference on the screen, between the ruins and their surroundings, shows that the process of change leaving these ruins behind has not yet done much to integrate and transform the others in the public space of the city.

Figure 7.2 Zhao Qiaoqiao walking through a demolished street in *Unknown Pleasures*.

In the movie, the new highways that the TV news says are going to be built to integrate Datong into the provincial and national network of transportation, and the few scattered new buildings appearing briefly on the screen, are purported to show, for sure, what the rest of the public space in the city would be transformed into, thereby becoming objects of desire in the eyes of the inhabitants. Indeed, the wasteland, the demolished houses, the shanty where the adolescent but jobless Guo Binbin and his father stay, the multifunctional railway station where, in addition to its railway function, old and new forms of entertainment intersect; the bleak old apartment buildings in which Xiao Ji and his mother live, the few glassy new buildings in the distance that the camera never takes us inside to see, and the new highways, all constitute an architectural order on the screen, whose varying difference in form and color would tell us a different story of individual well-being, social status, and historical change. In the meantime, they are also shown there to make up a hierarchical order of the objects of desire, with the new buildings and new highways at its top. The virtual existence of the integrating highways on the TV screen could be taken, in this light, as occupying an ultimate place in that order, and with the anticipated turning of its virtual existence into a real one, it forecasts that a bigger wave of historical change is now on its way to the city of Datong that so far is largely left behind by the expected changes. But before that arrives, the ruins and their inconspicuous difference from the rest of the city are used in the movie to indicate the city's current left-behind status. Simultaneously, they also serve the function of an ambient on the movie screen, reinforcing the general lackluster color and the depressing mood — combined with a veiled sentiment for some ineffable loss and with some anxieties of anticipation — of the present, seemingly uneventful public space that still lacks, at least in the eyes of the two jobless adolescents, Xiao Ji and Guo Binbin, an earth-defying hero that the soundtrack of a pop song repeatedly calls for in the film.

As a stark contrast to the dusty and bleak setting in the film *Unknown Pleasures*, the public space the film *The World* constructs is a bright and new cosmopolitan space, set in Beijing, whose structural point and focus of cinematic attention are a theme park of the world with lots of scaled-down exotic and famous landmark sites and buildings from around the globe. Among those shown on the screen, the seemingly pre-historical stones of Stonehenge, the yellow desert with the Sphinx rising in its midst, and the dilapidated column structure of some ancient Greek temple looking much like the Parthenon, are all filmed to maintain their isolated dignity as ruins, but they do not look much different from other landmark sites and buildings, such as the twin towers of the World Trade Center from New York, Big Ben from England, the Eiffel Tower from Paris, and the Taj Mahal mausoleum from India (see Figure 7.3). What is shared by all these world-famous landmark sites and buildings in the screened theme park here is the specter of destruction and death. It is a specter that Cheng Taisheng, chief of the security team in the park, inadvertently touches upon when he points out one can still see the complete twin towers in the park even after the original two in Manhattan were destroyed in September 11, 2001 — a spectral quality that could also be characterized as ruinous.

Figure 7.3   Cheng Taisheng showing friends from his hometown around the theme park in *The World*.

Indeed, like the specimens in the bag of an eighteenth-century European naturalist that were collected from around the globe to complete his abstract system of nature, the landmark sites and buildings in the theme park are collected here from around the world by the tourist company to sell to meet the demands of the Chinese for knowledge of foreign countries, and their global aspirations to "marching out toward the world." Just like the specimens in the naturalist bag that still give off an air of authenticity, the sites and buildings also emit an ideology of verisimilitude that the tourist industry makes efforts to promote, but they cannot avoid the fate nevertheless of being ruins — as leftovers and something transplanted from elsewhere, they are always haunted by the specter of violence and death exerted by the naturalist and the tourist company respectively to their original natural habitats and socio-historical environments as well as to themselves. In the meantime, they are seen on the film screen to be present on the local landscape of Beijing, being part of it but giving the viewers simultaneously an impression of not quite belonging there and being not yet fully integrated into it. Because of their ruinous nature, the on-screen landmark sites and buildings in the theme park cannot suppress the dialectic "Other" of their verisimilitude — the fakes and forgeries which we see in the movie hang in the minds of both the tourists and the theme park workers.

On the other hand, various as they are in terms of architectural and landscaping style, these scaled-down landmark sites and buildings in the park are rendered visually different on the screen from the surrounding buildings and landscapes. This spatial and architectural difference allows the image of the Eiffel Tower to stand out in the skyline from the forests of scaffolding and endless steel cables of the nearby construction site where the male worker named Little Sister suffers a fatal accident. It also allows the little zigzagging roads in the park to appear out of time beside the newly built broad and straight highway right outside of the park, the archaic appearance of the theme park palaces and mausoleums to be easily spotted among the newly built high-rise buildings, and the low and narrow hallway leading from the imperial stage of ethnic performance to the dressing room in the park to become such a sharp contrast to the futuristic hallway inside a KTV entertainment center to which Zhao Xiaotao and some of her fellow female performers at the park were once invited. It is apparent to see on the screen, that against the essentially ethnical and regional architectural styles inside the theme park, against the park as a structural point of spatial difference, the surrounding buildings and landscapes are able to acquire a conspicuous and uniform architectural character of being new and modern, thereby indicating Beijing as largely a modern and cosmopolitan city.

But, in the meantime, as a product of the transnationalized tourist industry, the theme park also radiates and spreads out on the film screen its insuppressible emissions of fakes and forgeries into other parts of the public space in Beijing, thus adding to the globalized city a spectral quality of being inauthentic, unfaithful, fake, ruinous, and also rootless. And such a spectral interaction between the theme park and the rest of Beijing is staked out on the film screen by a series of illegal moneymaking activities. It is meant, perhaps, to be at once ironic and suggestive of the pervasive and perverse dimension of the interaction that such activities are conducted first and foremost by the security chief at the theme park Chen Taisheng, who is supposed to safeguard the park of imitative and fake buildings. Yet, he is seen leaving the park to send fake IDs to his "business" partner Lao Song, so as to open some accounts for "globally reaching" wireless phone service. In the meantime, we also see some of Zhao Xiaotao's fellow female performers leave the park to fake passion and love with men in the KTV center in downtown Beijing; and Liao Aqun, the woman whom Cheng Taisheng dates behind his girlfriend Zhao Xiaotao's back, makes, in her workshop, all sorts of counterfeit brands of clothes, handbags, and other fashion products. In this light, the ruinous theme park, as a structural point of the public space in the film, seems to be turning the very modern and cosmopolitan space of Beijing into a vast theme park as well.

In the film *Still Life*, the debris from the apartment buildings, demolished due to the surging waters of the Three Gorges Dam under construction, appears on the screen — coming to us primarily through the eyes of Han Sanming and Shen Hong in search for their family members — to be something all the more overwhelming and devastating. And our impression of devastation is reinforced on the screen by the few visible signs of life from the ruins that, however, look particularly insignificant and pointless: homeless dogs emerging from the rubble and skulking around silently and aimlessly, the sanitizing workers in masks and white uniforms intently occupied with spraying chemicals all around on broken windows, deserted rooms and pile after pile of rubble and waste, and the sweating bare-chested laborers wielding heavy-duty hammers against the remaining standing walls and floors, with only the sound of hammers and falling bricks breaking the otherwise suffocating, heavy silence.

But, what these seemingly inconsequential human actions manage to achieve on the screen, frequently filmed in medium and long shots, is not just a cinematic reinforcement, in a contrastive light, of the devastating sight of the ruins already in place, but also to show the ruins in their making. Following the steps of Han Sanming, a coalminer from Shanxi Province, who is seen walking through the ruins in search of his long-separated daughter and divorced wife, and who later joins the bare-chested workers demolishing houses, we are able to see the violent production of ruins closely — how glasses get broken into fragments, windows taken off, walls pulled down, and a whole building blown up by dynamite. Turned from private apartments into debris on the demolition site, these ruins are presented on the screen as the wreckage and leftovers of a local place and a local mode of daily life that is being destroyed by the surging water that is to be used to generate electricity to power the booming and much globalized national economy. Furthermore, they appear in the camera frame to grow and spread out into other residential areas — following the sprawling routes of trucks transporting debris, accompanying the rapid appearance of the large white Chinese character 拆 or "demolish," tracing the threatening footsteps of those youngsters working for the demolition company to force inhabitants out of their houses, and finally emerging under the sweating bodies of the demolition workers like Han Sanming, who come to physically break down the residential buildings into countless pieces of rubble and debris.

In the meantime, following the steps and seen from the perspective of Shen Hong, who has also come from Shanxi to Fengjie looking for her husband, we are now allowed to see another type of ruins — those in the state-run factories that have been closed down after their properties were sold to private owners. The dark and dusty workshops, the rusty tall furnace, the gigantic tanks, and the huge rust-red pipes — no longer operating and staying motionless there without any maintenance — constitute the heroic site and sight of industrial ruins on the film screen, against which the noisy collapsing of a collective institution can still be heard and seen in the complaint and anger of its former employees. The industrial and residential ruins are both presented to take up so much narrative space and time in the film that the newly built high-rises, the new bridge across a tributary of the Changjiang river, the gigantic Three Gorges Dam, the distant grey network of power lines, the familiar green color of the disappearing natural landscape on the edge of the frame, and the strangely shaped architecture that is seen magically flying with certain grand ambition into the sky like a rocket, are all turned thereby into an ambient of the public space. The focus of cinematic attention in the film is placed firmly on the residential ruins, which is filmed in such a way as to become the essential structure and primary spectacle of the public space. Structured and manifested as such, the cinematic space registers unmistakably an ideological as well as an aesthetic preoccupation of the film with home, family, and post-socialist individuals whose lives are now reduced to their ruinous minimum in the age of globalization.

Grassroots and Cinematic Discontents

Jia's semiotic construction of the public space in his recent films as large and ruinous is consistent ideologically and aesthetically with the type of characters whose images he chooses to present as small and inconsequential on the screen. The visual combination of large mise-en-scène and small character becomes at once the vehicle and content of his cinematic interpretation, and a comment on the ongoing historical process of integration-cum-modernization that China is going through at present. The image of a small character dwarfed by a large mise-en-scène, constrained by the material and social environment, and pressed hard by the invisible hand of the emerging, at once abstract and historical world system represented and reified by the mise-en-scène on the screen, belongs to that of a new social group taking shape in the process of globalization — a group of people who have been increasingly debated and designated in contemporary Chinese media, if not yet so much among scholars, as *cao gen* or "grassroots."[17]

Estranged from the collective organizations and institutions of the past and present and in turn no longer able to be accommodated fully into current sociological and political categories of workers, peasants, proletarians, and the masses, the grassroots people are designated primarily as a social group opposite to the various social, political, intellectual, and economic elitist groups that have well benefited from China's present integration into the world system. They are struggling as the weakest link in the social, economic, and political fabric, and they are far away from various forms of power invested in other social groups. The image of grassroots brings to the Chinese mind the following properties that are associated frequently with this group of people: their lowly, rough, and minimal form of existence; their extraordinary capacity of surviving by any means, legal or illegal, and in all sorts of environments and conditions; and their unique bonding and attachment to soil and earth. For contemporary Chinese media and those in the West as well, the life stories of these grassroots people, discovered or constructed, constitute the rare picture of another type of the so-called "original eco-state of life" that lies locally beneath and beyond the glaring glamour of globalization in China today, and which, therefore, is viewed with much nostalgia to be fast disappearing from our globalized view.[18]

It is apparent that Jia's cinematic representation of the grassroots people, unassimilated into and so not benefiting much from the new historical change, is endowed, if not with an outright and open criticism, at least with some cinematic discontent toward the ongoing historical process of globalization. But, even from his early narrative films, we can find that the discontented and critical gaze comes to us not so much from the relationship between the characters as from the constructed tensions and conflicts between the characters and their material and social environments. This arrangement is made not only out of Jia's general perception of Chinese life as a reduced and squeezed existence in the historical process of change, but also — and more likely — from a realization on his part that the change, at once abstract and historical, is so pervasive and penetrating in Chinese life that, rather than being able to be personified in any particular character as its agency, it has to be spatialized in the material and social environment whereby it becomes an invisible but powerful presence. As a result, even tensions and conflicts between the small characters and their powerful environments are not dramatized and appear thereby as some unrelated incidents and accidents in the otherwise uneventful and largely biographical storylines of his films.

So we see, Xiao Shan, the peasant laborer from Shanxi in the film *Xiao Shan Going Home*, finds his displeasure in Beijing represented on the film screen not so much through his struggles with other people or through the coarse talk of his fellow natives about sex and politics in the dilapidated small room at night. Instead, it is articulated more in the shots of the seemingly unrelated winter street scenes of Beijing he witnesses in detachment and cold isolation, in the coffee-colored appearance of a tall female fellow native he suspects of prostitution, in the violent scene which his friend is involved in but which he comes too late to see and help, and in the black-and-white TV screen that, during the news hour, asks peasant laborers to stay in Beijing and not to go back home for the Chinese New Year so as to avoid burdening the already strained transportation facilities. Likewise, in the film *Xiao Wu*, the ineffable sense of loss experienced by Xiao Wu, the pickpocket in the city of Fenyang, is manifested not so much in the distancing of him from his long-time pickpocket friend, who now becomes a legitimized and much-acclaimed self-made entrepreneur, in the sudden disappearance of a female prostitute that he likes, or in the abrupt appearance of the police coming to arrest him. It emanates more from the out-of-pace or strained relationship between the inner dignity screened by his heavy eye-glasses and the fast-commercialized street scenes of stores and shops and the local and faraway social and political events broadcast on TV and radio.

No real dramatic conflict and tension between the characters, and the fact that the conflict and tension between the character and the mise-en-scène always make their appearance in seemingly unrelated incidents and accidents, are perhaps best shown in the film *Unknown Pleasures*. The jobless adolescent Xiao Ji's efforts to build up a real struggle and fight with Qiao San, the big moneyed man whose helpers once thrashed Xiao Ji for hanging out with his girlfriend Zhao Qiaoqiao, are undermined and deconstructed completely of their possible meanings by the death of Qiao San in a random car accident off-screen. In the meantime, we also see that, at the end of the film, the police's interest in Guo Binbin, the other major character in the film and Xiao Ji's jobless adolescent friend, is not so much for his real exploits as a bank robber as apparently and ironically for his karaoke-style of singing. And Xiao Ji's supposedly desperate escape from the failed bank robbery turns out to be a futile and unnecessary move because no police or any other law-enforcement personnel are seen as interested enough to come and pursue him.

It is significant for us to observe that all the major characters in *Unknown Pleasures* are struggling for a living outside of government, business, or any other institution. From the very beginning of the movie, we see that Xiao Ji does not have a job and Guo Binbin has just quit his job against his mother's will. Furthermore, both jobless adolescents live with their dysfunctional families: Xiao Ji stays in a shanty with his father who makes a living by repairing bicycles, and Guo Binbin lives in one of the bleak apartment buildings with his mother, who later in the film is also dismissed from her factory. Obviously, they all live under much financial pressure and have little social network as a recourse in their lives, thereby feeling different degrees of inactiveness, helplessness, and meaninglessness. On the other hand, Zhao Qiaoqiao, Qiao San's girlfriend whom Xiao Ji tries to date as well, does not have a regular job either and she also lives in a family with her single parent father who is now lying sick in the hospital. Of all these characters, Qiao San — though fired from his job as a physical education instructor in a school and thus having to struggle to survive for awhile — seems to be an exception, benefiting the most through legal and illegal business acts from the new historical change. For Xiao Ji, then, the competition with Qiao San for the same girlfriend would take on a double significance — it would offer him the excitement and comfort of adolescent fancy and also a target and a venue for fighting against the social establishment, thus elevating himself out of the current stagnant, boring, and meaningless life. Guo Binbin's girlfriend would also provide Guo with similar excitement and comfort in this indifferent and depressing world. But, the sudden death of Qiao San and the anticipated departure of Guo's girlfriend for college study elsewhere have destroyed the two jobless adolescents' hopes of a possible exit from such an environment.

Perhaps for the lack of real action between the characters, the material and social environment is presented and experienced on the screen by the grassroots people to be all the more pervasive and heavy. In Jia's early movies set in the historical period of reform and modernization, its pervasiveness can still be aestheticized in such a powerful way that, for instance, in the film *Platform*, the intrusion of the thick old wall as an obstacle into the tryst of the two theater troupe performers Cui Mingliang and Yin Ruijuan could still be arranged by the director with confidence to appear also as a shield to protect their budding love from other people on the screen and as a visual block to the viewers' penetrating gaze. But the no-exit material and social environment in *Unknown Pleasures*, set in the age of globalization, is presented largely from the perspective of Xiao Ji, Guo Binbin, and Zhao Qiaoqiao as predominantly indifferent, callous, and depressing. It is in such a depressing environment that not only do we see the sabotaging activities of blasting buildings and robbing banks as violent means of fighting against it, we also see that, as those who are left behind and ignored by the fast-changing society while still embracing their adolescent fancy, Xiao Ji and Guo Binbin frequently appeal, often in the space of an imaginary created and promoted by the then-pop songs, to becoming earth-defying heroes who would come and change the environment, or, to becoming somewhat like the ancient Taoist philosopher Zhuangzi's mythical bird that would fly high, far and carefree to ultimately transcend it.

The historical setting of *Unknown Pleasures* on the margins of China's globalization — the inland city of Datong — and in its early stage of change makes it cinematically possible for Jia to articulate some of the grassroots people's feelings and sentiments of discontent in such an explosive way on the edge of the film screen, and it is also capable, throughout the film, of making room on the screen both visually and acoustically for the characters to appeal for some imaginary escape from the depressing material and social environment. But the world, with room for such an outlet for the grassroots people to vent their discontentment, with such cinematic possibilities offered by the implied historical time and space, is to be completely changed in the film *The World*, which has a much more globalized space. In this space, the historically central position of Beijing in a much advanced stage of China's globalization forces the director to configure the public space with a totally new face and articulate the grassroots people's discontentment with some new cinematic means.

In *The World*, the theme park as a world of imitation, fake, and ruins and the whole public space structured by it are presented on the screen to be experienced by the characters, mostly coming from outside of Beijing, as a glamorous trap. Lured by the opportunities this space would offer, Cheng Taisheng, previously a farmer in Shanxi Province and now the security chief in the theme park, comes to Beijing in the hope of not only winning over his love, Zhao Xiaotao, but also of becoming somebody some day. But the public space of power, wealth, fake, and ruins in Beijing leads him astray, sending him down the wrong track which, as we have seen, involves him not only in making fake IDs but also in being unfaithful to his love. While the fake IDs are not seen in the movie to have any repercussions or to incriminate him, his unfaithfulness does comes back at the end, however, through the text message of a wireless phone, to haunt him and make him pay the price of losing his real love — perhaps forever. In the meantime, Zhao Xiaotao, who used to be a country girl in Shanxi and is now a lead performer in the theme park troupe, finds the seemingly glamorous life of performing and faking every day in the park to be boring and depressing, so much so that she wants to get away from the ruinous and fake park in the hope of landing on the real and solid ground of the outside world. For Zhao Xiaotao, it is her boyfriend Chen Taisheng, who safeguards the park of imitation and fake and often goes outside into the real world of Beijing, who represents not just the hope of love and comfort in her life but, more importantly perhaps, the only real and solid thing in the world of fakes, counterfeit, and unfaithfulness at large. So we see, when the text message suggesting Chen's betrayal reaches Zhao, she feels that not only have her trust and love been misplaced, the guard protecting the real from the fake forever lost, but also the whole glamorous world of wealth and prosperity is now imploding around her as a world of total imitation, fake, counterfeit, and unfaithfulness.

It is important to note that the grassroots people in *The World* are geographically and socially much more inclusive — or more cosmopolitan — than those in Jia's early films. In addition to Chen Taisheng and Zhao Xiaotao, we also see how their fellow natives from Shanxi, like Little Sister, came to Beijing to work on a construction site; Zhao Xiaotao's ex-boyfriend Liangzi stopped by at the theme park and then went abroad to Mongolia; Anna came from Russia to work in the theme park and then moved to work in a KTV entertainment center; and Liao Aqun, whom Chen Taisheng dated behind his lover Zhao Xiaotao's back, came from Zhejiang Province to make and sell counterfeit products in Beijing and finally went abroad to join her long-separated husband in France. Such an extended list of grassroots characters, like all the transplanted landmarks in the theme park supposedly representing the whole outside world for the Chinese, is purported nevertheless not only to offer us a broad view of how much and how thoroughly globalization has penetrated into Beijing, or how much Beijing and China have been globalized, but also to show us how the benefits and problems of globalization are distributed among different social groups in light of their respective positions in it.

No doubt, those benefiting the most from China's globalization are people like the businessman (played by the director Wang Xiaoshuai) who tries to seduce and harass Zhao Xiaotao in the futuristic hallway of the KTV entertainment center, and the least benefiting are those disintegrated ones, such as the shadowy garbage-collecting old man who, in the establishing shot at the beginning of the film, walks slowly to the foreground against the theme park and the modern buildings in its surroundings and then looks back at us for a moment. But what separate these two groups of people are not just their different wealth and social status but also — and in particular — the freedom to move and travel internationally. The businessman attempts to seduce Zhao Xiaotao not just with his money and fine food but primarily with what she lacks — the opportunity to travel to Hong Kong. For the majority of characters in the movie, who are grassroots people mostly integrated into the flow of globalization by either working in the theme park as part of a globalized tourist industry, using fake IDs to make illegal money, or producing counterfeits of world-famous brands circulating on the global markets, the freedom to travel internationally is still a marker of difference that separates them. In the eyes of Zhao Xiaotao, Chen Taisheng, and others, Zhao's ex-boyfriend Liangzi, the Russian woman Anna, and the fake-brand producer Liao Aqun become objects of admiration, much luckier and more successful in life, because they all have their own passports that would allow them to travel around freely. Likewise, for Zhao Xiaotao and Little Sister standing in the forest of steel cables on a construction site, those in the airplane flying right above their heads in the sky become the luckiest people in the world. In a contrastive light, the theme park and the rest of Beijing, primarily through the perspective of Zhao Xiaotao, Chen Taisheng, and Little Sister (people who do not have the freedom to travel but who have all the more desire to do so), are represented to be all the more restrictive, repressive, and depressing, and they are unable to offer any real excitement and happiness in the life of the trapped characters.

The theme park and the public space in Beijing are shown on the screen to be such glamorous traps of ruins, fakes, and unfaithfulness, that Jia has to use new cinematic means to represent the otherwise almost unrepresentable, deep-seated economy of feelings and desires of the grassroots characters. The abrupt and surreal burning of a sofa in the street in broad daylight can be viewed, in this light, as a calculated visual externalization of the repressed emotions surging inside Chen Taisheng, who at that moment is standing in Liao Aqun's office. And the "virtual realities," conspicuous visual differences from the rest of the film, are created by using the technology of flash animation to deliberately challenge the conventional principle of realism and to tear open the otherwise harmonized but imprisoning reality of the globalized city. Through the opening of the virtual, we are thus able to see how Zhao Xiaotao's desire to escape from the ensnaring park is animated on the screen as a bird-like flying lady in a blue uniform; the feelings of the female performers going to the KTV entertainment center as white dots of falling rain in certain street scenes; and, finally, against a black background, the emotions of Chen Taisheng going to see Liao Aqun as a budding pink flower and a green soldier riding a galloping horse that wears a wreath of rose petals; as well as Zhao Xiaotao's reactions to the text message indicating Chen Taisheng's betrayal as a lonely grayish fish with air bubbles floating to the surface of water. In the meantime, it seems that, outside of those "virtual realities," the only other effective means of communication of truthful feelings and serious commitment in the glamorous trap is, ironically, death. Little Sister's death from an accident on the construction site reveals clearly to other characters around him and us, in the few postmortem shots, not only his difficult financial situation but, more importantly, a sincere commitment, written on the back of a cigarette pack, to trust, and responsibility between members of a community that is, however, far away and absent from the screened world of the globalized city of Beijing. Finally, the supposed deaths of Zhao Xiaotao and Cheng Taisheng from a gas leak are turned, at the end of the film, into disembodied voices, speaking an otherwise unspeakable truth from the blackness of the screen — indeed, for the grassroots people in the dark, a death in the age of globalization is just the beginning of a new phase in life.

Jia's cinematic discontentment with China's globalization is nowhere more clearly manifested than in the representation of a devastating site of ruins and a massive displacement of people in the film *Still Life*. Yet, in order to examine the ideological content of the discontentment, what is of interest and significance to us for now is to see from what perspective the ruins and displacement are presented to us. Unlike the previous films that show us largely one story, *Still Life* gives us two stories — through the views of Han Sanming and Shen Hong — which are tangentially connected with each other but are closely related to two different aspects of the same historical event — the building of the Three Gorges Dam. Or, we may argue, as the two stories unfold in front of the searching eyes of Han Sanming and Shen Hong, the film provides us, essentially, with two different perceptions of the same historical event and two different sentiments toward it.

What Shen Hong's familial search leads us to see, corresponding with the sight of largely industrial ruins, are the collective frustrations and individual sense of helplessness experienced by the people toward the overall globalizing process that in the film centers on the project of the Three Gorges Dam. The collective frustrations are shown to us, however, through a spurious confrontation between the manager and former employees of the factory where Shen Hong's separated husband Guo Bin used to work. The former employees' anger over the sale of the factory to some businesswoman from Xiamen, though apparently not related to the Three Gorges Dam project in a direct manner, is revealed to be directed at the wrong person, the manager. For the manager is seen, from the outsider perspective of Shen Hong, to be also very angry and frustrated, and his intense attachment to the state property now being sold to a private owner is best seen perhaps in the shot of his yellow fingers rubbing against the blackish and bluish rusted surface of a disused giant furnace. But Jia does not let the frustration and anger of the workers-turned-grassroots people at the factory escalate into a large-scale and long-time social protest. They are soon cut on the screen to shots of the silent detachment of Wang Dongming, Guo Bin's old friend, who works at a county institute of cultural relic protection and now is burying himself in excavating some ancient tomb from the Han Dynasty. Indeed, the constructed historical temporality, with its isolated detachment and cold indifference exemplified visually in the dead watches and clocks hanging in Wang Dongming's apartment, poses such a sharp contrast to the present experiential time, to Shen Hong's controlled emotions over her husband's separation and irresponsibility, and to the incessant ongoing demolition of houses and office buildings, that they illuminate an undercurrent of helplessness felt by such institutionalized individuals as the factory manager and Wang Dongming.

Among all the characters coming into Shen Hong's view, her separated husband Guo Bin and his presumed mistress Ding Yaling, chairwoman of the company that runs the office of demolition in the city who is also suggested to buy the factory, are obviously among those benefiting the most in the film from the Three Gorges Dam and from the privatization of state property — a drive being part of China's reform and globalization. So, Guo Bin's final physical appearance on the screen, coming after all sorts of words about his success, his good ties with government officials, and his extraordinarily close relationship with his female boss Ding Yaling, who never shows up physically on the screen, becomes, naturally, the climax of Shen Hong's story of familial search. Yet this narrative climax of a reunion between Shen and Guo does not occur in an atmosphere expected for a successful man in the new age, nor does it end in some much expected dramatic action, such as an explosion of anger, crying, or laughter. It is arranged, obviously as another cinematic moment of discontentment, to end in a calm and seemingly meaningless ultimate separation, a final breakup of the hopeless marriage and dysfunctional family, which is nevertheless marked on the screen by a few impassionate and aimless steps danced by Shen and Guo in the foreground, against an epic prospect — ironically enough — of the Three Gorges Dam being successfully built in the not-far-off background.

It is evident that presented with Shen Hong's story of a familial search, reunion and breakup are also part of a grand vision of the non-grassroots nature that allows us to see not only the gigantic industrial ruins and the heroic collapsing of a collective but also the story of individual success in the new age. Under its far-reaching illumination, the narrative of China's historical and global ambitions and their successes is able to emerge and unfold on the screen. But as such, it is a brief vision in the film and it is engulfed and curtailed by a grassroots vision embedded in the story, of Han Sanming searching for his long-separated daughter and ex-wife in both the first and final part of the tripartite film. This grassroots vision in Han's story appears first in the film but it is anchored much lower, showing us largely a local view of the residential ruins and some seemingly random anecdotes in the life of grassroots people caught in the massive displacement.

The majority of characters whom Han Sanming encounters in his search are presented on the screen to be struggling outside of government or business institutions. Their world, without any effective institutional support, is unstable, chaotic, and tough. Little Brother Ma in the film compares it to that of the "*jiang hu*" or "river and lake," a term used frequently in Chinese language martial arts novels and movies to refer to the world on the margins of and even beyond the rule of law, where calamities occur and the good and evil fight it out, usually ending in the defeat of evil by the good. But the life of Little Brother Ma — who, in Han Sanming's eye, is good in nature, always inspired with some heroic spirit, and whose name is taken from an action hero played by Chow Yun-fat in a Hong Kong movie — is presented here to be one not so just, elevating, and heroic as homeless, jobless, and sometimes gangster-like, ending in a humble death in the rubble of residential ruins. While the evil hand behind Ma's death is never shown on the screen, the source of an unstable, tough, and chaotic life for the other characters is more directly suggested. In the eyes of Mr. He, the good owner of the hostel where Han Sanming stays throughout the film, the evil that forces him to close the hostel business and to move to live in a dark place under a bridge, is apparently what the Chinese character 拆 or "demolition" written on his wall signifies — forced relocation due to the surging water from the ongoing project of the Three Gorges Dam. For the same reason, we see that the middle-aged woman, whose daughter used to be in the same school as Han Sanming's daughter and whose husband lost one arm, has to leave her soon-to-be-demolished home. And Han Sanming's ex-wife, Little Sister Ma, and her brothers lose their homes to the surging water, and are shown on the screen having to live on boats, walking on the unsteady decks everyday and making a humble living in the world of "river and lake" — in its literal if not so symbolic sense.

Planted in Han Sanming's perception of the grassroots world that Jia presents as dominating the film screen is, as we have suggested, a moral lens of good and evil, and its focus is on home and family. The impressive visual display of demolishing the residential buildings and houses into countless rubble and ruins and the talk of family members being scattered to different parts of the nation are purported, thereby, to carry a moral weight and articulate discontentment of the Three Gorges Dam project. Yet, in showing us the human feelings and emotions emanating from the residential ruins and the falling-apart of families, Jia manages to have Han Sanming escape from such scenes as that of indignation and anger in the relocation office at the beginning of the film, so as to keep them on the margins and prevent them from exploding into a massive public protest on the screen. In line with the view of Chinese life in the new age as a reduced existence, he chooses to show human emotions and feelings here in the reserved and detached form of discontent, deliberately downsizing their passionate articulations on the screen. Han Sanming is seen, therefore, to talk to Mr. He almost expressionlessly and emotionlessly about his plan of looking for his separated daughter, revealed later in the film to work somewhere far away from the Three Gorges, and his ex-wife, turning out to make a living by serving the man operating a boat up and down the Three Gorges. Han also witnesses, in a quiet, sympathetic, and yet helpless manner, the scattering of the middle-aged woman's family, with her daughter working somewhere else and herself having to leave her jobless one-armed husband behind and going alone to the south in the hope of finding a job there.

While using the demolition of houses into ruins and the scattering of families into different places as a cinematic articulation of discontentment, Jia also lets us see the effort it takes to survive and reconstruct what the residential ruins are able to inversely signify — home and family being the emotional and spiritual core of the material conditions are already started in the film. The desire to rescue and reconstruct home is essentially what has motivated the stories of both Han Sanming and Shen Hong from the very beginning, and it is turned, through scenes of the very destruction and loss of its object, into a dominant structure of feeling in the film. Such a feeling, reinforced throughout the film by the use of various textualizing and intertextualizing cinematic techniques, finds its best articulation in such words as "without home, how would there be you?" from the theme song of the 1983 Hong Kong/Taiwan film *Papa, Can You Hear Me Sing*.[19] Yet the tremendously popular tear-jerking song of the Hong Kong movie is performed here, not by a well-dressed female performer as it was in the original movie, but by a bare-chested sweating male laborer in a parodist fashion to the laughter of the demolition laborers and others. The cinematic modifications are made here obviously to stem the feeling from falling nostalgically into that old expressive mode of bitter passion, but they simultaneously give off certain ideological emissions that identify Jia's position with the grassroots people. This ideological position is reinforced by the different endings of the stories of Shen Hong and Han Sanming: though they both see the cinematic mystification of a golden object flying in the sky as a star of fate connecting them together, Shen hopelessly breaks up with her now successful husband Guo Bin, but Han ends on a hopeful note that he will come back to remarry his divorced wife, Little Sister Ma, after going back to make some money in Shanxi Province so as to pay off his ex-wife's debt. In this sense, the image of Han Sanming, the demolition laborer, a human counterpart of the material ruins, a leftover and surviving element that cannot be fully assimilated and integrated into the new change, is endowed here with something more than discontentment — now we see a utopian impulse and vision are emerging at the time of devastating destruction and violence that reduces human existence to its "original eco-state of life."

In the meantime, we must see, Han Sanming is represented on the screen not as a unique individual but as merely one of the many — he is just one of the demolition workers whose work-honed and half-nude bodies are repeatedly and slowly panned over by the camera to reveal their natural and rough state that contains the most primitive and robust form of labor (see Figure 7.4). However, the labor-based embodied utopian vision of the grassroots people reconstructing home and making a living by physical labor is not yet endowed in the film with any ideological closure. The closure is in fact impossible to achieve at the present moment, historically because the Chinese grassroots people are still struggling just for a survival of their life and home in the age of globalization, and cinematically because the coalmines in Shanxi Province to which Han Sanming and his fellow demolition laborers are heading at the end of the film are said to be not a utopian enclave but a historical place not only of the money they are going to make but also of the death that they will have to face day in and day out.

Figure 7.4   Mostly bare-chested laborers demolishing houses in *Still Life*.

Part III.

Urban Space in Production and Disappearance

8

Of Humans and Nature in Documentary:
The Logic of Capital in *West of the Tracks* and *Blind Shaft*

Ban Wang

The deteriorating natural environment in China has gripped the attention of social scientists, humanists, and observers. Some blame environmental disasters on China's runaway economic growth, industrialization, and unregulated manufacturing practices. In the single-minded pursuit of growth and productivity, pollutants dumped into rivers and the air are causing egregious health and ecological consequences. In her book *The Rivers Runs Black: The Environmental Challenges to China's Future*, Elizabeth Economy vividly portrays the ravages inflicted on the valley of the Huai River in Anhui Province. Criticizing the government's failure to regulate the economy and to protect the environment, she tells a crisis story of "economic development run amok" along with the unfettered market and privatization.[1] Other observers stress the increasingly global role that China is playing in protecting the environment on the planet and in preserving worldwide natural resources. Environmental issues are now linked to China's drive to get on track with the world community. Still others trace the current environmental problems to a long-term developmental agenda of hasty modernization and industrialization already very much at work in Mao's era. Judith Shapiro's sensationally entitled book *Mao's War against Nature* attempts to go further than the familiar attribution of China's environmental problems to post-reform development and integration with the global economy. Shapiro traces the problems to Mao's or the Chinese government's erratic policy of development since the 1950s. Linking the arbitrary control of human beings with the assault on the environment, Shapiro seeks to show that the Maoists declared a war against nature, and that "coercive state behavior" such as forceful relocations, the suppression of political freedom, and ill-conceived social and natural engineering contributed to human suffering and environment degradation. The lessons from the negative examples of Mao's era, Shapiro hopes, may help us understand the human-nature relationship in other periods and parts of the world.[2]

To reduce environmental degradation to capitalist destruction or the socialist war of industrialization against nature is to simplify China's socialist past and the ongoing tension between these two conflicting motifs: economic development and the curbing of over-development in the name of society. What the above commentators seem to miss is the long-term contradiction between hasty development for the nation's wealth and power, which could be either capitalist or socialist or both, and the policy agenda to ensure the welfare and human development of the general population since the founding of the PRC. There has been a tug of war between development-driven policy orientations, often attributed to aggressive modernizers like Liu Shaoqi and Deng Xiaoping, and the socialist agenda, which attended more to community, human relations, all-round prosperity, and nature. The community-based, nature-friendly elements are in a tradition of socialist culture, a legacy barely audible on the forum of environmental discussion. Socialist modernity, by promoting the common ownership of productive means and natural assets by a nation-people acting in concert, aspires to a form of the human-nature relation. This alternative modernity insists on a harmonious relationship between city and countryside, intellectuals and manual labor, industry and agriculture. The debates over these issues in the 1950s through the Cultural Revolution signaled an attempt to achieve sustainable development and harmonious society.

While history reveals tremendous gaps between reality and these ideals, these notions are no stranger to the Marxist understanding of humans and nature. Indeed, they informed some elements of the socialist agenda in Mao's era. As John Foster demonstrates in his compelling study *Marx's Ecology: Materialism and Nature*, Marx's critique of capitalist production derives from an environmentally driven notion of "metabolism" between labor, human beings, and the earth. In *Capital: A Critique of Political Economy*, Marx defines the labor process as "a process between man and nature, a process by which man, through his own actions, mediates, regulates and controls the metabolism between himself and nature."

Contrary to the view that the productionism of campaigns against nature in the Mao era was anthropomorphic and arbitrary at the expense of external nature, genuine production is based on non-exploitive relations between human beings and between humans and nature.[3] Inherent in the Marxist conceptions of humans-nature relationship, this notion is crystallized in the dream image proposed by the French socialist thinker Charles Fourier. Fourier's social theory implied a utopian, environmentalist sensibility. In working on nature to produce goods, exploitation of nature is the direct result of the exploitation of humans by the profit-driving economy and production. It is true that human production and consumption persisted for centuries before capitalist economy and this process necessarily drew on and consumed natural resources. But production itself is not the problem. Rather it is a mode of society and the related economic organization of that society based on exploitation and profit motives that initiated the destructive process against nature. If humans are not exploited for surplus value, the value of consumer goods will not rest on the extraction of surplus value and exploitation of human labor. If humans do not exploit other humans for extra gains at the laborers' expense, human labor will focus on producing use value for satisfying the needs of survival and community. A number of aesthetic thinkers touched on this utopian image, which readily entails a concept of humans closely in tune with the environment. In his critique of the capitalist production of images and the dreamy consumerist world, Walter Benjamin proposed the genuine dream of children's play as a model of humans' relation with nature. In the harmony between man and nature, "human labor will then proceed in accord with the model of children's play, which in Fourier is the basis of the *travail passionné* [passionate labor] of the *harmoniens* [dwellers in his utopian communities]":

> Labor thus animated by play aims not at the production of value, but at an improved nature. And Fourier's utopia presents a model for it, one that can in fact be found realized in children's play. It is the image of an earth on which all places have become *Wirtschaften* [economy]. The double meaning of the word [economy/labor] blossoms here: All places are cultivated by human beings, made useful and beautiful by them; all, however, stand like a roadside inn, open to everyone.[4]

What has created exploitive relations between humans and nature is the modern system of profit-driven production. The capitalist relations of production produce an "irreparable rift" that constantly breaks apart this organic, natural metabolism. Exploitive, profit-driven production cynically and cyclically destroys the organic metabolism between human beings, labor, and nature. The extraction of surplus value from the producer gives rise to the antagonistic separation between capital and labor. The extraction of ground rent through the large-scale industrialization of agriculture results in the impoverishment of land and the nurturing environment.[5]

In the early industrial era, profit-driven production led to a drastic divide between the city as manufacturing center and the countryside as ghost towns and deserted wasteland. In the contemporary era of global capital expansion it has created a new divide between the metropolitan financial centers of the north and the desolate landscape of raw material and cheap labor in the south. Marx showed that the large scale concentration of agricultural capital "reduces the agricultural population to an ever decreasing minimum and confronts it with an ever growing industrial population crammed together in large towns; in this way it produces conditions that provoke an irreparable rift in the interdependent process of social metabolism, a metabolism prescribed by the natural laws itself."[6] In the historical case of England, the profit-driven, large-scale industrialization of agriculture destroyed small farmers and gave rise to a vast degrading of both laborers and materials for reproduction of life. It wrought havoc with labor power and thus the natural power of man and did damage to the reproductive power of the soil. The industrial system "applied to agriculture also enervates the workers there, while industry and trade for their part provide agriculture with the means of exhausting the soil."[7]

This irreparable rift recurs as a chronic cancer of capitalism production. It not only happens within industrialized countries but has also spread to developing nations. This is what happened in China's initial encounter with the capitalist mode of production at the turn of the twentieth century and is happening rapidly in the twenty-first. The combined social and environmental consequences were in part what prompted China's pursuit of alternative modernity in the Chinese Revolution and its socialist experience. Addressing the social and environmental ills of capitalist modernity, the socialist goals were to abridge the gaps between city and countryside, industry and agriculture, mental and manual workers. Although socialism, in its Enlightenment emphasis on productionism and conquest of nature, also yielded dire ecological and social consequences, the utopian goals draw energy and idealism from the notion of natural and social metabolism. Since the reforms of the 1980s, the socialist goals have been discredited in public debate and China has been moving ever closer to a capitalist mode of production. The result is a newly created, ever aggravated rift in natural metabolism and environmental and social consequences.

Environmental concerns might not be explicit in cultural scenes, but in retrospect we can discern their presence in the emergent socialist new culture of the 1950s through to the 1970s. Take Chinese films for example. Films depicting collective endeavors for mastering nature and building a livable socialist countryside evince a deep rationale about the interdependence between humans and nature. *Young People in Our Village* (*Women cunli de nianqing ren*, 1959) depicts how a small village in Shanxi Province modifies the natural environment, channels water resources, and solves the perennial problem of water shortage in agriculture. On the face of it, the whole endeavor to change the village's barren landscape may look like any routine modern project to conquer nature. Young village people educated in the city, the self-taught village engineer, and the revolutionary soldier from the army form an entrepreneurial vanguard, combating oppositions from different quarters. One typical opposition is the claim that the water source belongs to the Dragon — a superstition that the modern scientific project seeks to dismantle. The young people apply modern knowledge to investigating the local terrain and analyzing the feasibility of their water-channeling project. But the question for us is whether this constitutes a war against nature or a modification of nature for human needs. The film addresses this question by depicting how the organic relationship between humans and nature plays out, and how the collective implementation of the project proves vital to the human "improvement" of nature — not at the cost of depleting nature but for achieving a balanced form of resonance between human life and the environment. Since the project is conducted by the village as a collective, based on collective wisdom, it aims at altering nature for the common good and for the village's continued survival. Water is a gift from nature for nourishing and producing agricultural goods for villagers. The villagers' continued production relies on nature's bounty (water), which does not flow without help from science and engineering. But making improvements on nature enhances the cohesiveness of the community, creating the image of social metabolism or interdependence between humans and between humans and their natural habitat. This is one reason why any departure from the community-centered agenda, such as a desire for city life and consumer luxury, is portrayed as unethical in the narrative. On the other hand, as the film's theme song lyrics go, "after hard work the barren village will be in full bloom." This socialist image contracts sharply with the buying and selling of land, labor, and nature — what Karl Polanyi calls the "sole director of the fate of human beings and their natural environment."[8] Profit-seeking practices premised on the commodity conceptions of labor, land, and money in capitalist economy result in the demolition of community and the decay of nature.

The socialist model of human-nature relations is premised on the collective ownership of natural assets and on farmers as co-producers of a human habitat in tune with the natural environment. The powerful sway of profit economy and development in the last few decades, however, threatens to create a lopsided relation in which one group of humans mercilessly exploits other humans while relentlessly plundering nature. I will use two recent films to discuss the environmental and human costs of unfettered economic development. *West of the Tracks* (*Tiexi qu*, 2000) is a documentary film and *Blind Shaft* (*Mang jing*, 2003) is a feature film with powerful documentary effects. Both take a strong "objective" stance and depict Chinese reality in an unadorned fashion. The link between environmentalist consciousness and documentary reflects a growing trend, in China and in other parts of the world, to tell the inconvenient truth in documentary style. This may not be as surprising as it first seems. From a long historical perspective of representing reality, the drive to document a condition truthful to certain groups of people and to a certain historical era implies a materialist conception of history. And the materialist conception of history is grounded in an organic, ecological understanding of human beings deeply in touch with nature — humans as producers of their community in harmony with natural settings. Documentary is an effective medium in airing these concerns. In a runaway economy with over 10 percent annual growth for almost two decades, amid the growing appetite for fuel and in the euphoria for cars and big houses in suburbia, who are the visionaries telling the inconvenient truths about reckless development, damage to living conditions, and the depletion of rural communities? Documentary filmmaking is about telling the truth. In China's visual landscape, dominated by billboards, glamorous stars, gloried images of the nouveaux riches, what small territory can documentary stake out? What social and environmental conditions make documentary a hot topic? How does the documentary impulse impinge on feature films? To address these questions, it may be helpful to look at two documentary texts reminiscent of Marx's critique of capitalist accumulation.

The documentary *West of the Tracks* (*Tiexiqu*, 2000, dir. Wang Bing) begins with a long tracking shot, in which a moving train reveals a snow-covered landscape and deserted factory compounds. Under the desolate sky, human figures in the frame move around like tiny, ghostly scraps. The landscape lies in ruins and waste. The film's first part is titled "*Gongchang*" (factory) in Chinese but is translated into "Rust" in English, signifying the rusty remnants of the declining industrial infrastructure in northeast China. Located in the city of Shenyang, Liaoning Province, the industrial area had been China's longest-standing manufacturing center, dating back to Japan's colonizing drives in Manchuria in the 1930s. Following the model of Soviet-style heavy industry after 1949, the area became the pillar of China's centralized economy. While the film focuses on the aged steel plants on their last legs at the turn of the twentieth-first century, it also offers numerous shots of the workers scraping out a beastly, barbarous existence. These are directed at acts, at their crudest, of eating, chatting, cursing, talking dirty, taking showers, and watching pornographic videos. There is no proud socialist working class of the old days, but a disturbing series of gross animalism that lays bare showering bodies in front of the camera, with penises visible, completely empty of civilizational fig leaves or erotic touch. The body parts and genitals come across as crumbled pieces of human flesh, as boring as the pornography the workers are watching. The bodies are withering away, like the rotting factories, like waste products, in the midst of the gigantic machines and under the crushing weight of the unknown forces of global modernity.

In Lü Xinyu's analysis, this film registers lingering traces of China's earlier drive in building a national industrial base as part of the aggressive industrialization campaign during the Cold War era. But as globalization and market economy gained momentum in the early 1990s, the state-owned heavy industry gave way to privatization and the quick influx of global capital drew economic activity to the coastlines and the south. The once proud industrial base in the northeast started falling apart (Lü, 2004).

The film tells a tragic story of how uneven development in global capitalism erodes the national industry base, which gives way to capital-intensive, trade-oriented, information-related economic trends. This familiar advance of the "creative destruction" of capital accumulation and expansion leaves in its trail human victims and ruined landscapes. If they are not destroyed, the victims survive in sheer animality and beastliness, without hope or enough food.

The tracking shot of *West of the Tracks* is reminiscent of another documentary tracking shot, a text written more than a century and a half ago about the beastly conditions of industrial workers and the decayed environment where they lived. In his *The Condition of the Working Class in England in 1844*, Friedrich Engels offered an eyewitness account of the miserable and bestial conditions of workers' living quarters in Manchester and other cities in Britain during the high industrial era. The historical conditions of England may be far removed from contemporary China. But the similar logic of the profit-driven creative destruction of people and the environment is taking a similar toll across the centuries. The debasing of workers happened within the factory town of Manchester, while in China manufacturing workers lose their dignity by losing out to the trade centers of global capital. In human terms, the debasement and alienation are uncannily identical. Engels went to England in 1842, at the age of twenty-one, to learn the textile business. During the twenty-one months of his stay there, he turned himself into a "documentary" eyewitness and reporter. Taking numerous trips through the neighborhoods of "the helots of modern society," and through intimate conversations with workers, he documented the wretched conditions of the industrial slums and shanty residences, seeking to discover every nook and cranny of human misery. Packed with documentary details and a photographic language, supplemented with drawings of the city's layouts and voiced in an objective tone that scarcely hides mounting moral outrage, Engels's book offers a stark image of shaky houses, the suffocating density of living space, the residential tangles in which one house was crowded literarily one upon the other.[9] Reading Engels's book is like experiencing a long tracking shot carried out by a handheld camera as it penetrates into the winding alleys and obscure corners of a grimy maze of slums. At the entrance of many residential "courts," as the camera eye pinpoints, there is a toilet without a door, "so dirty that the inhabitants can only enter and leave the court if they are prepared to wade through puddles of stale urine and excrement" (58). In the communities of factory workers "there are several tanneries which fill the whole neighborhood with the stench of animal putrefaction" (58). A high-angle "shot" from a bridge above a shanty neighborhood by the river gives an overview of the Irk, a narrow, black, foul-smelling stream, full of debris and refuse, which were deposited on the banks, "creating a string of the most disgusting blackish-green slime pools" (60).

In *West of the Tracks* and Engels's book, the documentary stance reveals the waste products of reckless industrialization and capitalist modernity that keep piling up wreckage upon wreckage of wasted humanity and so expanding the wastelands. The film discloses a field of ruins strewn with scraps of body parts and withered penises, which in their sheer, unspeakable corporeality are stripped naked of dignity, humanity, community, and culture.

Against such an uncanny juxtaposition of two historical images, it seems no longer urgent to argue about the epistemological accuracy of documentary. If such beastly conditions are the chronic cancer of capitalist production and if documentary seems to be the sharpest diagnosis around, would it be useful to ponder the question of whether a documentary comes close to the reality that it aims to capture? Would it be leading anywhere to haggle over whether documentary authenticity is a matter of style, image, or narrative?[10] In the ceaseless shocks of these two "tracking shots," the controversy over whether documentary is itself fiction becomes so disingenuous as to be a defensive protection to divert the eye from the catastrophe or an attempt to dissolve the ugly referent into another feel-good simulacrum. Turning a foul-smelling reality into another sanitized image, the documentary-as-fiction thesis plays into the hand of the culture industry's image-making process that liquidates the reality of how the other half lives off-screen and shuts out the traces of devastated humanity from the private comforts of the living room equipped with the latest multimedia and soft drinks.

Engels already noted this habitual visual denial in the urban layout of Manchester. In the bourgeois thoroughfares and fashionable districts, the shop fronts served to hide from "the eyes of wealthy ladies and gentlemen with strong stomachs and weak nerves the misery and squalor which are part and parcel of their own riches and luxury" (55). In the era of globalization, capital accumulation crystallizes into palatable images around the world for profitable attentiveness and entertainment, melting the harsh reality of poverty and underdevelopment into thin air.[11]

Against this denial, documentary filmmakers are realists who are furious about such diverting of eyes and such media falsehood. True, documentary films are made with subjective intentions and designs, but they are not fiction and fantasy. Documentary filmmakers believe that all stories are as much constructed as they are found, but true stories must be constructed from scratch, not from the ossified and glamorous convention of the global visual regime, but by ordinary people on ground zero, living their lives and their stories as if they were acting out their own scripts and dramas in a given environment. Documentary involves different degrees of constructedness, a zero degree as it were, that is embedded in daily living and works at the grassroots level. This is the key to understanding the emergent documentary movement in contemporary China. As the visual field is increasingly dominated by fantastic representations promulgated by the transnational industry and Hollywood's dream factory, documentary arises as a wake-up jolt to the self-indulgence in dreamy self-denial and visual whitewashing. Documentary runs counter to cultural relativism and nihilism inherent in the view that "anything is a style or fabrication." It insists on a solid reality, not so much as a block of ontological substance or certainty, but as a risky experimental process and an earnest mode of engagement with social problems and lived experiences — engagements that have not been whitewashed into the visual spectacles of Hollywood or transnational media fantasies.

Documentary filmmaking in China presents a challenge to the newfangled mystifications in the atmosphere of global image production. The official media join commercial enterprises in promoting the triumphant prospects of development, prosperity, and a middle-class, consumerist lifestyle. Mainstream cinema turns Chinese history into a consumable spectacle and paints the current reality as nothing more than an endless stream of soaps, melodrama, and phantasmagoric visual stunts. Socially engaged filmmakers are aware that fast-paced modernization has given rise to new traumas of disintegration, displacement, loss, and life-and-death consequences. Yet, these disturbing developments are constantly belied by the smooth shining surface of new narratives and images. The documentary impulse aims at cutting through the veneer of fantastic lies to get at the hidden strata of reality.[12]

When the documentary shines a penetrating light into the obscure strata of reality, it produces a haunting effect. In reading *West of the Tracks* together with Engels's book, the fate of the workers in the steel plants in northeast China at the turn of the twenty-first century is haunted by the ghosts of textile workers in England in the 1840s. In Jia Zhangke's "documentary" feature film *Platform* (*Zhantai*, 2000), the ghosts come back to haunt a peasant who sells his body and soul to a local mining business that has total monopoly over his labor capacity as commodity. In an unforgettable episode, the peasant, apparently dim-witted and illiterate, signs a contract with the mining business without understanding a word of it. With the written contract pronouncing that his life and death are all in the hands of Heaven, the mining company is freed from any responsibility for his life and safety, thus permitting them to treat him worse than an indentured slave. Like millions of peasants uprooted from the land and village, this character is a floating labor particle, a victim of the unregulated market in league with political power. Unregulated and reckless in labor safety and workers' rights, the mining business offers an uncanny image of the exploitive practice and ruthless accumulation of capital reminiscent of the nineteenth-century industrial era. In large-scale industrialization, competition for accumulation of capital pushed capitalists to draw cheap laborers from the countryside and to inflict daily violence upon the workers. The ceaseless drive to gain surplus value beyond the value of labor power squeezes the last drop of blood and life from the worker. This process "devalues and depreciates labor power, to say nothing of the loss of dignity, of the sense of control over the work process, of the perpetual harassment by overseers and the necessity to conform to the dictates of the machine."[13] The history of capital accumulation "written in the annals of mankind in letters of blood and fire,"[14] and of the uprooting of peasants from the land and the reducing of their bodies into mere appendage to the machine, is repeating itself in China. In Jia Zhangke's *Platform*, a realist documentary camera seeks to dwell on this condition by taking a look at this uprooted job-hunting peasant, who sells his body and soul. The camera attempts to look into the brutal exploitation embedded in the unfair contract, and its many baffled long takes on this peasant intensify the enigma of a larger reality. The camera doggedly follows the peasant, gazing at his back for an agonizing stretch of time, as he walks towards to the mine, as if wondering about his unknown fate.

Though not a documentary film, *Platform* evinces an evident neorealist approach and inventiveness, which makes common cause with the contemporary documentary drive. Inspired by the legacy of Italian neorealism of the 1950s, Chinese critics and filmmakers have recently sought to apply realistic scrutiny to social and political problems and to delve into the grassroots life of the marginalized workers and peasants. Following the slogan "Carrying the camera to the streets," both neorealism and documentary seek to unearth a harsh and unwieldy reality. Compared with the straight genre of documentary, a neorealist feature film may be more effective in revealing the harsh truth. Although a documentary film may present the viewer with myriad facts and loosely connected scenes, it often loses the grip on the meaning of the facts and the attention of the viewer, often incapable of creating strong emotional resonance. The documented facts may be compelling, but they would be more compelling if the facts were interpreted or re-organized by virtue of an explorative, dramatic structure of narrative. It is in this mixture of documentary and creativity that John Grierson calls documentary film "a creative treatment of actuality," and that Pare Lorentz designates it as "a factual film which is dramatic."[15] In this light I would suggest that a feature film, endowed with the documentary's aesthetic and social message, makes a better documentary in the broad socio-historical sense as a witness to history, to the current landscape as well as mindscape. The French New Wave, Italian neorealism, and feature films by Jia Zhangke, Zhang Yuan, Wang Xiaoshuai, and others can be described as film practices premised on this twofold genre of drama and documentary.[16]

The film *Blind Shaft* (2003), directed by Li Yang and adapted from the novella *Sacred Woods* (*Shenmu*) by Liu Qingbang, fits very well into this mixed genre. Trained and employed as a documentary filmmaker in Germany, Li infuses into this film documentary, images, and aesthetics deploying familiar documentary and neorealist devices and weaving a seamless interface between documentary and feature film. These include shooting on location, firsthand experience of associating with the coalminers, going down the dangerous mine shaft to do real mining work, the use of nonprofessionals, the handheld camera, the scarce use of artificial lighting, eye-level shooting, and so on. There is absolutely no music throughout *Blind Shaft* to suggest any sentimental touch or drama. The director intended this film to be documentary in style.[17]

Although these features may produce a "reality" effect, they alone will not be effective in unraveling and tackling China's acute problems in economic development and environmental degradation. It is, rather, the film's social critique and political messages that make it "a factual film which is dramatic." Through documentary devices, the director aims to invite the audience to take a long, hard look at the impoverished survival of the workers, at the wretchedness of the earth, at the lingering residue of morality, at the traditional human relations swept away by the logic of capital, and at the natural environment mutilated by the obsession with growth. To do this, unfolding a narrative that lays bare human relations and strips them naked under the spell of money worship becomes an aesthetically powerful strategy.

In *Blind Shaft*, the figuration of the human body registers how the logic of capital accumulation, characteristic of the barbarous nineteenth-century industrialization and still rampant in the sweatshops of the metropolitan centers in the West, has penetrated into traditional human relations in China, reducing the human person to a thing. The mine workers and the prostitutes are pawns in a dehumanizing money-grabbing game. This situation need not be attributed to the corruptive power of money or psychologized into a greedy personality. Rather it is a structural problem that engulfs the whole population to varying degrees. In producing products for profit, the human body is reduced to a vehicle for making money and becomes a commodity. The workers use their muscles as a commodity to make money for the coalmines, but they only get back a tiny fraction of output value in order to keep body and soul together for another round of production, hence, the surplus value and the bare condition of subsistence in the mining camps.

The penetrating insight of the film reveals that the two miners, as main characters, work the reifying logic of capital to its grotesque, lethal extreme. Like other uprooted and dislocated peasants, they have to sell their labor power to obtain a living for themselves and their families back in the village, but that is a small-time operation for the minimum wage. How about becoming a capitalist in the image of the mine owner? How about using other human beings as a source of capital that can yield quick returns? The two men have a capital concept: they set up cave-in accidents in the mineshaft that kills the victim they claim to be their relative, and thus make bogus claims to the mining company to get compensation payment. The company usually complies, because cheating people of their lives is precisely what the company does in a lawful, contractual disguise. Co-partners in starting up what may well be called the business of death, using the raw material of human life, the two miners transform themselves from laborers into "business" owners in accordance with the logic of capital accumulation. Are not workers dying anyway in the mine due to frequent accidents and ruthless exploitation? The two workers-turned-con-artists know the secret and undertake to hasten certain fellow workers' deaths, gaining profit into the bargain. Their "business" operation is a truthful image of what the logic of capital encourages them to see: human beings as mere things. Workers are doomed in the grind of profit, and are disposable as means of capital.

The thing-like notion of human beings accounts for the film's dehumanized, zero-degree portrayal of working and living conditions. The opening of the film's narrative gives a striking example: under a leaden sky in the early morning, shivering in chilly winds and sharing a cigarette to warm up, the ghostly miners emerge out of the low cave dwellings and, in eerie silence, file in to the company office in order to go down the shaft. The shot of their descent into the "hell" down the shaft is visceral and symbolic. These stark shots, recalling Japanese director Yasujiro Ozu's desolate urban industrial scenes, turn the miners into prisoners trapped in a bare, vast, hostile landscape. The stripped-down human beings as things are consistent with the equally stripped-down landscape that looms large all around, threatening to swallow up the tiny crawling human animals. While the workers are maimed, the landscape, the whole physicality of nature indeed, is being mutilated, disemboweled, and crisscrossed by roaring trucks and machines.

Nothing illustrates the reifying logic more powerfully than the episode of murder down in the mine toward the ending. When a miner notices that the two murderous miners are up to something strange, Tang, the more "villainous" one, strikes him dead in an offhand manner. When Song, his partner, protests that no profit can come from such wanton killing, Tang replies, "Whoever stands in the way of my fortune will be eliminated." A supplement to this remark, often cited by the American press, is the observation by a mine owner that China lacks everything, but never lacks human beings. This view assumes that human life is disposable and cheap because of the huge size of the wretched, dislocated rural population. This quantitative measurement of the worth of human life is entirely complicit with the reifying logic of capital. The truth, indeed, is that the pervasive logic of capital already condemns human bodies, human integrity, and dignity as junk, whose value is to be measured only by the returns on their deaths, the majority of people being the means to the end of producing profit. This deadening logic is the structural principle embodied by the "villainous" character and the "lawful" owners of the coalmine who would not hesitate to cover up the villainy of business by paying off the murderers.

The naked logic of capital evidently seeps into the scenes involving nudity, which are glaring not because of their bold exposure, but because the logic of money has stripped everything naked in the first place. Only a while ago nudity in Chinese cinema was hailed as subversive and transgressive. Now the nudity in this film is banal, deadpan, and desexualized, as in a B movie; the human body is presented as a piece of meat. The two miners have sex as if they were eating an insipid meal, and Tang is put off by Song's complaint about not getting his money's worth. Sexual life becomes animalistic, indeed more debased than animal life: it is a discharge, like going to the bathroom, and Song could very well use sex toys rather than spend money on the girls. The transactions in the brothel are a mirror image of the way coalmines operate: like the miners, the prostitutes are nothing but a means of money-making. In a conversation between the two miners and the brothel girls, Song says women make money easily by spreading their legs, but men have to do hard work. One prostitute protests, but, as the brothel owner replies, the question as to why women sell their bodies and men sell their muscles, and women seem to have "easier" time, is for Heaven to decide.

The documentary thrust of *Blind Shaft* reproduces an authentic, earthy atmosphere in the confusion and chaos of the streets and market. Recording scenes of the runaway market economy, the documentary camera scrambles everything that is familiar and immerses the viewer into a giddy Chinese reality. On the other hand, the dramatic part of the film presents human agency and desire in tension with the naked logic of capital. The two murderous miners send money home and care about their families, like everybody else. Song, the "gentler" one of the pair, continuously defers the killing of the kid, their targeted victim, precisely because of his awareness that the kid is a human being like his own kid, having his dreams of education and providing for his family. The mixture of human drama and documentary serves to reveal more meaningfully and sharply the tensions and contradictions as Song tries to hold on to the last remnants of humanity. Documentary may lay bare a dark reality dominated by the logic of capital, but the light that illuminates the darkness comes from the lingering desire to be a human being entitled to dignity, education, and community.

Documentary and neorealism, exemplified by *West of the Tracks* and *Blind Shaft*, are two voices that participate in the cultural debate about environmental, social, and human consequences in China's fast development. In the rush to industrialization and urbanization and in its quest of new wealth and power, the questions of community, human dignity, equality, nature, and human habitat are thrown to the winds. The realistic cinematic approach intervenes by retrieving the forgotten motifs of socialist utopia, and attempts to give pause to the runaway development. Politically, the warnings of documentary and neorealist films alert the public and the government to the consequences of the blind faith in the global capitalist market.

9

Toward a Hong Kong Ecocinema:
The *Dis-appearance* of "Nature" in Three Films by Fruit Chan

Chris Tong*

On November 10, 2006, the *International Herald Tribune* published an article titled "Not even HK's storied Star Ferry can face down developers."[1] The article referred to the Hong Kong government's plan to demolish the historic Star Ferry terminal to create space for an expressway and a shopping mall. Concerned citizens, urban planners, legislators, and celebrities such as John Woo and Chow Yun Fat participated in petitions and protests as a last-ditch effort to stall the project. Against overwhelming public opinion, the government demolished the structure and eventually built a new Star Ferry terminal farther out in the harbor. This is not the first time Hong Kong has increased its urban space through land reclamations. Most notably, the new Hong Kong International Airport was built on an artificial island reclaimed from the sea north of Lantau Island.[2] While urban space is necessarily borrowed or earned from nature, urban cinema assumes urban space to be a "first nature" that people naturally inhabit. Hong Kong urban cinema thus lacks the opportunity to step outside of itself, into nature, to take a breath of fresh air. To conceptualize what might constitute Hong Kong ecocinema, it is therefore necessary to think through the nature of Hong Kong urban cinema.

This chapter takes a dual approach in rethinking the nature of Hong Kong urban cinema. It evaluates the form of Hong Kong urban cinema, on the one hand, and examines its content, on the other. I begin with an analysis of the current theories of representation in Hong Kong cinema. By reading Ackbar Abbas's notion of "disappearance" in the context of Jacques Lacan's *aphanisis*, I argue that "dis-

---

*   I would like to thank Sheldon H. Lu and Jiayan Mi for their guidance and patience during the writing and editing process. Many thanks to Simon Sadler and Colin Milburn for the helpful conversations. I benefited from the feedback on earlier versions of this essay at the Asian Visual Cultures Workshop at the University of California, Irvine (2008) and the Davis Humanities Institute Symposium at the University of California, Davis (2008).

appearance" is a theory concerned with the filmic representation of reality rather than the disappearance of Hong Kong in the literal sense. Films always already fall short of representing what is real. Therefore, the cinematic Hong Kong is never the real Hong Kong. Neither is the real Hong Kong merely its architecture. The "elusive subject" of Hong Kong manifests itself in bodily, urban, and natural spaces. I then introduce postculture, planetarity, and ecoscape as concepts that reorientate the notions of "nature" and "culture" and redirect the gaze of urban cinema. A Hong Kong ecocinema not only approximates the real Hong Kong more closely by debunking its misrepresentations, it also appropriates cinema as a tool to hold ourselves accountable for our society and environment. As examples of Hong Kong urban cinema moving toward a Hong Kong ecocinema, I undertake a closing reading of Fruit Chan's *Durian Durian* (*Liulian piaopiao*, 2000), *Hollywood Hong Kong* (*Xianggang youge helihuo*, 2001), and *Public Toilet* (*Renmin gongci*, 2002).[3] Rethinking the nature of Hong Kong urban cinema takes place at both the levels of form and content.

The *Dis-appearance* of Lacan in Film Theory

Ackbar Abbas's *Hong Kong: Culture and the Politics of Disappearance* is perhaps the most cited work on Hong Kong culture and is one of the major studies on the intersection between film and architecture. Published in 1997, the historical year in which Hong Kong was returned to mainland China, it diagnosed Hong Kong as a "space of disappearance."[4] While it was a timely eulogy for some and a premature one for others, his work continues to be central in the discourse of Hong Kong cinema. In the field of film theory, the timing of the book was no less ambiguous. It came a year after David Bordwell and Noël Carroll's collection of essays, *Post-Theory: Reconstructing Film Studies*, which marked the end of Lacanian film theory.[5] Abbas's theoretical reading of Hong Kong cinema, especially his use of psychoanalysis, is a marked departure from this trend. Nevertheless, his work was published at a timely inflexion point: not only has he imported film theory into the growing field of Hong Kong film studies, he has, through his discussion of the filmic representations of Hong Kong's cityscape, contributed to the growing field of urban visual culture.

Lacanian psychoanalysis has largely disappeared from contemporary film theory, despite the fact that it provided the foundation or point of departure for film theory since the 1970s. Film theorists such as Christian Metz, Laura Mulvey, Jean-Louis Baudry, Slavoj Žižek, Joan Copjec, Kaja Silverman, Mary Anne Doanne, and Carol Clover have all incorporated Lacanian psychoanalysis in their work. This list is by no means exhaustive, as many other film theorists have advanced, revised, and criticized Lacanian film theory to different ends. Bordwell and Carroll's *Post-*

Theory marks a juncture in the development of film theory in that the criticisms of Lacanian film theory, among others, finally gained a critical mass.[6] However, the project to re-assess and revive Lacanian film theory goes on. Most recently, Todd McGowan and Sheila Kunkle's *Lacan and Contemporary Film* is an attempt to look at Lacanian film theory beyond the old familiar ways: "What was missing in this [earlier] Lacanian film theory was any sense of the power of film to disrupt ideology…. This was the result of its too narrow understanding of Lacan, an understanding that elided the role of the Real in Lacan's thought."[7]

Lacan's tripartite system consists of the Imaginary, the Symbolic, and the Real.[8] These orders are multifaceted and do not reduce well to self-contained definitions, but they display several characteristic features. The Symbolic is the realm of signifiers where the structure of language is manifest. The subject emerges in and through this order, when it speaks for the Other, creating meaning. This moment marks the subject's entrance into socially determined meanings, into culture. The Real is the realm that exists beyond the Symbolic — beyond language, meaning, and culture. The Real is not simply nature or reality in itself, as "nature" and "reality" are discursive concepts. The Real is that which is undefined, or not accountable, within the frameworks of discursive knowledge. The Real manifests itself in moments of breakthrough or trauma when the Symbolic reveals a gap, rupture, or defect. Finally, the Imaginary, completely disconnected from the Real, is the realm of identification that works with and against the Symbolic. This pre-linguistic order allows for the recognition of surfaces and hence the sense of correspondence and wholeness. The Imaginary harbors the unregulated desires that are repressed by the Symbolic, the realm of culture. These orders are the context for Lacanian film theory.

Abbas's theory of disappearance, I argue, is a redeployment of Lacanian psychoanalysis in film theory. Here is one of the most cited passages in Abbas's work:

> Precisely because Hong Kong is such *an elusive subject*, there is a temptation to use, and to believe in, the available forms of representation and misrepresentation. This is *dis-appearance* in a very specific sense (imagine the term as hyphenated), in that it gives us a reality that is *not so much hidden as purloined*, a reality that is overlooked because it is looked at in the old familiar ways.[9]

The word "purloined" is a clue for the reader to reevaluate Abbas's theory in the context of Lacanian psychoanalysis. Lacan's reading of Edgar Allan Poe's "The Purloined Letter" is a well-known study of the realm of language, or the Symbolic order, as constitutive of the subject.[10] In the short story, the Queen who is having an affair intends to hide an incriminating letter from the King, but the Minister manages to steal it by replacing it with a copy. The Queen procures the help of the Prefect who meticulously searches every room in the Minister's hotel, where the letter is presumed to be hidden. All the while, the letter lies "hidden" on the Minister's desk — in plain view. Abbas uses a similar strategy to reintroduce Lacanian psychoanalysis to film theory.

Abbas's theory of disappearance can be traced back to Lacan's account of *aphanisis* (the process of becoming invisible; Greek *aphanes*: invisible): in a movement of division, the subject appears in the Symbolic order as meaning, while it is manifest elsewhere "as 'fading,' as disappearance."[11] The subject emerges in and through signification in the same movement that its being retreats from signification. In other words, "Hong Kong" appears in film (where film is not reality), while Hong Kong exists in reality (where "reality" is not film). In this sense, what we understand as "Hong Kong" is never what Hong Kong really is. "Hong Kong" is merely a signifier and is divided from Hong Kong's being. The Lacanian Real resists signification and stays just beyond the Symbolic order. It is therefore not difficult to argue that Hong Kong eludes *any* form of representation — with or without the *disappearance*. If Hong Kong is "an elusive subject" as Abbas argues, it is a necessarily "disappearing" one. "Hong Kong" always already *dis-appears*. Conversely, the Real is always already overlooked. What Abbas calls the *déjà disparu*, the already disappeared, is, in fact, the *toujours déjà disparu*, the always already disappeared. "The picture of the city that we carry in our mind is always slightly out of date," Abbas quotes from Jorge Luis Borges.[12] Likewise, the motion picture of the city is always slightly out of date and out of place. To take Abbas's "disappearance" literally is therefore problematic.

The Space of Subjectivity, the Subjectivity of Space

The signifier "subject" refers not only to *subject matter* (a "subject" as an object in discourse) but also *subjectivity* (a "subject" as that which acts on objects). It is therefore necessary to unpack Abbas's elusive subject of Hong Kong to better comprehend the object of analysis in his work:

> It should be noted ... that this new [Hong Kong] subjectivity that we are trying to describe and invent at the same time is not a mere psychologistic category. It is, rather, an affective, political, and social category all at once. It is, I am trying to suggest, a subjectivity that is coaxed into being by the disappearance of old cultural bearings and orientations, which is to say that it is a subjectivity that develops precisely out of a space of disappearance.[13]

This passage is purposefully remote. Not only do key terms remain vague, the theoretical parts do not add up to a stable, coherent whole. It is difficult to imagine a subject that is psychologistic, affective, political, social, and perhaps even linguistic and spatial all at once. A number of theories on the subject may be employed to imagine this yet-to-emerge subjectivity: a postcolonial subject found in between domains of difference (Homi Bhaba, Gayatri Chakravorty Spivak); a subjectivity formed by movement and travel (Gilles Deleuze, Paul Gilroy, Stuart Hall, Giuliana Bruno); a situated, corporeal subject derived in practice (Maurice Merleau-Ponty, Michel de Certeau); a subject formed in and through encounters with others (Jean-Paul Sartre, Jacques Lacan, Frantz Fanon); and a subjectivity constructed in and through performativity (Judith Butler).[14] In addition to the above theories, there is also Fredric Jameson's "'death' of the subject," the classic diagnosis that the subject either no longer exists in late capitalism or never really existed in the first place.[15] It is therefore not difficult to understand why the subject of Hong Kong is so elusive. On second thought, one can also see it as the attempt to posit an entirely new subjectivity through an unstable, contradictory, or perhaps impossible definition. The subsequent deciphering of the definition would yield infinite possibilities.

Lacan's mirror stage, or *le miroir stade*, serves as one of the models for interpreting the subject of Hong Kong. The passage cited above is reminiscent of the notion of *aphanisis*, as discussed earlier. The new Hong Kong subjectivity emerges out of a space of disappearance, through disappearance: precisely, it appears by *dis-appearing*. In Lacan's mirror stage, this logic is extended to the formation of the subject. The mirror stage is a spatial dialectic in bodily and architectural terms. It is the oscillation between the "fragmented image of the body" and the "'orthopedic' form of its totality" — between the objectifying externality of the body-image and the dominating internal coherence that the anatomical reflection provides. Conversely, it is the movement between "the shattering of the *Innenwelt* to *Umwelt* circle" and the "fortified camp or even a stadium," between the opening up of socialization and the closing in of isolation.[16] This "primordial drama" is the drama of the *degeneration* and *regeneration* of the body and the built structure — more specifically, their boundary elements. Anthony Vidler's reading of the mirror stage suggests the spatiality of this process: "Here two-dimensional physiognomy, the representation of the 'face,' is transformed into the three-dimensional space of subjectivity, place for the staging of social activity. That is, the plane of the mirror becomes the space of a theater."[17] The body is delimited by the skin, and the built structure by its walls. The boundary element is ultimately a property of space, as the words *Innenwelt* and *Umwelt* suggest: *Innenwelt*, the inner world, and *Umwelt*, the surrounding world. According to Giuliana Bruno, "self-identification is a *spatial* affair — a narrative drama set in intersubjective space and enacted on a *corps morcelé* [morcelated body], an imagined anatomy. ... [T]he mirror stage is a space, a screen, on which identity is constantly negotiated."[18] Likewise, Kaja Silverman calls the mirror stage a "territorialization of the infant's body."[19] If the new Hong Kong subject is to emerge from a space of disappearance, it is in and through the mirror stage — the space of subjectivity, the space of *dis-appearance* — that it appears.

Bodily and urban spaces illustrate subjectivity, as their boundaries divide the spaces of the subject and of the Other.[20] These spaces of subjectivity are delimited by degenerating/regenerating boundary elements that are not only permeable or porous but also oscillate between inside and outside. Mark Wigley's problematization of inside/outside in the discourse of deconstructivist architecture illustrates the permeability of the boundary as the negotiation between the private *Innenwelt* and the public *Umwelt*, between the *I* and the social *I*.[21] The Great Wall of China is an extended fortress that was built for defense and isolation, while Jacques Herzog and Pierre de Meuron's National Stadium in Beijing — a *stade* — is a structure that collects and disperses individuals with its permeable boundary. Likewise, the skin is a permeable, if not porous, boundary. The rim-like structures, or more specifically the erogenous zones, are sites of entrances and exits in the pursuit of desire. Lacan uses topological terms and diagrams to discuss the oral, anal, scopic, and invocatory drives and their relationship to the human orifices.[22] Intercourse, in this sense, is the complication of the inside/outside of bodily spaces and of subjects. The exchange of bodily fluids, surrogacy, and cannibalism are instances of intersubjective embodiment, as is the surgical transplant of tissues, organs, and limbs which breaches bodily space permanently. Similarly, cases of bodily trauma such as wounds, lacerations, and mutilation, and the body's subsequent healing illustrate the body's permeability and degeneration/regeneration. Body modification, self-inflicted injuries, and self-mutilation are various bodily manifestations of a subject in formation. The body's incorporation of technology or trans-species tissue, if taken far enough, may lead to the formation of a cyborg or human-animal subjectivity.

The subject of Hong Kong is elusive, because it is a subject in formation, an ongoing formation of subjectivity. The spaces of the subject and the Other — the *Innenwelt* and *Umwelt* — manifest themselves in bodily and urban spaces, and their boundary elements are permeable or porous. Complicating the notions of inside and outside, these boundary elements do not neatly separate the subject from the Other, but instead show their interdependence.

The Nature of Culture: Postculture and Planetarity

While nature and culture are often paired in discourse at various levels of binarity and opposition, their interrelations can be described as topological. However, since the "nature of culture" — the attributes and properties of "culture" and the culturally determined concept of "nature" — is an ongoing discourse, let us begin with the words "nature" and "culture" themselves. Raymond Williams traces the history of the word "culture" to its etymological root in the Latin *colere*, whose meanings include "to cultivate" and "to husband": "culture" in its early uses referred to "the tending of natural growth," usually of crops and animals.[23] While culture came into meaning through human interactions with nature, the history of "nature" finds its roots in culture: "Any full history of the uses of 'nature' would be a history of a large part of human thought," according to Williams.[24] Observing the implications of the latest technologies on the meaning of culture, Tony Bennett further problematizes the interrelations between nature and culture:

> Distinctions between nature and culture now ... have a weaker force as a result of the increasing sense that the relations between these are best thought of as *porous and permeable*. Developments in human genetics, biology, biotechnology, [and] genetic medicine ... have been especially important here, leading to a series of technological interventions in the human body and nature — from *in vitro* fertilization to genetically modified (GM) crops — which have called in question their separation from cultural processes. The new vocabulary of cyberculture, nanoculture, somatic culture, and technoculture reflect these concerns ...[25]

The "porous and permeable" interrelations between nature and culture are reminiscent of the degenerating/regenerating boundary elements of bodily and urban spaces, as discussed earlier, in that an entity's inside is not completely severed from its outside. If one were to view nature and culture topologically, one could problematize the respective inside/outside of nature and culture: since "nature" and "culture," unbounded, cannot be solely and completely themselves, they would be open to the other, to each other, in their potential to become more than themselves, other than themselves.

Postculture is a term of possibilities in the discourse of culture. Stephen Crook, Jan Pakulski, and Malcolm Waters define "postculture" as culture that is hyper-differentiated, hyper-rationalized, and hyper-commodified to the point of de-differentiation, de-rationalization, and de-commodification.[26] In a more self-referential move, Greg Urban puts forth the notion of "metaculture" as "culture that is about culture" to describe the dissemination and renewal of culture itself.[27] Unlike the above theorists, however, Abbas constructs a notion of "postculture" that is purposefully remote:

> [Postculture] is a culture that has developed in a situation where the available models of culture no longer work. ... A postculture, therefore, is not postmodernist culture, or post-Marxist culture, or post-Cultural Revolution culture, or even postcolonial culture, insofar as each of these has a set of established themes and an alternative orthodoxy. In a postculture, on the other hand, culture itself is experienced as a field of instabilities. ... Because it is *a set of anticipations*, postculture can be *a preparation for cultural survival*. Perhaps in the case of Hong Kong more than anywhere else, there is no chance of cultural survival unless we radicalize our understanding of culture itself.[28]

Defined against the available notions of culture, postculture is a set of infinite possibilities or even radical anticipations. Postculture encompasses but is not reduced to the various avant-garde, experimental, or alternative "-cultures" that attempt to go beyond the existing cultural paradigms and their predetermining edifices: subcultures, countercultures, cybercultures, nanocultures, technocultures, and other neologisms to come. As though it were a seed that embodies the various forms of vegetation that may emerge from it, postculture is the possibility and survival of culture itself. With its unstable definition, postculture defines itself through its afterness to culture. Postculture, in other words, is a "culture" of what is *beyond* "mere culture."

Lacan's tripartite system may shed light on what is beyond culture. In her Lacanian reading of culture, Catherine Belsey writes: "Culture ... is all we know. In that sense, we are always in culture — always in the game. ... [K]nowledge exists at the level of the *symbol*, and there is no way of showing that any specific set of symbols maps the world accurately."[29] Culture forms a grid, a coordinate system, or a type of mapping that negotiates what we perceive with what we experience and vice versa. If desire is the Imaginary fulfillment of a Real lack, then postculture constitutes the desire to expand culture, cultural knowledge. Postculture, therefore, is a turn toward not reality as we know it, but reality as we do not know it. Knowing what we do not know involves unknowing what we do know. Joshua Clover pinpoints these moments of revelation in what he calls the "Edge of Construct" genre of science fiction films.[30] The desire to know drives the protagonists of *The Matrix*, *The Truman Show*, and *Dark City*, for example, to their watershed discoveries. In a moment of breakthrough, both triumphant and traumatic, they come in contact with the Edge of Contruct and reorientate their mapping of the world. Postculture, in this sense, is a culture of wanting to know (beyond what we already know).

The idea of the "planet Earth" is significant in reorientating the nature of culture. *The Whole Earth Catalog*, published by Stewart Brand in 1968, showed on its front cover a satellite photo of the Earth released by the National Aeronautics and Space Administration (NASA), reportedly among the first ones to be circulated publicly.[31] The publication of the "whole Earth" photo was a *postcultural moment* that dramatically redefined "nature" and "culture," as Brand would later claim: "Those riveting Earth photos *reframed everything*. For the first time humanity saw itself from outside. ... Suddenly humans had a planet to tend to."[32] The image taken from beyond the Edge of Construct focuses our attention on the construct in and with which we live. This reframing or remapping of our environment finds a precedent, for example, in the contributions of Copernicus, Kepler, and Galileo whose advancement of heliocentrism eventually debunked the geocentric model or ideology. Nevertheless, debunking current models or ideologies is an ongoing process. The "whole Earth" photo falls short of representing the maximal extent of "nature," as Buckminster Fuller correctly observes: "Well, you can only see about half the earth at any given time [in the photo]."[33]

In a similar move, Gayatri Chakravorty Spivak proposes the notion of "planetarity" as an alternative to, if not a replacement of, the current notion of the "globe": "The globe is on our computers. No one lives there. It allows us to think that we can aim to control it. The planet is in the species of alterity, belonging to another system; and yet we inhabit it, on loan. It is not really amenable to a neat contrast with the globe."[34] The globe — a symbol associated with colonialism, capitalist globalization, and the exploitation of natural resources — disregards the sustainability of the space of the Other and the survival of other inhabitants on the planet. Planetarity aims to debunk this model or ideology. To conceive of the planetary, then, is to acknowledge and be responsible for the Other, the non-self-identical. As Timothy Morton puts it, "To truly love nature would be to love what is nonidentical with us."[35] Until the moment when other habitable spaces are discovered, planet Earth is what we know as the maximal extent of "nature."

Postculture and planetarity aim to express the ever-changing interrelations between nature and culture. Postculture seeks to posit a culture of survival, the survival of culture, while planetarity seeks to debunk the model or ideology of the globe. Precisely because the interrelations between "nature" and "culture" are porous and permeable, "nature" and "culture" are not outside of each other.

Viewing Hong Kong: From Ecoscape to Ecocinema

An ecoscape is not a landscape, an ecology, or "nature," but a way of viewing the planet and the planetary: it refers to the ongoing discourse on the materiality, spatiality, structures, and constructs of natural and cultural phenomena. Like "nature" and "culture," it is a cultural form — a form of postculture. An ecoscape appears at various temporal, spatial, and organizational scales. The topological qualities of an ecoscape are similar to the "fluid, irregular shapes" that Arjun Appadurai classifies under the suffix "-scape."[36] The notion of an "ecoscape," for example, may allow us to imagine the whole through seeing the parts and to imagine the parts through seeing the whole, depending on where we are situated. This is a logic based on fractal forms: "[T]he configuration of cultural forms in today's world [is] ... fundamentally fractal, that is, as possessing no Euclidean boundaries, structures, or regularities."[37] Whether we see fractal forms or simply chaos is an open question at any given point in time, over any period of time, given the limited time that we have. An ecoscape may manifest itself as topological or situated or both. Historical data, in the form of socio-cultural and political-economic discourses, would contribute to possible solutions to this problem. An ecoscape presumes a conceptualization of space that goes beyond the existing notions of the local and the global, on the one hand, and the regional, the national, and the international, on the other. An ecoscape manifests itself at the level of the planetary — somewhere, everywhere.

To view an ecoscape is to look at natural and cultural phenomena and to see the co-existing or co-occupying bodily, urban, and natural spaces. To move from looking to seeing requires naming the parts in view. Viewing an ecoscape would involve turning to that which we have seen and named as well as that which we have not — yet. We begin with elements of the weather such as sunlight, clouds, rain, snow, wind, heat, and cold as universal concepts. Natural phenomena such as earthquakes, tsunamis, hurricanes, snowstorms, floods, heat waves, and droughts intervene in urban space. The earthquake in the Sichuan Province of China, Hurricane Katrina in the state of Louisiana and the southern United States, and the Indian Ocean tsunami that affected multiple countries, most severely Indonesia, Sri Lanka, India, and Thailand, are recent cases of profound devastation, trauma, and tragedy that called for large-scale humanitarian efforts at various spatial and organizational levels. In addition to human beings, such catastrophes affect other creatures in the animal kingdom. The effects and aftermath ripple across national borders, across the spaces of wildlife. Concepts, if not actual phenomena, such as the greenhouse effect, global warming, and global climate change, affect more than one location on the planet — not only physically, but also discursively as political and scientific matters. Industrial pollution, radioactive and toxic waste, and unsustainable land use (agricultural and urban) contribute to the destruction of the environment and the quality of life. Finally, the AIDS epidemic, the outbreak of SARS, and the ubiquity of breast cancer are examples of public health concerns at the planetary level. Viewing an ecoscape would involve looking at, seeing, and naming these phenomena.

An ecocinema does not seek to reaffirm the old and familiar binarism of the urban versus the natural, by offering a counterpart to urban cinema. Rather, an ecocinema is the cinematic representation of an ecoscape and it seeks to problematize similarly the easy categorization of the "objects" it views. The "porous and permeable" interrelations between the urban and the natural can be thought of as being interrelated, mutually generative, non-bivalent — in a certain sense of yin-yang "binarism" or the Daoist notion, "These two, with different names, emerge from the same."[38] The bodily is likewise neither strictly "urban" nor strictly "natural," depending on the status of the human in terms of the social, the environmental, and the other-than-human.[39]

Hong Kong cinema is largely associated with urban cinema, and there are few mainstream features or documentaries that can be readily categorized as "ecocinema."[40] The preoccupation of Hong Kong cinema to represent urban space is strong, as Abbas observes: "One of the features of new Hong Kong cinema is its sensitivity to spatial issues, in other words, to dislocations and discontinuities.... We get a better sense of the history of Hong Kong through its new cinema (and architecture) than is currently available in any history book."[41] However, Hong Kong cinema does not represent urban space exclusively. Nor is Hong Kong merely an urban space. To conceive of the city and its architecture as the whole of

Hong Kong becomes a limited way of viewing and knowing Hong Kong.[42] Hong Kong's natural space disappears, precisely because space is looked at in this old familiar way.

What Abbas overlooks are other discontinuities and dislocations in the urban space represented in Hong Kong cinema. Natural space intervenes in this urban space as something we do see or as something we do not see. Natural spaces manifest themselves as discontinuities in urban space, when we focus on the parts that make up the whole. The iconic image of Hong Kong's Victoria Harbor is such an example (Figure 9.1). The view of the business district includes numerous modern skyscrapers in a jungle of concrete buildings. The whole is an image of Hong Kong's modernity, global city status, and, with a junk added to the mix, East-West hybridity. The parts that we may not immediately notice are the Peak, the subtropical vegetation lining the mountainsides, and the water of the harbor itself. Natural spaces reveal themselves in the urban space as gaps, if not ruptures or even defects. The natural spaces that we do not see are the dislocations: they are dislocated from the urban space entirely. Beyond this iconic image of Hong Kong are the parks, lakes, nature reserves, wetlands, mountains, remote coasts, and outlying islets. In fact, nearly 70 percent of Hong Kong's total area is farmland or the countryside, of which approximately 40 percent is protected as country parks and nature reserves.[43] The real Hong Kong eludes its representations, unless we relentlessly open our minds toward it, rejecting the ideologies of "reverse hallucination" and "disappearance."[44]

Figure 9.1   The iconic Victoria Harbor in *Durian Durian*.

The postcultural moment in Hong Kong cinema, if it has not already occurred, would be the turn toward natural space. It would involve seeing the urban space in Hong Kong cinema in a new unfamiliar way, thereby reorientating the realm of Hong Kong culture. Seeing the presence of urban space is not unlike seeing the absence of natural space. Land reclamation projects in Hong Kong, for example, have shaped the coastline into straight edges and narrowed the harbor. "Natural" space transforms into "urban" space, and seeing such "urban" space unveils a "natural" space that we no longer see. Three photographs in Abbas's book provide excellent examples.[45] The first, taken from a high elevation at a distance, focuses on a cluster of nondescript high-rise buildings surrounded by mountains and vegetation; in the background is the sea and outlying islets. The second shows the detail of a typical concrete-covered slope with vegetation piercing through and growing in abundance. In the third photo, what seems to be a retaining wall alongside a street is actually a façade left by rock-cutting. Seen differently, "urban" space is "natural" space without "nature." Hong Kong urban cinema is always already a Hong Kong ecocinema, if one redirects one's gaze toward the natural space in the filmic representation. An ecocinema does not focus on "nature" itself, but an ecoscape, a mixture of bodily, urban, and natural spaces.

Figure 9.2 High-rise buildings, mountains, islands, and the sea. Photo by Jamila Ismail.

Durian Durian: Between Home and the World

Durian Durian opens with the image of Victoria Harbor that separates Hong Kong Island from Kowloon and the New Territories. Hong Kong Island was the original concession to Britain in 1842, while Kowloon and the New Territories were conceded subsequently in 1860 and 1898. All territories comprising Hong Kong were returned to mainland China in 1997. In this sequence, the city is fragmented not only by the framing of the camera but also along the harbor between Hong Kong Island and the mainland, evoking a sense of what Gary Xu calls Hong Kong's "unattached attachment" to the mainland or what Wendy Gan sees as a manifestation of the policy slogan, "one country, two systems."[46] As the image of a fragmented Hong Kong cross-fades into the image of Mudanjiang in northeastern China, the water, followed by the whole image, turns blood red, alluding to mutilation and violence. After the opening credits finish, we see a one-legged man living in Hong Kong.

Victoria Harbor is the quintessential site/sight of Hong Kong's evolving subjectivity. The harbor is the original border along which Hong Kong was cut off from the mainland; it is also where one can observe the spectacular transformations that Hong Kong has undergone since. Through the sight of the camera, Hong Kong Island is able to "see" its own reflection. Yet, the city is merely the urban or architectural manifestation of Hong Kong. On the Kowloon side from which the opening sequence was filmed is a boardwalk well visited by tourists and locals alike. The site of the camera situates the viewer as a tourist, a local resident, or a combination of the two. The people in Hong Kong contribute to the other aspects of Hong Kong's subjectivity. As Stephen Teo notes, Hong Kong cinema is preoccupied with Hong Kong's identity and constantly asks the question, "Who am I?"[47] What is also pertinent, however, is the question, "Where am I?" or "Who am I in relation to where I am?" Although *Durian Durian* is a film about Hong Kong, the protagonists come from the mainland. They live in the mainland but find temporary work in Hong Kong, and their status is somewhere between tourist and local resident. Yan (or Xiaoyan), a native of Mudanjiang, enters Hong Kong on a temporary tourist visa and performs sex work in its love hotels, while the one-legged man brings his family from Shenzhen to Hong Kong where they overstay their visas to work at a restaurant. Their location changes their very identity.

Some of the sending cities in mainland China experience severe urban plight. Yan's hometown is in the northeastern region called Dongbei.[48] The rapid decline of the industrial sector coupled with a high unemployment rate has left many buildings in that region abandoned or in need of renovation. The establishing shots in the film show a ghostly cityscape devoid of workers and activity. The frozen river fortifies the isolation of Mudanjiang, leaving boats stranded on the banks as though it were a dried-up river (Figure 9.3).[49] While the harsh winter dampens the residents' mobility, the residents themselves have few options in life: they have nowhere to go. At Yan's homecoming dinner, one of her relatives, apparently unaware of the actual nature of Yan's previous work, asks Yan to take her teenage daughter along to Hong Kong. The community is portrayed, on the one hand, as warm and welcoming and, on the other, as unworldly and helpless. They are literally trapped in their space.

The protagonists are also trapped in their space in Hong Kong — and kept in place. The run-down love hotels where Yan engages in affective transactions are most likely in Mong Kok, one of the busiest urban centers on the Kowloon peninsula where one can find countless shopping malls, entertainment venues, and dilapidated residential complexes. Every time she enters the room, she appropriates a different regional identity from China to cater to each customer's curiosity and needs. The room acts as a prison cell or sweatshop that traps her body and extracts

Figure 9.3   Yan walks ashore from the frozen river in Mudanjiang.

its value, while her subjectivity disintegrates. When she exits the building, she re-immerses herself in Hong Kong society. Through her *flânerie* or "street-walking," she experiences the city as everyone else does, momentarily liberated from her work. It is on one of her strolls that she meets and befriends Fan (or Ah Fan), the daughter of the family from Shenzhen. Fan and her younger brother help their mother wash dishes in an alleyway behind the restaurant. A man of South Asian descent who speaks Cantonese also works there. The alley is the underbelly of the city and represents Hong Kong's other subjectivities.[50]

The degeneration/regeneration of the body is a recurrent theme for Yan. While the mainland Chinese migrants penetrate the spatial boundary of Hong Kong, Hong Kong men penetrate the bodily boundaries of the sex workers. Serving sometimes almost forty clients per day, Yan is constantly fatigued and in need of nourishment. In between jobs, she is often seen eating as her body demands recovery from the inside. On the outside, her skin peels away from the showers she takes with her clients, one of the degenerative effects of her work on her body. It is poignant to note that her skin does not regenerate despite returning home to Mudanjiang and quitting sex work. While she does the dishes after dinner one night at her parents' apartment, she notices that the skin on her hands is still peeling — this time from housework. Dishwashing seems to be a chore that Yan and Fan cannot avoid.

The urban space of Mudanjiang comes into focus upon Yan's return. In one scene, Yan waits for a friend outside a restaurant called *Wanjiao xiaochi* (Mong Kok Snacks). The reference is particularly ironic, because Yan has likely worked in this district, and now she literally "stands on the street," a Cantonese idiom for sex work. This short scene echoes an earlier one. Unable to go sightseeing in Hong Kong, she buys a calendar with photos of the city and hangs it up in her room. Now that she lives in Mudanjiang, she encounters Hong Kong again through a signifier. The symbolic Hong Kong, represented by the calendar and the restaurant's name, is split from the real Hong Kong. The representations generate value as products, while the work of Yan and Fan's family partly sustains the real city.[51] The film turns toward the real Hong Kong by telling these untold stories. Likewise, the relatively unknown post-industrial city in Dongbei provides a different representation of mainland China which is often associated with its modern cities and rural countryside.

In another scene, Yan and her old classmates visit the school where they trained to become dancers and opera performers. The brick building is vacant, and much of the furniture and equipment inside are worn out. The camera focuses on a mirror in the dance studio in a particularly memorable shot: the reflection shows the childhood friends performing their old routines (Figure 9.4). They re-enact, if not "perform," their childhood. This moment also marks a crossroads in their lives. Yan has just returned from Hong Kong after a short and discreet stint as a sex worker. Her male friends have lost their jobs and are contemplating mounting a variety show in which they will sing, dance, and strip. The dance studio is, in a literal sense, a mirror stage, a stage with a mirror. Chan ends the film with Yan performing a Chinese opera song on a makeshift stage on the street. Perhaps, reprising a role she learned at the studio, Yan repeats the lines and gestures mechanically. Her face is "frozen" in the traditional mask-like make-up, while her voice is controlled by the lyrics. She does not have access to the sort of language that is supposed to restore her subjectivity. Her subject formation continues without a clear resolution, as she disappears behind this rehearsal of the primordial drama.

Figure 9.4 Childhood friends perform routines in front of a mirror.

The durian reflects the condition of the protagonists. The Chinese title of the film, *Liulian piaopiao*, can be translated as "durian adrift." Native to Southeast Asia, the fruit is popular in Hong Kong where people love it for the creamy, bittersweet taste and avoid it for the pungent smell. In one sense, the durian adrift symbolizes the displacement of the mainland migrants who "export" themselves to Hong Kong where they are ambivalently received. In another sense, the contradictory qualities of the durian — being both bitter and sweet, rejected and appreciated, hard (on the outside) and soft (on the inside) — reflect the complexity of the migrant experience.

It is helpful to note that *liulian* (durian) is a homophone for "to linger." The title itself is almost an oxymoron, taken as "linger adrift." Yet, if to linger means to be in between departure and arrival, then to linger is also to be adrift. Reflecting the title, the protagonists are always somewhere between home and the world.

Hollywood Hong Kong: Between the Human and the Animal

The opening sequence of *Hollywood Hong Kong* shows the butcher and his two sons working shirtless, unloading pig carcasses from a truck. The father and the elder son each carry an adult pig, while the younger son carries a piglet. The three men are overweight, and the texture, color, and folds of their skin blend in with those of the pigs. As the father cuts up and roasts the meat, the opening credits appear as stamps on the human and pig bodies. The sound of chopping, sawing, and roasting fills the soundtrack along with the dreamy melody of a harp. The sequence ends, as the father takes a break. He shares his snack and drink with *Niangniang*, a sow whose name means "mother." The woman of the family ran away some time ago, presumably because of an affair, and *Niangniang* has become a replacement of sorts. From the beginning of the film, the boundary between the human and the animal blurs at the levels of visuality, signification, and affect.

The Chu (Zhu) family operates a small meat-roasting business in Tai-Hom Village (*Dakan cun*) in the Diamond Hill district of Kowloon. The village was originally founded by the pre-colonial inhabitants of Hong Kong (*yuanjumin*), among whom were the ancestors of the Chu family. However, the area has, since the 1950s, gradually transformed into a sprawl of illegal housing structures.[52] Many of the structures are made of wood and sheet metal, while some are built with more durable materials, but the overall living and sanitary conditions are poor. Residential structures are often mixed with businesses, stores, and restaurants, and these quarters are especially prone to fire. The Hong Kong government has demolished most of these villages and relocated the residents to urban public housing. At the time of the filming, Tai-Hom Village was one of the few of its kind remaining.

As one's location influences one's identity, one's identity also influences one's location. Social agents change their environments according to their identities. The question one asks here is: "Where am I in relation to who I am?" The formation and transformation of Tai-Hom Village, for example, is the accumulated effort of its inhabitants over the decades to create a place for themselves. The female protagonist, in contrast, prefers to relocate herself. A young woman from mainland China who goes by the aliases of Tong Tong (Dong Dong), Fong Fong (Fang Fang), and Hung Hung (Hong Hong), she is self-assertive, ambitious, and even manipulative.[53] While Yan in *Durian Durian* provides sexual services in exchange for money, Hung Hung takes a different approach. She seduces the men in the village, blackmails them with falsified documents showing her to be underage, and then extorts large sums of money from them. Fruit Chan explains in an interview: some sex workers in Hong Kong "are just trying to make a little money. Then there are those a bit more ambitious who plan on using that money to put themselves through school or go abroad. *Hollywood Hong Kong* is about the latter type."[54] Hung Hung eventually saves up enough money to go to Hollywood.

The degeneration/regeneration of urban space is a prominent theme in *Hollywood Hong Kong*. The location is itself a site of urban regeneration and growth. Instead of portraying the scenic Victoria Harbor or even the lively Mong Kok as symbolic of Hong Kong, the film turns toward one of the least picturesque areas to document the ongoing transformations in the real Hong Kong.[55] Across the road from the village is the newly built Plaza Hollywood, which consists of a shopping mall and five high-rise residential buildings. The average, middle-class estate has a not-so-average name, given its reference to the cinematic capital in the United States. In an economy of signs, urban spaces differentiate themselves and derive value by reproducing the names of better-known places. In *Durian Durian*, the Hong Kong–themed restaurant in northeastern China reproduces the signifier of Mong Kok. Places are teleported to faraway locations by means of the signifier. Film architecture, theme parks, and hotel resorts, for example, import places by reproducing their designs. On the one hand, place becomes depersonalized, deterritorialized, and dematerialized in a postmodern, globalizing era. On the other hand, place-making is relevant as long as social agents engage the spaces of their environment.[56]

The human body also experiences degeneration/regeneration. One of the most striking images in film is the surgical reattachment of a mismatched forearm. Wong Chi-keung (Huang Zhiqiang), a teenage pimp working in Tai-Hom Village, ignores Hung Hung's extortion scheme. Consequently, her lawyer-cum-client sends gangsters to chop off his forearm. In a case of mistaken identity, the gangsters chop off the wrong man's forearm, but eventually find Wong and finish the job. Having cut off the "wrong Wong's" left forearm and the "right Wong's" right forearm, they discard the body parts in the village. After a boy brings a severed forearm to him, Wong takes it to the local undocumented surgeon to have it reattached. As chance has it, the forearm is not his. Wong's arm and the severed forearm together show a montage of two tattoos, a tiger's head with a snake's tail (Figure 9.5). If the lion represents England, the dragon China, and the lion cub Hong Kong as in the emblem of the colonial Hong Kong government (Figure 9.6), then the resulting image of a tiger's head with a snake's tail can be seen as a symbol for the new Hong Kong, reflecting once again Hong Kong's "unattached attachment" — in this case, in bodily terms. This "Hong Kong" is represented as the awkward combination of a tiger and a snake (or, with some imagination, a lion and a dragon), depicting the trauma of severance and the subsequent project of reattachment. The left (incorrect) forearm is attached to the right (correct) arm. As the play of signifiers continues, one realizes that "a tiger's head with a snake's tail" (*hutou shewei*) refers to the Chinese idiom suggesting a premature or unsatisfactory finish. In an earlier sex scene with Hung Hung, Wong indeed finishes early. While their relationship may be "almost a love story," it is without a doubt a sex story.[57] The love-hate relationship between Hong Kong and the mainland has become one of love-hate-sex.

Figure 9.5   Wong's arm in a state of "unattached attachment" in *Hollywood Hong Kong*.

Figure 9.6   The emblem of the colonial Hong Kong government.

The clear division between the human and the animal becomes problematized in *Hollywood Hong Kong*. As the opening sequence shows, the human body and the animal body are conflated at the levels of visuality, signification, and affect. At one point, the undocumented doctor mentioned earlier approaches Boss Chu about a biological experiment to implant a human embryo in the uterus of *Niangniang*. She even suggests raising the human baby on the pig's milk, if the experiment is successful. The experiment breaches the boundary between the human body and the animal body and suggests a type of cross-species childrearing. If the human baby were to be born and raised this way, it would approach a human-animal subjectivity, something that the opening sequence playfully hints at. In another scene, the sow becomes the object-causing-desire for Boss Chu, when he dreams of a sexual encounter with Hung Hung who turns into a sow. In a later scene, the merging of the human body and the animal body takes place at a gruesomely literal level. Boss Chu kills one of his employees in a freak accident and disposes of her body by feeding it to *Niangniang*. The humans and the animals in the film co-exist in the same "ecology." The rule of law does not intervene in the actions of the human beings.

As in *Durian Durian*, mobility is expressed as an existential issue of being trapped. When Wong and Hung Hung engage in paid sex on the mountainside, they perform what is often seen in the stereotypical nature documentary: the mating of animals in the wilderness. After they finish, they climb toward Plaza Hollywood. Hung Hung likens the five high-rise apartment buildings to the Five Finger Mountain in *Journey to the West* (*Xiyouji*) (Figure 9.7). As Xu points out in his reading, the Five Finger Mountain (*wuzhi shan*) is a reference to the manifestation of Buddha's hand that traps the rebellious Monkey, Sun Wukong.[58] The characters find themselves in the position of the Monkey in the sense that they cannot escape their condition of existence altogether through mobility or place-making. While Wong is desperate to leave Tai-Hom Village, his manifestation of the Five Finger Mountain, Hung Hung wants to escape Plaza Hollywood, her manifestation of the Five Finger Mountain. After saving up enough money, she finally manages to travel to the West, to the real Hollywood. Wong is trapped by the signifier of his name and the location into which he is born, while Hung Hung plays with her aliases and moves constantly from place to place. Wong has his hand and forearm chopped off, and stays stagnated in his space. Despite her mobility, Hung Hung compares her hand to Buddha's hand, herself to the Monkey, and her location to the Monkey's prison. The physical spaces are mediated by and highly charged with their symbolic meanings. All is an illusion, as a Buddhist saying goes. Even "Hollywood." And, of course, "Hong Kong."

Figure 9.7   Hung Hung compares Plaza Hollywood to the Five Finger Mountain.

Public Toilet: Between Us and the Planet

In the opening sequence, a woman takes her young son to the women's bathroom, while a man takes his young daughter to the men's bathroom. Because both bathrooms are too crowded, they have to "go" outside — instead of using the public toilet, the children use the toilet in public. So begins the transnational or even planetary journey of *Public Toilet*. Shot in digital video (DV), the experimental film is reminiscent of the visual poetry of Matthew Barney, Dogme95's docudrama techniques, the globe-trotting *Qatsi* Trilogy, and the crude bodily humor of Wong Jing (Wang Jing).[59] Though made as a Hong Kong film, it features locations in Hong Kong, mainland China, Korea, India, and the United States. One of the premises of the film, as Chan admits, is that "all of humanity has to use the toilet."[60] Through the universal act of defecation, all of humanity on this planet is connected.

All of humanity uses language when it uses the bathroom. The signifier that marks a bathroom door evokes a classic Lacanian account of signification. In "The Instance of the Letter in the Unconscious," Lacan tells the story of two siblings, brother and sister, who arrive at a train station.[61] Sitting across from each other in a train compartment, they look out the window and see two bathroom doors. The brother exclaims that they are at the Ladies', while the sister says that they are at the Gentlemen's. The assumption is that they see only one of the two signifiers that designate the genders of the bathrooms, respectively. One must refer to the signifiers to differentiate the bathrooms, because the doors look the same. Lacan's interpretation is that the signifiers are barred from the signified. The signifier and the signified do not correspond one-to-one, and the signifier refers to nothing but other signifiers. In other words, when one enters a bathroom, one chooses the signifier, not the door. In one scene at the hospital, Dong Dong asks the question, as he enters, "Is this the men's bathroom?" Choosing the signifier is crucial, while walking through the door is all the same.

Cross-cultural casting illustrates how one's language and body do not necessarily correspond one-to-one to one's national or cultural heritage. The narrator, Dong Dong, is a native of Beijing in the film, but is performed by a Japanese actor who speaks Mandarin. His three friends are of Chinese, Italian, and African descent, and they speak fluent Mandarin as well (Figure 9.8). Tony, the Beijinger with dyed blond hair, speaks Cantonese without an accent. On a trip to India, he runs into two Indian brothers conversing in Cantonese; as it turns out, they are from Hong Kong. He meets their parents who do not speak Cantonese, and he switches to English with ease. In a particularly comic scene in the Korean storyline, a Chinese acupuncturist converses with his patients in Korean, pauses, and nonchalantly slurps up his lunch. He then switches to Mandarin to converse with Dong Dong. Finally, the two native Hong Kongers in the film never appear in Hong Kong, but instead in Beijing and New York City, respectively. The play with national, cultural, linguistic, ethnic, class, and other identities in the film evokes Kang Youwei's *datong*, which Sheldon H. Lu proposes as a way of imagining non-capitalist globalization.[62]

Figure 9.8   Actors converse in Mandarin in *Public Toilet*.

More than a film about globalization, *Public Toilet* is about the planet. By experimenting with the formal limits of urban cinema, the film turns toward the interpenetrating urban and natural spaces as content. The Indian people wash their bodies in the Ganges River, which is both a spiritual site and a river running through many cities in the subcontinent. The Great Wall of China is an architectural feat that extends into the vast landscape, but it cannot escape the snow that covers it. Manhattan, represented by the thoroughly urban space of Times Square, is actually an island located in the Hudson River. Excrement from the city is flushed into the sea, while fishermen in Korea take their catch to the fish market. The film does not attempt to present nature "as it is," outside the context of human activities, but it does turn toward the natural space that lies amidst, beyond, and adjacent to urban space.

Public Toilet turns away from the container and toward the content, away from the toilet and toward the crap. Instead of presenting the toilet as a construct that makes crap disappear, the film focuses on the slimy truth that it tries to expel. The toilet is a construct of cleanliness: flushing the toilet keeps our lives clean. It is also a construct of finality: once we flush, the crap disappears — forever. Instead of holding crap at bay (or in the sewage), the film goes beyond the toilet, toward reality as we do not know it. In one movement, Dong Dong is literally retrieved from the toilet to narrate the film. In another movement, he takes the filmic gaze through the sewage to the sea (Figure 9.9). This is to highlight the fact that "crap" — this includes other forms of "pollution," I suggest — does not disappear cleanly and forever. Nature unconditionally accepts our crap, all of it. The duty of ecological art, then, is to keep the crap in view.[63] Likewise, ecocinema ought to turn our gaze toward the crappy side of "nature." Rather than reaffirming the idyllic images of a pristine "nature," ecocinema should hold us accountable for our society and environment.

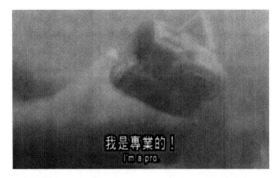

Figure 9.9   Dong Dong climbs into the sewer and finds a video camera.

Not only is *Public Toilet* about crap, it is also about the place of crap on the planet. There is no *shenyao* or "magical cure-all" that takes care of crapping. Crap is a necessary by-product of our survival. The point is not to stop crapping or to account for every ounce of crap, but to avoid messing up the bathroom for everyone. The planet, after all, is a public toilet. It serves all of humanity and, in turn, all of humanity is responsible for its maintenance.

Conclusion: Observing Mutations

The boundaries of self-identity exist as mutations. That is to say, the self ceases to be itself when it mutates, when it morphs into the non-self. "Gilles Deleuze writes: 'Godard says that *to describe* is to observe mutations.'"[64] To describe Hong Kong urban cinema, then, involves observing its mutations. The form of urban cinema reaches its limits in several ways. The Hong Kong it represents is never what the real Hong Kong is. Hong Kong is not merely its architecture; it consists of bodily, urban, and natural spaces. When the filmic gaze turns away from urban space toward natural space, urban cinema begins to redefine itself as a form through its changing content. While the director may facilitate this mutation of urban cinema, one also realizes that urban cinema has always included some representation of natural space. Fruit Chan opens up the form of Hong Kong urban cinema in the three films made after the Hong Kong trilogy. In *Durian Durian*, Chan takes Hong Kong urban cinema beyond its immediate territory to the northeastern region of mainland China. Although the setting of *Hollywood Hong Kong* remains in Hong Kong, he focuses on an urban "ecology" in which Hong Kong subjects oscillate between the human and the animal. Finally, *Public Toilet* focuses the filmic gaze on the planet in which people share universal conditions such as defecation, disease, and death. As Christoph Huber observes, "there's no great unifying theme in Chan's films, only the unmitigated surge of *the struggle to survive*."[65] Cultural survival and the survival of culture involve the re-orientation of the notions of "nature" and "culture": postculture and planetarity are two such strategies. Mutating toward a Hong Kong ecocinema, Hong Kong urban cinema transforms to represent Hong Kong more accurately as an ecoscape.

A City of Disappearance:
Trauma, Displacement, and Spectral Cityscape in Contemporary Chinese Cinema

Jing Nie

China has been undergoing enormous changes since the social and economic reforms unleashed by Deng Xiaoping. These changes are represented in various spaces, the most noticeable of which is cityscape, which has been commercialized, monumentalized, and globalized. This chapter will relate Henri Lefebvre's space theory to contemporary Chinese economy and urban landscape, and then examine the manifestations of space as represented in four Chinese films: *Shower* (*Xizao*, dir. Zhang Yang, 1999), *Beijing Bicycle* (*Shiqisui de danche*, dir. Wang Xiaoshuai, 2001), *The World* (*Shijie*, dir. Jia Zhangke, 2004), and *Cell Phone* (*Shouji*, dir. Feng Xiaogang, 2004). All four of these films depict spatial transformations in the Chinese city. The previously drab, politicized, and degendered space of Beijing has become commercialized, globalized, sexualized, and gendered. Instead of glorifying such a miraculous spatial reconfiguration, contemporary Chinese urban cinema tries to capture marginalized individual space, posing it as a resistant space against the grand narratives of modernization, globalization, and social progress, and it questions the rationality beneath the surface splendor of the modern metropolis.

Henri Lefebvre's Conceptualization of Space

Henri Lefebvre maintains in his groundbreaking exposition of the production of space that "formerly each society to which history gave rise within the framework of a particular mode of production, and which bore the stamp of that mode of production's inherent characteristics, shaped its own space."[1] Lefebvre's exposition primarily rests on Marxism (commodity, labor, class conflict, etc), prioritizes the power of production, and illustrates a top-down (mode of production — spatial arrangement) constitutive mode of space. In this top-down spatiological model, Lefebvre divides social space into three subcategories: spatial practice, representations of space, and representational spaces, and tries to link the triadic spatial system with subjects by shifting his focus to the *body* and its multiple relations with space. He thus offers a "perceived-conceived-lived" triad of concepts in his discussion of space, which correspond respectively in spatial terms: spatial practice, representations of space, and representational spaces.[2] Lefebvre elaborates: "That the lived, conceived and perceived realms should be interconnected, so that the 'subject', the individual member of a given social group, may move from one to another without confusion — so much is a logical necessity."[3] This approach enriches his previous top-down, production-oriented spatial system with psychological and aesthetical dimensions, and softens the rigidity and violence of the space that is dominated and inscribed by various discourses with dynamic spaces of appropriation and internalization.

The notions that bodies are spatialized entities, and that spaces and bodies mutually (re)produce one another are not new. Analyzing the policed boundaries of body caused both by brute action against individual bodies (e.g., imprisonment) and by the common social norms underpinning those actions, Michel Foucault maintains that bodies become the nexus at which power is produced through activation and resistance.[4] Michel de Certeau considers space as both the constitutive medium of embodiment and as something constituted by bodily practices.[5] The inscribability and trangressability of both space and bodies foreground their very nature of being narratives. Derrida's notion of the rhetoricity of all texts characterizes the sphere of space, which is, unarguably, also a certain kind of text.[6] In the filmic representations of Beijing that this chapter examines, we will see there is no lack of metaphors and rhetoric of Beijing, and of (re)inscribed bodies in this space that manage to retain, react to, and act upon their "being-inscribed" state. Lefebvre's most important contribution to the study of space is his linkage of the previous models with Marxism, highlighting the significance of economic factor that resonates with the process of globalization.

When discussing social space, Lefebvre refers to Marx's identification of "things/not-things" and adopts Marx's analysis of things as "ideological objects" into his interpretation of social space. Lefebvre explains: "This space qualifies as a 'thing/not-thing', for it is neither a substantial reality nor a mental reality, it cannot be resolved into abstractions, and it consists neither of a collection of things in space nor an ensemble of things related to space, it has an actuality other than that of abstract signs and real things which it includes."[7] Lefebvre's approach innovatively links the realm of capitalist economy with that of social space, and broadens its subject from the strictly defined "things qua commodities" to a more dynamic spatial actuality. As global capitalism and spatiology are indispensable to globalization, the torrent between things and not-things described by Lefebvre echoes that between the global and the local.

Using this "thing/not-thing" quality to analyze the process of globalization, we see that along with the process of global capitalism, the space of "not-things" (the abstract space fraught with discourses, ideological, political, and institutional powers) becomes subordinate to the space of "things," be they commodities or non-commodities; while the space of "non-commodities" becomes subordinate to the space of "commodities." Examples that testify to these tendencies are plenty: political powers across the globe tend to prioritize if not serve economic developments (for lack of any successful alternative, capitalist economy seems to be the only possibility); cultural and historical legacies are universally threatened with devastation; natural space on a global scale is invaded for commercial purposes; individuals, groups, or nations are threatened by the potential if not already actual danger of loss of identity (the increasing impossibility for subjects to live out of the categories of laborer and consumer). We will observe later in the chapter that "thing/not-thing" is a useful framework with which to analyze the tangled relations between economic development and urban space under the discourse of globalization in contemporary China as depicted in several contemporary films.

The Chinese Twist on Lefebvre's Space Theory

Although the movement from "production of things" to "production of space,"[8] as suggested by Lefebvre, is applicable to most capitalist countries, China is a special case. In contemporary China, the production of space, which fosters marketization and urbanization, is not initiated by a certain mode of production as one expects to find in capitalist countries. Before Deng Xiaoping's policy of "Reforms and Openness" (*gaige kaifang*) since 1978, China was an isolated country with a socialist planned economy. It was a political and administrative decision of China's government to designate Shenzhen, Zhuhai, and some other cities as Special Economic Zones (SEZs) in the early 1980s after observing the economic prosperity brought by the capitalist economic system in the West. The government experiments with market economy and privatization in SEZs and gives them special economic policies and flexible governmental measures to facilitate business operations. In other words, the "production of space" in the SEZs is initiated by the government to nurture a mode of production (the production of things), not the other way around. The economic success of these SEZs made the government open up first the coastal cities and then major inland cities to foreign investment, and promote marketization and privatization on a national scale.

The reversed order of movement from production of space to that of things is caused by China's special situation. As we all know, China has a long history of feudalism, a well-developed political system that dictated the production of space and things. In the ancient classification of Chinese citizens into four categories — "*shi* (officials, scholars) *nong* (peasants) *gong* (craftsmen) *shang* (businessmen)" — *shi* ranks the first, while *shang* is the last. As the social order of these categories was rooted in the Confucian emphasis on ethics, *shi*, who possessed the most cultural and ethnic capital, enjoyed enormous privileges over the other three categories and constituted the feudal government, which exercised its power over the production of space with the help of its army. This production and maintenance of space by the feudal government not only stabilized the feudal system, but also guaranteed sustainable production. The capitalist mode of production emerged in China in the sixteenth century, the late Ming Dynasty, but it failed to become a dominant mode of production and thus never had the power to produce corresponding spaces to facilitate its development.

After the establishment of the People's Republic of China, political space once again became dominant, dictating, coordinating, and penetrating all other spaces — including the space of the country's planned economy — and making them its subsidiaries. Deng's famous slogan, "Development is the key" (*fazhan caishi yingdaoli*) evolved from the never-admitted realization that the spaces in China, produced out of Marxism-Leninism-Mao Zedong thought, can generate and foster neither an efficient mode of production, nor a keen awareness of the global context in which China has positioned itself. Just as Liu Kang remarks, "Globalization is not simply a new international or global conceptual framework by which China's changes can be understood. Rather, it is both a historical condition in which China's *gaige kaifang* [reforms and openness] has unfolded and a set of values or ideologies by which China and the rest of the globe are judged."[9] The policy of *gaige kaifang* targets the economic sphere. It has reconfigured spaces to initiate, spur, and spread a single mode of production: capitalist economy. Obviously, the Chinese Communist Party wants to maintain its political, cultural, and ideological stability, while at the same time it is adapting its economic systems to the international economic system, which could bring in foreign capital and employment opportunities for the local laborers. The paradox of an ideology generating certain spaces and a mode of production that is opposite to its tenets reveals the shifting nature of the leading party under the inescapable impact of global capitalism. Nevertheless, the changes in the economic field inevitably affect and reshape the contours of ideology and local culture. When marketization and privatization take control of the mode of production in China, it inevitably produces spaces that facilitate that mode of production.

As the government has already taken the initiative by redefining spaces to reshape the mode of production, the subsequent spatial changes accelerated by the production of things have been manifested even more dramatically and arbitrarily. If China was under the supervision of ideological powers from its establishment in 1949 to the 1970s, then contemporary China is operated by economic forces, which dictate the ordering of the other dimensions such as ideology and culture. Succinctly put, the national priority of economic development instigated China's willingness to join the discourse of globalization, and its economic development is a natural product of this motivation, arguably at the expense of its culture and ideology.

China's enormous economic success has justified the mode of production (socialist market economy with Chinese characteristics) that the government fostered by reforming social spaces. The discrepancies between the country's institutions and its institutionalized spaces have been glossed over by its economic success and unprecedented consumption. In the Post-New Era (*hou xin shiqi*), a term used to refer to the period since 1989,[10] Chinese society has been cautiously diverting its attention from politics to economic development. Spurred by the slogan "Development is the key" and the promotion of the idea of "allowing a group of people to get rich first," the Chinese people are being driven single-mindedly to pursue material gains, bypassing or ignoring ambiguous political and ideological issues. The teleology of developmentalism has created an enormous disparity between rich and poor, uneven geographical development, corruption, crime, and instability, aside from severe moral and spiritual degradation. People are left to their own resources to survive materially and spiritually in China's turbulent climate of modernization and globalization.

The visual aspects of Chinese people's daily lives have undergone dramatic changes in the wake of China's marketization, urbanization, and globalization. These processes have radically transformed China's cities, wiping out their traditional architecture, erasing valuable cultural heritage, and replacing it with glamorous skyscrapers. People who occupy this transforming urban space also transform themselves. One can easily spot cool Western looks on the streets of big Chinese cities. Chinese urban youth are often seen in Starbucks with laptops and iPods, just like their counterparts in the West. Innumerable migrations (*mingong*) constitute another significant aspect of the monstrously attractive modern cityscape.

The cityscape has reshaped human relationships: the cozy and familiar sense of community has been supplanted by the coldness and indifference of (post) modernity. People are less tied to their birthplaces, but move around, usually from the countryside to the city, from inland to the coast, and from small town to metropolis in search of a more prosperous future. In China, mobility is necessary for survival. Only a few privileged Chinese citizens enjoy mobility for recreational purposes, although travel and the status of what Aihwa Ong has called "flexible citizenship" are now popular among the middle and upper classes.[11] The majority has to cope with the limited mobility imposed on them by China's government-fueled marketization and globalization and their relationship with place has become less ontological and more semiotic.

Filmic Representation of Contemporary Beijing

The emerging and expanding metropolis in China has become the representative locale where the conflicts and congruencies of globalization and localization,

Western and indigenous culture, and (post)modernity and convention are ostensibly staged. Many Chinese domestic films are set against such a glamorous space, and reflect upon its significance by visually and linguistically reshaping and redefining human relationships and socio-cultural values. By exploring four contemporary Chinese films, I examine the reconfiguration of space in contemporary China and the intricate relations of space within the framework of globalization.

Shower: A Nostalgia Fantasy of Disappearing *Hutong* Culture

Zhang Yang's *Shower*, well received both in China and abroad, is full of detailed cultural codes. Numerous scenes subtly present the contrast between the traditional and the modern, in terms of space, subjectivity, and interpersonal relationships. The shock of the futuristic opening scene in which we see someone using a "body washer" (an automatic shower machine) is contrasted instantly with a traditional bathhouse (owned by Master Liu) where men of all ages enjoy hot baths, massages, fire cupping treatments, pedicures, and intimate social interactions. With the arrival of Da Ming (Master Liu's elder son) from Shenzhen, a special economic zone in China, we observe the juxtaposition of the intimacy of the traditional community of Master Liu and Er Ming (Master Liu's second son, who is mentally retarded) with the estrangement embedded in Da Ming's relationship with his relatives and acquaintances.

In the film, place and location are tied to people's identity, shaping and regulating people's relationships. The traditional bathhouse is not only a place to become clean, but also a social place where neighbors gather, exchange news, help and entertain each other. It is a relaxing and healing place where a troubled marriage is rejuvenated (He Zeng and Wang Fang's marriage is saved by the "Mandarin Duck bath" arranged by Master Liu), and where suppressed talent is unveiled (Miao Zhuang can sing "O Solo Mio" only when water is pouring down on him). Though the bathhouse is old and in desperate need of repair, Master Liu and Er Ming find meaning and the pleasures of life in their daily ritual. Their enjoyment is subtly and humorously conveyed through the small tricks they play on each other in their daily chores. Although Er Ming is mentally retarded, his close relationship with Master Liu is contrasted sharply with the formality between the Master Liu and Da Ming. Both Master Liu and Er Ming belong to the bathhouse, where people care more about each other than about money; Da Ming belongs to Shenzhen, where money defines everything including interpersonal relationships.

The complicated attitude of local dwellers toward the old houses in the back alley is revealed by Master Liu's words to Da Ming on the roof of the bathhouse after repairing it one rainy night: "These houses are like old people. No matter how hard you try to fix them up, they're still old. But they're special. This is where

I've spent my life." (Figure 10.1). Master Liu knows that these old neighborhood houses will be torn down sooner or later, just as he himself will die. His words to Da Ming, not only the modern "intruder" but also Master Liu's heir, reveal his deep awareness and calm acceptance of social development. Nevertheless the downplayed meditating tone of the roof scene set against a pink morning sky intensifies the immeasurable loss of culture and memory in the processes of China's modernization and globalization in a seemingly casual and trivialized detail.

Figure 10.1 *Shower*. Father reveals the community's spiritual ties to the old bathhouse to his son on the roof top of the bathhouse after a clear-up from torrential rain.

With the tearing down of the old facilities in Beijing, the local people suffer from the loss of memories, communal customs, and genuine interpersonal connections. The harmony of the traditional bathhouse of *Shower* has been destroyed, and replaced by multilayered displacement on the level of culture, as well as individual psychology and temporality. As Sheldon H. Lu has insightfully pointed out, "*Chai* (demolition) is the very theme of much contemporary Chinese visual art. It points not only to the physical demolition of the old cityscape, but more profoundly to the symbolic and psychological destruction of the social fabric of families and neighborhoods."[12] What comes with the demolition of old architecture is a rationale rooted in developmentalism, the remoteness and coldness of which is hinted at in the scene in which Er Ming is tackled by three hospital attendants when Da Ming attempts to send him to the mental hospital after Master Liu's death. Though institutionalization and modernization can be degrading and impersonal, the fact that everybody in the neighborhood, no matter how reluctant, agrees to move shows that economic development is irreversible.

Lefebvre maintains that:

> Today everything that derives from history and from historical time must undergo a test. Neither "culture" nor the "consciousness" of peoples, groups or even individuals can escape the loss of identity

> that is now added to all other besetting terms ... Ideas, representations
> or values which do not succeed in making a mark on space, and thus
> generating (or producing) an appropriate morphology, will lose
> all pith and become mere signs, resolve themselves into abstract
> descriptions, or mutate into fantasies.[13]

Unfortunately, *Shower* is a "fantasy" that "offers a nostalgic look at a bygone way of life."[14] Because some of the local cultures and customs of Beijing displayed in the film had virtually disappeared by the time the film was made, some have criticized Zhang Yang for showcasing an "imaginary" local culture to appeal to the Western gaze. This criticism of Zhang's self-Orientalism is valid to a certain extent, as the globalized Western countries do eagerly seek heterogeneity and diversity to counterbalance their keenly felt homogenization.[15] Nevertheless, Zhang argued that he wanted to arouse the audience's awareness of and concern for the cultural loss associated with China's economic progress. He insists that he made the film not for film festivals, but for the Chinese, with attention to the relationships and feelings close to Chinese people's lives.[16] Numerous viewers' responses online testify that the film's international appeal rests in its subtle and nostalgic treatment of interpersonal relationships, not in its "exhibition" of indigenous cultures.

In other words, *Shower* successfully represents a social space, which, to use Lefebvre's words, qualifies as "'thing/not-thing." As Lefebvre claims, "Theory has shown that no space disappears completely, or is utterly abolished in the course of the process of social development — not even the natural place where that process began. 'Something' always survives or endures — 'something' that is not a *thing*."[17] Though the film is focused on disappearing (if not already gone), nuanced, and region-specific culture, it has been welcomed both domestically and internationally. Its extremely positive reception testifies that the represented conventional space on screen has not yet disappeared completely. Something not only survives the ruthless process of modernization but also comes back to haunt us. Despite the different orientations of Zhang Yang and those international-festival-minded Chinese filmmakers, they surprisingly reach the same target, which is reminiscent of what Sheldon H. Lu has pointed out: "The transformation of a new sensory economy in contemporary Chinese cultural production, through what some critics have termed the 'post-material' condition, is concomitant with the destruction of old spatial forms and the reconstruction of new cities."[18]

Stepping out of this marketized mindset of the argument on the film, we approach the complex relations among space, culture, and subject. Bathhouse (*zaotang*) and *hutong* (traditional alleyways) designate special spaces, different from private showers in individual homes and modern districts of apartment complexes. In bathhouses, one socializes in the nude with people whom one has usually known for decades. There is no modern equivalent of such spaces. Physical exposure, which belongs primarily to private or commercial spaces in the modern world, is naturally integrated into this semi-public space (bathhouse) where intimacy and formality are fused into an expected coziness. This space has an ambiguous color, and functions as a meeting place of the public and the private.

The buffering effect that these traditional spaces offer is different from those offered by such modern facilities and architectures as theme parks and shopping malls. The former is closely tied to people's everyday lives: people go to the bathhouses to clean, refresh, and entertain themselves; residents in *hutongs* smell and taste each others' meals and exchange help and favors. In contrast, the latter stands more separately from daily life: people take vacations and shop or "getaway" on weekends. The fake impression given by the internet of progressively more transparent relations between the public and the private (the publicizing of private spaces and privatizing of public spaces) can hardly penetrate the inertia and isolation of real spaces, and thus remains primarily in the imaginary virtual world. The demolition, reformation, and symbolization of these traditional spaces unavoidably change, reduce, and erase their subjects' practices within these spaces, and the residue of history and culture embedded in these spaces. The "fantastic" space represented in *Shower* thus presents a "third" space, which is differentiated and estranged from both the traditional space and the modern space, and projects a resistant space on screen to recollect the past while questioning and challenging the present and the future.

Analyzing a flashback sequence of trading grain for water in *Shower* which links the father with water, Lu keenly observes:

> The self-conscious evocation of *Yellow Earth* wraps up and inverts fifteen years of New Chinese Cinema (1984–1999), not by dismissing the Chinese father as a backward figure in the nation's quest for modernity but rather by returning to him as the root of harmony and life much needed in the time of mindless commercialization and globalization.[19]

If the Fifth Generation films have been preoccupied by vast rural areas and obsessed by a rebellious desire to overthrow the patriarchic figure of the "father" as a representation of "historical and cultural reflection" (*lishi fansi, wenhua fansi*) in the 1980s, then contemporary urban films refocus on the city, a fixed center which is surrounded by and privileged over peripheral areas, and which constitutes a hub in the global network. The "father" figure, present in or absent from contemporary urban cinema, has been inscribed with new meanings and intimately linked to space. In *Shower*, the father is closely associated with the bathhouse, which symbolizes the essence of China's traditional culture, and the father's death coincides with the demolition of the place. In the other three films, the patriarchic power has been disseminated in the urban space, which exercises omnipotent powers over its inhabitants.

Beijing Bicycle: Sacrificed Youth in the Heat of Concrete Buildings

The same juxtaposition of traditional and modern architecture also appears in Wang Xiaoshuai's *Beijing Bicycle*. Though this film depicts a confusing cityscape, the marks of modernity and commercialization are evident and aggressive. *Hutong*, as a form of space, becomes the embodiment of certain feelings. It marks out a private sphere, be it that of an individual, a family, or a neighborhood, confronting the outside — the Other: the modern and the unfamiliar.

Beijing Bicycle unfolds with the juxtaposition and intertwining of the lives of two teenage protagonists, Gui and Jian. Despite their obvious differences in class, fate, and background, both of them live in back alleys (Gui lives with his countryman, and Jian lives with his reassembled family) and their fates are linked by a bicycle, the once indispensable mode of transportation in Beijing, now a luxury boundary-setting symbol for urban youth. For most Beijing residents, owning a car has become a symbol of success. The busy modern street scene delivered in dazzling light with fast tempo is represented in the film as an alien "Other" to both Gui and Jian, whose lives are rooted in *hutong*s and entangled with a bicycle.

For Jian, a Beijing teenager, the fast-changing landscape and the prosperity of the city have nothing to do with him. Though this city is his birthplace, he is estranged, if not excluded, from its development and construction, physically and spiritually. He frequents deserted construction sites where he practices his bicycle skills with his friends and glimpses the busy swelling city from afar. He has no personal space at home either, where he shares a tiny room with his stepsister whom his father favors. He seeks refuge in courtyards and on rooftops. Scrutinizing the ambiguous relations between the conventional and yet still dominant rhetoric of improving one's *suzhi* (quality) through education and the inevitable early commodity envy caused by surging consumerism in contemporary China, Gary Xu points out in his analysis of this film that, "Early commodity envy is normally integrated in the image of improved and desirable *suzhi* when the commodity assumes transnational symbolic power, which, together with China's traditional valuation of education, disguises the fact that the body of the urban single child is as much an object of exploitation as that of the migrant laborer."[20]

The tyrannical, exploitative power of urban space exerts its power more cruelly on Gui, a migrant from the countryside, who is exposed to a living space that is completely different from that of his ancestors. His longing for the city is mixed and complicated by the desperation caused by discrimination, exploitation, and sometimes abuse of migrants. There are many scenes in the film in which we observe the urbanite treating Gui as a disposable being. The secretary at the Feida company where Gui works always talks to him in demanding tones and forces him to work one extra day beyond the limit of the agreed contract to obtain the bike. The hotel front-desk attendant would even detain Gui because of a misunderstanding for which she is partially responsible. Gui's innocence and stubbornness are juxtaposed against the caustic indifference and violence of the city. The silent trauma is stunningly depicted in the final scene in which the heavily bruised Gui swaggers through the crowded streets shouldering his damaged and yet finally owned bicycle (Figure 10.2). Urban space, once again, plays the role of the patriarchic power, dehumanizing people.

Figure 10.2 *Beijing Bicycle*. The wounded but defiant Gui carries his damaged bike on his shoulder walking against the dehumanizing urban space at the end of the film.

For Gui, the fantastic city scenes can only be glimpsed from far away as an invisible person. There are several voyeuristic scenes in which Gui and his countryman peep at a woman (played by Zhou Xun) who constantly changes her clothes and poses before the mirror in a big apartment. They later discover that this woman is only a maid in the household and comes from the countryside. This discovery informs the two men that the modern erotic urban body they gaze upon is actually a fake one. This, as Gary Xu has pointed out, reveals "the pure arbitrariness" of such an urban-rural divide, which is based on status symbols such as clothing.[21] The irony also, in many aspects, echoes the central theme in the film: the fakeness of the city's superficial prosperity and the oppressive nature of the new mode of production, which is embodied by the imported Fordism operating as the guiding principle for the express company for which Gui works.

In *Beijing Bicycle*, we see modernity exerting its power on an economic level. The government-sponsored developmentalism has generated a process of commercialization of space which seems to exert, on the one hand, an integrating power, motivating people to work and giving people hope, and on the other, an excluding, if not expelling, effect, trashing and destroying people's dreams and values. Dictated by economic forces, "place" is gradually stripped of its cultural and historical significances and becomes a monster with its own subjectivity. People who inhabit the space become marginalized and objectified by the "reformed" urban space.

The World: A Tale of the "Forbidden" Global Village

Set against the backdrop of globalization and China's commercialization, Jia Zhangke's *The World* meditates on the ironic and superficial relations among space, subject, culture, and identity. The word "place" in *The World* is devoid of its physical meaning. Place is no longer attached to any specific piece of soil, but assumes a more abstract, symbolic, and virtual significance. This significance heads toward a spectacular global sphere at the expense of specific historical or cultural depth. This tendency comes with China's shift from an agricultural economy to industry and information technology. The significance of place rests on its position as a nexus in a global network. The sense of substantiality associated with the word has been trivialized, and "place" has been supplanted by the multi-dimensional word "space," which can somehow penetrate the limits of place and time and create a space with more independence. "Real place" (the physical existence of location) has been turned into a stage (to represent) and a storage (to contain), both of which functions are captured by such a structure as the shopping mall, a representation of artificial culture and a container of conditioned subjects. This phenomenon exemplifies the irony that Arif Dirlik observes: "The very effort to manipulate places in the marketing of commodities and images is responsible also for the renewed awareness of places."[22] This irony has been captured and illustrated by Jia Zhangke's *The World*.

"The World" is actually the name of a theme park in Beijing, which exhibits scale replicas of landmarks from around the globe. "The World" is also a container of migrant laborers newly arrived from the interior to serve in the park. The Beijing marked by the World Park and populated by rural laborers obviously has nothing to do with the old Beijing, which housed characters such as those in Lao She's *Teahouse* (*Cha guan*) or *Camel Xiangzi* (*Luotuo Xiangzi*). The protagonists in the film, Zhao Tao and her boyfriend Taisheng, like many other characters, are not born in Beijing but come from Shanxi to seek opportunities. In their daily practices, they reshape and are reshaped by the space. As subjects, they experience a double displacement in the park: they move from the countryside to Beijing where they are surrounded, not by an urban Chinese culture, but by a fake and inaccessible global micro-environment.

The discrepancy between space and subject is evident in the beginning sequence of the film in which the camera follows the fully costumed Zhao Tao wandering in the showgirls' shabby and crowded dormitory and dressing room. The scene cuts directly to a glamorous show performed by these girls and then suddenly back to their quiet underground living space. The contrast of places reveals the temporal and commoditized nature of the subjects' presence. It also represents a collision of diverse dimensions of time: the migrant actor's psychological time, which is very much attuned to the temporal dimension in which he/she grew up; the time performed on stage — the representation of a historical spectacle of Mongolian culture following the latest Vegas-style act; and the stagnant real life time of these actors backstage.

These dimensions of time contradict and negotiate with each other. The psychological time of the subjects belongs to the past, which is conveyed by the lingering camera with a subdued sense of nostalgia. This past dimension is preserved by memory, manifested by habit, and challenged by the present. The present real live time is full of bleak darkness, which is meant to be endured temporarily, and which serves as a jumping board to the future. The only glamorous time is the fake time on stage. Regardless of the virtual nature of this staged time, it seems to be the only possible means of assisting the migrants to reach their dreams. The subjects in the film thus live in a gap of various temporal dimensions, neither in the past, the present, nor the future. It is a time in its own, constantly transforming process, which though thick with references to a vague future, belongs to no specific time zone.

This makes one think of David Harvey's contention that "progress entails the conquest of space, the tearing down of all spatial barriers and the ultimate 'annihilation of space through time.' The reduction of space to a contingent category is implied in the notion of progress itself."[23] It is a "progress of becoming, rather than being in space and place."[24] It is in this gap of multi-layered annihilation of space and time that the modern subjects are imprisoned. The spectacular cityscape of Beijing can be interpreted as a produced, commercialized space (using Henri Lefebvre's term[25]) intended to disguise the government-promoted reproduction of the capitalist mode of production and to seduce people into the unshakable circle of commodity, consumption, and production.

The opening sequence is followed by another silent scene, in which the Eiffel Towel and other world-famous landmarks are clearly identifiable in the background. A hunchbacked Chinese beggar walks slowly into the screen from the left, shouldering a heavy parcel. This old man walks to the middle of the screen, stops, and then turns to face the camera. Although completely in shadow, the face, one can sense, is a haggard one, marked by age, bitterness, and struggle (Figure 10.3). The "authentic" old Chinese man in the foreground contrasts sharply with the "imported" landmarks of the world in the background. Both the old Chinese man and the landmarks, regardless of their fakeness, are in Beijing, a city that seems to be neither the old man's birthplace, nor the original site of the landmarks. The sense of displacement of both subject and object is thus silently conveyed in this scene with its subtle irony and strong visual contrast. World Park unmistakably expresses China's wish to go global by globalizing and monumentalizing its local space even if it is accompanied by cultural and humanistic loss. As Sheldon H. Lu points out, "World Park is a monument to China's imaginary integration into the world at large, but the characters from Shanxi province are not part of this brave new world. They are vagrant people at the margins of China's modernization."[26]

Figure 10.3 *The World*. The ironical juxtaposition of China's artificial global space and its displaced authentic subalterns.

Xiaotao and Taisheng come to Beijing to pursue a dream. Though the capital city exposes them to many fresh facets of life, most of which are under the glamour of commodification, the two are actually on their way to self-destruction. Taisheng, as a park policeman, becomes involved in illegal activities, and then has an affair with a married woman who is waiting in Beijing to rejoin her husband overseas. Xiaotao eventually learns of the affair. Until this point Xiaotao has withstood the adverse effects of Beijing and the World Park, but now, disillusioned by her boyfriend's disloyalty, she kills herself and Taisheng with leaked gas, or so it appears in the ambiguous ending of the film.[27]

Urban phenomena such as adultery, work-related injuries and deaths, migrant laborers, petty gangsters, small-scale merchants, prostitutes, and showgirls all find their representations in the film. The dramatic turns of modern urban life upset the peacefulness and security the Chinese conventionally seek. Everyday life in contemporary Beijing is a drama on the concrete stage of the World Park, which stands as a miniature of the stage of the metropolis. Jia Zhangke shows us that the glorious high-rises of Beijing have been built at tremendous human and cultural cost. On the diverse stages presented in *The World*, though there are constant signs of the lack of governmental guidance and regulation, life's tragedies are, in general, downplayed and released in a subdued tragic tone. This kind of treatment also characterizes Jia Zhangke's other films, such as *Platform* (*Zhantai*, 2000), *Xiao Wu* (*Xiao Wu*, 1997), and *Unknown Pleasures* (*Ren Xiaoyao*, 2002). Nevertheless, the naturalistic acting and the subtle juxtapositions of the spectacular stage performances in the World Park with the bitterness of life in Beijing, intensify the silent suffering and invisible pain endured by Chinese people under China's modernization. Lu points out that "the miniature virtual world entraps its workers and is a mockery of globalization."[28] The film also represents a gendered space, subordinating female figures to the aggressive and masculine commercialization, globalization, and memorialization of space and reducing them to spectacles on the "global" stage, and to illegal sex workers. This sexualized and gendered space serves as a contrast to the previously degendered or gender-neutral Mao period, which is characterized very well by Mao Zedong's favorite proverb, "Women hold up half the sky."[29]

To summarize, in *The World* the migrants are displaced people. The relationship between people and place in the film is temporal, opportunistic, commercial, and staged. On the one hand, they are "global" beings living in "globalized surroundings"; on the other hand, they are trapped in this fake, unreal "prison" of the World Park. If we see a globalization of local specificities in *The Shower*, then in this film, we see a localization of the global where the significance of the local has been emptied out. The transaction between local and global conducted in *The Shower* is primarily on a cultural level (an imaginary visual space for the disappearing local culture and history), although economic development overpowers cultural needs at the end. In *The World*, we witness a more "mature" fusion of culture and economy, adopting Fredric Jameson's famous declaration, "the becoming cultural of the economic, and the becoming economic of the culture."[30] One notable point is that the "culture" that goes through the global economic filter, or that has been generated by that filter, is not the kind of "culture" that bears unique and irreplaceable tempo-geographic marks, but a commercialized culture. The immense reduplication capability of this kind of culture deprives its own dimension of temporality. Thereby in the theme park The World, a presumably cultural space, the transaction between the local and the global is conducted ironically on a practical or economic level with only a pseudo-global viewpoint and an ironic mimicry of misplaced minority shows which lack any specific cultural and historical depth or sincerity.

Cell Phone: The Intimate Foe of the Modern Being

Moving from *The Shower* to *Beijing Bicycle* and then to *The World*, we see that globalization and modernization have transformed space and subjects, and trivialized the significance of place. In Feng Xiaogang's *Cell Phone*, we continue to observe how the concepts of space and subject have been mobilized and redefined, and how the significance of location is trivialized by modern technology. Feng Xiaogang, the most popular commercial film director in China, is known for his series of highly acclaimed "New Year Celebration Movies." *Cell Phone* is extremely popular in China. At first sight, it seems to be a film about adultery. The underlying contrast between the traditional and the modern is, to a large degree, glossed over by the actors' hilarious acting. Nevertheless, we can trace the contrasts between the countryside and the fashionable modern places (such as luxurious hotels, or the protagonist's stylish home and office), between the literally unwired village and the wireless-phone-dominated city, and between the conventional community built on trust and mutual support and the modern casual relationships underlined by exchange value and deceit.

In *Cell Phone*, the complex relationships between men and women unfold in connection with cell phones. Arjun Appadurai points out that "electronic media give a new twist to the environment within which the modern and the global often appear as flip sides of the same coin. Always carrying the sense of distance between viewer and event, these media nevertheless compel the transformation of everyday discourse."[31] The cell phone, the most popular communication tool in contemporary urban China, transcends spatial constraints, mediates between the private and the public, and sparks numerous stories between men and women. It can both hide and reveal the protagonist's identity, and has become a symbol of the commercialization of interpersonal relations.

In the film, Yan Shouyi, the male protagonist, though not handsome, is very popular as he is at the zenith of his career. He has the power to recommend people for TV programs, and the money to own a car and a luxurious apartment — a living standard that can only be enjoyed by members of the upper class. In other words, he is a very successful migrant in Beijing. In contrast to the name of his TV talk show, *Youyi Shuoyi* (*Speak your mind*), Yan is deceitful in real life. He manipulates his cell phone to conceal his affairs: he takes out the batteries from his phone to make certain he "cannot be reached," using excuses like being in a meeting to cover his dates with other women; he often speaks as if the connection is bad and he is unable to hear the callers' voices; he changes his cell phone's mode to vibrate when he does not want to pick up his lover's call in the presence of his wife. All these scenes are delivered in such a humorous yet realistic tone that no audience can miss the underlying sarcasm.

Yan's splendid performance, nevertheless, demonstrates his subordination to his phone. No matter where he is, his lover can always intrude through his cell phone. His cell phone helps him hide his identity, but it is also ready to reveal his secrets at any time. He has only temporary power over his cell phone, while his cell phone always relays his lies back to him and, in the end, punishes him.

A remarkable example of the power struggle between Yan and his cell phone takes place when Yan, Shen Xue (Yan's wife), and Fei Mo (Yan's colleague) are getting their feet massaged. In this scene, Hu Yue (Yan's lover) calls. First, she sends Yan a text message informing him that she is in the same hotel room in the city of Qingdao where they once stayed together, and scolds him for lying to her. Upon receiving this, Yan deletes the message, switches the phone to vibrate mode, and then, after glancing at Shen Xue who is watching from a distance, declares that the next day has a fifty percent chance of rain. Shen Xue, who is obviously less complex than Yan, accepts this explanation (in China, one receives the weather forecast daily from one's cell phone or pager), and asks whether she should bring an umbrella. Fei Mo, who knows all Yan's secrets, answers yes, since nobody knows when it will rain. This answer alludes to the likelihood that Yan's relationship with Shen Xue will sooner or later be affected by Yan's affair with Hu Yue. Having barely escaped suspicion, Yan is reminded by the massage girl that his cell phone is vibrating. Yan pretends that he has just noticed, picks up the phone, and then cuts off the line, saying the caller had hung up. Shen Xue naively asks Yan to call the person back, but Yan replies that the number is unfamiliar, and might belong to one of the journalists he is avoiding.

This scene cuts to a night at Yan's home. Yan is looking for the newspaper to take to the bathroom, and finds Shen Xue cleaning his razor on it. Shen picks up the page that Yan is interested in, carefully cleaning it before handing it to him. Praising her for being considerate and family-oriented like his first wife, Yan takes the paper and goes into the bathroom, where he places the paper on the toilet cover, sits down, and calls Hu Yue. He covers his mouth when he whispers to Hu that he had been in meetings all day long and had no time to call her back. Just at this moment, Shen Xue breaks into the bathroom with one of her fingers bleeding. Shen searches the shelves for some bandages, and catches Yan sitting on the top of the toilet with a dumbfounded countenance in the mirror's reflection. "What are you doing there?" she asks.

Yan is startled and stands up. The camera pans Yan from head to foot. Just beside his feet lays his cell phone. "I'm using the toilet." He stumbles, and then, calculatingly turns back to flush the toilet. Yan's witty performance fails to cover his odd behavior. Back in the sitting room, Yan pretends to admit that he made a call to his ex-wife's brother and states that his precaution had been intended to protect Shen. He does not want Shen to mistake his care for his son and first wife as an attempt to rekindle their relationship. Shen says, "I still feel you are not absolutely loyal to me. I don't want to be a fool. I can live well without you. Write me a self-criticism."

From these scenes, we see how Yan manipulates his cell phone to hide his affair with Hu Yue, and how his cell phone puts him in embarrassing situations. He is eventually deserted by both his women and society, when Hu blackmails him with cell phone footage of their affair and replaces him in his job. In the final scene, he refuses to own a cell phone and is actually terrified by the newest model, which has GPS tracking on it. This final scene, strongly ironic, reveals Yan sitting alone in a shabby apartment in a skyscraper in Beijing, holding a global positioning cell phone in hand, and screaming out loud in horror. This reminds its viewers of the Foucauldian all-encompassing, prison-like surveillance system in modern society. What is absent from the film is the silent suffering of Yan's two ex-wives. As Yan still has an apartment in the global city Beijing, Yan's first wife leaves the city to live with their son elsewhere, and we are never told of the whereabouts of Yan's second wife. Modern city space, characterized by commercialization, globalization, and monumentalization, becomes the powerful new father figure, exerting patriarchal powers over modern beings.

In *Cell Phone*, we see how modern technology deprives place of its significance and reconfigures interpersonal relationships. The products of modern communication technology unwittingly encourage subterfuge and adultery. The virtual space that electronic media creates provides opportunities but also virtualizes and destabilizes conventional familial structures and interpersonal networks. Family, the fundamental unit of social relationships, is a place where one detects the deep roots of traditional Chinese culture and values. It is the site of possible resistance to the homogenizing forces of globalization and modernization. When this locale of groundedness and integrity is shaken, commercialized, and dismantled, subjects are thrown into the outer world, the abstract and commercialized spaces dominated by political, ideological, and capitalist discourses. This will confine the subjects to the market as laborers and consumers, and reduce their individual subjectivities to affiliations to commodities and signs. They will be possessed by secondary manifestations through commodities and services, only capable of temporary genuine emotional release over the Internet. As the modern cityscape comes to be populated by this kind of "shadow subjectivity" — bodies incapable of appropriating dominated spaces (in the real world), and subjectivities without bodies (in the virtual world) — this modern cityscape could be considered a spectral one.

Conclusion

Despite the diversity and plurality in their content and cinematic style, the four films discussed here are all representations of China's urban space in the context of commercialization, urbanization, and globalization. We see how modernization has transformed conventional notions of space and time, moving people from rural places to cities, and reshaping interpersonal relations. The urban space depicted in these films has very complicated characteristics. On the one hand, the space has been "modernized" and decorated with unmistakably modern architectural features and remarkable monuments. On the other hand, the space has shown its monstrous nature by erasing traditional cultures and reconfiguring human relations. Ironically, with the process of China's urbanization, its urban space, as we see in all four of the most popular and influential contemporary Chinese films, becomes virtual and homogeneous. The structures and objects bearing unique historical and cultural legacies (such as in *hutong*) are disappearing. Those that are remaining or newly constructed are commercialized and chiefly serve economic ends. Traditional substantive interpersonal connections, especially family relationships, are trivialized, traumatized, and commercialized. Modern beings are overwhelmed by a sense of nostalgia and are isolated and objectified by modernity and electronic media. To make the point, urban space as represented in the four films exerts tyrannical powers, determining people's way of life, alienating people from their pasts, and reorienting interpersonal relationships. Those who live in the urban space have to cope with the shifting environment, internalizing and appropriating its futuristic demands with no other choice. These films reflect and criticize the aftermaths of change in urban space and offer alternatives to the grand narrative of the government.

Frederic Jameson has explored the dialectical relations between standardization and differentiation, the two ends of the spectrum of globalization's effects. Globalization, especially global capitalism, has caused local economies to flourish, enabling subjects by exposing them to wider sources of information, and liberating local specificities on a global stage; at the same time, globalization has diminished the specialty of locality, reducing everything to its economic value. The cityscapes represented in the four films are, to a large extent, the result of these dynamic and interlocking effects. The metamorphoses of China's cities are above all governmental decisions made in the context of globalization. To remold China's production mode, spaces are redesigned and reformed first in SEZs and then on a national scale. Economic success and global connection are unfortunately not the only results caused by spatial changes. As we see in the films, in a global economy traditional customs and values become increasingly ghostlike, haunting and revisiting those people who still possess cultural heritage and historical consciousness, and leaving the majority disconnected from the past and tradition.

Depicting conflict between past and present, old and new, local and global, real and imaginary, these filmmakers ask their audiences a question: Do we have to forget who we are and where we come from in order to embrace economic prosperity? A clear message from these films is that we are found by global capitalism (not the other way around) and we are lost in it. The cost is devastating. It results not only in a spiritual void and loss of identity, but also a loss of the soul (as corruption, crime, and prostitution have become serious problems in contemporary China). Certain contemporary Chinese filmmakers have traced the root of the problem and proposed a different space — the assaulted, disappearing, shadowy, and always "in-between" space — in their films to spur contemplation and awareness. Brian Jarvis states that: "Marginalized spaces are always implied and central to any map's significance, they are a clue to the ideology through which space is seen and felt."[32] Although the cityscape represented on screen is fraught with trauma and displacement, and haunted by ghosts of both the past and the future, it has managed to represent a different, resistant space. The marginalized cultural and individual landscapes are captured and empowered on screen by contemporary filmmakers to analyze, contemplate, parody, and subvert the overwhelming utilitarian economic landscape.

Part IV.

Bioethics, Non-Anthropocentrism, and Green Sovereignty

11

In the Face of Developmental Ruins:
Place Attachment and Its Ethical Claims

Xinmin Liu

That land is a community is the basic concept of ecology, but that
land is to be loved and respected is an extension of ethics.
— Aldo Leopold, 1948

Places are "centers of felt values."
— Yi-fu Tuan, 1977

Like ecocriticism, ecocinema asserts its ethical claim. Yet how it does so in the
context of China's environmentalism remains intriguing and disputable. Facing the
sound and fury of China's urbanizing and market-driven economic boom, whatever
sociological and cultural roles ecocinema can play must at once help China press
on with progress and steer away from pitfalls. Should Chinese cinema, for instance,
continue to make films of idyllic simplicity of rural China or ethnic diversity and
exotica of the frontiers in the vein of memory retreats or imagined nostalgia? There
has been, admittedly, abundant footage of these in recent Chinese films, which are
apt to serve as redemptive or therapeutic foils in the "drama" of coastal commercial
outbursts and urban madness. Inevitably, I believe, the dilemma boils down to how
Chinese cinema confronts and critiques the law of modern development as it was first
construed and applied during the Western Enlightenment. By the same token, any
critique launched by Chinese ecocinema should aim at the particular and indigenous
context of China's modern development rather than being the mirror image of Euro-
American ecocriticism. Awareness of China's singular needs is derived not as much
from China's contingent need for development (which does not necessarily justify
her environmental negligence) as from the inherent bent of Western ecocriticism that
has evolved over a fundamental divide of nature versus culture, settlement versus
outback, and philanthropic conservation versus environmental justice.[1]

At the heart of American ecocriticism lies the issue of Nature (i.e. the wilderness
of the American West in colonial times) and the century-long debate among

American intellectuals as to whether one can adopt an ecocentric or anthropocentric approach to it. In disputing humans' conquest and control over nature as the root cause of today's environmental crisis, they remain divided, even to this day, as to whether wilderness is the absolute pristine Other or whether nature should be regarded as a "product" of human construction. Those holding the "preservationist" view deem wildness totally primordial, utterly independent of and ultimately unknowable to humans; it follows, they demand, that the greatest efforts be made to keep this wilderness out of human reach in order to prevent further corrosion or degradation caused by human greed. Opposing such a view is the "anthropocentric" school, whose penchant to put human lives above nonhuman forms has led them to chastise the legacy of the American wilderness as "the creation of very particular human cultures at very particular moments in human history."[2] While detecting the "fingerprints" of human intervention in the wilderness, they do not hesitate to expose the forgotten underside of this bucolic paradise: how its pristine landscape was once drenched in the blood of the slaughtered Native Indian tribes. Nor are they lenient towards the preservationists' obsessive nostalgia of remote lands and distant times, which, as they indict, is what makes nature lovers oblivious of the follies and injustices inflicted upon the urban poor right in their midst and the underprivileged elsewhere on the planet. Instead of giving philanthropic preservation to nature condescendingly, they try to be proactive in redressing social injustices and wrongs as well as in preventing the wilderness from being disfigured and animal species from being endangered. By way of stressing human "nature" being an inalienable part of Nature, they argue that it is precisely our empowered position that prompts humanity to acknowledge the wilderness and the nonhuman world as vulnerable objects of human-led endeavors, and for that very reason we ought to take moral responsibility for how we act upon them.

More and more have since realized that human alienation from nature is bound to occur when humans fail to detect the drawbacks of going to the extreme in both schools of thought; and it is to be noted that they have been attracted to the potential of mediating positions in the middle ground. But none have been as resourceful, embracive, and potentially effective as those that attempt to blend human survival with ecological well-being; one of these is the ethics of "place attachment" evolved from the phenomenological notion of *dwelling* which hearkens back to the ancient Chinese idea of *ren di qin he* (affinity between humans and the land) despite the different theoretical embryos out of which they each grew.[3] What makes this blending possible is the time-honored infusion of social relationships, communal values, and ceremonial rites grown in a natural setting. From the outset, the Chinese idea of an *Umwelt* valorized an ethical orientation that could avert the typical dilemma in modern Western ecological thinking; it was able to integrate areas of major philosophical differences in relation to the issue of "alienation from nature."

With her splendid land-tied antiquity and unfathomed ecological wisdom, it comes as no surprise that China's age-old agrarian civilization remains rooted to land-based habitats to date. They have lived in proximity with primal elements and tailored human rituals and life-sustaining skills in close affinity with ecological wellness; all this has retained such an ever-renewing hold on their cultural memory, e.g. how local communities would till the land, stay in tune with the ecosystem, revere their ancestral rituals, and endure social-environmental changes generation after generation. Being able to experience these socially oriented facts of existence was thus crucial in nurturing a sense of belongingness to a nascent habitat. Unmistakably, sociality laid the ground for this belongingness. The Chinese idea of a built human habitat would favor an intermingling of both so as to avoid partial and mistaken perception of nature versus human. And indeed, recognizing the belongingness of humanity to their living habitats offers a way out of the ontological deadlock Western critical theories are facing: it can tease out and negotiate the tension between humanity's being rooted to primal nature and nature being but human "constructedness" in the hope of resisting alienation. A humanist geographer like Yi-fu Tuan does precisely that.

"Belongingness" as Place Attachment

Known for his socio-psychological studies of geography, Yi-fu Tuan was among the first to adopt the term "belongingness." He has led the way in exploring and affirming what constitutes *sociality* in the context of building human habitats. Over the years he and other humanist geographers have pushed for the values of "place" in order to restore a house or a locale to its enmeshed "calculus of force-relationships."[4] Taking the cue from Western phenomenology, they have joined hands with humanity scholars in studying and conserving the *builtness* of human habitats. They have ardently advocated a "lived reciprocity" based on the dialectic between human experience and the lived ecological habitats. Drawing on Heidegger's idea of "dwelling," their critique has aimed at recovering the *oneness* of natural environs with human relationships that has been eroded and depleted by the intrusive effects of modern, capitalistic modes of existence. Their stress on a synthetic eco-community, an environmental palimpsest, if you will, helps them detect how places "are constructed in [our] memories and affections through repeated encounters and complex associations."[5] It is also their belief that the local inhabitants actively interact with the surrounding landscape to nurture and shape each other into a living totality, but Tuan's embedding of the cognitive human in the experiential world takes it beyond meditation on phenomenology into the realms of the human affect and literary imagination.

How did Tuan evolve and formulate such a position on the relational and dialogic perception of the human habitat? And what are the ways through which he affirms the point that there is "an intrinsic connectedness of spatial and social relationships?"[6] Returning to Tuan's term "belongingness," we find it handy to explore its meaning in his *Topophilia*, a book whose central theme spells out the interrelatedness between the *artifactual*, i.e. human architectural designs, and the *experiential*, i.e. human functional awareness and environmental perception in daily living.[7] It is precisely the human affective response, Tuan argues, that serves to trigger, drive, and maintain a cohesive affinity amongst these, an emotive bond that is fostered through habituation, embedded in the human unconscious, and often straddled across nature and culture. Tuan further defines it in a mostly existentialist manner: "Culture, through habitude, easily becomes second nature — like the graceful gesture that feels natural, always there, rather than chosen or constructed."[8] While positing sensations and feelings as part of human experiential reality, he construes *emotion* as a voluntary act being elevated from perceived reality to conscious action, and points out that "[Y]earning, desire, and other emotional states do not merely color perception; they *are* a way of perceiving, and they are also incipient actions."[9] Tuan has thus creatively installed emotion in the realm of human perception and has also instilled in "place attachment" a sense of fluidity and palpability to ward off charges of being limited by sedentary and deterministic inclinations.

The art of cinema evokes vivid memories through images and captures infusing moods of a place and its inhabitants as they are depicted through rapid social changes. Yet it is often the case that such visual evocations are accused of being overly sentimental and nostalgic when juxtaposed against the onslaught of modern conditions. It is even more pressingly true with China's booming development: spurred on by a frenzied rhetoric, people are overwhelmingly convinced that they should and can phase out the outmoded land-strapped agrarian tradition in favor of a commercialized, tech-savvy, and urbanized lifestyle. Induced by a tradition-versus-modernity dichotomy, they are oriented by a linear and ascensional path of human "progress," avidly striding from the rural (poor and backward) to the urban (wealthy and powerful). The flipside of achieving such "progress" is regrettably the sacrifice to be made of rural China's agrarian heritage and the wanton depletion of its ecosystem. When motivated by such teleological thinking, it is no surprise that one would regard being attached to one's native places, especially in China's least developed rural, interior, and border areas, as frail, regressive, deterministic baggage of the bygone times.

A case in point is how the idea of place attachment once triggered a political storm over the ethical orientation of China's open-door reform in the 1980s. In the summer of 1988, a group of pro-reform young thinkers released *Deathsong of Yellow River (Heshang)*, a TV documentary of social commentary in which they nearly pronounced a death sentence end for the land-based Chinese agrarian culture (dubbed the "yellow civilization") and asserted the supremacy of the ocean-going Euro-American industrialization (dubbed the "blue civilization") in their attempt to support the reformist faction within the CCP.[10] Besides its sweeping and even distorting generalizations, *Heshang* also resorted to evoking feelings of shame, dejection, and ultimately self-loathing toward the rigid and meager ecological settings of northwest China. Image after image was paraded of the loess highlands where China's Yellow River runs its main course and once nurtured the ancient "Central Kingdom" in her infancy. It was nothing short of insinuating that being attached to such a harsh, lifeless, and burdensome land amounted to only indignity and disaster. For all their good intent to stimulate political reform and social progress, the pro-reform thinkers led themselves onto a misguided course of "place-abandonment" as a result of being dictated by the binary opposites of country versus city. Even as they waxed nostalgic about the splendid cultural legacy of ancient China, they forfeited a much-needed ethical obligation in the course of pushing for human progress.

Regrettably, we are still faced today with the same moral dilemma, caught between ecological well-being and the human desire for progress. So how does place attachment, as espoused by Tuan, help filmmakers redress a dichotomized construal of culture in conflict with nature? In what ways can they exercise human accountability to avert a deadlock between ecological concern and social progress? The ethicist Geoffrey Harpham says: "Ethics does not solve problems. It structures them."[11] Rephrasing Harpham, I take it to mean that ethical judgment is evoked, not to deliver us directly final, one-size-fits-all solutions, but to fundamentally "reorient" our ways of conceiving the correct stakes in moral guardianship. Tuan's insight offers precisely one such act of reorientation: what literary and filmic arts do best is to impregnate the *built* world with feelings that "reorient" them towards attentive and proactive causes, be they social, cultural, and ecological, in the interest of the localities. It follows that the ethical obligation of literature and film is to explore and reflect diverse attachments to "places," which helps bridge the rural/urban gap, diffuses the unilinear and irreversible teleology behind the idea of modern progress, and holds the more developed urban (where are seated wealth, power, and privileges) accountable for poverty, injustice, and lack of progress of rural China.

It is therefore relevant and necessary to explore a few compelling acts of "emotive impregnation" of local places in recent filmic dramas about the desertion of rural habitats in the light of Tuan's espousal of place attachment. These films have fleshed out social and cultural displacement centering on the depletion and dismantling of the country by the city in the context of China's rapid modernization. Let us focus on scenes taken from two films, i.e. *Lao Jing* (Old Well, 1987) directed by Wu Tianming and *Nuan* (Nuan, 2000) directed by Huo Jianqi, to observe how the nexus of interrelationships unfolds amid *built* habitats that are emotively stirring and ethically uplifting, and help us steer through social apathy and moral limbo.[12] These scenes lay the grounds for the displacement and alienation of rural inhabitants from their attachment to local dwellings, a harsh but inevitable outcome in the wake of aborted rural development and massive drain of rural labor to urban construction. Through subtle but potent drama set against stunning landscape, they engage us dialogically in an emotive infusion with the local and rural people so that we can begin to *see*, *feel*, and *intuit* about how the spontaneous, the improvised, and often still inscrutable details of their harsh, humble, and non-toxic life are valorized as part of the nexus of human relations and its analogous ecological balance. Films like these should help us affirm how human relational ties with land-based habitats should end up being our ultimate home to which are brought back the rudderless pursuits of human greed and ruin.

Sociality in *Old Well*

While the literature of the "Root-Seekers" of the mid-1980s has seen better days, Wu Tianming's *Lao Jing* (Old Well, 1987), adapted from Zheng Yi's novel of the same title, defies critical wear and tear, remains vibrant in its ecological insinuations, and resonates with resurging interests in the upkeep of human habitats. What keeps up its enduring appeal may well be open to dispute, but the issue, i.e. water resource or the lack of it, is essential to understanding the native villagers' sacrifice of love, material comfort, and even human lives in their effort to dig wells. In her discussion on the "social fantasy" of labor as is depicted in the film *Old Well*, Rey Chow writes: "The production of images is the production not of things, but of relations, not of one culture but of *values between cultures*. ..."[13] I concur that "value" should be obtained through "relations" rather than mere "things," but I will stress that visual representation of local environs must be executed in such a way as to illustrate how precisely values are reflected through *relations*, i.e., humans are infinitely bound to their ecological and geological habitats, be they in Asian or Western cultures. Consequently, as depicted in the film *Old Well*, when such relations are re-enacted, they enable us to simultaneously recognize values in physical settings and manual labor; for it is through manual labor that the local peasants forge emotive bonds with their habitats from ancestry down to offspring. This, I argue, goes to disprove Chow's comments on the value production of the villagers' well-digging because she fails to appreciate the significant ties between them and the land, plants, and objects comprising their native habitat. Much less should their well-digging be seen as a pretext to cancel out the vital status of manual labor even if that labor has long been deprecated as backward, corporeal, and mostly futile.

Is the labor of the Old Well villagers random and contingent? Can their well-digging be no better than a social fantasy? The answer is decidedly in the negative if we are aware of the perils of the rural-to-urban trajectory of modern industrial development and the ruinous outcome of rural degradation on behalf of urban expansion. It is indeed true that the film *Old Well* leaves much to be critiqued in terms of CCP ideological baggage; for instance, the eventual success in well-digging occurs in 1983, which offers a handy curtain call for the drama of culminating the peasants' bitter, prolonged futility in well-digging with a triumphant coda, thereby adding a not-so-subtle shiny feather to the CCP's hat of infallible leadership. Chow's critique of "nonpresence" of the woman and bareness of romantic love as aspects of the futility of "nation-building" punctures this ideological self-aggrandizing. Yet to stretch her criticism further beyond by way of discounting the peasants' labor actually reveals her oversight of Old Well Village as the linkage between land and human labor, between sociality, history, and ecological settings.[14] What she misses is not only the enduring reality of the Chinese agrarian mode of living, of which Old Well Village is an illustrative instance, but the complex nature of city-country alienation that can reveal blind spots in our sociological and cultural understanding of China's modernity.

One such instance is the lack of water, which has plagued this habitat for ages by dint of its location high on the Taihang Mountains in north China. Situated on a peculiar geological terrain known as "calcareous stone," the physical settings around the village are the least favorable for forming and keeping water resources underground; when compounded by little rainfall, the ecological conditions make it almost impossible to dig wells that can draw and store water for long. Without access to the basic hydro-geological knowledge, peasants were, for generations, totally unaware of the true cause of water shortage and were led to believe that they were fated for water scarcity in this life because of some offense they had committed against the "Dragon King" of the "East Sea." On the other hand, living with water scarcity did not deter their ancestors from settling here, nor did it scare away generations of offspring for lands with water. Honoring obligations to their forefathers' endeavors, they accepted such a habitat as the conditions of their existence and carried on their search for water with an unthinkable "can-do" spirit known only to those who have accepted their birthplaces as a pre-existing given. It was practical and even sensible on their part as there were hardly any other solutions. For us however, it is more than necessary to acknowledge the fact that years of wresting a meager livelihood out of the teeth of a harsh climate has garnered for the local peasants hardy skills and toughened experience for making a self-sufficient, though strenuous and spartan, living which honed the local peasants' emotive rapport with such a habitat. Amid this down-to-earth attachment there is an undeniable sense, cherished by the villagers, of feeling duty-bound and responsible for the land, the objects, animals, and eco-environs bearing and rearing them. So too is there an obligation to fulfill for the well-being of their families and communities at their ancestors' behest.

Such an emotive attachment rejects any domination of or alienation from their locales. And Wangquan, the protagonist of the film, is just the perfect personification of it. Having attended high school, he has returned to his native village to farm the land with his grandfather and father, both skilled diggers of wells in the prime of their lives. Due to the dire poverty in this all-male household (his mother passed away prematurely), he succumbs to his elders' wish to be married to Xifeng, a well-off widow, so that part of his dowry can pay for his younger brother's marriage. Wangquan loves Qiaoying, his high-school sweetheart, and is unwilling to end it, but he reluctantly agrees to the arranged matrimony in the end. A character with compelling fortitude and ambiguity, Wangquan feels obligated to meet his father's dying wish (he has just become the latest fatality in a well-digging accident), declines to elope with Qiaoying to the city, bears with the indignity of being married off like a bride and having to do the unpleasant household duties (such as emptying the urinal every morning) normally expected of such a male "bride." Accepting all these constraints and limitations on his own self, however, Wangquan never fails to perceive that he is a member of the Old Well Village and a part of the interdependent whole of the local habitat. Thus, when called upon to design and sink a new well for the village, he devotes all his knowledge, skills, and passion to it. While caught in a bloody feud with the neighboring village over the ownership of a dried well, he does not hesitate to put his life on the line, jumping into the well to prevent others from filling it up with debris, hence nearly getting himself killed. It goes beyond doubt that the stakes laid out by Wangquan in such a life-or-death situation are not about obeying the CCP's "narcissistic" drive for the nation, still less for a masculinist "value-writing" against a "foreign enemy."[15] He is keenly motivated by a different "value-writing" — one of being in tune with the *genius loci* of his environs. As Zheng Yi says, "[This] is the bond between men's feelings and their land, a bond forged in flesh and blood whose depth no words can ever fathom."[16] It is precisely on the ethical level that Wangquan is able to renew confidence and respect, restore water and vigor to the Old Well community and, through them, work together towards the well-being of their natural habitat.

In light of the country-city rift, Wangquan's selfless and heroic act in well-digging indeed assumes ethical urgency in the context of China's misguided urban industrialism. Ironically, Zheng Yi, *Old Well*'s scriptwriter, was interviewed on-camera by the authors of *Deathsong* who then included his comments as part of the *Deathsong* script. It was during his interview that Zheng made the above-mentioned remark.[17] How perplexing and deplorable it is that these writers completely misinterpreted Zheng's point and went on to pass a death sentence on the entire Yellow River habitat! Since what led them to their conclusion was, among other things, the violent confrontation of local villagers over the ownership of a dried well, let us review closely what transpires in that sequence of action.

The violent feud is triggered by the discovery of a stele, with the inscription of an Imperial Edict, buried at the bottom of the dried well (Figure 11.1). Wangquan and other youths from Old Well Village are excited about the discovery as it gives them hope of finding out what to do to make the well work again. When peasants from the neighboring village learn about it, they come rushing to the well apparently to claim that they are the well's sole owner. In actuality they come to destroy the inscription on the stele before filling it up with debris (they are obviously blessed with ample water resources in their habitat and see no value in a dried well). So the two villages stage a standoff and when the truth about the defaced stele is out, violence erupts. Cinematically, this sequence of shots is well known for its true-to-life action, emotion, and immediacy, with the camera's swift, jerky moving shots to show fists punched, hair grabbed, farm tools flying, and blood spewing. But the lifelike appeal lies not just in its fluid and striking pictorial quality, but more so in the details of the storyline.

Figure 11.1 Bloody feud over a dried well in *Old Well*.

Contrary to the facile impression of peasants being rugged, stubborn, and uncivilized in their "country" manners, the plot here offers amazing wittiness and subtle sarcasm: firstly, there is the self-mockery of the peasants over the miserable fate during the Cultural Revolution, of one of the twin-steles of the Imperial Edict, which had them removed from the pedestal in the *Guanyin miao* (Temple of the Goddess of Mercy) to be used as the cover for a homemade toilet. And an ironic twist of fate now frees it from its stinky bondage to be a crucial witness in the public spotlight! Secondly, right under the noses of the local CCP chiefs, the peasants receive a lesson in social justice from the so-called *feudal* past: all must now be judged by what Emperor Daoguang in the Qing Dynasty (1821–1850) had to say. And what he said — a joint ownership of this particular well — turns out to be a daringly sarcastic stab at the CCP's leadership and its agenda of urban modernization.

Thirdly, the infamous behavior of two local CCP chiefs at the scene (one leaves to avoid responsibility, while the other instigates the violent clash), is almost symbolic of what the CCP has done in the name of socialist modernization either by turning its back on the rural once it reached the more developed urban, or by directing a relentless demolition of the rural ecosystem for the sake of urban development.

In the light of the above, it would hardly be fair to consider the old dried well a jaded icon of a historical "lack" or "fundamental nothingness." To the contrary, it attests to the fact that the objects (the mountainous terrain, the digging tools, and human strife in blood and sweat) represent the constituted nature of complex social relationships among the humans themselves and between them and their habitat; such relationships entail intriguing webs of correlation between the land and its physical surroundings inherited or constructed; it also reveals the historical cycle of the city's perpetuated betrayal and abandonment of the country: how these were blatantly committed in the form of sacrifice of things rural, e.g. their land and water and other raw resources, cheap labor, sexual servitude, unfair taxation, demanded and ransacked by the insatiable urban development. By contrast, the city, now modernized and developed by virtue of rural backing, has never genuinely desired to return to the country the favor and share the outcome of their social advance. Alas, history has repeatedly witnessed that progress or development often turns into renewed pretexts for the city to subject the country to its ever-growing arrogance and abuse.

Nuan and Moral Redemption

In *Nuan*, the drama of urban betrayal and its ruinous desertion of the rural delve deeper than the externality of the physical environs. It focuses on the revival of place-bound human passion and love and its hard-earned redemption which is staged with the renowned Huizhou-style architecture as its backdrop. There is no lack or void to struggle with in terms of its physical terrain, but an unhealed wound lingers by gnawing at our souls with pain and torture owing to hauntingly persistent memory. The story concludes with a surprising ending in need of further ethical inquiry and judgment. Directed by Huo Jianqi in 2000, *Nuan* is adapted from Mo Yan's "The White Dog and the Swing," a novella originally set in a dry and hilly region in Shandong, northern China. Huo Jianqi's attempt to transplant the story in a location south of the Yangtze River is primarily challenged by topographical problems as a result of the vast geographical and climatic differences. A yet bigger test of authenticity is posed by the task of putting the characters (all strangers to this region) in the settings of a Huizhou-style house whose layout and interior would take years to grow accustomed to. Success in such a topographical makeover would depend critically on the directors' ability to perceive the builtness of the vernacular architecture typically located in a hot, humid, and water-logged region. Huo, short of reinventing the entire story, accurately grasps the pivotal conflict between rural renewal and urban development embodied in the original tale and astutely weaves a web of narrative strands that blend seamlessly with the Jiangnan (the Yangtze Delta) topography (Figure 11.2).

Figure 11.2 Huizhou-style houses in south Anhui, China.

Yi-fu Tuan always believes that traditional architecture as a whole shows more environmental awareness than the modern — a point well taken by the director of *Nuan*. At first glance, his film brilliantly captures the marvels of Huizhou architecture, which he thoroughly blends with the captivating drama of the main characters' experiences of love, separation, and reunion. The artifactual appeal of the house, compounded with its functional suitability, stands out during critical moments of conflict, compassion, and sacrifice. The signature skywell, for instance, is a convenient and economical source of lighting for the enclosed courtyard, and for fresh cooling air to circulate around all the rooms on upper and lower floors. Such architectural ingenuity is given its worth by the director through its role of being "the center stage," where characters appear to welcome a guest, prepare for a meal, diffuse a confrontation, or bid a farewell. The skywell also offers ample space for the water-storing pots and vats, which are kept under drainage guards and close to the cooking stoves, rendering the house economical and energy-saving to meet the household's daily needs of water, as well as performing light-duty refrigeration of vegetables and fruits. The naturally ventilated interior is also crucial to raising a traditional local cash crop, silkworms, as its unique design of the upper-level rooms lends itself to not only the circulating airflow inside the house, but to the successful day-to-day operation of raising silkworms. Thanks to this ingenious layout, the house interior becomes remarkably accessible and cohesive, so that the inhabitants often have a meal, take a nap, and resume their work (such as weaving nesting mats for silkworms) without having to straighten their backs and move around. It comes as no surprise that the host of the family habitually asks guests to lend a hand in errands while entertaining them with local tea.

All these features, gems of crystallized architectural wisdom, bear witness to Tuan's insight that "*built* environment clarifies social roles and relations." It is these architectural surroundings that define and refine one's sense of reality and identity. To that end, the story of *Nuan* presents what at first appears to be another run-of-the-mill love triangle, but ends up in mounting a social critique on the injurious impact of modern urbanization and the ethical breakdown because of it. Jinghe, Nuan, and the village duck farmer who is a mute, are a trio of friends growing up in this local village since childhood. Little do they know that a decade later they will find themselves on opposite sides of a widening social rift owing to China's frantic urbanization. The story begins with the return of Jinghe, who is now a government clerk working in Beijing after graduating from college there, to his native village in southeast China where he unexpectedly meets Nuan, his childhood sweetheart. Only at this moment does Jinghe learn that Nuan, who had been crippled after falling from playing on a swing, is married to the mute duck farmer and leads the life of a handicapped housewife. Immediately engulfed in nostalgia and guilt (since he had been partially responsible for Nuan's disastrous fall), Jinghe realizes that he has broken his own promise to return after college and marry Nuan — a vow he took in front of the villagers years ago. Guilty of dashing Nuan's dream of leaving the village for a better life in the cities, Jinghe decides to visit Nuan's home to wish her family well and rid his soul of the burden of guilt. Jinghe's actual stay in her house is brief, for about five to six hours, but "time" is infinitely prolonged in his emotive world in which he now is able to relive Nuan's adolescent dream of being recruited by a Peking Opera troupe in a big city, and his bittersweet love for her in spite of and perhaps thanks to her city-going fantasy. The film, at the hands of a director already noted for his excellent directing of the bucolic film *Na shan, na ren, na gou* (Postmen in the Mountains, 1999), which was a box-office hit in Japan, does a sensational job of weaving Jinghe's remembered past (usually amid the outdoor setting of lush, breathtaking scenery of brooks, local-styled footbridges, and sun-bathed rice paddies) and his present visit (mostly within the indoor space of the Huizhou house). With a visual perception fermented by the local milieu, Huo's appreciation of the uncanny *genius loci* enables him to fuse emotion and memory in such a seamless flow that the audience cannot but feel drawn to the cozy ambience of the house.

It is indeed a guilt-stricken moment that sparks off Jinghe's remembrance and compels him to face what he has hitherto managed to forget owing to his successful career in Beijing and his marriage with a Beijing girl. As Tuan reminds us, architectural environment *educates* human awareness. In a manner of speaking, his home visit is prompted by the noise, smell, and objects whose familiarity momentarily descends on him like an enshrouding and caressing mist. When coming face-to-face with Nuan, Jinghe is presently seized by a momentous sensation of regret and guiltiness, which compels him to admit that:

> … meeting someone like her has completely changed my view about the value of my life. Sorrow has gulped me down like an enshrouding mist. At a moment like this, I can't run away from it even if it would cost my life.[18]

Jinghe feels the uncontrollable pull of himself down a memory lane infused with the scenes and feelings of love he used to cherish for Nuan. Yet, simultaneously, he is also reminded by his city-bred sense of the "equal match" and "comparable spouse" in judging Nuan's marriage with the rough and illiterate mute. Herein lies precisely the moral dilemma for Jinghe. The more he learns about what happened to the crippled Nuan during his long absence, the deeper he sinks into a guilt-stricken remorse, and the stronger his wish grows to make amends to Nuan. In the meantime, try as he might when communicating with Nuan, he cannot quit applying his city-bred sensitivity to drive a good bargain on her behalf in exchange value on the marriage market. "Why didn't you find a better match to marry?" he insists on asking her. He presumes, wrongly, that by so doing he is doing Nuan a favor. So, while adamantly uncovering the reason why Nuan would lower herself to marry the mute who, besides his apparent deformity, used to "bother" her and other village girls with his wordless pranks, Jinghe intends but fails to bring peace and consolation to Nuan or diminished guilt to himself.

Jinghe's failure is just another instance illustrating the continued legacy of non-encounters between the elite intellectual revisiting his/her native land/village. We are instantly reminded of the myriad guises of the "I" in the literary writings of Lu Xun, Shen Congwen, Wu Zuxiang, Mo Yan, and Han Shaogong, whose self-questing journeys have invariably had to pass this non-encounter on the way to their intellectual rediscovery and renewal. What differs in Jinghe's case is the insistent and durable ambience of the Huizhou-styled house and its moisture-engulfed habitat — what he used to see, hear, and smell daily as part of his nature in boyhood: the damp air, flooded fields, moldy walls, pitter-patter of rain, and grunting wooden doors and stairs, everything that is drenched in moisture imperceptibly yet unfalteringly. If the mist-induced yearning thrusts him back to a trance-like recollection of his past, then water, as the chief ecological force, is the indisputable catalyst. The film is thus studded with water-related objects, scenes, and occurrences that serve to cue up his remembered past, which in turn reminds him of his estranged present. Likewise, water-bound routines and actions bring alive an interplay reconnecting him with his native habitat, thus regaining his lost sense of belongingness. Gradually but winningly, Nuan's thoughts and deeds are put in perspective before Jinghe, especially the kind of love that once, in the days of innocent youth, warmed their hearts, purified their character, and always kept them in tune with the local habitat.

Estranged from and disregarded by modern and urban development, whether under the Maoist revolution or the recent pragmatic reform era, the rural community has, as their ancestors always did, drawn on their ecological awareness to hone a distinctive sense of whom to love, how to love and, when needed, how to forego love. That intuitive sense of love seems to be generic with the water-induced ambience of the local habitat. Analogous to the region's balmy, engulfing, and permeating weather, romantic love is typically expressed in a warm, encompassing, and unselfish manner. Local youths put a human face on this love in that their passions traverse as well as transcend the whole range of possibilities in expressing romantic love. Earlier in the film, Nuan is charmed by a handsome Peking opera singer whose troupe performs on a tour through the village before returning to the big city. Nuan seems so totally consumed by her swelling passion for the city hunk that she neglects the feelings of Jinghe who has cherished an unassuming love for her since childhood. Jinghe, on the other hand, still attuned to the local customs, feels little in the way of jealousy or aversion towards Nuan; instead it pains him to see Nuan in distress and he quietly wishes the singer to be man enough to openly return her love. Like a caring older sibling, he is ready as ever to share Nuan's longing for the opera singer, and to offer her words of comfort and encouragement when Nuan receives no news from him, while remaining unabated in his love toward her in private. Imperceptibly, like the pervasive mist, Jinghe suffers his share of sorrow as a neglected lover and demands the return of his love for Nuan because he sees it as a testimony of the city-dweller's respect and trust for the country girl. The same act of love is rehearsed when Jinghe finally wins back Nuan before leaving for college. This time the role of the lover is played by the mute duck farmer. When Nuan is once again in distress, waiting anxiously for letters from Jinghe in Beijing, the mute gladly replaces Jinghe in the role of a caring sibling. He is the first to get mail from the mail carrier, rushes to deliver it to Nuan and awaits her reaction of joy as if he would be pleased to hear from him. Like Jinghe before him, he shares her sorrow, loneliness, and anxiety, which is his expression of his generous and altruistic passions for Nuan. Love, in this case, is no longer merely a romantic act between individuals; it verges on social and ethical responsibility that enhances communal solidarity, and reverberates with sentiments of historical justice and social fairness in the Chinese context.

Lastly, it is no accident that two of the film's main cast are handicapped. We could read it as a subtle mockery at what is left of the rural existence if we honestly consider what a weak entity rural China has been reduced to after the huge exodus of her youths, skilled laborers and agro-technicians who have been lured away by money-making opportunities in the city. However, while the city has continued to behave as if it were only logical and proper for the country to bear the cost and burden for "progress," rural China, personified through these two handicapped persons, has harbored no grudges or biases against the city's hypocrisy, arrogance, and lack of interest or concern in return. In her own way, for instance, Nuan displays a noble and selfless love by voluntarily forgoing her love for Jinghe and warmly accepts the mute's affections, eventually marrying him. Her willingness to sacrifice any future prospects of a city life in favor of life with the mute rests as much on romantic love as on ethical righteousness, for she has come to realize that, whereas the city has twice betrayed her, the love offered to her by the mute is what she can call home, and so she remains true till the last. As the plot thickens for a climatic relief in the film, we are just as much surprised by her bold act as we are moved and inspired by it. When the mute delivers Jinghe's first letter to her, she tears it to pieces without a look. After marrying the mute, when Jinghe mails her a pair of fashion shoes from Beijing, Nuan does not hesitate to repeat the act, throwing away the shoes to assure the mute that nothing can distract her from their conjugal happiness.

If giving up her city-going dream, forgiving the broken promises, and reattaching herself to the future of her native village are the signposts that mark Nuan's coming of age, the mute's dream, by comparison, never takes him a step further than the streams and ponds which his flock of ducks daily frequent. While no verbal exchange ever goes on in his daily routine, the true meaning of love never gets lost in his inner world. Unable to hear or talk since birth, the mute relies mostly on his eyes to "see, touch and feel" people and physical settings. By the same token, he is equally sensitive to human physiological reactions and atmospheric changes around him. Ironically, that has brought him closer to the natural habitat than anyone else with normal sensory functions. To him, the muggy and sodden environment is almost like some extended organ or body part, conjoining him with the water holes, brooks, and streams through his senses of touch, smell, and taste. Indeed, he acts as if he were endowed with the nurturing power of Mother Nature: e.g. every spring he is seen cradling a few duck eggs to his bare chest to hatch a brood of ducklings by the sheer warmth of his body. Rain or shine, he defies the challenge of any physical or mental discomfort of the heat or the cold outdoors; his temperament waxes and wanes in unison with the cyclic change of seasons. For a human being whose body functions with these uncanny attributes of nature, it comes as no surprise that in the end he turns out to be the most perceptive, generous, and ennobling person of all. As the film proceeds, for all his boorish and uncouth manners, the mute is soon to discover that Jinghe truly wishes to amend his broken promises and his neglect of Nuan's dream for the city. And he plans to do something to help Jinghe accomplish that. The director astutely saves the best till the last, revealing the mute's selfless act during the very last shot sequence of the film as Jinghe takes his leave to return to Beijing. When it is time to part their ways, the mute abruptly asks Jinghe to take Nuan and their daughter with him to the city. Nothing can top this act of self-sacrifice in proving that the mute indeed best embodies the dynamic interplay between the rational, the inarticulate, and the subconscious, the human relationships and the natural habitat.

As if to head off any charges of utopian sentimentality, both directors have embedded threads of human fragility and humility in the mostly idyllic narratives of scenes and action (far more realistic than the original novels): fate is cruel to Wangquan from his birth; he has to follow his ancestors' footprints and keep digging wells in the mountainous village. Nuan is unfortunate in being naively captivated by an undelivered promise of a city-bound future. Moreover, the mute, besides being deprived of speech and hearing, could easily be dubbed as the walking specimen of undeveloped, close-minded, and outmoded behavior — exactly what China's rural, inland, and frontier regions are often accused of being. There is honestly very little that can be considered romanticizing if we are aware of the agonizing hardship and sheer monotony in inhabiting such places year in and year out; criticism such as the above misses the point about the historical changes undertaken in rural China in the socialist and reformist eras. In contrast, ironically, we have had no qualms over adopting a Western approach of "charitable preservationism" towards the ruinous conditions to which much of China's rural areas and the frontier have been reduced; we allow their rustic innocence and purity to move us in nostalgic moments occasionally as long as their appeal is emotive, ephemeral, and therapeutic. What both modes of urban modernization exhibit in common is that their projected trajectories of "development" in human conditions tend to extend away from the rural to the urban, which is touted as an inevitable, uplifting social betterment; but if this course is upheld as absolute and irreversible, then following this path of development is not unlike burning all the bridges after we have crossed them, leaving behind a gaping void of moral and social abandonment. Such a course of progress hastens its own demise by way of depriving itself of all the tried and proven wisdom and heritage from our forefathers.

What we need, following Harpham's view earlier, is the ethical choice of "re-orienting" our perception of modern progress by taking into account the disruption of human affinities with land demanded by a rampant urbanized lifestyle. The stance we take does not translate into a drastic moratorium of the "use" of nature to abruptly halt human progress, but it does call for a more balanced and durable co-habitation of our planet based on a genuine understanding of human interrelatedness with nature. There is a far weightier ethical liability facing us than bidding awe and reverence to our agrarian legacy. While ideas like "place attachment" are but the few known links to connect with China's vast and unfathomable trove of ecological, civilizational, and cosmological wisdom and knowledge, they go a long way in helping us discern fundamental flaws in urban and industrial development as the infallible mode of modernization and dispel the ecological demon we have unwisely created. It should incisively remind us that, though discounted as a lasting feudal remnant, China's agrarian tradition itself once led pioneering drives of "modernizing" agriculture centuries ago, long before most European nations did theirs, and that those prolonged ages witnessed how myriads of enduring forms of agriculture and agribusiness emerged, improved, and thrived with fewer and sparser lethal threats to the earth's ecological system on the whole. Its longevity and sustainability are precisely what modern commerce and industrialism prove hugely deficient in. It is in this sense that China needs to renew and sustain her agrarian heritages so that we may redesign blueprints for industrial and urban developments that allow the country to develop side-by-side with the city. Indeed, the true aim of our ethical indictment is not to make the cities disavow their social and material advances out of guilt, but to make them disavow their propensity to dispense with the country, its resource and status, for the sake of a misguided scheme of "progress," and remind them of their indebtedness to the country by way of repaying the latter with scientific know-how, education, and opportunities.

12

Ning Hao's *Incense:*
A Curious Tale of Earthly Buddhism

Xiaoping Lin

Ning Hao: I Film What I Saw

In summer 2006, *Crazy Stone*, a low-budget black comedy directed by Ning Hao, was an enormous success in China's domestic movie market and "an unlikely mainland hit" which "even brushed aside" Hollywood blockbusters such as *Superman Returns* and *Mission: Impossible III* released in the country at that time.[1] *China Daily*, the Chinese government's English language newspaper, hailed *Crazy Stone* as a film that "makes audiences laugh" and "Hollywood cry."[2] Ning Hao is a talented young filmmaker who, before his triumph of *Crazy Stone*, was actually unknown to a Chinese audience that had been bombarded with Hollywood offerings in the past decade. The director's two previous works, *Incense* (2003) and *Mongolian Ping Pong* (2004), were only shown abroad at internationals film festivals or in a few "art house" cinemas in the West.[3] In his first public interview with a CCTV anchor from "*xinwen huiketing*"[4] Ning Hao was teasingly called "a 29-year-old obscure director."[5] Yet the interview touched on a serious issue that critics and movie audiences had ignored, i.e. the director's "intense concerns with social problems — from peasant laborers' living conditions to laid-off factory workers' living environments."[6] As the CCTV anchor inquired of Ning Hao: "There is a very realistic [social] background to your film, including the crime of fraud, the bankruptcy of a state-run factory, and the problem of capital. Were these issues related to your own life? How did you observe such things?" Ning Hao answered: "I grew up at Taiyuan Iron and Steel Plant ... Many of my friends are factory workers, including a lot of my parents' friends. As a matter of fact, I know very well about these factories and I don't think those issues are really new to me. Just ask everyone: all of us understand the current situation of these factories and see those problems that are not complex at all. So I film what I saw."[7]

When the anchor inquired about the director's choice of Chongqing, a city in Sichuan Province where his film was shot, Ning Hao replied: "The glaring absurdity of the story [of *Crazy Stone*] can only be found in a place full of big changes and antagonistic contradictions ... Chongqing became a *zhixia shi*[8] [in 1997], which is developing rapidly. Against this background interesting things are taking place; and anything can happen here in the city. When we were looking for a location to shoot the movie, we sensed at once such an atmosphere there and hence the choice."[9] But the director's choice of the filming location was not only socio-political but also visual. He explains: "I sensed that atmosphere directly from the city's architectures. Looking from Luohan Temple, I saw instantly all kinds of buildings from three hundred years ago up to the present. Luohan Temple was probably a building from the Republic of China (1912–1949) or the early days of the People's Republic. Behind it are the glass walls [of skyscrapers]. The temple was not torn down so that it coexists with [modern architecture]. Under such conditions, there must be people of all social strata living in those buildings, old or new. Because of this there is a possibility of contradictions and a story as well."[10]

Clearly, a striking contrast between an old Buddhist temple[11] and new "glass walled" high-rises in Chongqing had inspired Ning Hao. In fact, his *Crazy Stone* starts with a Buddhist "cue." In the scene after the title credits, a developer asks a factory director to sign a foreclosure contract. This is because the state-owned factory is bankrupt and unable to pay back the loan from the developer's firm, which is buying the factory's land. Admitting that the workers have not been paid for eight months, the developer advises the director: "Lay everyone off. This is doing a good deed to them (*zhe caishi zuo shanshi*). The sooner they die, the sooner they reincarnate (*zao si zao chaosheng*)." In this speech, the developer appropriates the Buddhist concept of "reincarnation" (*chaosheng*) to justify his wanton disregard for human life.[12] For him, the laid-off workers will "shorten" their journey to Buddhist nirvana if they die "fast" symbolically — that is, the termination of their lifelong employment under socialism. No matter how callous the developer's discourse may seem, it conveys a grim reality in Chinese cities today. In a best-selling book titled *Zhongguo chengshi pipan* (A critique of Chinese cities), we read: "In Chongqing, one in five employees of state-owned enterprises is laid off, which results from the government's unwilling policy of 'reducing workforce and increasing productivity.' In 2003, 100,000 laid-off workers joined the army of unemployment, adding to the number of 400,000 laid-off workers before 2003. This figure is, without doubt, a disaster for Chongqing, a city that has a population of 222.79 million."[13] Thus, the success of *Crazy Stone* lies in its gritty cinematic realism. The movie is not only a poignant portrayal of the "life-and-death" matter of unemployment, but a biting satire on the greedy realtor's misuse of Buddhism.[14]

In *Mongolia Ping Pong*, Ning Hao shoots a scene of a lamasery rising from the grasslands of Inner Mongolia, where the child protagonists ask the learned lamas about the mysterious ping-pong ball (which is unknown to the children in the movie). In two other scenes, a teenage lama plays with the young protagonists but never speaks a word. However, his silent presence hints at a living tradition in the region. Since the Qing Dynasty (1644–1911), Mongolian parents would send at least one boy to a lamasery, for they believed that this child lama would bring benefits to the family through his "reincarnation in the next life" (*laishi zhuansheng*).[15] Obviously, Buddhism is a constant theme, or leitmotiv, in Ning Hao's work. In this chapter, I analyze his debut film, *Incense*, in terms of Buddhism as a living religion in contemporary China. As the new millennium begins, Chinese Buddhist leaders and scholars have advocated so-called "earthly Buddhism" (*renjian fojiao*) with regard to modernity and globalization. They consider it impossible for traditional Buddhism to "withdraw from the world" (*dunshi*) or evade the realities of globalization. As an alternative, they claim, "earthly Buddhism" must enter the world (*rushi*) and partake in the modernization of religious institutions and social life. For them, a domain in alliance with "earthly Buddhism" is that of "metropolitan Buddhism" (*dushi fojiao*), which is a ready response to rapid urbanization in the country. Moreover, they strongly endorse environmental protection and balance.[16] More recently, religious scholars outside China have also addressed this important issue of "earthly Buddhism," as illuminated by Charles B. Jones's study of Chinese Pure Land Buddhism.[17] In his study, Jones discussed the theologies of Taixu (1890–1940) and Yinshun (1906–), the two modern masters of Pure Land Buddhism who strongly advocated "earthly Buddhism."[18] In Yinshun's view, as Jones wrote, the historical Buddha left home to seek enlightenment, yet he did not take leave the human world but "the narrow confines of family" and he "made his way into the world of humanity as a whole with its troubles and travails."[19] And Yinshun believed that "this emphasis on human concerns and compassionate activity within the human sphere best suited the needs of the modern world."[20] It is in this context that I examine *Incense* as a film text which deconstructs "earthly Buddhism," especially its current efforts to adapt to China's economic reforms and capitalist globalization. To me, the film text of *Incense* also seems to concur with what Slavoj Žižek has lately said: the "very fact of capitalist globalization" is that "capitalism can accommodate itself to all civilizations, from Christian to Hindu and Buddhist."[21]

A Broken Buddha, a Shattered Faith

In *Incense*, Ning Hao chooses an impoverished Buddhist monk and his ruined temple as the central theme. The film opens with a vista of a long, snowy country road under a vast sunny sky. This bleak winter landscape is a mise-en-scène which symbolically frames the monk's existence, and which seems to designate his irrelevance to human society. As a truck enters the road, we first hear the driver singing loudly in front and then we catch sight of the monk curling up at back. In the next shot, the truck driver unloads a flock of sheep onto a stage-like building in a village. And the monk lifts up a box of incense — he is getting ready for his prayers at his temple during the Chinese New Year. On the top of the "stage" is a slogan from the Cultural Revolution (1966–1976), which reads: "Wishing Chairman Mao a Long, Long Life!" Apparently, the building was a place for political gathering in the village before, but now it functions as a "center stage" for economic activities — that is, a livestock shed where sheep are kept before butchery.

The subsequent shot is shocking: methodically and slowly, a butcher slays a sheep with a knife. This horrific scene of animal slaughter tells of the significant role that the monk serves in this village community. The butcher's home is next to the monk's temple, so both men are neighbors and good friends. On his way back to the temple, the monk teases his butcher/friend: "You are killing a living thing *(shasheng)* again!"[22] To which the butcher replies: "Look at your dress! You don't even seem a human!" This bitter verbal exchange between the two friends is perhaps a daily routine to chase away boredom. The butcher makes fun of the monk's "exotic" appearance, i.e. his bald head and drab clothing, while the monk's accusation of "killing a living thing" is theologically legitimate. Given that all of the villagers make a living by slaughtering sheep, he must maintain a temple to redeem their "sins." However, this religious legitimacy will soon be in question in the next sequence of "a broken Buddha."

Figure 12.1 Standing by the Buddhist statue in his temple, the monk examines his worn-out shoes. Ning Hao, *Incense*.

Back in his room in the temple, the monk inspects a pair of worn-out shoes that need repair. He looks around and walks to a small shrine that houses a clay Buddhist statue. He finds a piece of cloth tucked under a tree branch that sustains the already crumbling Buddha. Visibly the cloth was put under the branch to prevent it from slipping away, which would cause the statue to fall. Seeing that the gray color of the cloth matches his shoes, the monk pulls off the cloth from under the branch but makes sure the statue is fine. Then, he burns incense and prays to the Buddha, seeming to "repent" for what he has done. The monk returns to his room and mends his shoes with the cloth. Suddenly, a loud awful crash is heard off-screen. The monk rushes back to the chapel and he stares in shock: the clay Buddha has broken into pieces, except for the head. Next, we cut to a scene in which the monk is holding the "severed" head of the Buddha in despair. To the viewer, the monk's face and the Buddha head look eerily alike. Is the monk holding his own head that has survived the collapse but is "bodiless" now? And who is to blame for this terrible accident? Is this a symbolic "breakdown" of the Buddhist faith? Is the monk more concerned with his shoes than the welfare of a sacred Buddhist icon?

In fact, the shattered Buddhist statue is not a Buddha but an *arhat*. In Buddhism, arhat is one who has attained enlightenment and is free of the cycle of birth, death, and rebirth. Yet there is difference between an arhat and a Buddha. The Buddha attains enlightenment by himself, while the arhat achieves the same goal by following the teachings of others.[23] Theravada Buddhism, in particular, considers becoming an arhat as the goal of spiritual process.[24] (Later in the movie, after his arrest for illegal "alms begging," the monk tells the police that he was ordained in Foguang Temple in Huo County of Shanxi Province. So he was following the path of an arhat in that "spiritual process.") However, the difference between a Buddha and an arhat in *Incense* is important visually rather than theologically. As the monk curiously resembles the arhat that crashed to the ground, we may see this collapse as a "breakdown" of the monk's Buddhist faith. Actually, the accident presages the monk's own moral and spiritual downfall toward the end of the film.

But the accident also indicates that the monk lives in such appalling poverty that it may hinder him from keeping up the good works or achieving the goal of enlightenment. And the film text of *Incense* continues to present this pecuniary hindrance as a central motif. As noted, in that village the monk is the only person who runs the temple in order to redeem those who kill animals. His survival is inevitably linked to the Buddhist statue, without which no worshipers would come and donate money to the monk for his services. The broken Buddha needs to be repaired before the New Year, and that task requires funding. So the monk decides to get support from the local government. Before his first trip to town, the monk discovers that his bicycle is broken and he turns to his butcher/friend for help. The butcher has a younger sister who works as a school teacher in the village. In a sunny classroom full of noisy school kids, the sister calls her brother to come home to fix the bicycle through a speaker at her desk. She then lets all students go home, but a boy lingers on and mimics her tone of voice until she orders him out. This lively episode indicates that the young woman shares the monk's worry for the fallen Buddha, and she does everything she can to help him. Meanwhile, the boy's teasing hints at a warm relationship between the young woman and the monk. In a high-angle tracking shot that follows the classroom scene, we see the monk walk side by side with the schoolteacher in a courtyard, where children play around and watch the "couple" vanish into her house.

Inside the house, the brother is fixing the bicycle while the monk sits eating melon seeds offered by the sister.[25] Again, we are made to feel that daily intimacy between the monk, the butcher, and his sister. Though living alone in the temple, the monk is emotionally attached to a home that treats him like a family.[26] The monk stares at the framed family pictures on the wall and asks the brother: "Is this a photo of your sister?" Without looking to see which picture the monk means, the brother answers: "It's mine!" In a close-up shot, we see what the monk is looking at: a picture of a newborn baby whose gender is hard to tell. Next to it is a snapshot of the sister as a grown-up girl. In the movie, we never see the sister's face because she is always wrapped in a scarf during her brief screen presence. This obscured view of her may imply that the young woman is an "illusion" framed in a photograph which is elusive and unattainable to the monk, who is somehow attracted to her. (In fact, during that exchange of harsh words between the monk and the butcher, the monk complains that he looks "inhuman" because "no one takes care of" him, while the butcher shouts back: "Get yourself a wife!" And the monk confesses: "I think your sister is a good woman.")

A State and a Church for the Rich

The next long shot brings us back to that snowy country road. This time, the monk appears as a lone traveler, bicycling on the road with his back toward us. It is his first trip to town to visit the government agencies. The monk walks into the Section of Religion office and meets with the section chief. He explains to the chief that he runs his temple to redeem the sin of his fellow villagers, and that a temple without a Buddha is not functional (nor is a monk). The chief listens to him with sympathy but offers no help. He makes clear to the monk that the state's policy toward funding religious institutions is "*zhuada fangxiao*" (grasping the big and releasing the small). In other words, his Section of Religion can only use their limited funds to repair big temples but disregards the small ones. The chief advises the monk to "return to secular life" (*huansu*) if the "situation" becomes unmanageable. (This same advice of "returning to secular life" is given time after time by other characters to the monk.) But the monk answers that he is incapable of doing anything else other than being a monk. In the meantime, a well-fed, middle-aged woman enters the office with her boy. Both mother and child present "gifts" to the chief before asking for help to repair a Christian church. Feeling uneasy in the presence of the new visitors, the monk leaves the room. And we watch the chief promise the woman to fund her church repair work after the New Year. In this office, where staff members are playing cards on the job, the monk indeed looks "inhuman." His stern face and austere monastic outfit seem so alienating to others, especially compared with the Christian mother and her son.

Just before the monk walks away, the chief gives him another piece of advice: "You may go and see Xiao An of the Section of Cultural Relics about your problem." Puzzled by the chief's recommendation (why the "Section of Cultural Relics"?), the monk walks through the governmental compound as instructed. We cut to the office of the Section of Cultural Relics and, all of sudden, a man's sardonic voice is heard off-screen: "Xiao An! Who in your family goes to a monastery?" Ostensibly shaken by this reference to Buddhahood, Xiao An retorts: "Nonsense! And no one!" Yet the same mocking voice announces: "There is a *monk* waiting to see you!" Embarrassed by this encounter with the monk, Xiao An responds to his request for help in anger: "It's none of my business!" The monk continues to plead with Xiao An: "Without a Buddhist statue, how can I live?" The monk's tender appeal seems to soften Xiao An, who finally suggests that his Section is collecting "window frames" of antiquity, and that if the monk's temple has such stuff he may bring it in for cash. Like the chief of the Section of Religion, Xiao An thinks that the monk's temple is not worth saving, but its ancient assets or "cultural relics" might be profitable in China's booming antiquity market.

Such a governmental stance on religions, Buddhism in particular, poses a true challenge to the monk, who is too confined to his temple to understand an outside world. In *Incense*, the monk's visit to the government compound is staged like an unwanted "alien" intrusion. And the monk's "inhuman" appearance surely does a disservice to his fundraiser whenever he meets people. On the one hand, the "obscene power" of the state bureaucracy renders the monk helpless. On the other, a veiled yet "popular" prejudice against the Buddhist religion deprives the monk of his rights to government assistance. In contrast, the amiable Christian woman receives that same help denied to the monk. Such a social bias against Buddhism is most evident in the case of Xiao An, who feels insulted when a co-worker makes a crude joke about his family in connection with Buddhism.

While escaping from this hostile environment, the monk bypasses a room where the "cookhouse squad" (*chuishi ban*) is rehearsing a New Year song off-screen.[27] The song is about man's efforts to overcome hardship and achieve success. One line from the song says: "A body without a soul is like a scarecrow." Though we may ignore the banal words of the soundtrack, we cannot discount the images of a scarecrow that come into sight twice on screen. In the opening credit sequence, the truck driver and the monk pass by a scarecrow standing in the open fields by the country road. When the monk returns to his village from his first trip to town, he stops by the scarecrow and removes its hat. We are baffled by the monk's strange behavior: why would anyone steal a hat from a scarecrow? However, the mystery is soon resolved after the monk's return to his temple. In the shrine we find a "new" Buddhist statue. Or, what we see is that the old severed head of the arhat has been imposed upon the scarecrow's body! It seems that the monk's first fundraising trip has culminated with a comic twist. He carted off the scarecrow from the unattended fields, and he brought it to the temple to give the smashed arhat a new bulk! In his film, Ning Hao uses this bizarre makeshift arhat as a cinematic metaphor for Buddhism in general. Like the "soulless" scarecrow, Buddhism stands deserted in human society. The monk, in particular, is losing his relevance to the village community. Under the circumstances of personal poverty and government neglect, the monk is a Buddhist "scarecrow" that is doomed to fail in fulfilling its religious function.

The next day, the monk makes a second trip into town. On the road we see him riding his bicycle and carrying an old window frame that he has taken off the temple (an act of sacrilege by the monk who is under intense financial pressure). Again, the mise-en-scène of a wintry landscape frames the diminutive figure of the monk, whose existence has had to rely upon the "mercy" of the government officials. Soon the monk shows up in front of the office of the Section of Cultural Relics. Xiao An looks at the window frame and seems satisfied. "It could be from the Qing Dynasty," he says to the monk. But he gives the monk no "cash" (only after the New Year!) but a worthless "white receipt" (*baitiao*). Disillusioned with the state bureaucracy, the monk begins to wander along a busy downtown street. Abruptly, we hear a solemn Buddhist sutra being chanted on the soundtrack and in a long shot we see the monk walk toward a grand Buddhist temple. We then cut to the inside of the temple and find a tape recorder placed by the gate. It is the machine that is playing the chanting of the sutra, a task usually undertaken by monks. This mechanical recording of the human voice is, I think, an acoustic motif symbolic of "earthly Buddhism," which serves the faithful of the well-to-do middle class. At the suggestion of the chief of the Section of Religion, the monk comes here to seek help from the head priest, who is also a senior classmate (*da shixiong*) from back during his training years.

The two monks meet in front of the temple gate lavishly adorned in gaudy red and golden colors. This well-kept temple proves to be a success of the "state's policy" that the chief refers to as "grasping the big and releasing the small." While talking with the monk, the head priest is shining a brand-new motorcycle with a cloth. To his left is a huge screen wall which has an enormous Chinese character *fo* (i.e. the Buddha) written on it. This mise-en-scène is a quaint fusion of Buddhist ideology and modern technology, which epitomizes "earthly Buddhism," especially its close ally of "metropolitan Buddhism." As advocates of "metropolitan Buddhism" have pointed out, a "city monastery" (*dushi siyuan*) has economic advantages because donations from the faithful are not the only revenue. Under the state's policy of "self sufficiency" (*ziyang*), a city monastery can support itself by selling sutras, ritual implements, and other paraphernalia to pilgrims and tourists.[28] This viable "Buddhist economy" (*fojiao jingji*) may contradict the Buddha's teachings, yet it is an effective means for a monastery to survive and even prosper in a market economy. In history, the Buddhist church is never separated from the state in that "without depending on the state, the Buddhist service is hard to expand." It is a political doctrine adopted by the Buddhist church under socialism as well.[29] In this episode, the temple is typical of the "city monastery" which thrives on a self-sufficient "Buddhist economy." The monk's small temple in a poor village is bankrupt due to its lack of state funding, while the head priest's big temple is flourishing in a booming town because of wealthy donors and government support. Hence we see a Buddhist community that is divided between the "rich" townspeople and the "poor" villagers.[30] However, when the monk asks to borrow some money, the head priest refuses, alleging that his temple "business" is a bit "slow" before the New Year. And he suggests that the monk should desert his temple and come to stay in this one after the New Year, when he is taking office in another temple on Mount Wutai, the Holy Land of Chinese Buddhism. If the monk comes, says the head priest, he will have a "share" (*gufen*) in this temple which has adopted the joint-stock system. The head priest's offer provides an easy solution to the monk's personal crisis of survival. Yet the monk says: "I can't let a hundred-year-old temple ruin in my hands." "You can stay here for two hundreds years," the head priest answers coldly. In dismay the monk walks away and wonders what has become of his "senior classmate" with whom he had studied Buddhism.

Figure 12.2 The monk speaks with the head priest of a well-managed Buddhist temple asking for help. Ning Hao, *Incense*.

Denied help by both the government agency and the Buddhist establishment, the monk has to find some other means to raise money. On the street the monk sees a man posting a job advertisement on the wall. And he catches a glimpse of another man who is playing the two-string Chinese fiddle outside a house. A lady comes out of the house and gives the "uninvited" musician some money to send him away. Both men inspire the monk as to how he can "earn" his money. It is a free market where everyone can work a job or sell his/her skills. The "enlightened" monk then hurries home, traveling on that snow-covered country road. Unexpectedly, he falls off his bicycle and is thrown onto the roadside, an accident that signifies the monk's moral and spiritual downfall yet to come.

The Aborted "Alms Begging" and the Declined "Almsgiving"

Ironically, the monk's last trip to town also begins with a symbolic fall. In a long shot, we see the monk leave his village on a blue winter morning. The truck driver stands by that "stage" building, shouting at the monk: "Where are you going?" "To beg for alms (*huayuan*)!" the monk responds with great confidence. A second later the monk falls off his bicycle behind the "stage" building. These constant, awkward accidents may indicate that the monk is an inadequate bicyclist who has no control of his vehicle. Yet as we will learn from the movie, the monk's repeated falls stand for the failure of his "alms begging" mission and his moral bankruptcy thereafter. In Buddhism, "almsgiving" (*dāna*) is a key virtue and a source of great merit for the faithful. Buddhist laymen and laywomen give alms to monks in order to accumulate such merit.[31] For monks and nuns, "begging for alms" is to collect food or other gifts from the laypersons on the street. On his final trip the monk carries a "begging bowl" (*pātra*), a ritual implement used by monks to collect food on their daily alms round under Buddhist tradition.[32] The day before, the monk witnessed a capitalistic market place where everyone can make money by selling their expertise. Today, he is going to "beg for alms" — a rightful profession for a Buddhist monk in any society.

However, the monk's initial attempts at "alms begging" in the street prove disastrous. In a narrow alley, the monk comes upon two well-dressed young girls and starts to speak to them in a timid voice. Turning their faces away, the two girls dodge him like a disease. A moment later, the monk goes into a house in the alley but is forced to retreat because of a barking dog. The frustrated monk soon reappears in a swarming downtown area, where he approaches a middle-aged man. The man listens to the monk's words and asks: "Do you have a book of merit?" The monk answers "No" and the man gives him fifty cents as a "donation." Realizing his big mistake, the monk buys a notebook with a red flag on its cover and turns it into a "book of merit." In the next scene we see the monk beg for alms with his new "book of merit" in front of a fine house. A smiling old lady gives him plenty of cash after he assures her, in the name of the Buddha, that her pregnant daughter-in-law will give birth to a boy, not a girl as a recent hospital test confirms. In this "alms begging" job the monk seems to have achieved an instant success, and he walks into a bank to exchange small bills for big notes. As the monk continues his "alms begging" in the street, a policeman stops him and takes him to a nearby station, where two officers interrogate the monk, asking if he has a "certificate of monkship" (*dudie*). The monk answers "No." He is taken away for detention until the police verify his identity with the village head.

An officer brings the monk to a dimly lit room, where three young prostitutes are watching a TV program about "sexually transmitted disease" as required by the police. The officer orders the monk to join the prostitutes squatting against the wall on the left of the frame. The monk's arrival stirs up interest among the prostitutes, who begin to tease the monk by saying that he "looks more like a fortune-teller than a monk." The prostitute's view foretells what the monk will do after his release. Later, the girls mock him for watching the TV program "as a monk." In response, the monk makes a move across the room to the right of the frame, so that he is sitting next to the TV so as to be free of any accusations that he might be "watching." However, the monk's move is even worse, for he has inadvertently "repositioned" himself among the nude female mannequins on the floor (which have been confiscated by police). The monk's initial breakaway from the "living" prostitutes invokes a symbolic act of "spiritual purification," whereas his new alliance with the "lifeless" dummies forces him into a capitalistic fashion culture of explicit female sexuality. This entire "monk vs. prostitutes" sequence is filmed in a single long take. The camera's focus alters between the left and the right of the screen so as to show both parties, but it constantly registers the monk crouching amid the pretty faces and long legs of the female dummies. He looks embarrassed, holding his prayer beads as if to ward off the "evil spirit" of capitalistic commercial culture.

Strangely, after the monk reinstates himself through this ironic "split up," the prostitutes begin to take him seriously. They talk about the Buddhist faith and ask for the monk's opinion. He responds by preaching the Buddhist notion of *karma*: a person's good or evil deeds have consequences which are impossible to escape, and no one, not even the Buddha, has the power to exonerate evil deeds.[33] The girls agree that bad people get punished but there is always an exception. Although this conversation about *karma* is common among believers, it nonetheless reestablishes an agreeable relationship between the monk and the prostitutes. After the discussion, the prostitutes decide to raise 3000 yuan among their co-workers for the monk's project. And their motivation for this "good deed" is that since they are all "sinners" by profession, they must seek redemption by helping the monk rebuild the broken Buddhist statue. In this way, they will be able to accumulate "merit" and avoid being punished by burning in hell. Afterwards the officer returns to inform the monk that he has been cleared and is free to go. But, says the officer, his money has been confiscated because the state law bans "alms begging." He also orders one of the girls to go back to the karaoke bar where they all work and bring back "fines" to the station. As the monk is leaving with his bicycle, the girl asks him for a ride. In the following shot we see both of them ride together on the street, a scene which is somewhat uplifting. We cannot but hope that they will work out the "deal" as discussed earlier in the police station. When they arrive at the karaoke bar, the girl goes upstairs and asks the monk to come up with her. He first hesitates and then follows. We next cut to a dark sordid room where the girl is speaking to her boss about the police's penalty and the monk's need for money. "What monk? 3000 yuan?" the boss shouts. The girl hurries back to the staircase and finds the monk gone.

A Monk-Turned-Venture Capitalist

At that moment the monk seems to be caught in an impossible dilemma. The police have taken away the money he has rightfully "earned," while the prostitutes have offered money he is afraid to accept. In Buddhist doctrine, the money is permissible in either case: one is from the monk's "alms begging" and the other is from the prostitutes' "almsgiving."[34] Yet both are prohibited by state law according to the police. Following the karaoke scene is a medium shot in which the monk stands alone by his bicycle on a crowded street corner. He is visibly shaken by a world so blind to his sufferings. In anguish the monk walks away, but he is soon stopped by a young man lurking around the corner. The man asks the monk a "favor": Can he "play" the role of a fortune-teller for his girlfriend who believes in the Buddha? And he explains to the monk: the girl's parents do not approve of their relationship so he needs "help" from the monk to convince them. This request seems to give the monk a new chance to exercise the power of his Buddhist religion, and the youngster hastily teaches him how to do his job. The young man tears up a 100-yuan note, stuffs half of it into the monk's pocket and walks away. When he returns with his girlfriend, the monk blesses the "couple" as instructed. The girl leaves the scene happy, and the man gives the other half of the note to the monk. To our amazement, the street corner becomes a training ground for the monk, who, at this point, is willing to learn any skill to raise money. And he proves to be a quick learner in this new trade of "fortune-telling."

With the easy money of 100 yuan in hand, the monk buys a gilt figurine of the Buddha from a street vender for only 12 yuan. ("Stick them together," says the monk to the vender, as he hands over the broken note.) He also purchases a book on divination from another peddler. After that the monk opens his own business of "Buddhist divination" on the street. The sign the monk sets up in front of his vendor reads: *foyan kan shijie*, meaning, "The Buddha sees the world." It soon attracts a few old men who demand the Buddha's prophesy of their future. By using his Buddhist knowledge, the monk gains as prompt a success as he did with his "alms begging" venture earlier in the day. However, a man sitting across the street is watching the monk closely. He has been a "blind" fortune-teller in this neighborhood before the monk arrived. As more people are drawn to the monk's Buddhist divination, the "blind" fortune-teller grows apprehensive of losing customers. Unaware of this man's presence, the monk grabs the cash paid by his clients, puts it into a bag and is ready to go home — he has been miraculously transformed into a "venture capitalist." Out of the blue, a group of neighborhood youths surround the monk and demand "taxes" from him. Without waiting for a response from the monk, they beat him up, seize the money, and run away. The "blind" man, watching the situation, slowly removes his huge dark sunglasses and is evidently pleased. With disgust we realize that the man is not "blind" at all. He is just the leader of the street gang that has blasted the monk's last hope of raising money.

Figure 12.3   After all his efforts to raise a fund to rebuild the broken Buddha, the monk turns himself into a fortune-teller to make money. Ning Hao, *Incense*.

We cut to a night scene of the New Year's celebrations in this thriving town. Amid the cheering crowd we catch sight of the monk's bruised face darkened with grief. He looks lost and withdraws from sight. In a subsequent close-up shot, the monk's fortune-telling sign — "The Buddha sees the world" — is burning. Reasonably, we assume that the monk has given up all his efforts to rebuild the broken arhat. The next scene begins with the monk asleep in a sunny room. But the camera pans to show that this is the store of a coffin-maker, who has allowed the monk to spend the last night here. This ominous mise-en-scène may suggest that the monk has turned into a "living dead" — he is a wrecked man utterly defeated by those brute forces of state, church, police, and gangster.

Before returning home, the monk stops by a shop and buys a new pair of leather shoes with the money that he has kept hidden in the shoes he is wearing. This seemingly innocuous purchase, however, serves to remind us that the monk himself actually provoked the whole debacle of the broken Buddhist statute. That is to say, even from the outset, he was more concerned with his shoes than the well-being of his Buddhist icon. It is this spiritual lapse that the monk has been trying to redeem, but in vain. In the next scene, we find the monk again trudging along the snow-covered country road under a huge clear sky. This infinite winter landscape of the road, the fields, and the skies makes the monk a lonely diminutive figure that is about to fade away.

In a moment entering the frame from the far right is a red motorcycle minicab,[35] which comes out of nowhere and disturbs the cosmic tranquility of the scenery. Shortly, the minicab takes the road and approaches the monk from behind. Seeing the monk's bruised face, the cab driver is sympathetic. He offers the monk a ride home saying that he too is a Buddhist believer. Riding together in the car, the driver mentions to the monk that his neighbor's wife has been paralyzed for years and is not getting cured because he thinks that the woman is possessed by evil spirits. The driver asks the monk if he can help with this matter because the husband had asked him "to bring in an alms-begging monk" (*huayuan shifu*) if he was able to find one. The monk reacts to the driver's appeal immediately: "Shall we go now?" The driver then makes a U-turn and heads back to the place where he first picked up the monk. To me, this abrupt, spiral twist of "lift offering" is sternly surreal. In a way, the red motorcycle car looks like a spacecraft from American science fiction movies of the 1930s, while the driver's call for help sounds like a plea from another planet. In *Incense*, I think, the intrusion by such a man from "outer space" and the monk's ride with him is filmed like an "alien kidnapping" yet with the "hostage's" consensus. Both the monk and the driver act as if they have reached a secret Buddhist agreement.

Afterwards we cut to the same street scene, where the monk's career as a "venture capitalist" was cut short by the local gang. The following shot brings us into a shabby house in the neighborhood. In it, a sick woman is lying in bed while her husband is talking with the monk about the wife's incurable disease. He tells the monk that he has spent much money seeking treatment for her in hospitals but without success, and that he had asked a *fengshui* master and a Taoist exorcist for help but that both had let him down.[36] At that moment the driver joins in the conversation and asks: "Is this the fault of man or house?" The monk replies, "It is that of house." For me, this is an answer that the husband appears to have expected, just like the young man who paid the monk to "sanctify" the marriage between him and his girlfriend. The monk then gives another predictable *fengshui* speech: he detected something "wrong" in the ground when he first walked into the house. Until now, the monk has acted as if he were an expert on *fengshui*, which he is definitely not. As we recall, he only learned his fortune-telling skills on the street the day before. What happens next is, however, most surprising. The monk shows the husband the gilt figurine of the Buddha that he had bought for 12 yuan and says: "This Buddha has been blessed by a master of Mount Wutai with magic powers."

As noted, Mount Wutai is the Holy Land of Chinese Buddhism, and the monk is using this religious reference to put a high price on the gilt figurine, which has obviously never been "blessed" by anyone. So begins the monk's own descent into transgression. When the driver asks a price for the figurine, the monk plays a "Buddhist" trick. He cites the most auspicious numbers of "3, 6, 9" and picks "3" as a final answer. The camera shoots the next scene through a window frame, where we see all three men sitting in silence. A second later, we hear the husband choking. Then, we cut to a sunny courtyard outside the house where the monk is stashing the money with a sinister smile — he has got what he wanted by becoming a swindler. From this moment on, the monk starts to resemble the "blind" fortune-teller/gangster who orchestrated his brutal beating on the street the day before. Like the gangster who dupes customers with his faked physical disability, the monk gives the figurine a false religious identity to con a despondent husband out of 3000 yuan. In a long take that follows the courtyard scene, the monk is found riding his bicycle on the country road back home. Earlier in the film, we repeatedly saw the monk traveling this road but always with his back toward us. This time, however, the monk is coming head-on on screen, as if to ask us to join in his "celebration." In previous scenes, we watched the monk frequently fall off his bike like an inadequate bicyclist, but now he rides like a professional. In a bizarrely jubilant manner, he zigzags along the road from right to left and even takes his two hands off the handlebars. On the soundtrack the gong and drum music of a Chinese opera is played to accompany the monk's "joy ride," which nonetheless divulges his true face at last. Not only does he take advantage of the misfortunes of others but he also revels in his "success" at doing so. For the monk, the Buddhist belief has become a façade, like the "blind" gangster's enormous sunglasses, behind which he conceals his unscrupulous disposition.

In the film's final sequence, a brand-new statue of Amitabha Buddha represents the monk's dubious success. Amitabha means "boundless light" and he is one of the most important and popular buddhas in the Mahayana School of Buddhism,[37] which holds that people who speak his name with faith will be reborn in the paradise of Amitabha.[38] This glorious gilt statue of Amitabha Buddha contrasts sharply with the old broken one, which, as I have mentioned, was in the image of a humble *luohan/* arhat resembling the monk himself. Before the ceremony takes place, the butcher comes to congratulate the monk and gives him a modern gadget called *changjing ji*, i.e. the "sutra chanting" tape recorder which we saw earlier in the movie. The next close-up shot is the image of burning incense, followed by a critical scene which, I believe, forms the emotional core of the film text of *Incense*. In this scene, the butcher's sister is alone, playing the "sutra chanting" tape recorder in the same classroom that was once crammed with children but is lamentably empty now. In my judgment, the absent children embody a lost innocence and a blunt rejection of the monk, who has deviated from his Buddhist path and fallen into a moral abyss. In this light, even the sister's loyal support feels curiously empty — she has no one, not even the children, to listen to that recorded "sutra chanting." If this is the so-called "earthly Buddhism," which embraces modernity by substituting human "sutra chanting" for mechanical reproduction, it merely subjects itself to corruption rather than modernization. In reality, there are monasteries that have already abandoned the Buddhist practices (such as meditating and reciting sutra) in favor of "economic efficiency" (*jingji xiaoyi*).[39]

In the next medium shot, the monk is found leaning against a pole with a loudspeaker overhead, and the sutra chanting is blasting in the air. He seems to enjoy this "modernized" sutra chanting, a sacred duty that he should perform but shirks. When the monk returns to his temple, a small crowd of villagers gathers there, and the ceremony begins in a somber silence. The monk bows, burns incense, and prays to the Amitabha Buddha. The solemn ceremony reaches its peak when the monk steps out and holds up a mirror to refract the rays of sunlight onto the walls of his temple. Is it an attempt by the monk to bless the new Buddhist statue with "divine light"? Yet the monk's blissful endeavor is interrupted a second later, as he turns around to see two men with a white van parked in the proximity of his temple. The monk asks one of the men why he is here and the man answers: they are from the Bureau of Communications to survey the area; the temple is to be demolished in order to make way for a new "road to riches" (*zhifu lu*) for the villagers. The man then informs the monk that Xiao An from the Section of Cultural Relics asked him to take back the old window frame because it is dated from the Republic (1911–1949) rather than the Qing Dynasty, meaning that the item is worthless. In a subsequent medium shot, we see the monk, stunned and wordless, standing against a wall with a huge Chinese character "*chai*" (demolish) written on it. This final twist in Ning Hao's film plot is brilliantly tragic-comic. The monk, who made every effort to save his temple of "a hundred years old," is again crushed by brutal capitalistic market force, the same force that metamorphosed him from devoted Buddhist monk to pathetic "venture capitalist."

Earthly Buddhism and Social Ecology

In fact, the monk's eventual failure to preserve his temple is not caused by the government's oblivion to religion. On the contrary, the monk clashes with his fellow villagers from the very beginning. When the monk first tells the butcher that he is going to ask the government for help, the butcher complains that the government "has not built the road yet." In other words, his livelihood (and that of the whole village)

— slaughtering sheep — can only survive in a marketplace accessible through such a "road to riches." So, in the final scene of *Incense*, the sound of the sutra chanting is still hanging in the air, but the camera pans to show the snowy country road again, where we have witnessed the monk's (literal) ups and downs throughout the movie. Similar to the empty classroom, this country road is devoid of people, not even a solitary traveler. If the villagers welcome this yet-to-come "road to riches," the monk is surely not among them. His temple will be torn down even before the road is built. Therefore, a vexed question arises here: Is Buddhism relevant to people's lives? In the film text of *Incense*, such a problematic relationship of Buddhism to society is manifest in the image of the scarecrow, a central motif of alienation, which challenges all religions in contemporary China.

In February 2007, a survey on faith conducted by Tong Shijun and Liu Zhongyu, two professors at the East China Normal University in Shanghai, was published in the *Oriental Outlook Weekly*, a journal under the auspices of the Xinhua News Agency.[40] This latest survey found that in China, 300 million people consider themselves religious and about 200 million "are Buddhists, Taoists or worshippers of legendary figures such as the Dragon King and God of Fortune."[41] And 24.1 percent of the people surveyed said religion "shows the true path of life", while 28 percent said it "helps cure illness, avoid disasters and ensure that life is smooth."[42] In view of this survey, the Western media reported that "China is seeing a religious revival"[43] and "religion has been enjoying a resurgence in China over the past 20 years, as Communist Party disapproval eased."[44] Yet Liu Zhongyu offers another explanation: "After drastic changes in the past half a century, we now see bewildering moral decline, apathy between people, estrangement … All these have driven people to find new spiritual sustenance."[45] Evidently, Liu Zhongyu attributes the rapid growth of religious population in China to all of those "social ills" that force people to turn to religion for support. In *Incense*, for instance, the husband truly believes that Buddhism could "help to cure the illness" of his wife, while the monk tricks the poor man for his own material gain. In this case, the monk's devious deed stems from the "bewildering moral decline" within a Buddhist institution or community. Therefore, Buddhism is cinematically likened to the empty shell of a scarecrow which assumes a religious "bearing" but is devoid of any "spiritual sustenance."

In *Incense*, Ning Hao's harsh assessment of Buddhism might be compared with De Sica's "critical assault" on the Catholic Church in *Bicycle Thieves* (1948). As Millicent Marcus put it, "Just as the union failed to address Antonio's material plight, the Church offers no spiritual sustenance in his despair."[46] In Marcus's analysis, the Italian film is "a walk through Rome's social institutions, whose indifference to Antonio's plight forms De Sica's socio-political critique."[47] Similarly, the monk in Ning Hao's film hurries back and forth between the government agencies for nothing. Worse still, his desperate plea for help in the "big" Buddhist temple meets with equal "institutional" indifference. In the monk's plight, such a lack of institutional support within a Buddhist community is far more demoralizing than that in *Bicycle Thieves*. According to Peter Bondanella, De Sica himself suggests that the "only remedy" to Antonio's suffering is the "support and love" that the protagonist "receives from his family," especially "the love between father and son."[48] So, despite Antonio's failed attempt to steal a bicycle that horrifies his son Bruno, the boy, says Bondanella, offers "his father his hand before they both disappear into the alien crowd at the conclusion of the film."[49] In *Incense*, however, the monk is a loner who has no familial support whatever, just as the male protagonist in the novel adapted by De Sica's movie.[50] Although the monk's only human contact to "this world" is the butcher and his sister, he is treated as a pathetic social outcast by all the other characters in the film. In a sense, the monk's alienation is not *his* but that of the Buddhist religion, whose exotic "bearing" disaffects most people in a fast-changing Chinese society under economic reforms. As the monk is abandoned by his own Buddhist establishment, he finds no acceptance by other segments of society at large either. In *Bicycle Thieves*, Antonio's fall from grace is "redeemed" by Bruno's love, which, in Marcus's words, "makes the boy's generosity to the point of heroism."[51] By contrast, the monk in *Incense* is all alone in that cold, harsh world where his moral failure is beyond redemption. From a Buddhist perspective, the demolition of the monk's temple metes out retributive justice for his transgression. He must suffer the consequences of what "bad" karma he has done to the husband.

In *Bicycle Thieves*, the Catholic Church is "inadequate" in offering "spiritual sustenance" to people suffering from the war.[52] In *Incense*, both the state and the Buddhist church fail to assist ordinary people such as the husband (and even the monk himself). However, if Buddhism falls short in aiding the poor and needy in the film, it seems to have done well with the *nouveau riche* in real life. As Liu Zhongyu argues in his survey, it is naïve to think that poverty produces religion, and that if people get rich their zeal for religion would decline.[53] In fact, as he points out, "The increased interest [in religion] is not a result of poverty, as a large portion of new believers came from the economically developed costal areas."[54] Liu's widely publicized survey provides a broad backdrop to Ning Hao's *Incense*, especially in the context of "earthly Buddhism." For instance, the head priest is a clear example of "earthly Buddhism" whose service is orientated to the needs of the prosperous "new believers." His new motorcycle could be purchased with a fund from the temple's sales and tourist revenue, or a generous donation from the affluent faithful. Since he runs his temple efficiently, the priest is promoted to a higher office in a temple at Mount Wutai. This "earthly Buddhism" is not only well connected with the wealthy but also the state. It is the chief of the Section of Religion who recommends the monk to see the "business savvy" priest for help. And he makes a pledge of support to the well-off Christian woman, not the destitute monk!

In a sense, the monk's hardship is caused by his firm conviction of "no killing of living things," which is one of the "five rules" (*wujie*) of traditional Buddhism.[55]

Just recently, the advocates of "earthly Buddhism" have tied this old notion to a new ecological concern. They contend that the "five rules" should be reinterpreted in the context of a modern society, so that the notion of "no killing of living things" equates with environmental protection, ecological balance, and wildlife conservation.[56] On that account, we may identify the monk as an unwitting Buddhist ecologist. He sacrifices his personal life for redemption of "killing of living things" by his fellow villagers, yet he compromises his faith by yielding to a capitalist market economy. By playing a phony *fengshui* master in the husband's home, the monk runs afoul of another one of the "five rules" — that is, "no lying." Therefore, we find that "earthly Buddhism" is perhaps too eager to accommodate global capitalism by violating the fundamental principles of traditional Buddhism. In *Bicycle Thieves*, the Ricci character turns himself into a thief after he is denied justice. In *Incense*, the monk becomes a charlatan as soon as his "venture capitalist" cause brings success. So, in the final shot of the monk standing against the giant Chinese character "demolish," director Ning Hao delivers a simple and balanced judgment: even though he succeeds in rebuilding a broken Buddha, the monk will stand condemned under the Buddha's law for his own offense to human decency.

13

Putting Back the Animals:
Woman-Animal Meme in Contemporary Taiwanese Ecofeminist Imagination

Chia-ju Chang[*]

Animals are indeed a blank paper which can be inscribed with any message, and the symbolic meaning, that the social wishes.

—Tester 1991: 46

The invisibility of nonhuman animals (except pets) in our post-industrial society and our indifference to animal suffering reveal much about humanity as a species in relation to the current environmental crisis.[1] Our stubborn negligence is a powerful defense mechanism when facing daily life encounters with animals either at the dinner table or the department store, whether their body parts are used for food, clothing, or decoration. We shy away from talking about animal suffering, in part due to the extent to which human civilization has benefited, and continues to profit from their usage, capture, and decimation. Ingrained speciesism and utilitarian views toward them should be held responsible for the mass disappearance of animals from the face of our planet. One article from the online *Endangered Species Handbook* tells us that the "current extinction rate is estimated to be up to a thousand times higher than prehistory rates." Human activity such as killing for food or sport, and habitat destruction "lies at the root of this potentially catastrophic phenomenon" (Animal Welfare Institute, 2005). If we want to save the planet and redress the root problem of animal extinction, we need to extend the analysis of oppression of the human "other" to that of nonhuman species, and develop a reading strategy that helps integrate animals in our critical analysis.

[*] Here I would particularly like to express my gratitude to Professor Greta Gaard of the University of Wisconsin-River Falls, for reading my latest draft and giving me many helpful comments. This paper was first presented at 2007 AAS (Association for Asian Studies) in Boston, March 22–25, and then at ASLE (The Association for the Study of Literature and Environment) in Spartanburg, SC, June 12–16, 2007.

This chapter endeavors to redeem literal animals from human cultural production and language, to reinforce the need to rescue them from extinction due to endless, globalizing consumption and exploitation, to restore their intrinsic (as opposed to utilitarian) value, and to restore their proper place in the biotic community, the welfare of which should be seen as an "ultimate measure of moral value, the rightness or wrongness, of actions" (Aldo Leopold quoted in Katz's *Nature as Subject*, 15). Yet these endeavors are not independent from other humanistic calls for social reform or justice. In seeking a "notch" that intersects social and environmental ethics, I choose to focus on feminist and animal issues for the time being and to examine a prevalent "woman-animal meme," a cultural image or idea that associates women with animals to signify patriarchy's or modernity's double alterity.

This chapter builds on current ecofeminism,[2] particularly a branch called "vegetarian ecofeminist theorization of interspeciesist ethics," and critique of woman-animal meme to analyze contemporary Taiwanese films, as well as the literature and folklore on which these films are based. I first incorporate the insights from certain major American vegetarian ecofeminist theorists such as Carol Adams, Josephine Donovan, and Greta Gaard. Breaking the silence on the issues of animals, they see the "oppression of nonhuman animals (speciesism) as implicit within an ecofeminist analysis" and argue that "speciesism functions like and is inherently linked to racism, sexism, classism, heterosexism, and naturism" (Gaard 2002).

An examination of this meme is instrumental in illuminating the overlapping oppression and exploitation of both women and animals. I first look at current vegetarian ecofeminist views on woman-animal connection in American academia and then examine the ways in which this meme is appropriated by pro-feminist Taiwanese filmmakers and writers. The works to be analyzed include Li Ang's feminist dystopian novella *Shafu* (The Butcher's Wife, 1983), Zeng Zhuangxiang's filmic adaptation of Li Ang's *Shafu* (Woman of Wrath, 1988), and Wang Shau-di's ecofeminist animation *Grandma and Her Ghosts* (Mofa ama, 1998). While much has been said about domestic violence against women in patriarchy in Li Ang's and Zeng Zhuangxiang's *Shafu*, I argue that both versions should be considered as vegetarian ecofeminist texts. From the perspective of vegetarian ecofeminist theory, the theme of butchering and the overwhelming, detailed depiction of animal killing are direct accusations of violation against animals, rather than just a trope to dramatize psychological or emotional states such as the butcher's repressed anger and his wife's fear and wretchedness.

Working within a different genre, Wang Shau-di's animation, a genre meant for children, emphasizes a symbiotic relationship between humans (particularly elderly rural women and children) and animals. I argue that the filmmaker's ecofeminist strategy for envisioning a woman-centered ecological community in post-industrial Taiwan is achieved not only through returning to woman-centered religion but also through engaging and revising patriarchal oral tradition. Rather than rejecting the past, she allows the young generation to reconnect to their cultural tradition without absorbing the elements that would hamper feminist progress and violate animal integrity.

The "Woman-Animal" Meme: Culture, Nature, and Critical Theory

> Think literally!
> — Carol Adams

The association of women with animals is not a new philosophy.[3] It has been circulating in many cultures in mythology and folklore from antiquity to the present and has been a central site for ecofeminist interrogations of the sexism-speciesism linkage. In contemporary patriarchal-capitalist societies, the woman-animal meme is conceptualized and propagated by different groups to promote diversified agendas. On the one hand, the meme is appropriated to objectify women by fantasizing them as animal-like (e.g., Playgirl bunny, sex kitten, etc.) and sometimes even as deliciously edible: a transcultural example here is the globalizing "artistic" practice of *nyotaimori*, or "naked sushi" in Japanese restaurants around the world, which uses a naked young woman's body as a serving platter.[4] The fusion of culinary art form with naked women can therefore be interpreted as coalescing two forms of exploitation disguised under the names of aesthetics and tradition, that is, sexualizing *and* feminizing aquatic animals, and fantasizing women as food.[5]

On the other hand, the meme is also invoked by animal protection groups to chastise the unethical consumption and instrumentalization of animals. Here, women are criticized as complicit patrons who are the major consumers of animal products like cosmetics, leather goods, and fur coats. At the same time, women are employed as strategic instruments for terminating animal abuse. PETA, for example, has become infamous for its controversial appropriation of women's bodies in promoting animal rights and animal protection awareness.[6] The most notorious and protested example is the billboard image equating murdered women to slaughtered pigs in a specific reference to the case of Robert Pickton, a Canadian pig farmer and serial killer charged with twenty-six counts of first-degree murder.[7] PETA sees the use of women's bodies as a legitimate discourse on the interlaced devaluation of both women and animals under androcentric logic, but its approach, which shocks through objectification, runs counter to the values of spiritually-oriented ecofeminists, or spiritual ecofeminists, who view nature as holistic and sacred, and celebrate the woman-nature kinship as a form of empowerment and healing.[8] In an attempt to reverse patriarchy's devaluing attitude toward women and animals, they want to valorize the woman-animal or woman-nature connection as intimately linked.[9]

The linguistic aspect of the woman-animal meme has been explored by some social and vegetarian ecofeminists (Shapiro & Copeland 2005, Adams 1995, Dunayer 1995). For Joan Dunayer, "language is a powerful agent in assigning the imagery of animals vs. human," and she contends that a pejorative linguistic linkage between women and animals is "rooted in speciesism, the assumption that other animals are inferior to humans" (Dunayer 1995: 11). While Dunayer discusses the way animal imagery is applied to women so as to label them as inferior and, therefore, to justify abuse, Carol Adams argues that while the linguistic critique of the animal-woman meme has largely centered on the denigration of women by way of comparing them to animals, few feminists have challenged the cultural logic that denies the status of subjecthood to animals (Adams 2006: 56–58). It is noteworthy that the exclusion of nonhuman animals in the analysis derives partially from the "non-linguistic participation of animals in their own social construction" (Stibbe 2001: 146). Arran Stibbe, for example, points out that the Marxist-rooted Critical Discourse Analysis (CDA) in the study of language tends to focus on hegemony, in which "oppression of a group is carried out ideologically, rather than coercively" (Fairclough quoted in Stibbe 2001: 146). Stibbe contends that in the case of animals "the power is completely coercive"[10] because animals have no language. However, Max Scheler, a German phenomenologist (1874–1928), calls this judgment into question when he argues that humans need to "develop (or redevelop) their sympathetic intellectual capacities in order to decode the symbolic language of nature ... For instance when a dog expresses its joy by barking and wagging its tail ... we have here ... a universal grammar valid for all languages of expression" (quoted in Adams & Donovan 1996: 150).

This view of nature as expressive on its own terms runs counter to the conception of language typical of Western Cartesian rationality as well as modern critical theory, both of which view language as dualistic with a subject ("I")–object ("it") dichotomy. This view reflects the assumption that subjects use language to connect with objects: "[T]he underlying assumption within language is that the world is based in subject-object dualism and that language bridges between two or more *distinct* identities or objects" (Lorentz 2002: 62). The exercise of a dualistic language, in turn, reinforces the way we perceive the world as fragmented and separate in a vicious circle. There is an innate urge to connect through language, Lorentz asserts. The "ramifications of the use of [the dualistic] language" are to share and to unite with "the other" — but only "within [the human] family." This view of language is radically different from that of a "non-dualist," who sees the world as "innately communicative and seek[s] interconnectivity as a potential expression of our *fundamental* nature" (63). One example of a non-dualist perspective can be found in Buddhism. With its doctrine of *wuwo* (Pāli, *anatta*; Sanskrit, *anātman*) or no-self, Buddhism regards the subject-object split as illusory and mistaken because it sees both subject and object as creating and sustaining one another in a mutual and contingent way. From this perspective "language can be seen as both the primary method for asserting our individuality in the world *as well as* the principle bridging mechanism between that misconceived illusory identity and what's mistakenly perceived of as 'the other'" (Lorentz, 61, my emphasis).

The erasing of animal entities is best illustrated in vegetarian ecofeminist Carol Adams's idea of the "absent referent" in *The Sexual Politics of Meat: A Feminist-Vegetarian Critical Theory*. She contends that animals are constantly eliminated or being turned into what she calls the "absent referent" in both cultural and linguistic spheres. There are three ways of erasing animals from the human world, or turning animals into "absent referents," in Adams's scheme: the first is the literal, the actual killing of animals and the consumption of animal flesh, in which violence is the underlying fact beneath the practice of meat eating. The second way is the linguistic or rhetorical alteration to avoid coming to terms with animals. Linguistically, "absent referent" refers to the erasing of the signified by the signifier, for example, a cow is an "absent referent" in the word "beef." The "cow-transformed-into-beef" is "there and not there": "It is there through inference, but its meaningfulness reflects only upon what it refers to because the originating, literal, experience that contributes the meaning is not there. We fail to accord this absent referent its own existence" (42).

Similarly, in East Asia there is a prevalent self-deceiving discourse with regard to the idea of *sanjingrou*, the "threefold purity meat," often presented as a "means of expediency" for lay Buddhists. The idea is that as long as I (referring to the lay Buddhist) do not see, hear, or engage in the actual killing of animals or as long as I do not allow animals to be killed specifically for my consumption, then it is ethical to eat them.[11] Another similarly distorted view among certain Western Buddhists, as criticized by the translator of Shabkar Tsogdruk Rangdrol's *Food of Bodhisattvas: Buddhist Teachings on Abstaining from Meat*, is the idea that "animals gain a connection with the Dharma (and are therefore benefited) when their flesh is eaten by practitioners" (4). These two non-vegetarian rhetorics contribute to the practice of human hypocrisy, to the promotion of violence against animals in our daily lives, and to the deepening of the false sense of separation between the eater (human) and the eaten (animals).[12]

The third way of erasing animals is metaphorical and commonly found in cultural representations: "Animals become metaphors for describing people's experiences." Adams writes, "In this metaphorical sense, the meaning of the absent referent derives from its application or reference to something else" (2006: 53). A fitting analogy would be referring to woman prostitutes as *ji* (referring to "chickens") in Mandarin, where the entity of poultry is used to represent the ontological status of sex workers due to their homophonic association (雞/妓) and an ingrained patriarchal mentality that associates sexuality and animality. There is a new cultural phenomenon which refers to young male prostitutes as *ya* (duck) as a counterpart of *ji* in urban China. In order to turn an animal into food, one has to pretend that it is not an animal but an abstraction or an object. By the same token, in order to turn a human being into a sex object, one has to pretend she or he is not a human being but an animal.

According to Adams, radical feminists who seek to expose the patriarchal structure of oppression wind up "participat[ing] in the same set of representational referents, appropriating the experience of animals to interpret [women's] violation" (57). She argues for a two-way influence: "The structure of the absent referent in patriarchal culture strengthens individual oppressions by always recalling other oppressed groups" (2006: 54). In this sense, "feminists have used violence against animals as metaphor, literalizing *and* feminizing the metaphor" (57). Women are similarly made into "absent referents" in the language of eroticizing animals. In rejecting the use of metaphoric language that appropriates the materiality of animals, she asks: "Could metaphor itself be the undergarment to the garb of oppression?"

Adams's analysis of the linguistic split between signifier and "absent referent" is further developed by another ecofeminist scholar, Josephine Donovan. She points out a tendency for replacement and elision, or a shift from the material reality to the symbolic in contemporary critical theory, and she argues that such a habit of displacement is embedded in the practice of structuralist and post-structuralist language theory, in which language is seen as a sign system, and the system of signification, referent, signified, and signifier designate a symbolic discourse. Then she appropriates the term "thing-in-itself" to redeem the repressed or omitted signified. Donovan's concept of "thing-in-itself" does not refer to the Kantian notion but one that often appears in ecofeminists' writing as the "literal, the natural" referent (Donovan 1998: 76). In other words, building on Adams's theory of "absent referent" and feminist language theory, Donovan embarks on restoring the referent erased in the metaphor. In an effort to restore the absent referent as a "thou," Donovan then sees texts as "reconceived as vehicles for the disclosure of being ... thereby helping to reconstitute the 'objects' of discourse as 'subjects'" (74). Once the relationship shifts from "I-it" to "I-thou," the old oppressive paradigm will yield to one that views all forms of relationships as non-hierarchical but reciprocal or symbiotic.

Recognizing the animal "other" as a subject does not mean the substitute "thou" is conceptualized as human-like. Rather, animals should not be "considered 'persons' [who] have rights similar to those held by citizens — that is, the basic rights to have their territory (their selves, their bodies, their space) held inviolate from unwarranted human intrusions and/or abuse" (Adams & Donovan 1996: 14). To see the situation of animals in terms of rights is to embrace "a male bias toward rationality, defined as the construction of abstract universals that elide not just the personal [but also] the contextual, and the emotional" (147).[13]

Rejecting the rights-based theory that privileges reason over emotion, vegetarian ecofeminists instead develop a care-based ethical theory for the treatment of nonhuman animals and for bioregional community building. Recognizing differences between human and nonhuman animals, they focus on the unequal power relations between humans and nonhuman animals, particularly for domestic animals since their survival depends on human care. These theorists also see feelings, including those of empathy, compassion, and interdependency, as basic principles undergirding feminist care-based ethics.

The sense of empathy for others is notably exhibited among children, as Kenneth Shapiro, the executive director of Animal and Society Institute and a clinical and personality psychologist, points out: he notes that a child's understanding of the world starts with something that is closer to empathy than to objective knowledge (Shapiro 1996: 133). Children's genuine feeling of connecting to nonhuman animals is evidenced in their refusal to eat meat when they find out about its origin (Gaard 2002). Unfortunately, in order to enter the patriarchal order, one has to suspend that innocent feeling experienced as a child. These issues of empathy and the care-based community will be further explored in Wang Shau-di's *Grandma and Her Ghosts*.

A Study of the Household: "Women-Battering and Animal-Slaughtering" Narrative in Li Ang's *The Butcher's Wife* and Its Cinematic Adaptation

Li Ang's *Shafu* (The Butcher's Wife) and Zeng Zhuangxiang's filmic adaptation *Shafu* (Woman of Wrath)[14] exemplify François Lyotard's etymological understanding of the word "ecology." He writes, "The word *ecology*" is "a word made up of *oikos* [meaning house] and *logos* [meaning study]." In Greek, the word connotes domesticity and is in opposition to the public sphere. "The *Oikeion* is the women, whose sex is *oikeion*; the children, whose generation is also *oikeion*; the servants, everything that can be called 'domesticity' in the old Latin sense, that which is in the *domus*, like the dogs, for example. In the final analysis, *oikeion* is everything that is not [public] … the *oikeion* is the space we call 'private.'" He continues, "It is the shadowy space of all that escapes the light of public speech, and it is precisely in this darkness that tragedy occurs" (2000: 135). This sense of ecology, which Lyotard calls, "discourse of the secluded," comprises elements of femininity, subalternity, and domesticity. The last one sense of "domesticity," as derived from *domus*, denotes a realm beyond the human species.

Seen in this light, Li Ang's *Shafu* is de facto a Lyotardian eco-text that delves into the dark corner of Taiwanese patriarchal society where "tragedy occurs." The oppression of women in Taiwanese society was conspicuously present in two consecutive political regimes: the Japanese colonial rule that "intensifie[d] the already existent submissive nature of women's position in Taiwan" and the Nationalist government's retreat to Taiwan in 1949, which "sought to tighten social" controls by encouraging women "to play supportive and subservient roles both at home and in society" (Ng 1993: 268–269). Since the 1970s, Taiwanese writers and filmmakers have been examining "the social, economic, and political roles of women, and [have been] demonstrat[ing] in their portrayal of women, both lexically and stylistically, a sense of self-reflection and contemplation on their roles" (Chung 2000: 146).

Shafu is an accusation against Taiwanese patriarchal society. The dystopian vision of its rural community conveys a strong sense of alienation, victimization, and hostility toward women. In the preface, Li Ang talks about her preference for the original title, *Furen shafu* (a woman kills her husband) over *Shafu* (husband-killing). The former title as well as the English titles — the literary *The Butcher's Wife* or the filmic *The Wrath of Woman* — place the emphasis on woman. The meaning of the current Chinese title *Shafu* is more ambiguous and therefore allows a different reading. The word "Shafu" is polysemic: it not only denotes "killing the husband" but also refers to someone whose career is related to killing, as in *"tufu"* (屠夫). This interpretation would tie the three themes together: the killing of the husband, the killing of animals and, on a more subtle level, the killing of the husband for the sake of the animals. The last is evidenced in the prologue. According to the news report, Lin Shi confesses that her killing of her husband is not only to end her misery but also to avenge the numerous pigs he has murdered: "Toward dawn, after making sure he was fast asleep, she cut him up like a pig, just as she had seen him do at the slaughterhouse. In her own mind this deed also served to avenge the deaths of the countless poor animals that had met their end at his hand" (Goldblatt 3) .

Shafu was inspired by local news in Shanghai in the 1930s about a woman, Zhan Zhou, who was abused by her drunkard butcher husband and decided to avenge the animals he had slaughtered in her presence as a demonstration of his masculine mastery (Chen 2000: 41). Transplanting the locale to her native hometown, Lugang, in Taiwan, the author fictionalizes the life and marriage of a rural woman, Chen Lin Shi. Both Lin Shi and her mother are social outcasts of a patrilineal community. Lin Shi is sold to a pig-butcher, Chen Jiangshui, by her paternal uncle in exchange for pork. Her husband's life revolves around pig-killing during the day time, sexually abusing her at night, and frequent visits to the brothel. He eventually attempts to starve her and kill her ducklings after her obstinate resistance to his sexual advances. One day, she is forcefully brought to the slaughterhouse where Chen Jiangshui works and made to watch him demonstrate pig-dismembering. Eventually, she dismembers him the same way in a delirious mental state after coerced sex.

Male critics from a middle-class, intellectual backgrounds often read the story as too violent, too pessimistic, and lacking in empathy and human warmth, or intended to scare young women away from marriage. Female critics read it as a "feminist novella that discusses the socio-economic nature of women's victimization" (Ng 1993: 267). Chen Yü-ling's reading of *Butcher* incorporates Luce Irigaray's idea of "female writing," which intends to show patriarchal oppression of women's bodies, law, and economics, and this is achieved by virtue of revealing its oppressive structure in order to make accusation (2000: 41–42). Taking a different outlook on feminist literature, Li Ang herself professed that the "ultimate concern of 'feminist literature' is, after all, human nature." Her interests reside not only with women under the rules of traditional Chinese society but also with issues of "humanity, such as hunger, death, sex." In this light, the cross-references between woman and pig throughout the text, as a feminist strategy to reveal a violent side of human behavior, help intensify the grave social status and living conditions of the female protagonist. Take the name of the heroine, Chen Lin Shi, as an example. When pronounced in Taiwanese, it sounds like "waiting for you to feed." The name is a parallel between her existence and that of food animals, particularly pigs. Clearly this degrades the woman's ontological status, but it also does the same to animals, reducing both to absolute subalterns.

However, given the fact that the character of the butcher Chen Jiangshui serves to interlock the narratives of ruthless animal-killing and of domestic violence, it would be an anthropocentric blindness to treat violence against food animals as a mere backdrop to a feminist story. In this light, the vegetarian ecofeminist Carol Adams's analysis helps flesh out the overlapping exploitation of woman's "flesh" for sex and labor and animals' "meat" for food. As Adams's study of "battered-women-and-harming-of-animals" social texts in Western society shows, a male perpetrator may torture his partner's pet as a form of psychological abuse: "The killing of an animal [can function] as warning and to instill terror" (1995: 56). However, animal harming is not only a means of expressing masculine mastery over women; the animals themselves are erased both literally and metaphorically while women are abused. After Chen Jiangshui finds out that Li Shi has begun to raise ducklings, he chops up their bodies:

> Without waiting for her to finish, he reached behind him and picked up his butcher knife. Lin Shi was terrified, thinking that he was going to use it on her, and she backed away in panic. But he thrust his hand into the cage and began hacking away in a frenzy, using so much force that he broke the bamboo cage in a number of places. The ducklings cried pitifully at first, but before long, all was silence. (Goldblatt 119–120)

Here, the ducklings are not just a symbol of Li Shi's existential vulnerability and hope for economic independence, which are brutally smashed by her sadistic husband. From a nonhuman-centered standpoint, the narration also evinces a menacing threat that defenseless, domestic animals face at the mercy of their human male "master."

In both literary and filmic versions of the story, animals are not completely objectified.[15] In the case of the literary version, animal subjectivity is asserted skillfully in the butcher's inner reflection. In the scene after he chops up the bodies of the ducklings, Chen remembers an episode in his youth. He recalls that once he killed a pregnant sow whose eyes, as they seemed to him, bore "extraordinary sad looks" but he simply dismissed it as his own imagination. Here Chen's eye contact with a sow indicates that he is aware of the fact that a sow also has subjective states, such as emotions (definitely fear) and the power to gaze back, despite the fact that the look is the gaze of despair. But this awareness must be rationalized and thus denied as his own fantasy so as to disguise guilt and justify killing. Justice for animals is also reified in the form of folk belief or "hearsay," which is incorporated to instill a deeply felt sense of guilt concerning daily violent enactment against nonhuman animals. For example, we learn that there are social taboos in the butcher's world: "People in the slaughterhouse were saying that when an expectant sow was killed, her piglets would demand their right to life from the person responsible, who was thus fated to die a horrible death." This theme of animal vengeance underlying these folk beliefs has a broader ecological implication and reverses what is often trivialized as superstitions. The broader eco-cosmic dimension of folk religion, particularly the rite of "Middle Primordial Universal Salvation Festival" (*zhongyuan pudu*), will be discussed in the following section.

The richness of the butcher's inner reflection, which opens up a space for an intersubjective discourse, is dismissed in the film due to the limitations of both the film medium and the social realist genre. Within a visual medium, the butcher's subjective, internal activity is either exteriorized through the use of symbolic visual imagery or is constructed through external events. For example, the scene of "releasing the water lantern" (*fang shui deng*) has been added by the director to show the butcher's fear of animal vengeance.[16] The butcher's fear, disguised under his hypermasculinity, is represented through visual imagery such as the staggering iron hooks in the slaughter house and the visceral image of the blood-stained slab crawling with flies.[17] The butcher's repressed anxiety relating to animal slaughter is expressed in a series of shots beginning with one in which he worships at a "tablet of the ghost of the animal" (*shouhun bei*), thus signifying his desire to pacify the ghosts of the slaughtered animals. A point-of-view shot is employed to further highlight his unspoken anxiety about animal killing. The site of the slaughterhouse is carefully examined under the butcher's deliberate gaze to further concretize his inner anxiety over slaying the animals.

Generally speaking, Zeng Zhuangxiang's filmic version remains "faithful" to its literary "prototype" from the standpoint of plot. Yet there are a few places in which the director alters the ambiguous aspects that are unique to literature to render a more direct and dramatic effect through visual means. For example, in the novel, the omnipresent third-person narration conjecturing the whereabouts of Lin Shi's mother after she is caught having sexual intercourse with a soldier (e.g., Is she thrown into a river or driven into exile, or does she elope with the soldier?) is replaced by a dramatic suicide scene to give closure and to render an action-oriented visual effect. After the arrival of the Lin clan, Lin Shi's mother, out of embarrassment, stabs herself with a knife and this is followed by Lin Shi's attempt at saving her mother by pulling the knife out of her body. The disturbingly violent imagery of stabbing (both thrusting in and out) adheres more to the overall theme of killing: it echoes the imagery of Chen Jiangshu's routine thrusting into the throats of pigs and it reaches its climax with Lin Shi's later repeated stabbing of her husband. The dramatic effect helps bring forth the theme of violence.

The scene of "husband-killing" places Jiangshui in the position of a pig. In the literary version, Li Ang draws an analogy between Jiangshui and a pig on the wedding night:

> A short, stocky body and a prominent paunch — more fat than a man ought to have — he walked with a sort of waddle, kept his hair cut very short and had such a sharply sloping crown that the back of his skull seemed to be missing altogether. Fairly ordinary features, except that his small beady eyes were sunk deep into a swelling of flesh around the sockets. Lin Shi was told sometime later that these were known as pig-eyes and that they always belonged to people whose fate was tied to pigs. (Goldblatt 12)

In the filmic version, the butcher-pig analogy is carried out visually, as most prominently shown in the scene where Jiangshui carries a pig head on his back as he is walking toward home. In it, we are shown the rear view of Jiangshui walking away from us with the pig head superimposed on his back. This "surrealist," montage-like visual imagery symbolically breaks the boundary between human and animal, but only momentarily; ultimately the separation remains in place. By contrast, Wang Shau-di's animated film goes beyond Shafu in its attempt to reconfigure animal and woman memes. Starting with the children's experience living in a rural community, it boldly imagines a woman-centered eco-community.

Re-Envisioning Mu Lian and His Mother: A Creation of Postmodern, Woman-Centered Community in Wang Shau-di's *Grandma and Her Ghosts*

> The unwritten priorities of the culture enable even that which is in full view to be rendered effectively invisible — or if still visible to be drained, by common consent, of any significance. The dominant cultural view that the subject of animal is essentially trivial, or is associated principally with memories of childhood, is a clear case in point.
>
> —Steve Baker 1993: 8

Wang Shau-di's animation *Mofa ama* (Grandma and Her Ghosts), which came out more or less fifteen years after *Shafu*, subverts the previous tragic representation of a traditional Taiwanese rural community. Working within a children's genre, it offers an optimistic, "comic" alternative-community cohesion. Joseph Meeker in *The Comedy of Survival* argues that the universal, comic mode of cultural production celebrates the life of the common people and other animal species, maintains equilibrium among living beings, and restores that equilibrium once such a balance is lost: "Productive and stable ecosystems are those which minimize destructive aggression, encourage maximum diversity, and seek to establish equilibrium among their participants — which is essentially what happens in literary comedy" (Meeker 1996: 160). However, in *Mofa ama*, what goes beyond the biological confinement of Meeker's formulae of a necessary comic spirit and sense of humor for "the survival of our own and other species" is an injection of the religious, mytho-ritual dimension that communicates with the supernatural realm.[18] The harmony of the eco-community is actualized via the hybridity of human beings and nonhuman animals, *and* the participation of the invisible realm — a symbolic gesture of positive human and nonhuman animal interconnectedness. Furthermore, such a vision is enacted by way of a folk ritual that warrants the continuity of all sentient beings.

Though inspired by Miyazaki Hayao's *anime*, *Mofa ama* has acquired its own distinct local cultural, artistic sensibility, and humor that is very "Taiwanese." The animation narrates the tale of a city boy whose name is Doudou (*dou* can be translated as "bean" in English), who is sent to stay with his "superstitious" grandma — "superstitious" as perceived from the urban viewpoint of Doudou's mother — in the countryside for the summer due to a family emergency. His grandma, whom he has never met, is a Daoist priestess who performs funeral rituals and guides the deceased to the next stage of existence during the Daoist Ghost Festival or the so-called "*Yulan pen*" on the fifteenth of the seventh lunar month. Grandma has a cat (Shilo) and a dog (Kulo), which are not only her companions but also helpers, guarding over the urns of the deceased. One day, Doudou breaks into the house that stores the ashes of the dead and breaks an urn. An evil spirit gets out of the urn and possesses Shilo who then turns into a demonic creature and eats up all the spirits in the neighborhood. Eventually, by turning into a dog, grandma, together with Doudou, catches the bad ghost and restores her cat and the spirits who are able to make it to the festival for their reincarnation.

Seen from children's eyes, the world is enchanted. The universe is magical and fantastic (e.g., talking mushrooms, a whale learning how to walk, and the magic of grandma's tears that allow one to see the *hao xiongdi*, meaning good brothers, a euphemism for ghosts). Through their participation in the fantasy dimension of the world, Doudou and his friend Ah-ming learn to pay attention to other sentient beings and learn to feel empathy toward both the visible and invisible worlds. Here, empathy is defined as "a way of relating to the world that focuses on and directly apprehends the feelings, motives, and interests of other beings" (Shapiro 1996: 132).

These supernatural and ritual elements are the props for a coming-of-age story for two boys: Doudou goes through a character arc after being more involved with the world of the invisible; he eventually changes his worldview and learns to accept folk values and ways of life that have been forsaken by the modernized urban lifestyle as represented by his mother. Similarly, in a narrative of *bildungsroman*, Ah-ming (*ming* literally means "people," it is also a homophone of "ming," which means bright), who is the only child untainted by "civilization" and able see the ghost world, pays the price of growing up by losing his sight/vision of the other world.[19]

This film was nominated for the best film but failed to receive the Golden Horse Award in Taiwan as it was criticized as superstitious, and permeated with "strange happenings, the use of force, disorder, or the spirits" (*guai li luan shen*).[20] However, what is yet to be explored is its revision of a Buddhist myth and the *pudu* rite in the ecological and women-centered context. I posit that the subject matter of *Grandma* should be viewed as a post-industrial, nativist allegory of a women-centered, organic, eco-community rather than one that subscribes and proselytizes a certain religious or folk belief.

Mofa ama challenges an anthropocentric vision of community and an androcentric view in reference to leadership by way of evoking a Han Chinese folk religious practice called *zhongyuan pudu*. "The Pudu rite, or rite of 'Universal Salvation,'" writes Wen Chen-hua, "held in the seventh month, was developed to deal with the wandering souls ... These days, the Pudu rite blends not just Han beliefs about spirits and dead souls, but also Taoist and Buddhist thought, and so it's often called the 'Chungyuan [zhongyuan] Pudu' or the 'Ullambana Rite' ["*Yulan pen*" in Chinese]."[21] The *pudu* ritual, which involves offering food to the spirits of the dead and rescuing them from their suffering, serves as the backdrop for the animation and sets a cosmic tone. Underneath the fabric of ritual enactment between the human and the ghost realms is the director's purposeful ecofeminist reversal of gender and animal hierarchy. One symbolic dimension of the *Yulan pen* ritual, according to Stephen Teiser, is as an "annual celebration of renewal." While the ritual "mark[s] the symbolic passage of monks and ancestors to new forms of existence, it also usher[s] in the completion of a cycle of plant life" (1988: 3–4). Death as point of departure is not tragic in the sense of a terminus of one's existence, but a transition to another existence.

Overall, the grandma figure as a Daoist spiritual guide for both humans and the spirits conjures up the pre-modern image of a matriarch. But on the mythological level, the grandma character reactivates and also revises the archetypal "sinful" mother and her canine transformation in the folk narrative of "Mu Lian Saves His Mother," on which the *Yulan pen* ritual of releasing the hungry ghosts is based. The grandma tells part of the Mu Lian story to the curious future adept, Doudou, who would be recognized by a Chinese audience as the modern reincarnation of Mu Lian himself. As an agent of the oral tradition, the grandma omits from her retelling of the Mu Lian narrative the details about the "evil" mother who, when she dies and becomes a ghost, is unable to swallow food due to her needle-thin neck (Chow 2002: 5).[22] In this modern revision of the ritual and myth, the elderly woman is presented as a strong-willed priestess with an ability to exchange her form with that of her companion dog. In a sharp contrast to her urban, rational-thinking daughter, the grandma, as a mediator of the human, animal, and ghost realms, reverses the patriarchal hierarchy, not by turning the structure upside down but by making it egalitarian.

If, as Teiser suggests, the Mu Lian myth reflects the medieval Chinese preoccupation with the salvation of the mother after death (12), then the reworked animated narrative is concerned with rectifying the negative women-animal meme and women's role in a rural community. While in ancient times the woman-animal connection was often construed as a threat to social stability, the matriarch-animal metamorphosis reveres the conventional bias. The grandma's bodily exchange with her dog explicitly subverts the Mu Lian narrative: in the original story, the "evil" mother is penalized for her transgression by being reincarnated as a dog after her release from her initial condition as a hungry ghost. But in the film, the grandma transforms herself into a dog in order to save humanity, then returns to her human body.

To put it differently, while the dog in the earlier version of the Mu Lian story serves as a signifier of dangerous excess (Sterckx 2000: 231–232), *Mofa ama* draws on the other image of dog as both human companion and apotropaic animal, like the guardians of the land of the dead Bull Head (Niutou) and Horse Face (Mamian), the Chinese equivalents of the Greek Cerberus. There is a positive dimension of dogs in Chinese culture with regard to their symbology in ancient China. "Meditating on the boundaries between domesticity and wildness, inner and outer, the human and the bestial," Sterckx writes, "dogs in China and elsewhere were associated with the threshold of the household" (231). Therefore, in order to restore the cosmic order, the grandma has to rely on her dog to carry her over to the other realm. In this regard it is noteworthy that the film's treatment of the cat is different. Unlike dogs, which are pack animals, cats are solitary. There is also a color prejudice toward black according to Irvine's research on people adopting and surrendering animals (Irvine 2004: 95). Therefore, the black cat does not fare as well as the dog, probably due to an ingrained cultural prejudice.

Even though this prejudice remains in play, the film profoundly refigures the relations between humans and animals. In the Greek myth of Io, her transformation into a cow results in a complete loss of language. But the grandma-as-a-dog maintains her mental autonomy. By imagining that human mental capabilities, including thinking and verbal communication, might be contained in a canine form,

Mofa ama challenges the way we perceive human subjectivity. A human-animal intersubjectivity is formed, which is neither simply anthropomorphizing the dog nor animalizing the grandma. In saying this, however, I need to qualify the term "intersubjectivity" for my further analysis: instead of using a reflexive, cognitive model of intersubjective relations that risks privileging humans over animals, I resort to the prelingual, emotive, and somatic one that emphasizes a "shared subjective experience" between humans and animals (Irvine 2004: 10). Extending the prelinguistic intersubjectivity beyond that normally confined within mother-infant relations, Irvine argues that animals not only have a sense of self, but also "intersubjective capacities" to "share intentions and feelings" (3).

The intersubjective relationship, as in its most intensified form of "grandma-dog" bodily exchange, opens up another discourse that has already embedded itself in this ritual practice. According to Wai-yin Chow in the study of the Daoist Ghost Festival in contemporary Hong Kong, which is also applicable to contemporary Taiwanese society, this festival upholds "certain Chinese social values," one of which is the practice of care and giving, particularly to ghosts who are considered to be "closely associated with 'suffering'" (2002: 9), though this act is not completely disinterested (21). This festival also teaches, writes Chow, "the importance of mutual concern and solidarity between different groups in a society where fierce, unrelenting, and oppressive competition has come to be the norm" (21).

Conclusion

In Taiwanese culture as well as other cultures, the woman-animal meme has traveled a long way from antiquity to the present time and will probably continue to exist. While some feminists find it problematic to incorporate nonhuman animals into analyses of women's issues, others, such as vegetarian ecofeminists, argue that such a discourse needs to be developed so as to unveil the logic of androcentric oppression. I see it as an opportunity to address the complexity of interaction between the human and nonhuman world without taking an essentialist position that could wind up justifying the inferiority of both women and animals or nature. In this chapter I have shown different ways to carry out such a task: Li Ang's social realist novella is re-interpreted as a harsh attack against androcentric rural society in which both subaltern women and food animals are treated as mere flesh/meat. Wang Shau-di's animation is analyzed from a broader cosmic and mytho-ritual context in which elderly women and companion animals are re-conceptualized as guardians of a yet-to-be-modernized community. The appearance of these films suggests a shift away from both patriarchal and anthropocentric tradition towards a gender and species equal perspective.

14

"Reconstructing the God-Fearing Community":
Filming Tibet in the Twenty-First Century

Donghui He*

Since the turn of the new millennium, Tibet has been a popular filming location for Chinese filmmakers of all stripes — mainstream or independent, commercial or art house, fiction or documentary. In part because of environmental issues and energy problems that have snowballed in China since the 1990s, Tibet, located far away from China's industrialized center, has increasingly demanded public attention as an example of ecological stability. This new endorsement of ecological ethics in the Chinese public media has contributed to a recently acquired Chinese conviction in the Tibetan religion, a conviction that is mutually illuminative with an appreciation of the Tibetan landscape. For example, Tibet is typically referred to in tourist guides as an accessible Buddhist "pure land" (*jingtu*), two words that allude to the paradisiacal realm of Amitabha Buddha but are now used to evoke a land that is culturally innocent and uncontaminated by industrial pollution.[1] This ecological/religious turn signifies an important shift in public discourse in China. However, such whitewashed projections of the Tibetan landscape, presented as documentation of the actual ecological condition of geographically diverse Tibetan regions, or as an illustration of Tibetan Buddhist ideas of the "pure land," do not go unchallenged, especially when inside views from indigenous directors become available.

*   I would like to thank Wanma Caidan for interviews and correspondences since summer 2006, and Sean Deitrick, Elizabeth McGuire, and Steven Taubeneck for reading versions of this chapter and for the constructive comments. Research for this project was supported by a Professional Development Award from the University of Tennessee and by one semester of residence at the Central University of Nationalities.

The quotation used in the title comes from Zhang Haiyang, "*Gaojian hexie shehui yu chongjian you 'shen' de shequ*" (The construction of a harmonious society and the rebuilding of the God-fearing communities), *Zhongguo Minzubao* (Chinese Ethnic News), March 24, 2006, 4.

In this chapter, I will discuss recent documentary-style film representations of Tibetan ecology by experimental-mainstream Chinese director Tian Zhuangzhuang and Tibetan director Wanma Caidan, giving special attention to the ways they shape perceptions of the Tibetan religion and relate it to ecological connectedness in the everyday setting. I suggest that a major contribution these films make to the reappraisal of Tibetan ecology and to the theorizing of ecocinema not only lies in providing glimpses of Tibetan life but also in mobilizing culturally conditioned perceptions of ecological "connectedness" — a widely used but vaguely defined concept in ecocriticism. In other words, as a visual medium, film has the potential both to clarify and obscure the dynamics of ecological interconnectivity, according to the limitations, self-awareness, or insight of the director. While documenting the different contacts the directors have with Tibet, these films bear witness to the different perceptional frameworks within which Tibetan and Chinese directors perceive and create ecological connections. My hypothesis is that the examination of culturally conditioned positions embedded in the taking, selecting, and editing of footages can be expected to contribute to a more self-reflective practice of ecocriticism across disciplines.

Specifically, this discussion proceeds in four parts. It begins with an overview of the changed environmental discourse in mainstream Chinese documentary-style film, starting in the late 1980s before massive industrialization programs were launched in China. The second part proceeds to Fifth Generation director Tian Zhuangzhuang's subtitled documentary *Delamu* (2004). Critically acclaimed by film academics in China, Tian's documentary film will be used as an example of the evolving mainstream aesthetic background against which Wanma presents his work. Although Tian would object to his inclusion in the mainstream, I use the word "experimental mainstream" to direct attention to the emerging hybridized mainstream "ethnographical" genres of which Tian's work is a part, despite its self-differentiation from government-sponsored propaganda documentaries and popular entertainment films.

The next two sections concentrate on Wanma Caidan's two Tibetan-language documentary-style fiction films — *The Grassland* (2003) and *The Silent Holy Stone* (2005) — in correspondence to his two-phase redefinition of Tibetan culture. Although there is little secondary literature on his works, Wanma's films are crucial to the discussion of film representation of ecological connections informed by Tibetan Buddhism. Despite Tibet's lure for film directors and academics, Tibetan Buddhism is almost always represented in terms of formal ritual or Bon mysticism. Similarly, even in volumes devoted to the discussion of Buddhist ecological views such as *Buddhism and Ecology: The Interconnection of Dharma and Deeds*,[2] Buddhism is only studied in relation to Chinese, Japanese, and Thai Buddhisms to the complete exclusion of Tibetan Buddhism. Wanma's Tibetan-language films therefore are a valuable response to this omission.

Documenting Discursive and Landscape Changes

Wanma's films and Tian's documentary are loosely categorized as documentary-style films in this chapter because they straddle fiction and non-fiction film genres: Tian's film is a staged documentary and Wanma's fiction films contain a generous amount of documentary aesthetics. The blend between documentary and fiction genres constitutes a new trend with Chinese film directors and is particularly favored in films with ecological interests. To analyze fiction/documentary-mixed ecocinema, a brief review of the connection and distinction of the two different genres is a necessary introduction. As Bill Nichols observes in his broad definition of documentaries:

> Every film is documentary. Even the most whimsical of fiction gives evidence of the culture that produced it and reproduces the likeness of the people who perform within it. In fact, we could say that there are two kinds of film: (1) documentaries of wish-fulfillment and (2) documentaries of social representations. Documentaries of wish-fulfillment ... give tangible expression to our wishes and dreams, our nightmares and dreads. They make the stuff of the imagination concrete — visible and audible ... Documentaries of social representation ... give tangible representation to aspects of the world we already inhabit and share. They make the stuff of social reality visible and audible in a distinctive way, according to the acts of selection and arrangement carried out by a filmmaker. They give a sense of what we understand reality itself to have been, of what it is now, or of what it may become.[3]

Differently put, both fiction films and documentaries are simultaneously fictional and non-fictional in the sense that they both reflect reality as we want it to be and archive the cultural realities of the time and place of its production. However, in China the objects of both wish-fulfillment and social representation have been radically changing.

From 1949 to the late 1980s, documentary film in China was largely identified with newsreels and montage-style news magazines modeled after those by Soviet director Dziga Vertov.[4] Documentaries as such spoke prophetically, guiding the public to bring their lives in line with a grand vision of the future. The future prospect was boundless because resources were inexhaustible. The public had never been instructed otherwise until 1988 when a six-episode television documentary, *The River Elegy* (*Heshang*), aired nationwide on CCTV. *The River Elegy* raised a sense of crisis with the help of a geopolitical reinterpretation of the Yellow River — popularly known as the cradle of Chinese civilization. Defying the glossy socialist vision of the future as well as populist sentiment over national roots, it spotlights a well-known but little discussed facet of the Yellow River — the environmental hazard embedded in "agricultural civilization" or the "yellow earth civilization."[5] Due to continuous deforestation in the upper reach of the river, the Yellow River has been severely sedimented as far back in time as the Yellow River is known in literary sources or historical records. With the riverbed raised twenty-eight feet above street level in the most populous area of China, the Yellow River resembles a bomb suspended over the historic lowlands. *The River Elegy* goes further than sociologist Murray Bookchin's famous position statement that "all ecological problems are social problems."[6] The scriptwriters of the TV documentary use the Yellow River ecology as an allegory for China's socio-political crisis. The voice over the murky river declares: "Our civilization is too old. It needs to be rejuvenated with new cultural cells. Like the sediment at the bottom of the Yellow River, this old civilization has blocked the blood vessels of our nation. It requires a powerful flood to wash it off."

Sluggishness of Chinese cultural and social structure is visualized, among other things, in a sweeping shot of religious devotees at the beginning of each episode: Chinese Buddhists praying with their hands, Muslims on their knees with their bottoms facing the camera, and Tibetan pilgrims prostrating on all fours. This picture of slow, rhythmic, and collective body movement resonates with communist and intellectuals' ideas about blind superstition as well as the cultural elite's conception of stagnant agricultural civilizations.

Socialism, the realization of which relied heavily on peasant revolutions in China, offers no real solution to the crisis embedded in agricultural civilization. Instead, the attempt to tame the Yellow River by building dams has only made the situation more precarious. The Sanmen Xia Dam on the Yellow River — one of the tombstones of Sino-Soviet cooperation — serves as a testament to socialist deviation from the West. Indeed, the sole opposition to the dam enthusiasm came from American-trained geologist/hydrologist Huang Wanli. His disenchanted voice had been suppressed for decades until *The River Elegy* created a forum for him to speak out on behalf of the rational West. Initially entitled *Breaking Out of Yan'an* (*Zouchu yan'an*), *The River Elegy* proposes to draw directly on enlightenment truth — progress, as exemplified by the real West — "industrial civilization" or the "civilization of ocean blue." The series prepares audiences for what it sees as the inevitable: "In fact, this flood has already arrived. It is industrial culture. Industrial culture is beckoning us."

Despite the remarkable consistency with which water metaphors are explored in the documentary (powerful ocean waves flushing off the muddy deposits from a blocked waterway), the elements are secondary, except for being metaphors employed to trumpet the cause of socio-political reform.[7] From where it stood in the 1980s, *The River Elegy* cannot be expected to predict the events of the 1990s or be completely "real" about the environment. This is evidenced by the fact that it identifies industrial culture with one monolithic color — the crystal-clean ocean-blue — and expects industrialization to solve China's long-standing environmental problem. Nonetheless, *The River Elegy* is groundbreaking in bringing the environment to public attention, preparing public intellectuals to discuss environment problems in terms of national crisis, as well as the other way around.

When unrestrained economic development in the 1990s prompted reflections on its environmental and social cost, the intelligentsia's attitudes towards "agricultural civilization" softened. The idea of revisiting the holistic worldviews of premodernity — especially where they seamlessly integrate with ecological awareness — has gained momentum among intellectuals. Religion, when perceived as reverence to nature, is now valued as an enduring form of wisdom in contrast to the short-term profit of rapid development and China's anxieties about modernity and globalization. Many public intellectuals — including environmental activists — attribute the deteriorating environment to a lack of reverence of nature, of God, or of social scruples. If the country still needs to pursue economic development for the well-being of the majority of its population, anthropologist Zhang Haiyang offers the "reconstruction of God-fearing communities" as the solution to social and environmental problems brought about by modernity.[8] In this context, "God-fearing communities" refers in particular to ethnic regions where religious beliefs and practice are retained and integrated into everyday life.[9] The Tibetan-Qinghai plateau offers the chief source of such imagination because of its geographical isolation, comparatively coherent culture, and the well-known spiritual pursuit of its people.

This 180-degree change in public discourse has implications for both the wish fulfillment and the social representation of film. Significantly, the desire to preserve prevails over the desire to predict. Tibet and the rural regions inhabited by ethnic minorities were the first locations where new documentary filmmakers such as Duan Jinchuan committed themselves to preserving in film what appeared to be the pre-industrial condition. The seemingly unedited, unpolished, and non-dramatic everydayness characteristic of this new wave of amateur anthropography documentary films was subsequently appropriated in fiction films that ride on what Yomi Braester describes as "documentary impulse."[10] In this regard, Tian's documentary and Wanma's fiction films provide concrete examples as to how documentary aesthetics can be used in the service of two important strands of ecocinema — recreating rural stability and/or documenting ecological changes in Tibetan areas.[11]

Delamu — Vision into Landscape

"Maybe a couple of mountains, monks, and stuff like that" — this sparse imagery is enough to convert a young Californian into a Tibetan enthusiast.[12] Indeed, mountains and monks comprise the quintessential images of Tibet in Chinese as well as Euro-American film representations of the Tibetan ecology. Tibetan spirituality, conceptually entwined and identified with the snow-clad mountains, is found in Hollywood blockbusters such as *Seven Years in Tibet* (dir. Jean-Jacques Annaud, 1997), the French movie *Himalayas — l'enfance d'un chef* (dir. Eric Valli, 1999), and Chinese blockbusters such as *The Story of the Sacred Mountain* (literally *The Red River Valley*, dir. Feng Xiaoning, 1997).

A practical explanation for such shared concentration on a few iconic images of Tibetan natural landscape and spirituality can be found in Tuan Yifu's observation of the use of landmark imagery. Tuan maintains that landmark image for a region is "a mnemonic device ... people's concept of a place or region which they have not directly experienced and which can be expressed in words, pictures, or maps."[13] In comparison, Tian's documentary *Delamu* is more complicated in terms of landscape or scenic construction. Tian has made serious attempts to go beyond popular postcard images of Tibet — the snow-clad mountains are nowhere to be found in *Delama*. Before the shooting of the film, he spent three years touring the area and still takes pride in the authenticity of his on-site observation. As further evidence of his on-site interactions with indigenous people, the film is mostly comprised of interviews with locals. Nonetheless, landscape or scenic construction is still his preferred approach as long as landscape construction can be understood as a projection of natural harmony between human beings and the natural environment.

Tian is well known, among other things, for his infatuation with Tibet. Although his first film set in Tibet (*Horse Thief*, 1987), is primarily remembered for its record box-office failure, Tian was partly right in claiming to make films for the audience of the twenty-first century because Tibet's popularity as a film setting has soared since the turn of the new millennium.[14] After years of relative obscurity, Tian Zhuangzhuang resurfaced in the limelight in 2004 with *Delamu*, a documentary set on the border between Yunnan and Tibet. Its focus is on the indigenous people (*yuanzhumin*) residing on the border of Yunnan and Tibet, along the ancient tea-and-horse route that linked trade between China, Tibet, and Burma, beginning in the twelfth century. The region is still underdeveloped by any standard; its residents live in considerable isolation in the natural environment. Their primary connection with the outside world is caravans that periodically arrive with commodities. However, the situation is to change. At the time the film was shot, a highway was under construction and was expected to be finished in three to five years' time. *Delamu* was designed to record that which would soon become history.

Characterized by a mellow nostalgia for an environment in which human beings live in harmony with nature and at peace with one another, *Delamu* has been celebrated by film academics as "a special kind of documentary."[15] Technically, this means that the film is between genres. For example, one could justifiably classify *Delamu* as a travel narrative — an existential traveler's search for the meaning of life and adventure. It is essentially about Tian's discovery of a hidden utopia — a model of the imagined original China as opposed to the China of the world processing center. The filming of this remote region of ethnic minorities is described by the director as an escape from the SARS (Severe Acute Respiratory Syndrome)-seized city to a place of "fresh air, natural, healthy people, and the essential *qi*." This trajectory of escape is recorded in a special feature that accompanies the documentary on a separate DVD — an uncommon feature for a documentary whose focus is supposed to be indigenous people and their everyday life, instead of stars and celebrities. The opening scene of the special feature is symbolic of a jailbreak: the director is confined in a hotel room, reporting to Beijing that the film crew is stranded while on its way to the filming location. As the director observes, in order to stop the rapid spread of SARS from coastal cities, "the entire country [was] trapped in a state of suspension"; in Spring 2003, traffic between counties was suspended even in the southwest end of the remote Yunnan Province.

In the special feature, SARS is explicitly attributed to "the crowds of big cities in China." The city is represented by the imagery of dubious entertainment quarters, an ambulance, and shops deserted by customers. Compared with urbanites who, according to Tian's description, spent their lives "making a living, getting around in traffic jams, pursuing career ambitions, and dealing with pollution," the ancient tea-and-horse route constitutes a dreamland where life is essential, meaningful, and even leisurely. Although this imagination is not completely sustained by screen images or the indigenous people's life stories, the film crew believes that it has unearthed an organic China — one that differs from the artificial China that is held responsible for ruining the world climate, polluting the water system, and accelerating global warming.

The two aspects of indigenous culture that Tian attempts to explore are nature and religion in everyday life.[16] The way he emphasizes observation draws *Delamu* close to being an ethnographic film that, according to David McDougall's description, aims to show "some discernible intention of recording and revealing cultural pattern."[17] However, the total of thirty-two days allotted to shoot the film and interview residents scattered along ninety kilometers of the ancient trade route was not sufficient for any in-depth exploration of the subject. In addition, Tian was too creative to be satisfied with the role of simply taking, selecting, and editing footages, as a documentary director is normally obliged to do. In short, he refused to be restricted by any genre limitations commonly associated with documentary making. The lofty but ultimately subjective goal Tian set for himself was to "reveal the spirit and poetry of the place and its people at any cost."[18] For this purpose, he applied his expertise in fiction film direction to the making of a documentary.

To start with, nature is conveniently introduced as pictures. The film opens with a breathtaking landscape of mountains partly veiled by white mist. The color scheme of pure blue (mountains) framed in white (clouds) hammers in the idea of uncontaminated and mysterious nature. The sense of nature is further enhanced with the use of montage in the form of soundtrack and aggressive editing. The meditative music that accompanies the pictures conveys a sense of natural serenity. This imagery of uncontaminated nature hereafter serves as the overarching framework into which locals and other landscape images are placed.

However, many scenarios that Tian planned to use to create the atmosphere and impression of a completely natural environment were non-existent at the time the film was shot. Staging was therefore extensively used to add "natural" touches to the picture and to properly situate the locals within it. Staging started with the assembling of a caravan. The caravan that was expected to lead the film crew "naturally" to the indigenous people was not available. The one shown in *Delamu* was assembled especially for the sake of the film. Moreover, the postman who is supposed to ride his bike across the rope bridge hung above the river had long stopped delivering mail on his bike. He was requested to resume the practice for the film and to deliver a half dozen letters posted from Beijing and Guangdong to a family hotel.[19] While the family hotel is real, the letters are not.

More often, staging in *Delamu* takes on the form of still life posing against a designated background — grafting the interviewed onto dramatic vistas. This way the indigenous people can be best framed in the picture as museum pieces ("living fossils" in Tian's words). For example, in the filming of a 104-year-old blind Tibetan woman, the fire in the pottery stove and the mist rising from the cooking constitute the stage set for Tian's signature picture of aboriginal life. The film crew waited for three days before she could enter the scene and tell her story to the camera as expected. Despite or because of these carefully staged scenarios, *Delamu* is applauded by film academics as a "new classic" in Chinese documentary film.[20] It is critically acclaimed for "discovering the people living in harmony with nature" and "breathing the fresh air from the mountains and rivers"[21] because each piece fits into some conventional Chinese imagination of spontaneous unity between human beings and the natural environment. Compared with Chinese blockbuster films in which fabrication is usually rushed, flawed, and not to be taken seriously, *Delamu* designs a nearly seamless "real life." It is not my intention to critique Tian's staging as a kind of professional misconduct or to suggest that it is mutually exclusive from documentary making. More relevant to this discussion is the prior perception of undisturbed natural life that the director (un)consciously acts on in the filming of indigenous people.

Delamu is, nonetheless, ambiguous in another area that Tian promises to clarify — the indigenous people's relationship with religion or the relationship between nature and religion. This connection remains loose throughout the film. Although a church gathering is the focus of one episode and a lama tells his life story in another, the film makes no effort even to differentiate Tibetan Buddhism from Catholicism in their approaches to nature and their nuanced influence on the indigenous people. Instead, religion is generally identified in the film as the feeling of gratitude and/or the ability to endure adverse circumstances. Nearly all the life stories the villagers tell directly to the camera are about coping with poverty and adversities. Still the role of religion is not clear. For example, a Tibetan man in his late twenties reveals that he and his brother are compelled by poverty to share one wife. Although he has come to terms with the situation, it is questionable whether he is inspired by religion or can be described as religious. Indeed, both the people and their religion are imagined as products of the spirit of the place, although Catholicism and Buddhist are both imported and Catholicism was not introduced to this area until the nineteenth century.

This ambiguity could be deliberate. In *Delamu* the discovery of religion among ethnic minorities is prioritized over defining religion. Intertitles are placed between scenes to lead the audience into associating nature and religion where the connection is largely imagined. Apart from the use of short informational intertitles for the purpose of contextualizing screen images, intertitles in the form of two- or four-line poems are used to help the audience discern subtle but significant signs of the divine. In the first episode of the documentary, "The Song of the Returned Traveler," for example, the intertitle is a four-line poem that reads: "This tiny green leaf on the deserted mountain/ has absorbed a thousand years of quietude/ Tested by furious wind/ and the scorching sun/ the peace in your apples is divine." Passages like this invite the audience to follow the connection between indigenous life, nature, and religion the director makes on behalf of the locals. However, in its lyrical tone, *Delamu* loosely identifies religion with something ancient and lasting, suggesting that whatever survives naturally contributes to cultural conservation as well as acquires a dimension of divinity. Like the mist-veiled mountains, religion constitutes a mystery as well as an atmosphere. *Delamu* reveals as well as creates this mystery.

This organic China is a child born from the marriage of non-fiction and fiction. *Delamu* blurs the boundary of the director's mindscape and the land, substantiating his vision of ecological harmony with concrete landscape images. As Tian recalls, "When first coming into contact with that place, I was completely under the influence of the people, rivers, mountains, and culture of that place, free from any preconceptions. That was the most exciting condition. It is painful to realize that the making of the film restrains and trims these things little by little."[22] It is the Daoist, Confucian, and Chinese Buddhist imagination of ecological harmony that shapes the view and excludes what is irrelevant from the picture. This mindscape both motivates the director to look for the non-industrial landscape and blocks it from him.

Admittedly, Tian is not the only one who has encountered difficulties in "getting real" about Tibet.[23] In fact, by the time Tian embarked on his discovery journey to the Tibetan area, younger filmmakers, who contributed to the first wave of documentaries on Tibet in the 1990s, had already withdrawn from Tibet, having outgrown their initial, mostly visual, infatuation with Tibet. This vanguard group included Ji Dan, an independent documentary filmmaker, who learned the Tibetan language, lived for two years in a Tibetan village, and finished two well-known documentaries on Tibetan rural life — *The Happy Life of the Gongbus* (*Gongbu de xingfu shenghuo*, 1997) and *The Elderly* (*Laoren men*, 1997). Admitting to the fact that her Chinese cultural background frequently interfered with her perception of Tibetan culture, she left Tibet in order to pursue a subject within her reach.[24]

Although non-fiction is no longer considered as mutually exclusive with imagination and fantasy as suggested by some critics,[25] to classify a film documentary is to create expectations for reality and to promise to meet these expectations.[26] It is questionable whether such promises are delivered by *Delamu*. As a "special documentary," *Delamu* actually reveals more about the position of the director than that of the indigenous people. The film is extremely informative of ecologically wise Tibetans as imagined by urban intellectuals in China. However, what do Tibetans think about the environment?

The Grassland — Wanma Caidan's Middle Landscape

A recent graduate from the Beijing Film Academy, Tibetan director Wanma Caidan is a newcomer on the film scene. Nonetheless, his two low-budget Tibetan-language films are well known in Tibetan areas and at international film festivals, not because a Tibetan filmmaker is a novelty, but because his films invite reflections and imaginations on the deeper landscape of Tibet. For example, his films are mostly appreciated as documentaries on Tibet despite the director's repeated attempts to verify that they are fiction films. This section explores Wanma's construction of a deeper or inner landscape of Tibetan life, which is conventionally presented as a spectacle.

Wanma's graduation project, *The Grassland* (2004), marks the first film made by a Tibetan director. It is also Wanma's first attempt to define Tibetan culture in cinematic language. As a thesis project, the film presents a slice of Tibetan life in a conventional aesthetic framework — a recognizable landscape of Tibet that is frequently accepted by critics and audience as the epitome of Tibet. Within the time restraint of fifteen minutes, the film tells a moving story about the theft and recovery of a sacred yak (a yak set free by its owner). Releasing domestic animals to the wildness is a way of showing respect for life in the Buddhist tradition. It is primarily in Tibetan areas that the tradition lives on among the lay population as an integral part of life and celebration. In this regard, *The Grassland* tells a story geo-culturally marked as Tibetan.

However, *The Grassland* is atypical of Tibetan films, as the term is conventionally understood by Chinese directors. Instead of focusing on the magnificent religious rituals and mysticism of Lamaism, it concentrates on commoners who revere the Buddha and local deities. Rather than reinforcing the religious atmosphere with the sound of trumpets or the view of monasteries, the film starts like a detective story (a lost and found story) that could happen at any time — the village head Chieftain Tsedrunk and the elderly Ama Tsomo are in the neighboring Meilong Grassland to look for the latter's missing sacred yak. Like any religion, Buddhism rates stealing as a crime; however, the stealing of a sacred animal is alarmingly profane to religious Tibetans. It is nothing short of a deliberate violation against the divine connection among human beings, living things, and the mountain god. Tsedrunk's determination to pursue the matter to the end is supported by the entire community in an attempt to restore the disrupted order in the Meilong Grassland.

Next, the audience is presented with the equivalent of a courtroom drama. No lawyers and judges in the conventional sense of the word appear. However, it is no less solemn than any formal trial because it is presided over by the divine. Chieftain Dorlo of Meilong Grassland summons three suspicious youths to confess their sin or swear their innocence in front of a *mani* stack — pebbles and stones Tibetans pile up on roadsides to serve as altars for prayer — against the background of the distant mountain range. Though the suspects decry the unfairness of being fingered by the chieftain, they never doubt the justice and presence of the divine.

Contrasted with this communal determination to pursue justice is Ama Tsomo's uneasiness about the trial. She is willing to forgive whoever stole the yak because she feels uneasy about disturbing the mountain god with what must be a trivial matter to the divine; in addition, she is concerned that the revelation of the truth may lead to the thief's arrest and imprisonment. In her own words, "it would be a grave error of mine if people are punished for stealing the yak." Her generosity extends from a vague concept of "all living things" to include someone who has taken advantage of her religious devotion. This concern for fellow human beings contrasts significantly with the stereotypical representation of Tibetans as more conscious of animal life under the influence of Buddhist idea of reincarnation. For example, in *Seven Years in Tibet*, the monks assigned to build a cinema for the young Dalai Lama are more concerned about relocating worms dug up from the soil than actually building the cinema. In *The Grassland*, it is not the fear of bad karma or concern with incarnation but Ama Tsomo's generosity that moves the thief to confess. The final scene sees Chieftain Dorlo and his son — the yak thief — heading towards Ama Tsomo's village to return the sacred yak.

While directing attention to religion in the lives of the lay people in Tibet, *The Grassland* still follows the aesthetics of mainstream Chinese film representations of Tibet somewhat, in terms of landscape construction. It starts with what may be described as the iconic landscape of Tibet: the camera traces an eagle as it hovers in the crystal-clear blue sky. The association of a pure, unpolluted, and spiritual Tibet embedded in the imagery is reinforced by a high-pitched Tibetan folk song sung over the screen — the well-known sound of Tibet or the expression of nomadic life in a vast, empty space. The opening scenario is followed by a horizontal shot of the grassland that extends to distant mountains. When two human figures — Trusdesh and Ama Tsomo — finally appear, their conversation is accompanied and almost drowned out by the singing over the screen. The lyrics of the song offer an interpretation of the Tibetan herdsmen to the effect of identifying them with the grassland: "the sheep are stars/ herds people are the moon/ herdsmen are the sun/ sheep are the dew on the grassland." As a predication of the story to take place, the lyrics emphasize the generosity of Tibetan nature: that the heart of a Tibetan is comparable to "a silver milk bowl. It is filled with sweet and pure milk." As is often the case with Chinese films, ethnic minorities are admirable, presented for their transparency, which reversely implies their lack of subtlety or psychological depth.

The Grassland is critically acclaimed for its story, film aesthetics and all. Film critic Cui Weiping, for example, speaks of the film as an "excellent arthouse film"; director Xie Fei sees in it the potential of Tibetan film in China.[27] Wanma, however, has much higher expectations for himself. When asked about his opinion, Wanma told the author that he "dislikes the film because it was derived from a concept (*gainian hua*). It is driven by the desire to present something emblematic of Tibet."[28] Wanma resists simplistic representation of Tibetans because he sees himself responsible for making films that mirror and reflect the nuanced geo-cultures of Tibetan regions. His second film *The Silent Holy Stone*, which is also his first full-length film, presents a comprehensive endeavor to this effect.

The Dynamic Holy Stone

Wanma refers to the subject of his first full-length film, *The Silent Holy Stone* (2005), as the "condition of life in a Tibetan area." "Condition" in the context of this film has both spatial and temporal implications, encompassing the geo-cultural condition of the region and the socio-economic structure of the community. Significantly, Wanma uses *zangqu* (Tibetan regions) instead of "Tibet" when referring to areas inhabited by Tibetans. The concept of Tibetan regions places emphasis on geo-cultural differences embedded in Tibetan life. As Wanma observes:

> Non-Tibetans tend to mistake the Tibetan regions for Tibet. The Tibetan regions actually extend beyond Tibet to encompass three big areas — Amdo, Kampa, and Ütsang. Identified with three major dialects, the three areas form an interrelated organic entity. Ütsang, for example, overlaps with the Lhasa dialect area, Amdo is formed of a part of Qinghai province, a part of Gansu and Sichuan provinces. Kampa spreads over Tibet, Qinghai, Sichuan, and Yunnan.[29]

Lhasa is identified with Tibetan aristocrats and the clergy elite who lived in the city when it was the cultural and political center of the Tibetan regions. Although it is popularly accepted as being emblematic of Tibet, Lhasa is not demographically representative of the rest of Tibet, much less of other regions such as Wanma's hometown, Amdo. Wanma emphasizes that Amdo "has a half agrarian and half herdsman economy. Up in the mountains, people herd their cattle; down in the plains, farmers grow their crops."[30] In other words, residents of Amdo are not completely represented by the herdsmen in *The Grassland* or the clergy in *Seven Years in Tibet*.

What Wanma conceives as the "condition" of Tibetan life refers to a lived-in environment, an environment firmly grounded in everyday specifics. To this end, wide-angle observatory shots characteristic of non-fiction film are frequently used in his recent films. The stark, overexposed images convey the visual effect of looking at the arid land of the Tibet-Qinghai plateau under the unfiltered natural light of the glaring winter sun. The film also employs completely non-professional actors. The characters play their role in life: the Little Living Buddha is actually a Buddha and the little monk is also a monk in real life. They were given permission to revise the script in order to play themselves.

At the same time, by "condition," Wanma refers more emphatically to the dynamics embedded in everyday situations. It underscores interconnected transition instead of a fixed state of things. Tibetan Buddhism has absorbed significant influence from India after the seventh century. Chinese and Japanese Buddhist ideas about original nature and "pure land" as the ultimate refuge from the worldly concerns are foreign to Tibetan Buddhism. Although the standardized Tibetan landscape of snow-clad mountains could satisfy popular imaginations of ecological stability, still nothing could be more remote from the concept of stability in Tibetan Buddhism. One especially emphasized tenet in Tibetan Buddhism is the concept of emptiness in the phenomenological world (*samsaric*) — emptiness defined in terms of the absence of fixed essence. The phenomenological world is temporal and impermanent; it is formed of a network of an ever-changing flux of atoms or a chain of dynamic causations instead of atomic unity. Tibetans who spend their lives earning good karma for the next life are acting on their awareness of the intransient nature of existence. Because the totality as well as any portion of the environment rests on the chain of causations, "stability" is inherently impossible. In addition, in Tibetan Buddhist concepts, "pure land" or the Buddha field can be located in everyday life scenes rather than in some cosmic paradise. The essence or ideal of the Buddha field is that the individual should respond to interconnectedness through sharing (*dana*) and constructive action (*attacariya*). Doing things for others' benefit is instrumental to the Tibetan Buddhist ideas of interconnectivity.[31]

The Silent Holy Stone explores changes and new balances in Tibetan life, although nothing dramatic happens in the film on the surface. The storyline is simple: a Buddhist monk in his early teens visits his parents on New Year's Day. The parents entertain the little monk with a television adaptation of *The Journal to the West*, a popular classic loosely based on the legendary pilgrimage of Xuanzang to India to fetch Buddhist scriptures in the seventh century. The next day, the little monk takes the VCD (video compact disc) with him to the monastery and watches the television drama with his friends and tutors.

The little monk's two-day home visit is, nonetheless, integrated with a multitude of revealing details about Tibetan community structuring. A major cohesive tissue in traditional Tibetan community — the Buddhist value of giving and sharing — is forged through *Drimed Kundan*, one of the Jataka tales (about Buddha Sakyamuni's earlier incarnations) in the Crown Prince Sudana Sutra. The traditional venue of the play is the Tibetan theater — an operatic theater that dates back to the fourteenth century. The play is staged twice during the little monk's home visit. Drimed Kundan is seen to distribute his wealth from the treasury to the poor, to give away his three children, and finally to offer both his eyes to a blind man, on stage in the community center. The play is traditionally expected to be treated as moral example for the community instead of as mere entertainment. It is in the observation of this tradition that the younger generation departs from the old. For example, the little monk's elder brother plays Drimed Kundan on stage but moves out of that role immediately after the performance is over. By contrast, his grandfather recommends Drimed Kundan as a model for his grandchildren to emulate in their own lives. The grandfather reprimands the actor for failing to live up to Drimed Kundan's example when he is reluctant to lend the little monk his television and VCD player to show *The Journey to the West* in the monastery.

The traditional idea of interconnectedness is further illustrated by Wanma's portrayal of the little Buddha. "Don't be childish. You should not push your way around just because you are a Buddha. People are waiting to get your blessing. You have to see them." This is the scripture tutor's response to the little Buddha's request to see one more episode of *The Journey to the West*. The eight-year-old little Buddha is portrayed as an ordinary child in every sense of the word. His childishness contrasts with the extraordinary wisdom of young Dalai Lama in *Seven Years in Tibet*. The young Dalai Lama's lifelong friendship with Heinrich Harrer, his "yellow head" Austrian mentor, stems from His Holiness's unquenchable desire to "know everything about the [outside] world." The little Buddha in Amdo, on the other hand, is not interested in world politics. He finds state leaders boring because "adults do not know how to play." In the film, his contribution to the community is mostly symbolic, similar to that of the child emperors in Chinese history. The little Buddha embodies the connection with spirituality required by the community. The little Buddha, as such, is a symbol around which the communal bond is forged and imagined.

Wanma's de-exoticizing of Tibetan Buddhist institutions is only counterbalanced by examples of the pervasive influence of Buddhism in everyday life, ranging from releasing animals to celebrate new life to philosophically reflecting on the inevitability of death. However, *The Silent Holy Stone* shows an underrepresented aspect of Buddhist ecology in that it recognizes the dynamics, including changes, in the environment. Like other communities, Wanma's Tibetan community is built on changing economic realities. With increased social mobility and market development, the traditional and newly introduced value systems are competing with one another for attention. For example, the young no longer limit their career choices to the clergy or farming. The little monk's elder brother does business; his younger brother studies Chinese, planning to move to the city when he grows up; and two other boys who were sent to the monastery by their families renounce it. Changes in the rural community and monastery are expected to continue beyond the bounds of the film screen.

A significant change spotlighted in the film is the appearance of new media. The arrival of television marks the beginning of what Wanma refers to as "a negotiation between Tibetan culture and the outside world" on an everyday basis.[32] It is not only an antenna that brings in the outside world (as in the rest of the world, Iraq is in the headline news in Tibetan television): it is also a phenomenon with cultural and economic implications locally. The presence of the machine at home and in the monastery suggests a new pedagogical interest in technology, perhaps with varying degrees of entertainment value. As an invited guest, the machine is handled with care, suspicion, or reverence. Parental figures try to figure out how to accommodate and harness this piece of modern machinery to purposeful service. At home the father ensures that "the machine should be treated like us humans. It should not be overworked." In the monastery, the watching of the television and VCDs is monitored by another parental figure. The scripture tutor sees to it that the little monks and the little Buddha are not overexposed to the world outside the monastery or distracted from their study of the scripture.

Due to technological and geographical reasons, the reception of television transmission in most regions in the Tibet-Qinghai plateau is extremely limited. Some areas, like the one in the film, can only receive one or two channels, and only a portion of these programs are in the Tibetan language. VCD, therefore, provides a much desired additional choice. *Drimed Kundan* and *The Journey to the West*, widely circulated in Tibetan regions in the form of storytelling or theatrical performance, are now represented on VCD. Buddhist stories, which represent familiar values to Tibetans, serve as the "translation code" with which the new medium is introduced.[33]

The Silent Holy Stone traces the gradual unfolding of what will be a long process of cultural interaction. Its minimalist depiction contrasts with the drama of *The Cup* (dir. Khyentse Norbu, 2000), an Indian film that focuses exclusively on Tibetan Buddhist monks' reception of television. *The Cup* evokes the idea of a global village, with football as the global language and television its carrier. Even exiled Tibetans prove themselves part of this international community despite their isolation as monks living in a monastery in a foreign country (India). The monastery in Wanma's film, on the other hand, is closely affiliated with a network of local Tibetan communities; the introduction of television in the monastery represents a more complex negotiation between Tibetan culture and mainstream entertainment. It is neither a completely secular nor a totally global development.

The introduction of religious and quasi-religious VCDs could even be described as facilitating a fresh take on Buddhist materials. To some extent, the legendary stories of Drimed Kundan and *The Journey to the West* are reintroduced through a new medium. In this regard, the little monk's experience with Drimed Kundan provides a good example. Bored by having seen the play countless times in the village community center, the little monk is, nonetheless, drawn to the VCD version. The play becomes new to the little monk when it appears on the television screen.

As a fictional work, *The Journey to the West* presents a complex interpretation of Buddhism. Although the text uses Xuanzang's pilgrimage to India as its framing story, Xuanzang only serves as the nominal protagonist. His dogmatic approach to the Buddhist scriptures makes him ill equipped for his turbulent journey to India. In the novel and the television drama, Xuanzang is deceived whenever evil spirits disguise themselves as innocent people. He would have died many times if not for the help of his disciple, the Monkey King. Despite his lack of respect for the hierarchy of organized religion, the Monkey King proves himself a more sophisticated Buddhist, free from illusions and immune from temptations. Among Han Chinese the text is mainly read as an adventure story; its targeted audience is children. Tibetans, on the other hand, have a more serious take on the television drama, owing to their Buddhist background and high regard for pilgrimage.[34] Not only are children enthusiastic about the television drama, but adults, including the grandfather and little monk's tutor, also like it. Since Buddhist messages are well mixed with adventure stories in the text, it is possible that they are emphasized differently by adults and children. The little monk's elderly tutor sees his own pilgrimage to Lhasa as a continuation of Xuanzang's pilgrimage to India. He not only spends ten years preparing for the journey but is willing to die for it. The little monk and the little Buddha, on the other hand, are both drawn to the adventure story, casting themselves into the role of the Monkey King, wearing a monkey mask and mimicking his voice. Just as the outside world is drawn to the Tibetan community for its mystery, members of the community are also drawn to the outside world. They may lure each other as illusions before they come into deep contact. It is the contact and negotiation between them that will shape the future of the Tibetan community.

The monastery and parents purchase VCD players only to explore the desired offerings of the new technology. The fact that Hong Kong crime fiction is shown in a dark shed outside the community center where *Drimed Kundan* is staged reminds the audience that the new medium has the potential to affect the Tibetans in many more ways that are contrary to Buddhism as well. That a 1988 television drama from China can create a new sensation in Tibet in the early twenty-first century is a concrete example of Tibet's belated modernity. However, precisely because it is late in the race for modernization, Tibet may be blessed with the opportunity to make informed decisions about its future. Like the film, the future is open-ended.

Conclusion

Tibet is almost always perceived as the object of modern people's wishes, whether they be modernization or the escape from modernization. The drastically increased interest in the Tibetan religion in China since the turn of the twenty-first century is significant in terms of critical reflection on the environmental cost of modernization. Cinematic imagery of Tibet is particularly instrumental in visualizing and forging connections essential to ecological imagination. Scott Slovic maintains that "ecocriticism has no central, dominant doctrine or theoretical apparatus — rather, ecocritical theory, such as it is, is being re-defined daily by the actual practice of thousands of literary scholars around the world ... If you're looking for ecocritical theory, look for it in our practice."[35] The diverse cinematic landscapes of Tibetan areas are metaphorical of different localities and perspectives from which film directors engage the subject. Even the idealized vision is highly informative of what we wish for and how we position ourselves in relation to ecological conservation. In this regard, Tian Zhuangzhuang's documentary is both representative and remarkable for its persistent use of cut-and-paste imagery to fit Tibet into the Chinese cosmological imaging of ecological harmony.

Wanma, on the other hand, shows that Tibet has more to offer towards ecological consciousness than we imagined, precisely because it challenges the concept of ecological harmony as a feasible description of Tibetan ecological consciousness. Despite its ancient appearance, Tibetan Buddhism, with its special emphasis on the instability of the phenomenological world, is surprisingly pertinent to what is referred to in secular terms as ecological consciousness. Informed by Tibetan Buddhism, *The Silent Holy Stone* refuses to be deluded by a perfectly stable ecological past as envisioned in *Delamu*. What it suggests is a sense of being on the move, a Tibet that is cautiously and yet steadily changing while attempting to reach a new balance.

Although Tibet is reconstructed and imagined as a remote domain from industrialization, Wanma reminds the audience that Tibetans will not stand still just to satisfy the romantic imagination of urbanites. Whether this is seen as an illustration of the Tibetan Buddhist concept of the flux or the impact of modernization, *The Silent Holy Stone* encourages the audience to rethink what happened in China not long ago. If they could start all over again in China, would they do it differently?

Notes

Introduction. Cinema, Ecology, Modernity

1. Cheryll Glotfelty, "Introduction: Literary Studies in an Age of Environmental Crisis," in *The Ecocriticism Reader: Landmarks in Literary Ecology*, ed. Cheryll Glotfelty and Harold Fromm (Athens and London: University of Georgia Press, 1996), xviii. For other comprehensive anthologies of ecocriticism, see, for example, Steven Rosendale, *The Greening of Literary Scholarship: Literature, Theory, and the Environment* (Iowa City: University of Iowa Press, 2002); Michael P. Branch and Scott Slovic, eds., *The ISLE Reader: Ecocriticism, 1993–2003* (Athens and London: University of Georgia Press, 2003); Michael P. Branch, Rochelle Johnson, Daniel Patterson, and Scott Slovic, eds., *Reading the Earth: New Directions in the Study of Literature and the Environment* (Moscow, Idaho: University of Idaho Press, 1998). For a study of Hollywood films from an ecological point of view, see Pat Brereton, *Hollywood Utopia: Ecology in Contemporary American Cinema* (Bristol, UK and Portland, Oregon: Intellect Books, 2005).

2. A preliminary effort in this direction is my book *Chinese Modernity and Global Biopolitics: Studies in Literature and Visual Culture* (Honolulu: University of Hawai'i Press, 2007).

3. Ecocriticism (*shengtai piping*) was introduced to mainland China in the early twenty-first century. Indigenous critics attempt to grasp the relevance of this critical trend to their own historical situation as they acclimatize something foreign to Chinese soil. See Chen Jianlan, "Shengtai zhuyi huayu: shengtai zhexue yu wenxue piping" (Ecophilosophy and ecocriticism: Some aspects of ecologism), *Wenyi lilun qianyan* (Frontiers of Literary Theory) No. 1 (April 2004): 3–43; Song Lili, "Lun wenxue de 'shengtai wei'" (On the niche of literature), *Wenyi lilun qianyan* (Frontiers of Literary Theory) No. 3 (April 2006): 126–161. Publicized as the first international conference on ecocriticism in Beijing, the conference "Beyond Thoreau: American and International Responses to Nature" is held at Tsinghua University, Beijing, China, October 10–12, 2008. See the website http://web.ku.edu/~beyondthoreauchina/ (accessed April 21, 2008). In Taiwan, there has been a stronger awareness of ecological criticism. For instance, Tamkang University has organized several international conferences on ecological discourse. The fourth such conference is called "Crisscrossing Word and World: Ecocriticism: Crisis, and Representation," held on May 23–24, 2008. Presentations on film were included in the conference. I thank Chia-ju Chang, a contributor to this volume, for bringing this to my attention. In China and Taiwan,

the phrases of "*shengtai dianying*" 生態電影 and "*yuan shengtai dinaying*" 原生態電影 have been used to designate what we call "ecocinema" in this volume.

4. Suffice to repeat here that the academic currency of the term "New Chinese Cinema," or "New Chinese Cinemas" in the plural, was established by the publication of the anthology *New Chinese Cinemas: Forms, Identities, Politics*, ed. Nick Browne, Paul G. Pickowicz, Vivian Sobchack, and Esther Yau (Cambridge: Cambridge University Press, 1994).

5. For an understanding of China's New Documentary Movement, see the groundbreaking work by Lü Xinyu, *Jilu Zhongguo: dangdai Zhongguo xin jilupian yundong* (Recording China: The New Documentary movement in contemporary China) (Beijing: Sanlian, 2003).

6. These ideas are developed and propounded by the Han Confucian scholar Dong Zhongshu (ca. 195–105 B.C.) in his magnum opus *Chunqiu fanlu* (Luxuriant gems of the Spring and Autumn). English studies on this scholar and his text are rarer. See Sarah A. Queen, *From Chronicle to Canon: The Hermeneutics of the Spring and Autumn Annals according to Tung Chung-shu* (Cambridge: Cambridge University Press, 1996).

7. The key text is the chapter "Tian Lun" (Treatise on Heaven) in *Xunzi*. For relevant scholarly studies in English, see John Knoblock, *Xunzi: A Translation and Study of the Complete Works*, 3 vols. (Stanford: Stanford University Press, 1988–1994); Edward Machle, *Nature and Heaven in the Xunzi: A Study of the Tian Lun* (Albany: State University of New York Press, 1993); T. C. Kline III and Philip J. Ivanhoe, eds., *Virtue, Nature, and Moral Agency in the Xunzi* (Indianapolis: Hackett, 2000); *Xunzi: Basic Writings*, trans. Burton Watson (New York: Columbia University Press, 2003).

8. David Harvey, *A Brief History of Neoliberalism* (Oxford: Oxford University Press, 2005), especially Chapter 5, "Neoliberalism 'with Chinese Characteristics,'" 120–151.

9. Bruce Robbins, "The Sweatshop Sublime," *PMLA* 117.1 (2002): 84–97.

10. For an informative discussion of sinascape and ideascape in reference to *Hero* by Zhang Yimou, see Gary G. Xu, *Sinascape: Contemporary Chinese Cinema* (Lanham, Maryland: Rowman and Littlefield, 2007), especially 36–43.

11. Walter Benjamin, *Illuminations*, ed. Hannah Arendt (New York: Schocken Books, 1969), 256–258.

12. Theodor W. Adorno, "The Idea of Natural History" (1932), trans. Bob Hullot-Kentor, *Telos* No. 60 (Summer 1984): 122.

13. Ibid., 121.

14. Masao Miyoshi, "Turn to the Planet: Literature, Diversity, and Totality," *Globalization and the Humanities*, ed. David Leilei Li (Hong Kong: Hong Kong University Press, 2004), 35.

Chapter 1   Framing Ambient *Unheimlich*

1. Upon completion of this essay, news was announced that *On Behalf of Water* or *In the Name of Water* (*Yin shui zhi ming* 因水之名), which claimed to be "the first green Chinese ecofilm," has started shooting and is scheduled to be released in 2009. This film, directed by Jiang Xiaoyu, consists of three parts — revenge of water, the uncanny world of endangered water, and images of horror.

2. 這是一溝絕望的死水，
    清風吹不起半點漪淪。

不如多扔些破銅爛鐵，

爽性潑你的剩菜殘羹。

這是一溝絕望的死水，

這裡斷不是美的所在，

不如讓給醜惡來開墾，

看他造出個什麼世界。

Wen Yiduo, "Sishui" (Dead water), in *Zhonghua shige bainian jinghua* (*Anthology of the Best Modern Poems in One Hundred Years*) (Beijing: Renmin wenxue chubanshe, 2003), 41–42.

3. World Water Assessment Program (WWAP), "Water for People, Water for Life," 2003, http://www.unesco.org/water/wwap/ (accessed March 20, 2007).

4. United Nations Development Programme (UNDP), "Beyond Scarcity: Power, Poverty and the Global Water Crisis," 2006, http://hdr.undp.org/en/reports/global/hdr2006/ (accessed March 25, 2007).

5. Ma Jun, *China's Water Crisis* (Norwalk: Eastbridge, 2004).

6. Elizabeth C. Economy, *The River Runs Black: The Environmental Challenge to China's Future* (Ithaca and London: Cornell University Press, 2004).

7. Slavoj Žižek, *The Sublime Object of Ideology* (London: Verso, 1989), 95.

8. In this article I focus more on water-themed feature films that picture China's water crisis. There are more feature films about the river, including Chen Kaige's *Bian zou bian chang* (Life on a string, 1990), Liu Yan's *Nuhou ba, Huanghe* (Roar! The Yellow River, 1979), and Teng Wenyi's *Huanghe yao* (Ballad of the Yellow River, 1989). In the genre of television documentaries, there are three important productions: the forty series *Huashuo Huanghe* (Tales of the Yellow River, 1986–1987), *Huashuo Changjiang* (Tales of the Yangtze River, 1986–1987), and *Huashuo Yunhe* (Tales of the Grand Canal, 1987).

9. Sigmund Freud, "The 'Uncanny'," in *Collected Papers* Vol. 4 (London: The Hogarth Press, 1957), 375.

10. Ibid., 399.

11. Nicholas Royle, "Déjà Vu," in *Post-Theory: New Directions in Criticism*, ed. Martin McQuillan, et al. (Edinburgh: Edinburgh University Press, 1999), 3–20.

12. For further reading on Zheng Yi's novel from which this film was adapted, see Jiayan Mi, "Entropic Anxiety and the Allegory of Disappearance: Toward a Hydro-Utopianism," *China Information* 21, No. 1 (March 2007): 104–140; for more discussions on its filmic adaptation, see Rey Chow, *Primitive Passions: Visuality, Sexuality, Ethnography, and Contemporary Chinese Cinema* (New York: Columbia University Press, 1995), 55–78.

13. For more discussions on *Suzhou River*, see Jerome Silbergeld's *Hitchcock with a Chinese Face: Cinematic Doubles, Oedipal Triangles, and China's Moral Voice* (Seattle: University of Washington Press, 2004); Sun Shao-yi's essay, "In Search of the Erased Half: *Suzhou River*, *Lunar Eclipse*, and the Sixth Generation Filmmakers of China," in *One Hundred Years of Chinese Cinema: A Generational Dialogue*, ed. Haili Kong, et al. (Norwalk: Eastbridge, 2006), 183–198; and Andrew Hageman's chapter in this volume.

14. Jean-Pierre Rehm, et al., *Tsai Mingliang* (Paris: Dis Voir, 1999), 34.

15. Freud, 399.

16. Homi Bhabha, *The Location of Culture* (London and New York: Routledge, 1994), 11.

17. Frank Martin, *Situating Sexualities: Queer Representations in Taiwanese Fiction, Film and Public Culture* (Hong Kong: Hong Kong University Press, 2003), 178.

18. For further readings on Tsai Mingliang's films, see "Tsai Mingliang Symposium" in *Reverse Shot* (Winter 2004), http://www.reverseshot.com/legacy/winter04/intro.html (accessed March 27, 2007).

19. Shelly Kraicer, "Chinese Wasteland: Jia Zhangke's Still Life," *Cinema Angle* 29 (2007), http://www.cinema-scope.com/cs29/feat_kraicer_still.html (accessed March 14, 2007).

20. There are four methods of resettlement: in the neighborhood/on-the-spot resettlement; nearby settlement; settlement at a distance; and settlement through relatives or friends. For detailed information on resettlement, see Gorild Heggelund's work *Environment and Resettlement Politics in China: The Three Gorges Project* (Burlington: Ashgate Publishing Limited, 2004) and Sukhan Jackson, et al., "Resettlement for China's Three Gorges Dam: Socio-economic Impact and Institutional Tensions," *Communist and Post Communist Studies* 33:2 (June 2000): 223–241. For documentary film on resettlement and inundation in the Three Gorges reservoir area, see Yan Yu and Li Yifan's *Yanmo/Before the Flood* (2005), which was said to have inspired Jia Zhangke's *Still Life*, as Jia served as president of the jury of the Cinema du Reel documentary festival in March 2005 when Yan Yu's film was submitted for competition. See Ian Johnston's review of Jia Zhangke's *Still Life*, http://www.brightlightsfilm.com/58/58stilllife.html (accessed January 21, 2008).

21. For more discussions on demolition in the city, see Sheldon H. Lu, "Tear Down the City: Reconstructing Urban Space in Contemporary Chinese Popular Cinema and Avant-Garde Art," in *The Urban Generation: Chinese Cinema and Society at the Turn of the Twentieth-First Century*, ed. Zhang Zhen (Durham, NC: Duke University Press, 2007), 137–160.

22. Perhaps the most uncanny and spectral episode about inundation and dislocation can be seen in Zhang Yang's latest film *Getting Home* (*Luoye guigen*, 2007): before his sudden death, a migrant worker expressed the wish for his body to be buried in his hometown, located in the reservoir area. Through a tortuous journey, the dead body was carried on the workmate's back all the way home, but could not be buried because his hometown was flooded and the natives had already moved elsewhere downstream. Thus the dead soul became homeless and unhomely in the flooded world. Such a motif of the drifting soul is also explored in another film about the Three Gorges reservoir areas of the Yangtze River, *Floating Lives/Fu Sheng* (Sheng Zhimin, 2006).

23. Lewis Kirshner, "Rethinking Desire: The *Object Petite a* in Lacan's Theory," *APSA*, http://www.apsa.org/Portals/1/docs/JAPA/531/Kirshner-post-p.83-102.pdf (accessed March 19, 2007). For more discussions on Lacan's *object petit a*, see Slavoj Žižek, *Interrogating the Real* (London/New York: Continuum, 2005).

24. See Nick Kaldis's chapter in this volume.

25. Wei Ming, "The Three Gorges Dam Will Turn the Fast-Flowing Yangtze into Stagnant, Polluted Reservoir," *Three Gorges Probe* (November 1999), http://www.threegorgesprobe.org/probeint/threegorges/tgp/tgp12.html (accessed June 4, 2007).

26. Tseng Chen-chen, "Myth as Rhetoric: The Quest of the Goddess in Six Dynasties Poetry," *Journal of National Chung Cheng University Sec. I: Humanities* 6.1 (1995): 235–278.

27. Song Yu, "The Gao Tang Rhapsody," in *An Anthology of Translations: From Antique to the Tang Dynasty*, ed. John Minford and Joseph Lau (New York: Columbia University Press, 2000), 272–278.

28. One can identify more parallels between the two characters in this film. See Nick Kaldis's chapter in this volume.

29. For this point, see Greg Garrard, *Ecocriticism* (London/New York: Routledge, 2004), 33–58.

30. For more discussion on this issue, see Rey Chow's *Primitive Passions: Visuality, Sexuality, Ethnography, and Contemporary Chinese Cinema* (New York: Columbia University Press, 1995).

31. Zhang Yingjin, *Screening China: Critical Interventions, Cinematic Reconfigurations, and the Transnational Imaginary in Contemporary Chinese Cinema* (Ann Arbor: Center for Chinese Studies of the University of Michigan, 2002), 32.

32. Lawrence Buell, *Writing for an Endangered World: Literature, Culture, and Environment in the U.S. and Beyond* (Cambridge: Harvard University Press, 2001), 66.

33. For more discussions on the affective relationship between human beings and space/place, see Gaston Bachelard's *The Poetics of Space* (Boston: Beacon Press, 1994) and Yi-Fu Tuan's *Topophilia: A Study of Environmental Perceptions, Attitudes and Values* (New York: Columbia University Press, 1989).

34. For the ecological degradation of the Loess Plateau and the restoration projects, see Wang Tao, et al., "Sandy Desertification in Northern China," in *China's Environment and the Challenge of Sustainable Development*, ed. Kristen A. Day (New York and London: M. E. Sharpe, 2005), 233–256; John D. Liu, "Environmental Challenges Facing China Rehabilitation of the Loess Plateau," 2005, http://unep.org/pcmu/project_reference/docs/ BB_170707Large_scale_ecosystem_restoration_JPMorgan_Essay_2005.pdf (accessed December 3, 2007).

35. Liu Jianguo and Jared Diamond, "China's Environment in a Globalizing World: How China and the Rest of the World Affect Each Other," *Nature* No. 435 (June 2005): 1179–1186.

36. Ni Zhen, *Memories from the Beijing Film Academy: The Genesis of China's Fifth Generation*, trans. Chris Berry (Durham: Duke University Press. 2002), 177.

37. All the following references are from Bonnie McDougall's translation of the filmscript; see Bonnie S. McDougall, *The Yellow Earth: A Film by Chen Kaige with a Complete Translation of the Filmscript* (Hong Kong: The Chinese University Press, 1991), 177, 231, 241, 245.

38. Jerome Silbergeld, *China into Film: Frames of Reference in Contemporary Chinese Cinema* (London: Reaktion Books, 1999), 15–16. The water jar, which appears during the rain prayer ceremony at the end of the film, according to Jerome Silbergeld, is the reincarnation of the drowned Cui Qiao.

39. McDougall, 34.

40. Silbergeld, *China into Film*, 30.

41. Ibid., 34.

42. One of the principal causes for ecological degradation in post-1949 China is the massive deforestation, largely through the conversion of forested land into arable land to meet the needs of a growing population. "*Kaihuang zhongdi*" (cultivating wilderness for arable land) is the most charged Maoist slogan that not only reflects the instrumental anthropocentrism and Mao's agricultural expansionism, but also the blind ideology of Mao's political economy of land. What are at stake are not the literal methods used for the land reclamation — such as slash-and burn, logging, and clear-cutting, which are devastating to the forests — but the power, labor, capital, and social justice that operate at the center of the ecological transformation. There are quite a few "green movies" and novels dealing with deforestation, such as *The Savage Land* (Ling Zi, 1979), *King of the Children* (Chen Kaige, 1988), *The Foliage* (Lü Le, 2004), *The Forest Ranger* (Qi Jian, 2006), and Ah Cheng's novella, *King of the Trees* (Shuwang, 1984). In particular, Ah Cheng's *Shuwang*, which was written in

the same period as *Yellow Earth*, foregrounds the chopping down of the ancient sacred tree and its subsequent tragic impact on the cohabitation of nature and human beings. For the worship of the beneficent power of trees in ancient myths, see James G. Frazer's influential work, *The Golden Bough: A Study in Magic and Religion* (New York: The Macmillan, 1922), particularly Chapter IX "The Worship of Trees" (109–135).

43. Walter Benjamin, "A Small History of Photography," in *One-Way Street and Other Writings*, trans. Edmund Jephcott and Kingsley Shorter (London: Verso, 1992), 243.
44. Walter Benjamin, "The Work of Art in the Age of Mechanical Reproduction," in *Illuminations*, ed. and intro. Hannah Arendt, trans. Harry Zohn (New York: Schoken Books, 1968), 236–237.
45. Benjamin, "A Small History of Photography," 244.
46. Ibid., 243.
47. Benjamin, "The Work of Art in the Age of Mechanical Reproduction," 234.
48. Susan Buck-Morss, *The Dialectics of Seeing: Walter Benjamin and the Arcades Project* (Cambridge, Mass.: The MIT Press, 1989), 267–268.
49. Andrew Ross, *The Chicago Gangster Theory of Life: Nature's Debt to Society* (London: Verso, 1994), 171.
50. Buell, *Writing for an Endangered World*, 18–26.
51. Wang Yuejin, "The Cinematic Other and the Cultural Self? Decentering the Cultural Identity on Cinema," *Wide Angle* 11, No. 2 (1989): 35.
52. Hwang Sung-uk, "Ecological Panopticism; the Problematization of the Ecological Crisis," *College Literature* 26.1 (Winter 1999): 137–149. Hwang Sung-uk, by incorporating Foucault's conception of the panopticism of power and domination, defines "ecological panopticism" as a kind of unethical play of power and exploitation in the Greenism discourses so as to "construct an ecological grammar that conceptualizes and encodes ecological issues in order to rescue a capitalism in impasse." In other words, ecological panopticism, according to Hwang, "serves to maintain the present relations of power by forging subjects themselves and fabricating their interests" (140).
53. Buell, *Writing for an Endangered World*, 246.
54. Hu Kanping with Yu Xiaogang, "Bridge Over Troubled Waters: The Role of the News Media in Promoting Public Participation in River Basin Management and Environmental Protection in China," 125–139, http://www.ide.go.jp/English/Publish/Spot/pdf/28_08.pdf (accessed December 10, 2007).
55. Cynthia Deitering, "The Postnatural Novel: Toxic Consciousness in Fiction of the 1980s," in *The Ecocriticism Reader*, ed. Cheryll Glotfelty and Harold Fromm (Athens and London: The University of Georgia Press, 1996), 246.
56. Bruce Sterling, *Schismatrix Plus* (New York: Ace Books, 1996), 226.
57. Ibid., 232.
58. Ibid.

Chapter 2 Gorgeous Three Gorges at Last Sight

1. Walter Benjamin, *The Arcades Project*, trans. Howard Eiland and Kevin McLaughlin (Cambridge: Belknap-Harvard University Press, 1999), Convolute N, 2a, 3, p. 462.
2. Georg Lukács, *Studies in European Realism* (London: Hillway Publishing Co., 1950), 40.
3. For book-length critical discussions of the social, economic, and cultural transformations of

China in the 1990s in the context of globalization, see Sheldon H. Lu, *China, Transnational Visuality, Global Postmodernity* (Stanford: Stanford University Press, 2001); Kang Liu, *Globalization and Cultural Trends in China* (Honolulu: University of Hawai'i Press, 2004).

4. Max Horkheimer and Theodor W. Adorno, *Dialectic of Enlightenment*, ed. Gunzelin Schmid Noerr, trans. Edmund Jephcott (Stanford: Stanford University Press, 2002), 1.

5. Shelly Kraicer, "Chinese Wasteland: Jia Zhangke's *Still Life*," *Cinema Scope* no. 29, http://www.cinema-scope.com/cs29/feat_kraicer_still.html (accessed February 2, 2007). More detailed studies of Jia Zhangke's film aesthetics prior to the release of *Still Life* are given in Xiaoping Lin, "Jia Zhangke's Cinematic Trilogy: A Journey Across the Ruins of Post-Mao China," in *Chinese-Language Film: Historiography, Poetics, Politics*, ed. Sheldon H. Lu and Emilie Yueh-yu Yeh (Honolulu: University of Hawai'i Press, 2005), 186–209; Jason McGrath, "The Independent Cinema of Jia Zhangke: From Postsocialist Realism to a Transnational Aesthetic," *The Urban Generation: Chinese Cinema and Society at the Turn of the Twenty-First Century*, ed. Zhen Zhang (Durham: Duke University Press, 2007), 81–114.

6. The intertextual relationship here is rather interesting. Wang Hongwei is the actor who portrays Four Eyes in *Balzac and the Little Chinese Seamstress*. He is the lead actor in several Jia Zhangke films: *Xiaoshan Going Home* (*Xiaoshan huijia*), *Xiao Wu* (*Xiao Wu*), and *Platform* (*Zhantai*). He also briefly appears in Jia's *Unknown Pleasures* (*Ren xiaoyao*) as a hawker of bootlegged DVDs, asking the buyer if he needs a copy of *Xiao Wu*.

7. This issue is taken up in Sheldon H. Lu, "Tear Down the City: Reconstructing Urban Space in Contemporary Chinese Popular Cinema and Avant-garde Art," in *The Urban Generation*, 137–60; Yomi Braester, "Tracing the City's Scars: Demolition and the Limits of the Documentary Impulse in the New Urban Cinema," in *The Urban Generation*, 161–80.

8. Liu Xiaodong regards himself as a participant in the New Chinese Cinema movement. He and his wife Yu Hong, another painter, were the main characters in the first film directed by Wang Xiaoshuai, *The Days* (*Dongchun de rizi*), based on the personal life of Liu Xiaodong and Yu Hong. Liu Xiaodong and Wang Xiaoshuai also had cameo appearances as upstarts in Jia Zhangke's film *The World* (*Shijie*).

9. Liu Yong, "Wu Guanzhong's *People's Dwellings at Sanxia* shown to the Public in Chongqing, Estimated Price 5 Million" 吳冠中《三峽民居圖》亮相重慶，估價 500萬，*Chongqing shangbao* (Chongqing Commerce Newspaper), February 9, 2007. Available at http://cq.qq.com/a/20070209/000027.htm (accessed April 16, 2007).

Chapter 3   Submerged Ecology and Depth Psychology in *Wushan yunyu*

1. Larissa Heinrich. "Souvenirs of the Organ Trade: The Diasporic Body in Contemporary Chinese Literature and Art," in *Embodied Modernities: Corporeality, Representation, and Chinese Cultures*, ed. Fran Martin and Larissa Heinrich (Honolulu: University of Hawai'i Press, 2006), 126–145: 134.

2. Estimates of the total cost of the dam run from U.S. $34–$40 billion, to as high as $75 billion. For details, consult Dai Qing, *The River Dragon Has Come!: The Three Gorges Dam and the Fate of China's Yangtze Rive and Its People*, ed. John G. Thibodeau and Philip B. Williams, trans. Yi Ming (Armonk: M. E. Sharpe, 1998). In addition to Dai Qing's

book, more recent works on the subject include Gørild Heggelund's *Environment and Resettlement Politics in China: The Three Gorges Project* (Hampshire: Ashgate, 2004) and Deirdre Chetham's *Before the Deluge: The Vanishing World of the Yangtze's Three Gorges* (Hampshire: Palgrave Macmillan, St. Martin's Press, 2002). Other sources for statistics on the dam, its cost, its benefits and drawbacks, how many people it has dislocated, etc. abound on the internet.

3. Patience Berman, "The Three Gorges Dam: Energy, the Environment, and the New Emperors," *Education about Asia* Vol. 3, No. 1 (Spring 1998): 31.

4. 1996, Beijing Film Studio and Beijing East Earth Cultural Development Co., Ltd.; screenplay by Zhu Wen, based on an idea by Wang Xinyu, Liu Yongzhou, Jiang Yuanlun, and (according to one source) Tian Zhuangzhuang. ASIAN Film Connections, 2002, "In Expectation," http://www.usc.edu/isd/archives/asianfilm/china/. The English title "In Expectation" comes from a comment by Zhang Ming at a press conference: "This is a film about expectation" (*dianying yao biaoda de zhuti shi qidai*), Song Guoliang, "Zhang Ming yu 'Wushan yunyu'" (Zhang Ming and "Wushan Clouds and Rain"), *Shenzhou yingshi wanhuatong* (Shenzhou TV-Film Kaleidoscope, 1997), 1. Additionally, in one scene in the film, a poster can be seen opposite the hotel entrance, advertising the movie "In Expectation" (*Zai qidai zhizhong*). The original title literally translates as "Wu Mountain['s] Clouds and Rain," the meaning and significance of which are discussed in detail later.

5. Michael Eigen, *Rage* (Middletown: Wesleyan University Press, 2002), 181.

6. For a powerful argument proceeding from a similar conviction, see Rey Chow, "The Seductions of Homecoming: Place, Authenticity, and Chen Kaige's *Temptress Moon*," in *Cross-Cultural Readings of Chineseness: Narratives, Images, and Interpretations of the 1990s*, ed. Wen-hsin Yeh (Berkeley: Institute of East Asian Studies, 2000), 8–26; See also Sheldon H. Lu, *China, Transnational Visuality, Global Postmodernity* (Stanford: Stanford University Press, 2001), 107; and Zhang Yingjin, *Screening China: Critical Interventions, Cinematic Reconfigurations, and the Transnational Imaginary in Contemporary Chinese Cinema* (Ann Arbor: Center for Chinese Studies, 2002), 251, 253, passim.

7. Yin Hong has similarly noted that: "The film uses a nearly emotionless factual documentation and the 'disastrous' metaphor of the Three Gorges relocation as a backdrop … to narrate the 'sexual' core of the existential states of a few average men and women" (*yingpian yi jinhu wuqing de jishi, yi sanxia banqian de "zainan" xing yinyu wei Beijing … xushule yi "xing" wei hexin de jige putong nannu de shengcun zhuangtai*). Yin Hong, "Zai jiafengzhong zhangda: Zhongguo dalu xinshengdai de dianying shijie" (Growing up in a crevice: Mainland China's "Newborn Generation" and their cinematic world), *Ershiyi Shiji Shuangyuekan* (Twenty-First Century Bimonthly) Vol. 49 (October 1998): 91. Yin does not, however, attempt to explain the key relationship between the Three Gorges backdrop and characters, nor does he analyze the "'sexual' existential states" in any depth. I will address both of these issues later.

8. One of Zhang Ming's own appellations for the characters. Zhang has asserted that the film attempts to portray "the most normal of characters, the simplest of lives, the plainest language, the most basic emotions, even the most familiar of stories, but it also wants to express that the main characters have their own extraordinary and moving attributes." See Yin Hong, 91.

9. Beijing Film Studio & The Beijing East-Earth Cultural Development Co., Ltd., 1997. "In Expectation (Clouds and Rain in Wushan)" (Advertisement & Informational Flier), 1–3 (emphasis added).

10. For a masterful analysis of the relationship between environmental degradation, politics, development, and culture during the Mao era, see Judith Shapiro, *Mao's War against Nature: Politics and the Environment in Revolutionary China* (Cambridge: Cambridge University Press, 2001). Shapiro is particularly perceptive in her analyses of CCP propaganda, tracing the connections between the rhetoric of warfare/domination and the treatment of people, the environment, and nature.

11. Mao, whose poem pictured the dam being built in Wuxia gorge, was not the first to come up with the idea of a large dam on the Yangtze. Sun Yat-sen proposed a Yangtze dam project in 1912, according to Audrey Ronning Topping, "Foreword: The River Dragon Has Come!" in Dai Qing, xviii; and similar ideas "were discussed from time to time during the 1920s and 1930s, and some preliminary explorations were made," as documented in Lyman P. Van Slyke, *Yangtze: Nature, History, and the River* (Reading: Addison Wesley, 1988), 181. Premier Li Peng, an engineer, is the leading proponent of the Three Gorges Dam project.

12. Several essays in Dai Qing's book discuss the Three Gorges Project in terms of the rhetoric and events of the Great Leap Forward.

13. It can be argued that the film is a textbook example of what Shih has termed "Sinophone articulation," in that it uses "visual images" in ways that "exceed the containment of ideology" (2008: 10), and represents "visually mediated identities that ... make a difference locally, regionally, or globally" (ibid.: 23). This is the case, despite Shih's unnecessary exclusion of PRC ("continental Chinese") cultural products from her notion of the Sinophone.

14. NETPAC/USA, and the Asia Pacific Media Center at the Annenberg Center for Communication, USC, "The 1997 Asian Film Tour [Promotional Flier]," 1.

15. Beijing Film Studio & The Beijing East-Earth Cultural Development Co., Ltd., 1997. "In Expectation (Clouds and Rain in Wushan)" (Advertisement & Informational Flier), 1–3. The movie was filmed on location in and around Wushan, the director's hometown. Significantly, Zhang does not attempt to present Wushan as he might nostalgically recall it from his younger days; rather, he foregrounds its imminent submersion and the psychological turmoil of citizens currently living under this impending catastrophe.

16. Fredric Jameson, *Signatures of the Visible* (New York: Routledge, 1990), 133.

17. Wang Xinyu, "Mosheng de daoyan yu mosheng de yingpian: Mantan Zhang Ming ji qi dianying 'Wushan Yunyu'" (An obscure director and an obscure film: A casual look at Zhang Ming and his movie "Wushan Clouds and Rain"), *Dianying Yishu* (Film Art) Vol. 3 (1996): 75–79.

18. Patricia Rae, cited in Kevin Ward, "From the Pens of 'Leaping' Poets: Parataxis as a 'Leap' between Robert Bly and Wallace Stevens," *Parataxis* (Spring 2003), 1. http://writing. colostate.edu/gallery/parataxis/ward.htm (accessed June 7, 2008).

19. This last sentence, of course, implicates the current interpretation in these psychological dynamics.

20. Zhang Ming studied painting in college, making for some interesting parallels between the artist in the film and the artist behind the camera.

21. The irony of this scene is brilliant; Mai Qiang is hauling two buckets of water up from the river, metaphorically "raising the water level," with a far greater degree of control over that event than he — or any of the other characters — will have in the near future. The scene might even be an ironic commentary on the complicity of the local residents in not resisting this project that will bury their homes under hundreds of feet of water.

22. One VCD version of the film includes occasional musical scoring that is absent from the original.

23. According to the director, the film uses "the most frugal lighting, the most authentic settings, the flattest frames, the driest arrangements, the most low-key acting, the most primitive editing methods, the cheapest costumes, and the most permissive directorial attitude, yet it wants to achieve the freshest of imagistic expressions," as quoted by Yin Hong, 91.

24. This type of narrative ambiguity as one of the distinctive features separating the Sixth Generation from the Fifth; Yin Hong, 90.

25. On the way jump cuts (*tiaojie*) and other cinematic devices solicit audience conjecture and contribute to this novel viewing experience, see Wang Xinyu, 75–79.

26. That filth is partially—if not largely—responsible for the recent extinction of the Yangtze River Dolphin (白鱀豚), "the first large animal to be wiped from the planet for 50 years, and only the fourth entire mammal family to disappear in 500 years." Jeremy Laurance, "Extinct: The Dolphin That Could Not Live Alongside Man," http://environment. independent.co.uk/wildlife/article2843953.ece (accessed 2007).

27. Other modes include: metaphor, tropes, figures of speech such as parapraxis, ellipsis, denial, digression, irony, litotes, etc., most of which are mentioned by Shoshana Felman in her discussion of a [Lacanian] "*rhetoric* of the unconscious" in *Writing and Madness (Literature/Philosophy/Psychoanalysis)*, trans. Martha Noel Evans, Shoshona Felman, and Brian Massumi (Ithaca: Cornell University Press, 1985), 119–125, 180–183. Laplanche and Leclaire list "timelessness, absence of negation and contradiction, condensation, displacement" ("The Unconscious: A Psychoanalytic Study," in Jean Laplanche, *The Unconscious and the Id: A Volume of Laplanche's Problématiques*, trans. Luke Thurston and Lindsay Watson (London: Rebus Press, 1972), 248). See the work of Charles Rycroft for numerous analyses of primary process thinking (*Rycroft on Analysis and Creativity* (Washington Square: New York University Press, 1992); *Psychoanalysis and Beyond*, ed. Peter Fuller (Chicago: University of Chicago Press, 1985).

28. The director himself has stressed his goal to communicate his message through visual grammar rather than spoken word. In a press conference, Zhang Ming faulted his own script for having too much dialogue in the second half, and that "relying on dialogue to resolve problems *causes images to lose vigour*" (*shi xingxiang fali*). Song Guoliang, 1 (emphasis added).

29. The intertitle introducing the policeman, Wu Gang, also mentions his recent engagement and, consistent with the misleading nature of the previous intertitles, his relationship with his fiancée is not treated in the film.

30. Fish have long been symbols of sexuality in China. The scholar Wen Yiduo, for example, did much research on the sexual nature of fish symbols in ancient China and published an essay on the subject entitled "Shuo yu" (On Fish). A comment made by Lili also links fish to the other narrative theme of development: she notes that the Wushan area will someday be "home to fishes."

31. A bucket of fish also appears in one of the police station scenes.

32. Bhaskar Sarkar has recently argued: "... In the absence of a clear cognitive grasp of the vast transformations of their lives, many Asians turn to generic narratives and mythic structures to make sense — allegorically — of their lived experiences"; see Bhaskar Sarkar, "Hong Kong Hysteria: Martial Arts Tales from a Mutating World," in *At Full Speed: Hong Kong Cinema in a Borderless World*, ed. Esther C. M. Yau (Minneapolis: University of

Minnesota Press, 2001), 173. *Wushan yunyu* portrays "Asians" who have been deprived of visual recourse to shared cultural myths that might help them make sense of the vast transformation of their lives.

33. Jacques Lacan, *The Four Fundamental Concepts of Psycho-Analysis*, ed. Jacques-Alain Miller, trans. Alan Sheridan (New York: Norton, 1981), 20.

34. Fredric Jameson, *The Geopolitical Aesthetic: Cinema and Space in the World System* (Bloomington: Indiana University Press, 1992), 4–5.

35. I borrow this apt phrase from Chris Berry, "Happy Alone? Sad Young Men in East Asian Gay Cinema," in *Queer Asian Cinema: Shadows in the Shade*, ed. Andrew Grossman (New York: Harrington Park Press, 2000), 188.

36. The title of the film, an aphorism referring to sexual intercourse, is a later contraction of two lines from the poem "Gaotang Fu" (The Gao Tang Rhapsody): "Dan wei zhao yun / mu wei xing yu" (In the early morning I am the clouds of dawn; in the evening I am the passing rain), attributed to Song Yu, "The Gao Tang Rhapsody," trans. Arthur Waley, in *Classical Chinese Literature: An Anthology of Translations: Volume I: From Antiquity to the Tang Dynasty*, ed. John Minford and Joseph S. M. Lau (New York: Columbia University Press, 2000), 273. See also Edward H. Schafer, *The Divine Woman: Dragon Ladies and Rain Maidens in T'ang Literature* (San Francisco: Northpoint Press, 1980), 43–48.

37. The film's reference to the "Gao Tang Fu" might also be an indirect political statement; the poem ends with a "little homily on good government," as described by Burton Watson, *Early Chinese Literature* (New York: Columbia University Press, 1962), 259. Allegorically, the succubus of that poem could today stand for the ideology of progress and modernization; when we awaken to its concrete reality, we feel disappointed, abandoned, alone.

38. Van Slyke, 32–33.

39. Ibid., 33.

40. The Wushan setting is doubly ominous in contemporary times, for mankind is about to violate and destroy this mythical and mystical (historical) place, and cause great social and ecological damage. As noted earlier, natural landscapes and phenomena are the indispensible elements of much (Chinese) mythology and legend, allowing a society to project, engage, and sustain its cultural unconscious, the repressed dramas and conflicts that must be excluded from human habitats and disavowed in social relations.

41. Chen Qing and Lili are also inexplicably associated with one another, in twin scenes showing each of them holding a piece of currency up to the light. Lili is apparently bored or hinting that she can be bought, while Chen Qing is checking for counterfeit money received from hotel customers. As with the toilet paper scene discussed earlier, here the film again portrays the crass instrumentalization and alienation of subjectivity that result from a "modernization and development at any costs" mentality. The circulation or exchange of people as objects is also evident in Ma Bing's attempts to force Lili and Mai Qiang to have sex.

42. Anne Sytske Keyser, "PRC and Hong Kong Films at the 1997 International Rotterdam Film Festival," *China Information* Vol. 11, No. 4 (1997): 119.

43. Derek Elley, "In Expectation (Wushan Yunyu)," *CineEast* (1997): 1–2. Though her status is never made clear in the film (as with many other facts), the latter seems more likely.

44. Several scenes in this film which can be paralleled with other "ambivalent homoerotic films set in Asia and Oceania" are very briefly touched upon by Ki, "*In Expectation*," *Queer View* (1997): 1. Located at: http://home.snafu.de/fablab/queerview/079regenwolkenuber/qw79ef.htm.

45. Jameson has used this terminology in his efforts to show how contemporary films, especially conspiracy films, often capture nascent/new aspects of and formations in the stages of capitalism. I find his term particularly apt here, with reference to the way a film can represent "this epistemological problem, this ultimate challenge to cognitive mapping," Fredric Jameson, *The Geopolitical Aesthetic*, 88. See also the epigraph at the beginning of this section.

46. Shu-mei Shih argues forcefully for the centrality of visual dynamics and representation to the notion of identity, which she defines as "the way we perceive ourselves, and others perceive us" in the process of "seeing and being seen." Shu-mei Shih, *Visuality and Identity: Sinophone Articulations across the Pacific* (Berkeley: University of California Press, 2008), 16.

47. In one formulation, Lacan refers to the "cut in the signifying chain [which] alone verifies the structure of the subject as discontinuity in the real," and how analysis reveals "'holes' in the meaning of the determinants of its [the subject's] discourse." Jacques Lacan, *Écrits: A Selection*, trans. Alan Sheridan (New York: Norton, 1977), 299.

48. Ibid., 71, 68.

49. Ibid., 70.

50. Ibid., 70.

51. Ibid., 68. Recent developments in the "new Lacanian film theory," as in the works of Copjec, Žižek, and McGowan, have departed from the apparatus-theory (Althusserian) of the cinematic subject. They propose a more optimistic version of subjectivity as "a mode of resistance to ideology rather than the product of ideology," (Todd McGowan, *The Real Gaze: Film Theory after Lacan* [Albany: SUNY Press, 2007], 173), and view the theorist as "cinema's ally in the struggle to reveal the gaze" and "expose the functioning of ideology" (Ibid., 171, 173).

52. Tony Williams, "Thatcher's Orwell: The Spectacle of Excess in Brazil," in *Crisis Cinema: The Apocalyptic Idea in Postmodern Narrative Film*, ed. Christopher Sharrett (Washington, D.C.: Maisonneuve Press, 1993), 216.

53. Dai Qing has gone so far as to claim that the support or rejection of the ongoing Three Gorges Project and the official interpretation of the Tiananmen events of June 1989 have constituted the two major "fault lines running under the Chinese Communist Party," as quoted by John G. Thibodeau and Philip B. Williams, "Preface," in Dai Qing, xii.

54. Dai Qing, 4.

55. C. Nadia Seremetakis, *The Senses Still: Perception and Memory as Material Culture in Modernity* (Boulder: Westview, 1994), 21.

Chapter 4 Floating Consciousness

1. This exchange is from a passage in Neal Stephenson's 1995 novel, *The Diamond Age or a Young Lady's Illustrated Primer* (New York: Bantam Books, 1995), 270, in which the media mogul Carl Hollywood employs the urban mise-en-scène of one of the major Shanghai thoroughfares to explain the complexities of global interconnectedness.

2. For a detailed history of ecocriticism and speculations on its future, see Lawrence Buell's *The Future of Environmental Criticism: Environmental Crisis and Literary Imagination* (Oxford: Blackwell Publishing, 2005), especially 1–29.

3. The increase in conference calls for papers (cfps) on ecocinema that followed the release of *An Inconvenient Truth* evinces its significance, along with other films such as *Grizzly Man* (2005) and *The March of the Penguins* (2005), in generating activity in this still nascent field of study. The Film and History League's 2006 Biennial Conference issued one of the first calls to use Gore's film. The conference featured five full panels in the "Nature and the Environment" area; perhaps suggestively, though, none were dedicated exclusively to *An Inconvenient Truth*.

4. This chapter uses the terms "videographer" and "narrator" interchangeably. Though there is room for debate about this identity, the interchangeable use should not compromise the arguments of this chapter.

5. Zhang Zhen's chapter on *Suzhou River*, "Urban Dreamscape, Phantom Sisters, and the Identity of an Emergent Art Cinema," in *The Urban Generation: Chinese Cinema and Society at the Turn of the Twenty-First Century*, ed. Zhang Zhen (Durham: Duke University Press, 2007), 344–387, makes a similar assertion that the river symbolizes the material interconnectedness between people and their environs, though the emphasis there is on gender relations and the idea of the "maternal river" (359).

6. See Gary G. Xu's chapter on *Suzhou River* in his *Sinascape: Contemporary Chinese Cinema* (Lanham: Rowman & Littlefield Publishers, 2007) and Linda Chiu-han Lai's chapter "Whither the Walker Goes: Spatial Practices and Negative Poetics in 1990s Chinese Urban Cinema," in *The Urban Generation*, especially 220–24.

7. For Lacan's discussion of the gaze through the story of the uncanny feeling of being looked at by a sardine can floating on the waves, see Jacques Lacan, *The Four Fundamental Concepts of Psychoanalysis*, ed. Jacques Alain Miller, trans. Alan Sheridan (New York: Norton, 1981), 95–96.

8. Even when this quote is invoked in conjunction with *Suzhou River*, as in Zhang Yingjin's chapter, "My Camera Doesn't Lie? Truth, Subjectivity, and Audience in Chinese Independent Film and Video," in *From Underground to Independent: Alternative Film Culture in Contemporary China*, ed. Paul G. Pickowicz and Yingjin Zhang (New York: Rowman & Littlefield, 2006), 23–45, it tends to be applied analytically to wider issues such as contemporary filmmakers who have "interven[ed] in Chinese media and have succeeded in reestablishing the artist's subjectivity …" rather than to sustained critique of the film itself (40).

9. For details on the production history of *Suzhou River*, including its origins in a ten-part television series entitled *Super City*, see Jerome Silbergeld's *Hitchcock with a Chinese Face: Cinematic Doubles, Oedipal Triangles, and China's Moral Voice* (Seattle: University of Washington Press, 2004), especially 121, and Zhang Zhen's chapter on the film in *The Urban Generation*, 457.

10. For a select view of the Portman buildings in Shanghai see the John Portman corporate website: http://www.portmanusa.com/index1.html. One could also consider the incredibly suggestive architectural juxtaposition in the 1300 block of West Nanjing Road where Portman's collection of gothic monoliths known as the Shanghai Center faces (albeit the posterior of) the Stalinist-style, Soviet-designed Shanghai Exhibition Center.

11. A similarly provocative instance of architectural symbolism in Shanghai is found in the adjacent proximity of the trendy urban complex Xintiandi and the site of the First National Congress of the Communist Party of China, both of which promise versions of "New Heaven on Earth."

12. While living in Shanghai from 1996–2002, I encountered numerous urban legends about official manipulation of this situation but do not have resources suitable for hazarding assertions about the matter.

13. "Mardar" is the spelling used in the film's English subtitles while this chapter has used the standard *pinyin* romanization, "Mada" to refer to this character.

14. Thank you to Timothy Morton for sharing, on multiple occasions, the ecocritical utilities of deceleration. See Morton's excellent *Ecology without Nature: Rethinking Environmental Aesthetics* (Cambridge, MA: Harvard University Press, 2007).

15. The displacement, or outsourcing, of responsibility for contributing to ecological crises from America to China appears in a variety of locations, from statements on global warming and other ecological crises by George W. Bush and other politicians to Ted Nordhaus and Michael Shellenberger's *Break Through: From the Death of Environmentalism to the Politics of Possibility* (Boston: Houghton Mifflin Company, 2007) and Thomas L. Friedman's *Hot, Flat, and Crowded: Why We Need a Green Revolution — and How It Can Renew America* (New York: Farrar, Straus and Giroux, 2008).

16. Connecting the ecological aesthetics of *Suzhou River* with science fiction is quite pertinent since, while he seems to have opted for different aesthetic approaches in films subsequent to *Suzhou River* (*Purple Butterfly* and *Summer Palace*), Lou Ye's rumored next project is a science fiction film entitled *Restorer*, and his writing sample for the 2006 University of Iowa International Writing Program is a provocative synopsis of a science fiction film entitled *Passion* set in Shanghai during 1905, 2005, and 2105. See http://www.uiowa edu/~iwp/WRIT/documents/LouYeformatted.pdf.

Chapter 5 The Idea-Image

1. Shelley Kraicer, "Absence as Spectacle: Zhang Yimou's *Hero*," *Cinema Scope Magazine* 5: 1, Issue 14 (Spring 2003): 9. http://www.chinesecinemas.org/hero.html (accessed March 23, 2007).

2. Jia Leilei, *Wu zhi wu — Zhongguo wuxia dianyingde xingtai yu shenhun* (The dance of martial arts — Form and meaning in Chinese martial arts films) (Zhengzhou: Henan renmin chubanshe, 1998), 130.

3. Leon Hunt, *Kung Fu Cult Masters: From Bruce Lee to Crouching Tiger* (London, Wallflower Press, 2003), 184–200.

4. George Miller, Interview with Marilyn McMeniman, Sydney, screened in Brisbane, March 13, 2007.

5. Roger C. Anderson, "Ecocinema: A Plan for Preserving Nature," *Bioscience* Vol. 25, No. 7 (July 1975): 452. First published in Arboretum News of the University of Wisconsin Arboretum and Wildlife Refuge in 1966.

6. Linda Sunshine, ed., *Crouching Tiger Hidden Dragon: A Portrait of the Ang Lee Film* (New York: New Market Press, 2000), dustjacket.

7. Peter Pau, "In the Bamboo Forest," in *Crouching Tiger Hidden Dragon*, ed. Linda Sunshine, 122.

8. Stephen Teo, "Love and Swords: The Dialectics of Martial Arts Romance, A Review of *Crouching Tiger, Hidden Dragon*," *Senses of Cinema* Issue 11 (December 2000–January 2001), http://www.sensesofcinema.com/contents/00/11/crouching.html (accessed March 26, 2007).

9. Mary Farquhar, unpublished interviews at Animal Logic with the *Hero* and *Daggers* visual effects (VFX) teams, Sydney (April 12, 2005). The discussion around Animal Logic's visual effects (VFX) relies on these interviews, arranged by Anna Hildebrand, and an earlier interview with Murray Pope and his team, Sydney (September 21, 2004). A much more focused theoretical and practical discussion of *Hero*'s digital imaginary and VFX (using the same interviews and follow-up material) will be found in Mary Farquhar, "Visual Effects Magic: *Hero*'s Sydney Connection," under review for publication.

10. John R. Stilgoe, "Foreword," in Gaston Bachelard, *The Poetics of Space: The Classic Look at How We Experience Intimate Places*, trans. Maria Jolas (Boston: Beacon Press, 1994), x.

11. Bob Strauss, "A little 'Hero' worship is in order," http://u.dailynews.com/cda/article/print/0,1674,211%7E24684%7E2360551,00.html (accessed December 17, 2004).

12. Simon Schama, *Landscape and Memory* (London: Fontana Press, 1996), 10, 14.

13. Ng Ho, "Jianghu Revisited: Towards a Reconstruction of the Martial Arts World," in *A Study of the Hong Kong Swordplay Film (1945–1980)*, ed. Lau Shing-hon (Hong Kong: Urban Council, 1981), 85.

14. James Schamus, "Location: Shooting in China," in *Crouching Tiger Hidden Dragon*, ed. Linda Sunshine, 46.

15. Ang Lee, "Finding China," in *Crouching Tiger Hidden Dragon*, ed. Linda Sunshine, 40.

16. Jia Leilei, *Wu zhi wu*, 163.

17. Bai Xiaojun, "Xinjing, yijing-shanshuihua chuangzuode zhudao yinsu yanjiu" (The realms of the heart and the idea-image — A study of the guiding principles in the creation of landscape painting), *Shehui kexuejia* 48: 4 (1994): 53.

18. Mary Farquhar, unpublished interview with Zhang Yimou, Hawai'i, 1995. For a discussion of *Yellow Earth*'s landscape see Chris Berry and Mary Farquhar, "Post-Socialist Strategies: An Analysis of *Yellow Earth* and *Black Cannon Incident*," in *Cinematic Landscapes: Observations on the Visual Arts and Cinema of China and Japan*, ed. Linda C. Erhlich and David Desser (Austin: University of Texas Press, 1994), 85–95. See also Mary Ann Farquhar, "The 'hidden' gender in *Yellow Earth*," *Screen* 33: 2 (Summer 1992): 154–164.

19. Mark Cousins, "The Asian Aesthetic," http://www.prospect-magazine.co.uk/ArticleView.asp?P_Article=12875 (accessed October 29, 2004). In English language scholarship, Linda Erhlich and David Desser's edited book *Cinematic Landscapes* is a rare study of cinematic landscapes in Japanese and Chinese Fifth Generation (or post-Mao) film, but the work does not include Chinese martial arts movies. Other scholarship often touches on martial arts landscape, including essays in the studies of Hong Kong martial arts in Chinese-English catalogues attached to the Hong Kong International Film Festival: Lau Shing-hon, ed., *A Study of the Hong Kong Martial Arts Film* (Hong Kong: Urban Council, 1980); Lau Shing-hon, ed., *A Study of the Hong Kong Swordplay Film (1945–1980)*, and Law Kar, ed., *Transcending the Times: King Hu and Eileen Chang* (Hong Kong: Provisional Urban Council, 1998).

20. Jia Leilei, *Zhongguo wuxia dianying shi* (The history of Chinese martial arts film) (Beijing: Wenhua yishu chubanshe, 2005), 212.

21. James E. Cutting, "Perceiving Scenes in Film and in the World," in *Moving Image Theory, Ecological Considerations*, ed. Joseph D. Anderson and Barbara Fisher Anderson (Carbondale: Southern Illinois Press, 2005), 17, 9–27.

22. Ran Ruxue, "Jingzhong fengjing" (The scene in the camera), *Dianying chuangzuo* 239, No. 4 (2001): 74.

23. "Bonus Features," in *Quentin Tarantino Presents Jet Li: Hero* (DVD) (Miramax Home Entertainment, no date).

24. Bai Xiaojun, "Xin jing, yijing," 54. "Spirit" is related to creative energy, called *qi* or matter-energy in Chinese philosophy, which animates a work of art just as it animates the cosmos. This is another core concept in Chinese aesthetics but it is not commonly used in Chinese film scholarship.

25. Jia Leilei, *Wu zhi wu*, 135, 139.

26. Chen Mo, *Zhongguo dianying shi daoyan, Langman yu youhuan* (Ten Chinese film directors, Romanticism and suffering) (Beijing: Renmin chubanshe, 2005), 20.

27. Ran Ruxue, "Jingzhong fengjing" (The scene in the camera), *Dianying chuangzuo* 239, No. 4 (2001): 74.

28. Mao Zedong, "Xue" (Snow), in Ding Li, *Mao Zedong shici da cidian* (A dictionary of Mao Zedong's poems), ed. Ding Li (Beijing, Zhongguo funu chubanshe, 1993), 148. For a discussion of landscape and power, see W. J. T. Mitchell, "Preface to the Second Edition of *Landscape and Power*: Space, Place, and Landscape," in *Landscape and Power*, ed. W. T. J. Mitchell (Chicago and London: University of Chicago Press, 2002), x.

29. Wang You, "Luobai Aosike *Yingxiong* weihe nanguo Meiren guan" (Why *Hero* failed to win an Oscar and enter the gateway to America), http://www.people.com.cn/GB/yule/8222/30797/30798/2230905.html (December 5, 2003) (accessed March 27, 2007). A spate of reviews followed *Hero*'s international release in 2004. For example, Yao Xiaolei calls the story of the King's enlightenment "nonsense": Xu Haofeng claims that his enlightenment is so thinly portrayed it is like a painting in which "the ink is spared as if it were gold"; J. Hoberman labels the film "fascinatin' fascism." See Yao Xiaolei, "Jingdiande jiegou yu chongjian, yishuzhongde xia, tianxia, yu yingxiong — ye you Zhang Yimoude *Yingxiong* shuoqi" (Classic constructions and reconstructions: *xia, tianxia*, and heroism in art — speaking from Zhang Yimou's *Hero*), *Zhongguo bijiao wenxue* 51, No. 2 (2003): 46–48, 49–51; Xu Haofeng, "Zhang Yimoude *Yingxiong*" (Zhang Yimou's *Hero*), *Dianying yishu* No. 2 (2003): 8; and J. Hoberman, "Review of *Hero*," *The Village Voice* (August 23, 2004). http://www.villagevoice.com/issues/0434/hoberman2.php, in mclc@lists.acs.ohio-state.edu (accessed August 27, 2004).

30. For a discussion of *Hero*'s controversial narrative and blockbuster status see Chris Berry and Mary Farquhar, *China on Screen: Cinema and Nation* (New York: Columbia University Press, 2006), 163–168 and 211–213.

31. Eng, Robert Y., "Is *Hero* a paean to authoritarianism?" (August 25, 2004), mclc@lists.acs.ohio-state.edu (accessed November 27, 2004).

32. Jia-xuan Zhang, "Hero," *Film Quarterly* 58, No. 4 (2005): 51–52.

33. Tan Dun, in "Bonus Features" in *Hero* (DVD).

34. Michael Berry, *Speaking in Images, Interviews with Contemporary Chinese Filmmakers* (New York: Columbia University Press, 2005), 116.

35. Jia Leilei, *Zhongguo wuxia dianying shi*, 192–193.

36. Clarissa Oon, "Multi-Coloured Hero soars," *The Straits Times* (January 15, 2003), http://global.factiva.com/en/arch/print_results.asp (accessed March 11, 2003).

37. Roger C. Anderson, "Ecocinema," 452.

38. Michael Berry, *Speaking in Images*, 117–118.

39. Stephen Short and Susan Jakes, "Making of a Hero," Timeasia.com, http://www.time.com/time/asia/features/hero/story.html (accessed January 18, 2002).

40. "Hero Defined" in "Bonus Features," in *Hero* (DVD).

41. Gaston Bachelard, *The Poetics of Space*, xv, xxxv–xxxvi.

42. Jet Li, in "Bonus Features," in *Hero* (DVD).

43. "Regulation issued to protect natural reserves," *Xinhua Newsagency* (March 1, 2007), http://www.china.org.cn/english/government/201123.htm (accessed March 12, 2007).

44. "Ministry identity comes second to the environment," *China Daily* (May 22, 2006), http://www.chinadaily.com.cn/chinagate/doc/2006-05/22/content_596694.htm (accessed March 20, 2007).

45. "Jiuzhaigou scenic area says no to film shooting," NewsGD.com, http://www.newsgd.com/travel/travelnews/200703080008.htm (accessed March 20, 2007).

46. "Zhang Yimou criticized for damaging environment of famous scenic lake," People's Daily online (November 1, 2006), http://english.people.com.cn/200611/01/eng20061101_317255.html (accessed March 23, 2007).

47. "Film shooting banned in nature reserves," http://www.radio86.co.uk/china-insight/news-today/1833/film-shooting-banned-in-nature-reserves (accessed March 12, 2007).

48. Quoted in Tang Yuankai, "Action Plan, China translates its awareness of environmental protection into workable laws," beijingreview.com, http://www.bjreview.com.cn/ender/txt/2006-12/22/content_51643.htm (accessed March 20, 2007).

49. Tang Yuankai, "Action Plan."

Chapter 6   Façades

1. Jim Yardley, "In grand Olympic show, some sleight of voice," *New York Times*, August 12, 2008, A1. "Miaoke, a third grader, was judged cute and appealing but 'not suitable' as a singer. Another girl, Yang Peiyi, 7, was judged the best singer but not as cute. So when Miaoke opened her mouth to sing, the voice that was actually heard was a recording of Peiyi. And it is unclear if Miaoke even knew." Zhang Yimou's two thousand-strong, mechanistic, cogs-in-a-wheel drum-thumping troop seems almost to have leapt off the screen of his earlier film *Hero* (2002) and uncannily confirms the links which can be drawn between that film in visual style and political orientation with Leni Riefenstahl's two films, *Triumph of the Will* (1935) and *Olympia* (1938).

2. John Branch, "Go figure: So many fans, yet so many empty seats," *New York Times*, August 13, 2008, D1.

3. A story broken by Loretta Chao and Jason Leow, "Chinese children in ethnic costume came from Han majority," *Wall Street Journal*, August 14, 2008, A5.

4. The question of whether five of China's six-member gold-medalist women's gymnastics team met the minimum age of sixteen, despite the ages listed on their Chinese passports, provoked a formal investigation by the International Olympics Committee; see Juliet Macur, "I.O.C. is seeking proof of Chinese gymnasts' ages," *New York Times*, August 23, 2008, D3.

5. See note 6, below.

6. See Tim Oakes, "The Village as Theme Park: Mimesis and Authenticity in Chinese Tourism," in *Translocal China: Linkages, Identities and the Reimagining of Space*, ed. Tim Oakes and Louisa Schein (London and New York: Routledge, 2006), 166–192. Also, Wu Hung, *Remaking Beijing: Tiananmen Square and the Creation of a Political Space* (Chicago: University of Chicago Press, 2005); Duanfang Lu, *Remaking Chinese Urban Form: Modernity, Scarcity and Space, 1949–2005* (London: Routledge, 2006).

7. Opened 1993; filmed both there and at Shenzhen's World Park.

8. Nicholas Kristof, "Malcontents need not apply," *New York Times*, August 16, 2008, A11. The Xinhua news agency reported that of the first seventy-seven applications to protest, all were withdrawn, suspended, or rejected by authorities. Several were reportedly arrested for attempting to apply, including two women, aged seventy-seven and seventy-nine, whose Beijing homes had been seized for redevelopment, who were sentenced to a year of re-education through labor. Audra Ang, "China has not approved Olympic protest requests," Associated Press in Washington Post online, August 18, 2008, http://www.washingtonpost.com/wp-dyn/content/article/2008/08/18/AR2008081800699.html; Andrew Jacobs, "Too old and frail to re-educate? Not in China," *New York Times*, August 20, 2008, A1.

9. Audra Ang, "China has not approved."

10. Jason McGrath, "The Cinema of Jia Zhangke," in *The Urban Generation: Chinese Cinema and Society at the Turn of the Twenty-First Generation*, ed. Zhang Zhen (Durham and London: Duke University Press, 2007), 81–114; Jason McGrath, "The Cinema of Displacement: The Three Gorges Dam in Feature Film and Video," in Wu Hung, with Jason McGrath and Stephanie Smith, *Displacement: The Three Gorges Dam and Contemporary Chinese Art* (Chicago: Smart Museum of Art, University of Chicago, 2008), 33–46; James Quandt, "Unknown Pleasures: The Films of Jia Zhangke," in Julia White, et al., *Mahjong: Art, Film, and Change in China* (Berkeley: Berkeley Museum of Art and Pacific Film Archive, University of California, 2008), 109–114.

11. Zhang Yuchen's palace-for-rent is a near-replica of Francois Mansart's famous Baroque original near Paris, completed in 1651.

12. Cf. Jeffrey Kinkley, *Corruption and Realism in Late Socialist Literature: The Return of the Political Novel* (Stanford: Stanford University Press, 2007). Prosecutions for corruption like theirs may have more to do with internal party competition than with genuine efforts to clean up the system.

13. Mark Elvin, *The Retreat of the Elephants: An Environmental History of China* (New Haven and London: Yale University Press, 2004); Judith Shapiro, *Mao's War against Nature* (Cambridge and New York: Cambridge University Press, 2000); and note 15, below.

14. See Jerome Silbergeld, et al., *Outside In: Chinese x American x Contemporary x Art* (Princeton, New Haven and London: Princeton University Art Museum, The P. Y. and Kinmay W. Tang Center for East Asian Art, and Yale University Press, 2009), 211–213.

15. Elizabeth Economy, *The River Runs Black: The Environmental Challenge to China's Future* (Ithaca and London: Cornell University Press, 2004); Thomas Campanella, *The Concrete Dragon: China's Urban Revolution and What It Means for the World* (New York: Princeton Architectural Press, 2008); Andrew Mertha, *China's Water Warriors: Citizen Action and Policy Change* (Ithaca and London: Cornell University Press, 2008).

16. Hai Bo is engaged in a photographic series documenting the disappearance of north China's agricultural landscape; Zhang Dali has long been recording the demolition of old Beijing; Liu Xiaodong has focused on the displacement of the local population of the Three Gorges Dam project; Ji Yunfei has made the Three Gorges Dam and its social impacts the prime subject of his painting for the past several years; Maya Lin has made both American and Chinese landscape history and ecology a major object of her installation work. For Liu Xiaodong and Ji Yunfei, see especially their interviews by Wu Hung in Wu Hung, et al., *Displacement: The Three Gorges Dam*, 122–135 96–109.

17. Interview with the author in Jerome Silbergeld, et al., *Outside In*, and in Jerome Silbergeld, "Double-Vision: Art out of Joint," in *Reason's Clue: 8 Artists* (New York, Taipei and Beijing: Queens Museum of Art and Lin and Keng Art Gallery, 2008), xviii–xxxiii.

18. Cf. Jerome Silbergeld, "Drowning on Dry Land: *Yellow Earth* and the Traditionalism of the 'Avant-garde,'" in Jerome Silbergeld, *China into Film: Frames of Reference in Contemporary Chinese Cinema* (London: Reaktion Books, 1999), 14–52.

19. Sima Qian, *Records of the Grand Historian*, trans. Burton Watson (New York: Columbia University Press, 1993), 1: 45.

20. Sima Xiangru, "Sir Fantasy," trans. in Burton Watson, *Chinese Rhyme-Prose: Poems in the Fu Form from the Han and Six Dynasties Periods* (New York: Columbia University Press, 1971), 29–54. For an extensive collection of such poetry, see Xiao Tong, translated by David Knechtges, *Wen xuan, or Selections of Refined Literature: Volume 1, Rhapsodies on Metropolises and Capitals* and *Volume 2, Rhapsodies on Sacrifices, Hunting, Travel, Sightseeing, Palaces and Halls, Rivers and Seas* (Princeton: Princeton University Press, 1982, 1987).

21. James Hargett, "Huizong's Magic Marchmount: The Genyue Pleasure Park of Kaifeng," *Monumenta Serica* 38 (1988–89): 1–48.

22. Régine Thierez, *Barbarian Lens: Western Photographers of the Qianlong Emperor's European Palaces* (Amsterdam: Gordon and Breach, 1998).

23. Philippe Forêt, *Mapping Chengde: The Qing Landscape Enterprise* (Honolulu: University of Hawai'i Press, 2000).

24. See Wu Hung, *Remaking Beijing*, 108–126.

25. Zong Bing, "*Hua shan shui xu*" (Preface on painting mountains and water), trans. in Jerome Silbergeld, "Re-reading Zong Bing's Fifth-Century Essay on Landscape Painting: A Few Critical Notes," in Michael Sullivan *festschrift* volume, ed. Li Gongming (Shanghai: Shanghai shudian and Guangzhou Academy of Fine Art, forthcoming).

26. See John Hay, *Kernels of Energy, Bones of Earth: The Rock in Chinese Art* (New York: China House Gallery, 1985); Rolf Stein, *The World in Miniature: Container Gardens and Dwellings in Far Eastern Religious Thought* (Stanford: Stanford University Press, 1990); John Hay, "Values and History in Chinese Painting," *RES* 6 (Fall 1983): 73–111 and 7 (Autumn 1984): 103–136; Lothar Ledderose, *Ten Thousand Things: Module and Mass Production in Chinese Art* (Princeton: Princeton University Press, 2000); Kiyohiko Munakata, "Concepts of *Lei* and *Kan-lei* in Early Chinese Art Theory," in *Theories of the Arts in China*, ed. Susan Bush and Christian Murck (Princeton: Princeton University Press, 1983), 105–131. The fourth-century B.C. philosopher Zhuangzi put this in terms that any postmodernist could find delight in:

> There is a beginning. There is not yet beginning to be a beginning. There is not yet beginning to be a not yet beginning to be beginning. There is being. There is nonbeing. There is a not yet beginning to be nonbeing. There is a not yet beginning to be a not beginning to be nonbeing. Suddenly there is nonbeing. But I do not know, when it comes to nonbeing, which is really being and which is nonbeing.

Zhuangzi, *The Complete Works of Chuang-tzu*, trans. Burton Watson (New York: Columbia University Press, 1970), 43.

27. For Xie He's (active ca. 500–535) *Liu fa* or six canons/laws/principles/elements/standards of painting, see William Acker, *Some T'ang and Pre-T"ang Texts on Chinese Painting* (Leiden: E. J. Brill, 1954), xiv–xlv, and numerous other articles on this text.

28. Wen Fong, "The Problem of Forgeries in Chinese Painting," *Artibus Asiae* 25.2/3 (1962): 95–140.

Chapter 7 Ruins and Grassroots

1. For Chinese theories of globalization, see Cao Tianyu, ed., *Xiandai hua, quanqiu hua yu zhongguo daolu* (Modernization, globalization and the Chinese road) (Beijing: Shehui kexue wenxian chubanshe, 2003) and Zhonghua kongzi xuehui, ed., *Jingji quanqiu hua yu minzu wenhua: duoyuan fazhan* (Economic globalization and ethnic cultures: multiple developments) (Beijing: Shehui kexue wenxian chubanshe, 2003). For recent Chinese discussions on modernity and China, see Zhang Yiwu, ed., *Xiandai xing zhongguo* (Modernity and China) (Kaifeng: Henan daxue chubanshe, 2005).

2. For M. M. Bakhtin's theory of chronotope, see "Forms of Time and of the Chronotope in the Novel," in *The Dialogic Imagination: Four Essays by M. M. Bakhtin*, ed. Michael Holquist (Austin: University of Texas Press, 1981), 84–258.

3. Schematic discussions are made of the various styles of Chinese cinema in mainland China since the 1980s in Yingjin Zhang, *Chinese National Cinema* (London: Routledge, 2004), 189–239 and 281–196. Analyses of some of these styles can also be found in Ying Zhu, *Chinese Cinema during the Era of Reform: The Ingenuity of the System* (Westport, Conn.: Praeger Publishers, 2003).

4. For a discussion of the discourse of "civilization vs. savage wilderness" in Chinese films since 1980s, see Dai Jinhua, "Liangge wutuobang zhijian" (Between the two utopias), in *Wuzhong fengjing: zhongguo dianying wenhua 1978–1998* (Scenes in the fog: cinematic culture in China 1978–1998) (Beijing: Beijing daxue chubanshe, 2000), 70–80.

5. For Gilles Deleuze's time-image and movement-image concepts, see his *Cinema 1: The Movement—Image*, trans. Hugh Tomlinson (Minneapolis: University of Minnesota Press, 1986).

6. See Jason McGrath, "The Independent Cinema of Jia Zhangke: From Postsocialist Realism to a Transnational Aesthetic," in *The Urban Generation: Chinese Cinema and Society at the Turn of the Twenty-First Century*, ed. Zhang Zhen (Durham, NC: Duke University Press, 2007), 81–114.

7. For a recent discussion of the cultural politics on nature in Taiwan and mainland China in the age of globalization, see Robert Weller, *Discovering Nature: Globalization and Environmental Culture in China and Taiwan* (Cambridge, UK: Cambridge University Press, 2006).

8. For Henri Lefebvre's ideas on the "contradictions of space" and the "differential space," see his *The Production of Space*, trans. Donald Nicholson-Smith (Oxford UK: Blackwell, 1991), especially Chapter 6: "From the Contradictions of Space to Differential Space."

9. See Zhang Zhen, ed., *The Urban Generation: Chinese Cinema and Society at the Turn of the Twenty-First Century*.

10. For an interesting discussion of cinematic presentation of the police in contemporary Chinese films, see Yaohua Shi, "Maintaining Law and Order: New Tales of the People's Police," in *The Urban Generation: Chinese Cinema and Society at the Turn of the Twenty-First Century*, ed. Zhang Zhen, 316–343.

11. The version of *The World* released in Japan, Europe, and North America for film festivals is about 143 minutes long and in it the police show up on the screen briefly investigating into a theft by a security guard in the theme park. In the shorter version (109 minutes) released in Hong Kong and mainland China for public view in theaters, the police part and the security guard's love gestures toward a fellow female worker are cut and the plot is thus rendered less melodramatic. I think here the cuts are made more for aesthetic and practical reasons than for "political" or state censorship reasons that Western viewers may tend to associate with.

12. Wu Hung, "Ruins, Fragmentation, and the Chinese Modern/Postmodern," in *Inside Out: New Chinese Art*, ed. Gao Minglu (Berkeley, Calif.: University of California Press, 1998), 59–66.

13. Sheldon H. Lu, "Tear Down the City: Reconstructing Urban Space in Contemporary Chinese Popular Cinema and Avant-Garde Art," in *The Urban Generation: Chinese Cinema and Society at the Turn of the Twenty-First Century*, ed. Zhang Zhen, 138–140.

14. Yomi Braester's "Tracing the City's Scars: Demolition and the Limits of the Documentary Impulse in the New Urban Cinema," in *The Urban Generation: Chinese Cinema and Society at the Turn of the Twenty-First Century*, ed. Zhang Zhen, 162.

15. In the article "Jia Zhangke's Cinematic Trilogy: A Journey across the Ruins of Post-Mao China," in *Chinese-Language Film: Historiography, Poetics, Politics*, ed. Sheldon H. Lu and Emilie Yueh-yu Yeh (Honolulu: University of Hawai'i Press, 2005), 186–209, Xiaoping Lin uses Maurice Meisner's historical characterization of present China to designate the world in which the stories of Jia Zhangke's *Xiaoshan Going Home, Xiao Wu*, and *Platform* take place as "the ruins of post-Mao China." The ruins are used more metaphorically to refer to the destruction of Mao's egalitarian socialist society and China's old traditions by the new capitalist market economy, than literally to talk about the debris and rubble in the mise-en-scènes of the movies.

16. Some of the buildings and street scenes in this film have also appeared in Jia Zhangke's 2001 documentary film *Gonggong changsuo* (In public) shot in the city of Datong in Shanxi Province. In an interview done in 2005, Jia Zhangke identifies most of the "monument-like" buildings in the documentary and *Ren xiaoyao* as from the 1950s and 1960s. The video interview, the documentary, and Jia's *Xiao Shan huijia* are now available in the DVD *Jia zhangke zuopin ji* (Jia Zhangke collection) issued by Anhui wenhua yinxiang chubanshe in 2005.

17. This term and the debates related to its use in designating exactly which social group with what kind of characteristics can be found in many Chinese websites and some popular magazines. Some special websites for the grassroots social group have also been set up in China. As far as I know, there is not yet much Chinese scholarship on the new sociological use of the term to describe the current social formation in China.

18. The term "*yuan shengtai*" 原生態 has become such a fashionable word in China today that it appears both in the media and in critical works by scholars. Its popularity can be established as closely related to the fast and massive changes brought by globalization to the life in China today.

19. The Hong Kong film *Papa, Can You Hear Me Sing* was directed in 1983 by Yue Ham Ping. Since the release of the film, the theme song and many other songs in the movie, sung by Julie Sue, have become very popular in Hong Kong, Taiwan, and mainland China, and they were part of the pop songs that Jia Zhangke's generation grew up with.

Chapter 8   Of Humans and Nature in Documentary

1. Elizabeth Economy, *The River Runs Black: The Environmental Challenge to China's Future* (Ithaca and New York: Cornell University Press, 2004), 10.

2. Judith Shapiro, *Mao's War against Nature: Politics and Environment in Revolutionary China* (London and New York: Cambridge University Press, 2001), xii.

3. Productionism is often deployed to characterize the aggressive drive in search of wealth and power in Mao's China. The idea has origin in both the liberal and Marxist understandings of progress. Andrew Janos notes that in modern times England's agricultural and industrial revolutions focused attention on the means and modes of production. As Promethean man grappling with the forces of nature became *homo oeconomicus*, a narrowing productionist paradigm became enshrined in the great classics of political economy — the Scottish moral philosophers and Marxian economic theorists of history. These schools of thought propose a logical progression that is technical and instrumental: when human means of production or technologies change, they change the social division of wealth and labor. These then compel changes in the structure and exercise of public authority. On the other hand, when politics is changing, it is motivated by administrative efficiency and improvement of a technical nature. What is left out in this picture is ethical consideration for community and political, public authority for stemming excesses of change. The productionist view underlies today's neo-liberal faith in the market as a panacea for political and environmental problems. See Andrew Janos, "Paradigms Revisited: Productionism, Globality, and Postmodernity in Comparative Politics," *World Politics* 50.1 (1997): 118–149.

4. Quoted in Susan Buck-Morss, *The Dialectics of Seeing: Walter Benjamin and the Arcades Project* (Cambridge, Massachusetts: The MIT Press, 1989), 276.

5. John Bellamy Forster, *Marx's Ecology: Materialism and Nature* (New York: Monthly Press, 2000), 141–142.

6. Karl Marx, *Capital* Vol. 3 (New York: Vintage, 1976), 949–950.

7. Ibid., 950.

8. Karl Polanyi, *The Great Transformation: The Political and Economic Origins of Our Time* (Boston: Beacon, 2001), 76.

9. Friedrich Engels, *The Condition of the Working Class in England*, trans. W. O Henderson and W. H. Chaloner (Stanford, CA: Stanford University Press, 1958), 57. Further references to this book will appear with page numbers in the text.

10. Chinese critics debate whether through standard documentary conventions, such as long shots, long takes, interviews, and synchronic sounds, etc., the documentary film can address the question of what is real. This debate, centering on the medium, inevitably leads to the questions of content, to the obscured layers of Chinese society in terms of socio-economic status. The debate becomes a socio-historical enquiry into the current circumstances in a time of confusion and change. See Lü Xinyu, "*West of the Tracks*: History and Class Consciousness" (*Tiexiqu: lishi yu jieji yishi*), *Dushu* (book review) 1 (January 2004): 3–15.

11. The close relation of capital expansion and visual spectacle is becoming a fruitful line of inquiry in critiquing the global visual regime. This inquiry is to reveal how image-making is part of the global economy. For a discussion of capital as cinematic spectacle, see Jonathan Beller, "Capital/Cinema," in *Deleuze and Guattari: New Mappings in Politics, Philosophy, and Culture*, ed. Eleanor Kaufman and Kevin J. Heller (Minneapolis: University of Minnesota Press, 1998), 77–95.

12. For an excellent account of Chinese documentary, see Lü Xinyu, *Recording China: Contemporary Documentary Movements* (*Jilu Zhongguo: dangdai zhongguo xin jilu yundong*) (Beijing: Sanlian, 2003). Also see Cheng Qingsong and Huang Ou, eds., *My Camera Does Not Lie* (*Wode sheying ji bu sahuang*) (Beijing: Zhongguo youyi chuban gongsi, 2002).

13. David Harvey, *The Limits to Capital* (London: Verso 1999), 32.

14. Quoted in David Harvey, 414. This is Karl Marx's phrase for the bloody process of primitive accumulation of capital.

15. Richard M. Barsam, *Nonfiction Film: A Critical History* (New York: Dutton, 1973), 2.

16. For a more detailed treatment of this double genre and its engagement with street realism, see Ban Wang, *Illuminations from the Past* (Stanford, CA: Stanford University Press, 2004), especially Chapter 8, "Remembering Realism: The Material Turn in Chinese Cinema and Street Scenes of Globalization."

17. Stephen Teo, "There Is No Sixth Generation": Director Li Yang on *Blind Shaft* and His Place in Chinese Cinema," *Senses of Cinema* (June 2003), available online at http://www. archive.sensesofcinema.com/contents/03/27/li_yang.html.

Chapter 9   Toward a Hong Kong Ecocinema

1. Ng Tze-Wei, "Not even HK's storied Star Ferry can face down developers," *International Herald Tribune*, November 10, 2006, http://www.iht.com/articles/2006/11/10/news/ferry. php (accessed May 30, 2008).

2. The artificial island consists of two former islands called Chek Lap Kok (*Chiliejiao*), after which it is now named, and Lam Chau (*Lanzhou*). See G. W. Plant, C. S. Covil, and R. A. Hughes, *Site Preparation for the New Hong Kong International Airport: Design, Construction and Performance of the Airport Platform* (London: Thomas Telford, 1998), 43.

3. Fruit Chan's *Made in Hong Kong* (1997), *The Longest Summer* (1998), and *Little Cheung* (1999) are commonly called the "Hong Kong Trilogy" or "1997 Trilogy." His incomplete "Prostitution Trilogy" consists of *Durian Durian* and *Hollywood Hong Kong*. For a comprehensive (Marxian) analysis of Chan's films, see Wimal Dissanayake, "The Class Imaginary in Fruit Chan's Films," *Jump Cut* 49 (Spring 2007), http://ejumpcut.org/archive/ jc49.2007/FruitChan-class/text.html (accessed May 30, 2008).

4. Ackbar Abbas, *Hong Kong: Culture and the Politics of Disappearance* (Minneapolis: University of Minnesota Press, 1997), 1. Hereafter cited as *Hong Kong*.

5. David Bordwell and Noël Carroll, *Post-Theory: Reconstructing Film Studies* (Madison: University of Wisconsin Press, 1996).

6. Bordwell and Carroll summarize the objections to "Grand Theories" of film in their history of film studies (6–12).

7. Todd McGowan and Sheila Kunkle, "Introduction: Lacanian Psychoanalysis in Film Theory," in *Lacan and Contemporary Film*, ed. Todd McGowan and Sheila Kunkle (New York: Other Press, 2004), xi–xxix, xvi.

8. For a discussion of Lacan's model of the subject, see Kaja Silverman, *The Subject of Semiotics* (New York: Oxford University Press, 1983), 149–193.

9. Abbas, *Hong Kong*, 25. My emphasis.

10. Jacques Lacan, "Seminar on 'The Purloined Letter,'" in *Écrits: The First Complete Edition in English*, trans. Bruce Fink in collaboration with Héloïse Fink and Russell Grigg (New York: W. W. Norton & Company, 2006), 6–48. Hereafter cited as *Écrits*.

11. Jacques Lacan, "The Subject and the Other: Aphanisis," in *The Four Fundamental Concepts of Psychoanalysis*, ed. Jacques-Alain Miller, trans. Alan Sheridan (London: The Hogarth Press, 1977), 216–29, 218. Hereafter cited as *Concepts*. See also Lacan, *Concepts*, 207–208.

12. Ackbar Abbas, "Play It Again Shanghai: Urban Preservation in the Global Era," in *Shanghai Reflections*, ed. Mario Gandelsonas (New York: Princeton Architectural Press, 2002), 37–55, 55.

13. Abbas, *Hong Kong*, 11.

14. See Steve Pile and Nigel Thrift, "Mapping the Subject," in *Mapping the Subject: Geographies of Cultural Transformation*, ed. Steve Pile and Nigel Thrift (London: Routledge, 1995), 13–51.

15. Fredric Jameson, *Postmodernism, or, The Cultural Logic of Late Capitalism* (Durham, NC: Duke University Press, 1991), 14–5.

16. Lacan, *Écrits*, 78.

17. Anthony Vidler, *The Architectural Uncanny: Essays in the Modern Unhomely* (Cambridge: MIT Press, 1992), 223.

18. Giuliana Bruno, *Atlas of Emotion: Journeys in Art, Architecture, and Film* (New York: Verso, 2002), 113. Her emphasis.

19. Silverman, 155.

20. Lacan, *Concepts*, 207–208 and 218. For topological diagrams of the subject/Other, see Lacan, *Concepts*, 187 and 211.

21. Philip Johnson and Mark Wigley, *Deconstructivist Architecture* (New York: The Museum of Modern Art, 1988), 18.

22. Lacan, *Concepts*, 168–169, 178, 187, and 195.

23. Raymond Williams, *Keywords: A Vocabulary of Culture and Society* (New York: Oxford University Press, 1983), 87.

24. Ibid., 221.

25. Tony Bennett, et al., *New Keywords: A Revised Vocabulary of Culture and Society* (Oxford: Blackwell Publishing, 2005), 63–69. My emphasis.

26. Malcolm Waters, *Modern Sociological Theory* (London: Sage, 1994), 211–212.

27. Greg Urban, *Metaculture: How Culture Moves through the World* (Minneapolis: University of Minnesota Press, 2001), 3.

28. Abbas, *Hong Kong*, 145–146. My emphasis.

29. Catherine Belsey, "What's Real?" in *Critical Zone 1: A Forum of Chinese and Western Knowledge*, ed. Q. S. Tong, Wang Shouren, and Douglas Kerr (Hong Kong: Hong Kong University Press, 2004), 21–36, 27. My emphasis.

30. Joshua Clover, *The Matrix* (London: British Film Institute, 2004), 8.

31. R. Buckminster Fuller, *Your Private Sky: R. Buckminster Fuller, the Art of Design Science*, ed. Joachim Krausse and Claude Lichtenstein (Baden, Switzerland: Lars Müller Publishers, 1991), 491.

32. An example of the postcultural desire to know is Stewart Brand's movement to acquire a photo of the whole Earth. See Stewart Brand, "Photography Changes Our Relationship to Our Planet," *Smithsonian Photography Initiative*, http://click.si.edu/Story.aspx?story=31. (accessed May 30, 2008). My emphasis.

33. Brand, 1+.
34. Gayatri Chakravorty Spivak, *Death of a Discipline* (New York: Columbia University Press, 2003), 72. My emphasis.
35. Timothy Morton, *Ecology without Nature: Rethinking Environmental Aesthetics* (Cambridge: Harvard University Press, 2007), 185.
36. Arjun Appadurai, *Modernity at Large: Cultural Dimensions of Globalization* (Minneapolis: University of Minnesota Press, 1997), 33. Indeed, Henri Lefebvre reminds us of the political-economic quality of land, if not the planet: "[M]ost significantly, Marx ... proposed his 'trinity formula,' according to which there were three, not two, elements in the capitalist mode of production and in bourgeois society. These three aspects or 'factors' were the Earth (Madame la Terre), capital (Monsieur le Capital), and labour (the Workers)." See Henri Lefebvre, *The Production of Space*, trans. Donald Nicholson-Smith (Oxford: Blackwell Publishing, 1991), 324–325.
37. Appadurai, 46–47.
38. Chen Guying, *Laozi zhuyi ji pingjie* (Hong Kong: Zhonghua Shuju, 1987), 53. The line is taken from the first chapter of *Dao De Jing*. Author's translation from the Chinese: *ci liang zhe, tong chu er yi ming*.
39. The status of the human in terms of the social, the environmental, and the other-than-human would benefit from historical, political, and ethical analyses, which are beyond the scope of this essay. For extensive discussions of these issues, see the following works: Giorgio Agamben, *The Open*, trans. Kevin Attell (Stanford: Stanford University Press, 2004), Alain Badiou, *Ethics: An Essay on the Understanding of Evil*, trans. Peter Hallward (London: Verso, 2001), Donna Haraway, *When Species Meet* (Minneapolis: University of Minnesota Press, 2008), and Bruno Latour, *Politics of Nature*, trans. Catherine Porter (Cambridge: Harvard University Press, 2004).
40. For a history of Hong Kong urban cinema, see Leung Ping-kwan, "Urban Cinema and the Cultural Identity of Hong Kong," in *The Cinema of Hong Kong: History Arts, Identity*, ed. Poshek Fu and David Desser (Cambridge: Cambridge University Press, 2000): 227–251. Hong Kong public television routinely airs educational shows on Hong Kong's nature parks and travelogues featuring less urbanized locations around the world. These television shows may constitute a "proto-ecocinema" of Hong Kong.
41. Abbas, *Hong Kong*, 27.
42. Cf. Abbas, *Hong Kong*, 91.
43. Hong Kong Tourism Board, December 27, 2006, http://discoverhongkong.com/eng/touring/hiking/index.jhtml (accessed May 30, 2008).
44. Abbas, *Hong Kong*, 25.
45. Abbas, *Hong Kong*, 92, 99, and 100. For a photo essay on Hong Kong, see David Clarke, *Reclaimed Land: Hong Kong in Transition* (Hong Kong: Hong Kong University Press, 2002). The chapter titled "Beyond the Concrete Forest: Village and Island Life" brings the gaze closer to the natural space of Hong Kong (140–159).
46. Gary Xu, *Sinascape* (Lanham, MD: Rowman & Littlefield Publishers, 2007), 134. See also Wendy Gan, *Fruit Chan's Durian Durian* (Hong Kong: Hong Kong University Press, 2005), 1–2.
47. Stephen Teo, "Local and Global Identity: Whither Hong Kong Cinema?", *Senses of Cinema* April 19, 2000, http://www.sensesofcinema.com/contents/00/7/hongkong.html (accessed May 30, 2008).

48. Fruit Chan discusses in an interview his quasi-ethnographic research on mainland Chinese sex workers in Hong Kong. See Michael Berry, "Fruit Chan: Hong Kong Independent," in *Speaking in Images: Interviews with Contemporary Chinese Filmmakers*, ed. Michael Berry (New York: Columbia University Press, 2005), 458–483, 474–476.

49. The frozen river is a contradictory symbol: it is dry, but it has not dried up. It has no movement (on the surface), but it has not stopped flowing (underneath). It is land made of not soil, but water. The frozen river challenges the binary oppositions of stagnant/flowing and dry/wet. For a discussion of river symbolism, see Jiayan Mi, "Entropic Anxiety and the Allegory of Disappearance: Hydro-Utopianism in Zheng Yi's *Old Well* and Zhang Wei's *Old Boat*," *China Information* 21.1 (2007): 109–140.

50. Leung, 249.

51. Xu argues that Hong Kong, as "nothing but a cinematic product" in an economy of signs, sustains the "real, breathing, inhabited Hong Kong" (136). *Durian Durian* shows how regulated bodies sustain the real Hong Kong and, in turn, provide the subject matter for a film.

52. These quarters are commonly referred to in Hong Kong as *muwuqu* (district of wooden houses) or *liaowuqu* (district of temporary houses). For a history of such settlements in Hong Kong, see Alan Smart and Wing-Shing Tang, "Illegal Building in China and Hong Kong," in *Restructuring the Chinese City: Changing Society, Economy and Space*, ed. Laurence J. C. Ma and Fulong Wu (New York: Routledge, 2005), 80–97.

53. The three aliases — Dong Dong, Fang Fang, and Hong Hong — together make up *dongfang hong*. Literally "The East Is Red," *dongfang hong* is a reference to the revolutionary song dedicated to Mao Zedong during the founding of the People's Republic of China. For an example of the use of this song, see Xiaomei Chen, *Acting the Right Part: Political Theater and Popular Drama in Contemporary China* (Honolulu: University of Hawai'i Press, 2007), 54.

54. Berry, "Fruit Chan: Hong Kong Independent," 478.

55. For a discussion of the socio-psychological effects of urban spatial transformations, see Esther M. K. Cheung, "The City That Haunts: The Uncanny in Fruit Chan's *Made in Hong Kong*," in *Between Home and World: A Reader in Hong Kong Cinema*, ed. Esther M. K. Cheung and Chu Yiu-Wai (Hong Kong: Oxford University Press, 2004), 353–368.

56. Places are created through the social and political actions of agents. Yingjin Zhang argues that Abbas's work neglects the agency of people in place-making. See Yingjin Zhang, *Screening China: Critical Interventions, Cinematic Reconfigurations, and the Transnational Imaginary in Contemporary Chinese Cinema* (Ann Arbor: Center for Chinese Studies at the University of Michigan, 2002), 257–258. For a similar criticism, see also Gordon Mathews, "Book Review of Ackbar Abbas, *Hong Kong: Culture and the Politics of Disappearance*," *Journal of Asian Studies* 57.4 (November 1998): 1112–1113.

57. See Sheldon H. Lu, *China, Transnational Visuality, Global Postmodernity* (Stanford: Stanford University Press, 2001), 111.

58. Xu, 148.

59. Wong Jing, a Hong Kong director and producer of popular commercial films, is (in)famous for his crude humor involving *shi-niao-pi* (crap-piss-gas). His films and the mass culture they cater to serve as a context for understanding why Fruit Chan might have picked such a topic for his experimental film.

60. Berry, "Fruit Chan: Hong Kong Independent," 479.

61. Lacan, *Écrits*, 416–417.

62. Sheldon H. Lu, *Chinese Modernity and Global Biopolitics: Studies in Literature and Visual Culture* (Honolulu: University of Hawai'i Press, 2007), 200–203.

63. Morton, 159–160.

64. Abbas, *Hong Kong*, 49.

65. Christoph Huber, "Curious about Crap: Fruit Chan's Public Toilet (2002)," *Senses of Cinema* January 2003, http://www.sensesofcinema.com/contents/03/24/toilet.html (accessed May 30, 2008). My emphasis.

Chapter 10   A City of Disappearance

1. Henri Lefebvre, *The Production of Space*, trans. Donald Nicholson-Smith (Cambridge, Massachusetts: Blackwell, 1991), 412.

2. Ibid., 38–40.

3. Ibid., 40.

4. Michel Foucault, *Power/Knowledge: Selected Interviews and Other Writings, 1972–1977*, ed. Colin Gordon (Pantheon: New York, 1982).

5. Michel de Certeau, *The Practice of Everyday Life* (Berkeley: University of California Press, 1984).

6. Jacques Derrida, "White Mythology: Metaphor in the Text of Philosophy," in his *The Margins of Philosophy*, trans. Alan Bass (Harvest Press, 1982), 207–272.

7. Lefebvre, 402.

8. Lefebvre, 410.

9. Liu Kang, *Globalization and Cultural Trends in China* (Honolulu: University of Hawai'i Press, 2004), 2.

10. Sheldon H. Lu, *Chinese Modernity and Global Biopolitics: Studies in Literature and Visual Culture* (Honolulu: University of Hawai'i Press, 2007), 204–210.

11. Aihwa Ong, *Flexible Citizenship: The Cultural Logics of Transnationality* (Durham, NC: Duke University Press, 1999), 6. Ong illustrates that "'Flexible citizenship' refers to the cultural logics of capitalist accumulation, travel, and displacement that induce subjects to respond fluidly and opportunistically to changing political-economic conditions."

12. Lu, *Chinese Modernity and Global Biopolitics*, 167.

13. Lefebvre, 416.

14. Lu, *Chinese Modernity and Global Biopolitics*, 172.

15. For the concept of Orientalism, see Edward Said's *Orientalism* (Vintage, 1979). Ray Chow coined the term "self-Orientalism" in her *Primitive Passions: Visuality, Sexuality, Ethnography, and Contemporary Chinese Cinema* (New York: Columbia University Press, 1995).

16. Augusta Palmer, "After 'Spicy Love Soup,' Zhang Takes 'Shower,'" Indiewire, http://www.indiewire.com/people/int_Zhang_Loehr_000707.html (accessed May 29, 2007).

17. Lefebvre, 403.

18. Sheldon H. Lu, "Tear Down the City: Reconstructing Urban Space in Contemporary Chinese Popular Cinema and Avant-Garde Art," in *The Urban Generation: Chinese Cinema and Society at the Turn of the Twenty-First Century*, ed. Zhang Zhen (Durham: Duke University Press, 2007), 138.

19. Ibid., 144.
20. Gary G. Xu, *Sinascape: Contemporary Chinese Cinema* (Lanham: Rowman & Littlefield Publishers, 2007), 76.
21. Ibid., 77.
22. Arif Dirlik, "Place-Based Imagination: Globalism and the Politics of Place," in *Places and Politics in an Age of Globalization*, ed. Roxann Prazniak and Arif Dirlik (Oxford: Rowman & Littlefield Publishers, 2001), 23.
23. David Harvey, *The Condition of Postmodernity: An Enquiry into the Origins of Cultural Change* (Cambridge, Massachusetts: Blackwell, 1990), 205.
24. Ibid., 205.
25. Lefebvre, 36–46.
26. Lu, *Chinese Modernity and Global Biopolitics*, 153.
27. The ending does not show directly that Xiao Tao killed Taisheng and herself. After Taisheng goes into Xiao Tao's room, the scene is cut immediately to one in which people are dragging their dead bodies out of the gas-filled room. Xiao Tao is the biggest suspect, though it could be an accident.
28. Lu, *Chinese Modernity and Global Biopolitics*, 154.
29. For more information on gender issues in the Mao's era, see Emily Honig's "Maoist Mappings of Gender: Reassessing the Red Guards," in *Chinese Femininities/Chinese Masculinities: A Reader*, ed. Thomas Laqueur (Berkeley and Los Angeles: University of California Press, 2002), 255–268.
30. Fredric Jameson, "Notes on Globalization as a Philosophical Issue," in *The Cultures of Globalization*, ed. Fredric Jameson and Masao Miyoshi (Durham and London: Duke University Press, 1998), 60.
31. Arjun Appadurai, *Modernity at Large: Cultural Dimensions of Globalization* (Minneapolis and London: University of Minnesota Press, 1996), 3.
32. Brian Jarvis, *Postmodern Cartographies: The Geographical Imagination in Contemporary American Culture* (New York: St. Martin's Press, 1998), 8.

Chapter 11   In the Face of Developmental Ruins

1. My sources on Western ecocriticism include: Cheryll Glotfelty and Harold Fromm, eds., *The Ecocriticism Reader: Landmarks in Literary Ecology* (Athens: University of Georgia Press, 1996), William Cronon, ed., *Uncommon Ground: Rethinking the Human Place in Nature* (New York: W. W. Norton & Company, 1996), Lawrence Buell, *The Future of Environmental Criticism* (London: Blackwell Publishing, 2005).
2. William Cronon, "The Trouble with Wilderness; or Getting Back to the Wrong Nature," *Uncommon Ground*, 69.
3. For a detailed explication of "dwelling" as Heidegger did with his "Being-in," see Hubert Dreyfus, *Being-in-the-World: A Commentary on Heidegger's Being and Time* (Cambridge, MA: The MIT Press, 1991), 40–59.
4. Yi-fu Tuan has published voluminously on humanist studies of geography. His major works include: *Topophilia: A Study of Environmental Perception, Attitudes and Values* (New Jersey: Prentice-Hall, Inc., 1974), *Space and Place: The Perspective of Experience* (Minneapolis: University of Minnesota, 1977).

5. Edward Relph, "Geographical Experiences and Being-in-the-World: The Phenomenological Origins of Geography," in *Dwelling, Place and Environment: Towards a Phenomenology of Person and World*, ed. D. Seamon and R. Mugerauer (Malabar, FL: Krieger Publishing Co., 2000), 26–29.

6. Yi-fu Tuan, "Literature, Experience, and Environmental Knowing," in *Environmental Knowing*, ed. Gary Moore and Reginald Golledge (Stroudsbury, PA: Dowden, Hutchinson & Ross, 1976), 46

7. Yi-fu Tuan, *Topophilia*, 75–128.

8. Yi-fu Tuan, *Passing Strange and Wonderful: Aesthetics, Nature, and Culture* (Washington, D.C.: Island Press, 1993), 8.

9. Yi-fu Tuan, "Structuralism, Existentialism, and Environmental Perception," *Environment and Behavior* 4.3 (Beverly Hills, CA: Sage Publications, 1972), 328.

10. Su Xiaokang, Wang Luxiang, et al., *He Shang* (Deathsong of the Yellow River) (Hong Kong: Zhongguo dushu kanxingshe, 1988), 14. This is one of the earliest published film scripts.

11. Geoffrey Golt Harpham, "Ethics," in *Critical Terms for Literary Study*, ed. Fran Lentricchia and Thomas McLaughlin (Chicago: The University of Chicago Press, 1995), 404.

12. Incidentally, both films are adapted from fiction. Director Wu adapted *Old Well* from a novel by the same name written by Zheng Yi in 1985. Huo Jianqi adapted *Nuan* from Mo Yan's novella named "The Swing and a White Dog" written in 1986.

13. Rey Chow, *Primitive Passions: Visuality, Sexuality, Ethnography, and Contemporary Chinese Cinema* (New York: Columbia University Press, 1995), 60.

14. See comments by Chow, *Primitive Passions*, 72–78.

15. For readers interested in Chow's comments, see ibid., 74–75.

16. See Su, et al., *He Shang*, 14.

17. See note 10 above.

18. Jianqi Huo, *Nuan*, DVD (Beijing: Jinhai Fangzhou Cultural Development Inc., 2003).

Chapter 12   Ning Hao's *Incense*

1. See "The *Crazy Stone* Craze," available online at http://www.cctv.com/program/cultureexpress.

2. See Vivien Wang's review, "*Crazy Stone* makes audiences laugh, Hollywood cry," available at http://www.chinadaily.com.cn/entertainment.

3. For instance, in July 2006, Ning Hao's *Mongolian Ping Pong* was shown in the cinemas of two U.S. cities, Seattle and Washington D.C. One year later, however, the DVD of the movie is one of "the hottest in town" in Beijing. See *Le Mingpai shijie* (*Time Out Beijing*) issue 115 (June 2007): 65.

4. The CCTV program is an imitation of CNN's "Meet the People."

5. See the transcript of Ning Hao's interview with CCTV broadcast on August 8, 2006, which is titled "Ning Hao: The Stone is crazier than I," available online at http://news.cctv.com/wangbo.

6. Ibid.

7. Ibid.

8. *Zhixia shi* means municipality directly under the Central Government. See *Xin shidai han ying da cidian* (New Age Chinese-English dictionary) (Beijing: The Commercial Press, 2005), 1992.

9. Ibid.

10. Ibid.

11. Luohan Temple is much older than Ning Hao thought. It was originally built in the Song Dynasty (960–1279) and was rebuilt in 1752 during the Qing Dynasty (1644–1911). In 1940, the temple was bombed by the Japanese and was rebuilt in 1945. During the Cultural Revolution (1966–1976), five hundred statues of *luohan* (meaning arhat "the worthy one") were destroyed and rebuilt in 1984. The temple was reopened to the public in 1986. See Ji Xianlin, et al., eds., *Zhongguo chansi* (China's Chan Buddhist temples) (Beijing: Zhongguo yanshi chubanshe, 2005), 274.

12. In *Crazy Stone*, officially released by Warner China Film HG Corporation, the English subtitles for this speech is far from a faithful translation: "Lay everyone off early. Give them time to find a new job. Now that would be a good deed."

13. See Hai Mo, *Zhongguo chengshi pipan* (A critique of Chinese cities) (Wuhan: Changjiang wenyi chubanshe, 2004), 174–175.

14. After the huge success of *Crazy Stone* in the summer of 2006, a Chinese critic pointed out: the movie is so popular among ordinary Chinese because it shows how much those greedy realtors, who, together with corrupt government officials, control and manipulate the real estate market in almost every city in China, are hated nowadays. In the movie, the callous developer is shot dead by his boss, who is also killed by an international jewelry thief from Hong Kong whom he had hired to steal the "crazy stone" — the priceless green jade, which is an object of desire for every character in the film.

15. See De Lege, *Nei Menggu lamajiao shi* (A history of Lamaism in the Inner Mongolia) (Huhehot: Nei Menggu renmin chubanshe, 1998), 153. In the past century, both Nationalist and Communist governments banned "the forced child lama." Ibid., 185 and 741.

16. See Huang Xianian, "Dushi fojiao yu renjian fojiao taolunhui zongshu (A summary of the Conference on Earthly Buddhism and Metropolitan Buddhism)," in *Dushi zhong de fojiao: Shanghai yufo chansi jinian jiansi 120 zhounian yantaohui lunwenji* (*Buddhism in the metropolis: Proceedings of the Symposium in Commemoration of the 120th Anniversary of the Founding of Yufo Chansi in Shanghai*), ed. Jue Xing (Beijing: Zongjiao wenhua chubanshe, 2004), 1–12.

17. See Charles B. Jones, "Transitions in the Practice and Defense of Chinese Pure Land Buddhism," in *Buddhism in the Modern World: Adaptations of an Ancient Tradition*, ed. Steven Heine and Charles S. Prebish (Oxford and New York: Oxford University Press, 2003), 125–142.

18. According to Jones, it was Yinshun who chose to use *renjian fojiao* (which is often rendered "Humanistic Buddhism") instead of *rensheng fojiao* (which means "Buddhism for human life") as termed by his teacher Taixu. Ibid., 132.

19. Ibid., 133.

20. Ibid.

21. See Slavoj Žižek, *The Parallax View* (Cambridge: The MIT Press, 2006), 181.

22. In Buddhism, one of the "five rules" for monks and laymen is "no killing of living things (*bu shasheng*)," an important concept that I will discuss in detail later on in this essay.

23. See the entry for arhat, in Damien Keown, *A Dictionary of Buddhism* (Oxford and New York: Oxford University Press, 2003), 18.

24. See the entry for arhat, in *Merriam-Webster's Collegiate Encyclopedia* (Springfield: Merriam-Webster, Incorporated, 2000), 86.

25. Melon seeds are a kind of "holiday snack" that people enjoy during the Chinese New Year.

26. In Chinese, monks and nuns are called *chujiaren*, literally meaning "persons out of home."

27. In most Chinese government facilities and "work-units (*danwei*)," there are "canteens (*shitang*)" where the "cookhouse squad (*chuishi ban*)" prepares daily meals for employees.

28. See Jue Xing, "Dushi siyuan yu renjian fojiao jianxing" (The practice of the city monastery and earthly Buddhism), in *Dushi zhong de fojiao* (Buddhism in the metropolis), ed. Jue Xing, 15.

29. See Xu Wenming, "Dushi fojia de zuoyong yu yiyi" (The role and significance of metropolitan Buddhism), ibid., 90–92. The historic statement — "Without depending on the state, it is difficult to expand the Buddhist service"—was made by Dao An (312–385), a renowned Buddhist leader and scholar of the Eastern Jin Dynasty (317–420). Advocates of "earthly Buddhism" regard Dao An as a role model for modern Buddhism. See Tong Liao, "Cong Dao An fashi tan renjian fojiao zhi jianshe (Master Dao An and the building of earthly Buddhism)," ibid., 355–366.

30. According to a recent study, monks who work in a well-managed "city monastery" receive a stipend of several thousand yuan plus free accommodation, while monks from a "rural monastery (*shanlin siyuan*) live in poverty and their daily meals are a steamed bun, fried noodles, and rice soup. See Banban Duojie, "Jianlun dushi siyuan yu shanlin siyuan zhi bijiao" (A comparison between city monastery and rural monastery), ibid., 402–405. In *Incense* such a wide gap between the "rich" and "poor" monasteries is exemplified by the head priest and the monk.

31. See Damien Keown, *A Dictionary of Buddhism*, 69.

32. Ibid., 30.

33. Ibid., 137–138.

34. Legend has it that Sakyamuni Buddha (565–486 B.C.) accepted donations from a rich prostitute in Vaisal, a city on the north bank of the Ganges River in India. See Du Jiwen, ed., *Fojiao shi* (A history of Buddhism) (Nanjing: Jiangsu renmin chubanshe, 2006), 27.

35. Motorcycle "taxi" is called *modi* in contemporary China. It is a "refitted" motorcycle that can take a few passengers. In Beijing it was banned in the summer of 2006 but it is still available as a "taxi" in the suburbs of the Chinese capital and many other cities of China, especially in small towns and rural areas.

36. *Fengshui* (wind and water) is traditional Chinese method of arranging the human world in auspicious alignment with the cosmos. Specialists in *fengshui* use instruments to determine the cosmic forces that affect a site for buildings. See the entry for *fengshui* in *Merriam-Webster's Collegiate Encyclopedia*, 570.

37. See *The Shambhala Dictionary of Buddhism and Zen* (Boston: Shambhala, 1991), 5.

38. See John Powers, *A Concise Encyclopedia of Buddhism* (Oxford: Oneworld Publications, 2000), 18–19.

39. See Song Lidao, "Dushi fojiao de xiandai yiyi" (The modern significance of metropolitan Buddhism), in *Dushi zhong de fojiao* (Buddhism in the metropolis), ed. Jue Xing, 81.

40. It is an official news agency of the People's Republic of China since 1949.

41. See a People's Daily online report, "Religious believers thrice the official estimate," available at http://english.people.com.cn/200702/07.

42. Ibid.
43. See a MWC News report, "China is seeing a religious revival," available at http://mwcnews. net.
44. See a BBC News report, "Survey finds 300m China believers," available at http://newsvote. bbc.co.uk.
45. MWC News, op. cit.
46. See Millicent Marcus, *Italian Film in the Light of Neorealism* (Princeton: Princeton University Press, 1986), 65.
47. Ibid.
48. See Peter Bondanella, *Italian Cinema: From Neorealism to the Present* (New York: Continuum, 1999), 62.
49. Ibid.
50. According to Marcus, the Bruno character is "an inspired addition to the literary source, the novel *Lardi di biciclette* by Luigi Bartolini, whose protagonist is a childless loner." See *Italian Film in the Light of Neorealism*, 59.
51. Ibid., 75.
52. As Marcus argues that in De Sica's *Bicycle Thieves*, "The Church's charitable efforts are portrayed as not only inadequate to the task of rehabilitating a war-ravaged population, but downright dehumanizing in its wholesale approach to processing bodies and souls." Ibid., 65.
53. See Liu Yiwei, "Dangdai Zhongguoren zongjiao xinyang diaocha" (A survey of contemporary Chinese religious beliefs), in *Liaowang dongfang zhoukan* (Oriental Outlook Weekly) issue 6 (February 8, 2007): 29.
54. See Canadian Press, "Poll shows almost one-third of Chinese consider themselves religious," available at http://www.canada.com. One of those wealthy "new believers" of Buddhism is Chen Xiaoxu, a former actress and business celebrity, who became a household name in China in the 1980s after playing the character Lin Daiyu in a TV series adapted from the Qing Dynasty classic, *Dream of the Red Mansion*. During Chinese New Year 2007, Chen Xiaoxu took the tonsure at a Buddhist temple in Changchun, capital of Jilin Province, which became headline news in the media. In the public's eye, however, Chen Xiaoxu's conversion to Buddhism was a traumatic event. Many fans of the former actress felt sad at the news and they speculated that Chen must have a terminal disease that had prompted her conversion. Chen died of breast cancer in early May 2007. She was a generous donor to Jingang Temple in Lujiang County, Anhui Province. In 2005, she spent 5.5 million yuan renovating the Temple, a charity that won her high praise from the locals. See Ma Jun, "Sister Lin's conversion raises issues of materialism, spirituality, happiness," available at http://www.shanghaidaily.com and a report titled "Chen Xiaoxu spending 5.5 millions rebuilding the temple" available at http://news.tomcom.
55. The "five rules" include: 1) no killing of living things; 2) no stealing; 3) no sex; 4) no lying; 5) no drinking. See Ren Jiyu, ed., *Zhongguo fojia shi* (A history of Chinese Buddhism) (Beijing: Zhongguo shehui kexue chubanshe, 1981), 181.
56. See Yang Zenwen, "Renjian fojiao yu xiandai chengshi wenming jianshe (Earthly Buddhism and the building of modern city civilization), in *Dushi zhong de fojiao* (Buddhism in the metropolis), ed. Jue Xing, 27.

Chapter 13 Putting Back the Animals

1. Ecofeminism or "ecological feminism," a term coined in 1974 by French feminist Françoise d'Eaubonne, is a social and political movement as well as a philosophy that combines environmentalism and feminism. It is an "umbrella term which captures a variety of *multicultural* perspectives on the nature of the connections within social systems of domination between those humans in subdominant or subordinate positions, particularly women, and the domination of nonhuman nature" (Warren 1997). For a further introduction on ecofeminism, see Carolyn Merchant's *Radical Ecology: The Search for a Livable World* (New York and London: Routledge, 1992). For a Chinese reference, see Yang Ming-tu's "Shengtai nuxing zhuyi pingxi," from *Shengtai renwen zhuyi 3* (*Ecohumanism*), ed. Lin Yao-fu (Taipei: Shu-lin Ltd., 2006), 1–36.

2. There is, of course, an animal-man meme, but it is beyond the scope of the current chapter to explore this.

3. *Nyotaimori* in Japanese is 女体盛り, which is literally translated as "female body presentation." There is also a male version call *nantaimori* but the female version is more popular.

4. This practice was introduced into China but was banned by the Chinese government. See BBC NEWS: "China Outlaws 'Naked Sushi' Meals": http://news.bbc.co.uk/2/hi/asia-pacific/4570901.stm.

5. PETA is an acronym for "People for the Ethical Treatment of Animals." For a critique of PETA's controversial use of women, see http://www.nostatusquo.com/ACLU/PETA/peta.html (January 28, 2007). See online CityNews: "Robert Pickton to Stand Trial/Case Overview," Sunday, January 21, 2007: http://www.citynews.ca/news/news_7102.aspx.

6. See online CityNews: "Robert Pickton to Stand Trial/Case Overview," Sunday, January 21, 2007: http://www.citynews.ca/news/news_7102.aspx.

7. See Charlene Spretnak's "Earth Body and Personal Body as Sacred," from *Ecofeminism and the Sacred*, ed. Carol Adams (New York: Continuum, 1993).

8. There is still a distinction that needs to be made about spiritual ecofeminists: that is, anti-essentialist spiritual-ecofeminists, who view nature as sacred and holistic, and spiritual-essentialist ecofeminists, who believe that women are closer to nature — that there is an "essential" affinity between women and the natural world. The latter group risks "regress to harmful patriarchal sex-role stereotyping" (Murphy 1995: 62).

9. For a further analysis of language, power, and the oppression of animals, please see Stibb, "Language, Power and the Social Construction of Animals," *Society and Animals* 9/2 (2001): 145–161.

10. See an online article on *sanjingrou* from Corporate Body of the Buddha Educational Foundation: http://www.budaedu.org.tw/doctrin/d61.php3 (in Chinese).

11. Val Plumwood, on the other hand, favors what she called the "ecological animalist" model of animal defense, which disrupts more thoroughly the ideology of mastery. For a detailed explanation, see Val Plumwood's "Animals and Ecology: Towards a Better Integration," http://hdl.handle.net/1885/41767. See http://www.radicalleft.net/blog/_archives/2006/5/18/1962217.html.

12. For a more thorough critique of rights-based ethical theory for animals, see Josephine Donovan's "Attention to Suffering: Sympathy as a Basis for Ethical Treatment of Animals," in *Beyond Animal Rights: A Feminist Caring Ethic for the Treatment of Animals*,

ed. Josephine Donovan and Carol Adams (New York: Continuum, 1996), 147–169. One point worthy of noting here is that while Donovan disputes male bias toward rationality, which derives from Immanuel Kant in Western philosophy, she also points out a male version of sympathy theoretical tradition that can be traced back to David Hume, Arthur Schopenhauer, Martin Buber, Edmund Husserl, and other phenomenologists (148).

13. For a brief survey of Taiwanese film history and New Cinema filmmakers, see Chang Te-Chuan's doctoral dissertation, "Taiwan xin dianying zhong de nuxing jiaose: ershi nian yihou" (Women's roles in Taiwanese New Cinema: After twenty years), 2006, 8–13.

14. There are some gendered differences between female writers' novels and male directors' films. See Chang Te-Chuan's dissertation, 110–123.

15. See the director's comment on the scene, Chang Te-Chuan, 120.

16. The function of these hooks is to hang pigs after they are slaughtered and disemboweled.

17. By "supernatural," I refer to Karl Kao's definition within the traditional Chinese context as those that "represent phenomena that exist beyond the observable world" (1985: 2).

18. For a more detailed synopsis, see the film study guide for *Mofa ama* prepared by University of Hawaii's National Resource Center for East Asia and Cynthia Ning, UH center for Chinese Studies, http://www.hawaii.edu/nrcea/Grandma&Ghosts.pdf.

19. This film has won several awards including the 1999 Taipei International Film Festival's Best Film award in the commercial film category; the 1999 Chicago International Children's Film Fest's Certificate of Merit Award for Feature Film and Video — Animation category, etc.

20. See "Nongli qiyue pudu yu Taiwan shehui" (Ghost Month and the *pudu* rite): http://www.twhistory.org.tw/20010827.htm.

21. For a detailed account of the Ghost Festival and this story "Mu Lian Saves His Mother," see Wai-yin Chow's "Religious Narrative and Ritual in a Metropolis: A Study of the Taoist Ghost Festival in Hong Kong," *Inter-Religio* 41 (Summer 2002): 5–7.

Chapter 14   Reconstructing the God-Fearing Community

1. See *Xueyu qiriyou* (Seven-day tour of the Snow Domain) (Beijing: yinxing zhilü, June, 2006).

2. Mary Evelyn Tucker and Duncan Ryuken Williams, eds., *Buddhism and Ecology: The Interconnection of Dharma and Deeds* (Cambridge: Harvard University Press, 1997).

3. Bill Nichols, *Introduction to Documentary* (Bloomington & Indianapolis: Indiana University Press, 2001), 1.

4. For a discussion of Chinese documentary films from 1949–1976, see Shan Wanli, *Zhongguo jilu dianying shi* (A history of Chinese documentary films) (Beijing: zhongguo diangying chubanshe, 2005), 113–298.

5. For discussions of the international and national, global and local dialectics in intellectual discourse in the 1980s, see Chen Xiaomei, *Occidentalism: A Theory of Counter-Discourse in Post-Mao China* (New York: Oxford University Press, 1995); Jiayan Mi, "The Visual Imagined Communities: Media State, Virtual Citizenship and *TELE*vision in *River Elegy*," *The Quarterly Review of Film and Video* 22.4 (October–December 2005): 327–340; Wang Jing, *High Culture Fever: Politics, Aesthetics, and Ideology in Deng's China* (Berkeley: University of California Press, 1996).

6. Murray Bookchin, "Society and Ecology," in *Debating the Earth: The Environmental Politics Reader*, ed. John S. Dryzek and David Schlosberg (Oxford: Oxford University Press, 1998), 415–428, 418 (emphasis original).

7. For an example of government-endorsed criticism of *The River Elegy*, see Ji Ren, "*Zhao Ziyang de jieru shou he <Heshang> de 'xin jiyuan'*" (Zhao Ziyang's theory of non-interference and the "New Epoch" in *The River Eulogy*), *Guangming Ribao*, August 15, 1989, 1.

8. Zhang Haiyang.

9. Liao Guoqiang, "Zhonguo shaoshu minzu shengtaiguan dui kezhixu fazhan de jiejian he qifa" (China's national minorities' ecological consciousness as a reference and inspiration for sustainable development), *Yunnan minzu xueyuan xuebao* (Journal of Yuannan Institute of Nationalities) 9 (2001): 160–163; Jia Qinglin, "*Minzu, zongjiao gongzuo yao wei gaojian hexie shehui zuo gongxian*" (Ethnic and religious policy should contribute to the building of a harmonious society), www.xinhuanet, February 2, 2005, last retrieved July 6, 2007; Xue Cheng, "Zongjiao — goajian hexie shehui de dutie jingshen ziyuang" (Religion — the unique spiritual resources for the building of a harmonious society), www.Zhongguonet, March 8, 2006, http://www.lianghui.org.cn/chinese/zhuanti/2006lh/1147512.htm, last retrieved July 5, 2007.

10. Yomi Braester, "Tracing the City's Scars: Demolition and the Limits of the Documentary Impulse in New Urban Cinema," in *The Urban Generation: Chinese Cinema and Society at the Turn of the Twenty-First Century*, ed. Zhang Zhen (Durham: Duke University Press, 2006), 161–180, 162.

11. China's new wave of documentaries is alternatively referred to as new independent documentaries. Wu Wenguan's *Liulang Beijing* (Wandering in Beijing, 1990) is commonly credited as the beginning of this cinematic revolution. Duan Jinchuan started to make documentaries of Tibet in the mid-1980s. He was employed by Tibetan Television Station during his tenure in Tibet. There are controversies surrounding the classification of his early works. For an overview of documentary films by independent filmmakers see Lü Xinyu, *Jilu Zhongguo* (Recording China) (Beijing: Sanlian shudian, 2003), 1–23; for analysis of cinematic language of independent documentary films of the 1990s, see Wang Gang "90 *niandaihou zhongguo jilupian de 'zhenshigan' he fengge yanbian*" (The concept of "reality" and stylistic change in Chinese documentary film in the 1990s), Master's thesis (Beijing; Beijing Film Academy, May 2007); for introduction to independent documentaries in China, see Zhu Jinjiang and Mei Bing, eds., *Zhongguo duli jilupian dang'an* (The archive of Chinese independent documentary film) (Xi'an: Shaanxi shifan daxue chubanshe, 2004).

12. Orville Schell, *Virtual Tibet* (New York: Metropolitan Books, 2000), 36.

13. Tuan Yi-Fu, "Images and Mental Maps," *Annals of the Association of American Geographers* Vol. 65, No. 2 (June 1975): 205–213, 210.

14. For Tian Zhuangzhuang's reflection on the making and distraction *Horse Thief*, see Michael Berry, *Speaking in Images: Interview with Contemporary Chinese Filmmakers* (New York: Columbia University, 2005), 60–66.

15. Tian Zhuangzhuang, in Ma Yufeng and Li Bin, eds., "*Xuanze le yisheng zhong zuiyukuai de shiye*" (The most enjoyable project in my life), *Beijing dianying xueyuan xuebao* (The Journal of Beijing Film Academy) 6 (2004): 62–92, 63.

16. Ni Zhen, "Huimou <delamu>" (Reflecting on *Delamu*), *Dangdai dianying* (Contemporary Cinema) 4 (2004): 4–7, 4–5.

17. David MacDougall, "Ethnographic Film: Failure and Promise," *Annual Review of Anthropology* Vol. 7 (1978): 405–425, 405.

18. Zhang Jinghong, "Tianye hezuozhong de qidai" (Expectations for cooperation in field work), *Minzu yishu yanjiu* (Studies in Ethnic Arts) 3 (2004): 69–76, 70.

19. For the staging and recreation of indigenous life in the film, see Zhang Jinghong, 70–71.

20. Zhang Huijun, "Guanzhu pingjing" (Concentrating on quietude), *Beijing dianying xueyuan xuebao* (Journal of Beijing Film Academy) 6 (2004): 74–83, 75.

21. Ibid.; Tian Zhuangzhuang interviewed by Zhang Tongdao, Xie Yuzhang, "<Delamu>: huxi shanshui" (*Delamu*: breathing in mountains and rivers), *Dianying yishu* (Cinematic Art) 5 (2004): 31–36, 36.

22. Tian Zhuangzhuang interviewed by Zhang Tongdao, Xie Yuzhang, 36.

23. "Getting real" is a phrase borrowed from Chris Berry. Berry uses this phrase to describe the drive for realism in China's independent documentary films of urban life in the 1990s. See Chris Berry, "Getting Real: Chinese Documentary, Chinese Postsocialism," in Zhang Zhen, 115–134.

24. Ji Dan, "Yu huoshenshen de mingyuan xiangyu" (Encounters with the fate real life), in *Zhongguo duli jilupian dang'an* (The archive of Chinese independent documentary film), ed. Zhu Jinjiang and Mei Bing (Xi'an: Shaanxi shifan daxue chubanshe, 2004), 230–247, 237.

25. For debate on the creativity of non-fiction, see Raymond Spottiswoode, *A Grammar of the Film* (Berkeley: University of California Press, 1959).

26. For "practical, everyday differences between fiction and nonfiction," see Dirk Eiitzen, "When Is a Documentary?: Documentary as a Mode of Reception," *Cinema Journal* Vol. 35 (Fall 1995): 81–102, 82.

27. Cui Weiping interview with Wanma Caidan, March 2007.

28. Wanma Caidan interviewed by author, July 30, 2006.

29. Cui Weiping.

30. Ibid.

31. For different emphases placed on "pure land" by Chinese, Japanese, and Tibetan Buddhists, please see Paul Williams, *Mahayana Buddhism* (London and New York: Routledge, 1993), especially 152–153, 274–275, 222–224; for evolution of Tibetan Buddhism, see Kenneth Ch'en, "Transformations in Buddhism in Tibet," *Philosophy East and West* Vol. 7, No. 3/4 (1957–1958): 117–125, 122.

32. Wanma Caidan, personal correspondence with author, October 20, 2006.

33. "Translation code" is borrowed from Stephen Hutchings, "Ghosts in the Machine," *International Journal for Cultural Studies* Vol. 5.3 (2002): 291–315, 291.

34. For discussion of the novel's relationship with canonical Buddhist works see Giancheng Li, *Fiction of Enlightenment* (Honolulu: University of Hawai'i Press, 2004), 49–52.

35. Qtd. in Robert E. Burkholder, review "*The Song of the Earth*," *Comparative Literature Studies* Vol. 39 (2002): 253–256, 253.

Chinese Glossary

A Cheng 阿城
Ah-ming 阿明
Anding yiyuan 安定醫院
Anduo 安多

baitiao 白條
Bian zou bian chang 邊走邊唱
Bingzhongluo 丙中洛

cao gen 草根
caoyuan 草原
cha guan 茶館
chai 拆
Chama gudao 茶馬古道
changjingji 唱經機
Chen Guo 陳果
Chen Jiangshui 陳江水
Chen Kaige 陳凱歌
Chen Lin Shi 陳林市
Chen Qing 陳青
Chen Yü-ling 陳玉玲
Chenmo de Nujiang 沈默的怒江
Chiliejiao 赤鱲角
Chongqing 重慶
chuishiban 炊事班
ci liang zhe, tong chu er yi ming
　　此兩者同出而異名
Cui Qiao 翠巧

Da cuo che 搭錯車
Dahong denglong gaogao gua
　　大紅燈籠高高掛

Dakan cun 大礐村
dan wei zhao yun / mu wei xing yu
　　旦為朝雲，暮為行雨
Danshui (Tamsui) 淡水
Daoguang 道光
Daoma zei 盜馬賊
Dashixiong 大師兄
Datong 大同
Delamu 德拉姆
dianying yao biaoda de zhuti shi qidai
　　電影要表達的主題是期待
Dong 東
Dong 洞
Dong hai 東海
Dongbei 東北
Dongfang hong 東方紅
Doudou 豆豆
dudie 度牒
dunshi 遁世
dushi fojiao 都市佛教
dushi siyuan 都市寺院

fang shuideng 放水燈
fazhan shi yingdaoli 發展是硬道理
feixu 廢墟
Feng Xiaogang 馮小剛
Fengkuang de shitou 瘋狂的石頭
fengshui 風水
fo 佛
Foguang Si 佛光寺
fojiao jingji 佛教經濟

foyan kan shijie 佛眼看世界
Fu sheng 浮生
Furen shafu 婦人殺夫

gaige kaifang 改革開放
Gaotang fu 高唐賦
Gaobie Sanxia re 告別三峽熱
gongchang 工廠
Gonggong changsuo 公共場所
Gu Qing 顧青
guai li luan shen 怪力亂神
Guangyin miao 觀音廟
gufen 股份

Haizi wang 孩子王
Han Shaogong 韓少功
Heliu 河流
Heshang 河殤
Hong gaoliang 紅高粱
hou xin shiqi 後新時期
Huang tudi 黃土地
Huanghe yao 黃河謠
Huangtu Gaoyuan 黃土高原
huansu 還俗
Huashuo Changjiang 話説長江
Huashuo Huanghe 話説黃河
Huashuo Yunhe 話説運河
huayuan 化緣
huayuan shifu 化緣師傅
Huizhou 徽州
Huo Jianqi 霍建起
Huoxian 霍縣
hutong 胡同
hutou shewei 虎頭蛇尾

Jia Zhangke 賈樟柯
Jiangnan 江南
Jinghe 井河
jingji xiaoyi 經濟效益
Jingjing de manishi 靜靜的嘛呢石
jingtu 淨土
Ju you zhongguo tese de shehuizhuyi
　　具有中國特色的社會主義
Judou 菊豆

kaihuang zhongdi 開荒種地
Kala shi tiao gou 卡拉是條狗
Kang Youwei 康有為
Kangba 康巴
Keke xili 可可西裏

Lanzhou 欖洲
Lao jing 老井
Lao Mo 老莫
Lee Ang 李安
Li Ang 李昂
Li Bin 李彬
Li Yang 李楊
Li Yu 李玉
liaowuqu 寮屋區
Liechang zhasa 獵場紮撒
Lili 麗麗
Ling Zi 淩子
lishi fansi, wenhua fansi 歷史反思，
　　文化反思
Liu Qingbang 劉慶邦
Liulian 留連
Liulian 榴槤
Liulian piaopiao 榴槤飄飄
Long wang 龍王
Lou Ye 婁燁
Lü caodi 綠草地
Lu Chuan 陸川
Lü Xinyu 呂新雨
Lu Xuechang 路學長
Lu Xun 魯迅
Lugang 鹿港
luohan 羅漢
Luohan Si 羅漢寺
Luotuo Xiangzi 駱駝祥子
Luoye guigen 落葉歸根

Ma Bing 馬兵
Mai Qiang 麥強
Mamian 馬面
Mancheng jindai huangjin jia
　　滿城盡帶黃金甲
Mangjing 盲井
Meiren cao 美人草
Mingong 民工

Mo Yan 莫言
Mofa ama 魔法阿媽
Moudanjiang/Mudanjiang 牡丹江
Mulian jiumu 目蓮救母
muwuqu 木屋區

Nashan, naren, nagou 那山，那人，那狗
Ning Hao 寧浩
Niutou 牛頭
Nuan 暖
Nuhou ba, Huanghe 怒吼吧！黃河

Piaoliang mama 漂亮媽媽
Pingguo 蘋果

qian 遷
qiangjian 強姦
Qiaoying 巧英
Qing Ti 青提
Qingchun ji 青春祭
qingcui 青翠

ren di qin he 人地親和
ren ding shengtian 人定勝天
Ren xiaoyao 任逍遙
Renjian fojiao 人間佛教
Renmin gongci 人民公廁
rushi 入世

Sanxia gongcheng 三峽工程
Sanxia haoren 三峽好人
Se, jie 色戒
Shafu 殺夫
Shandong 山東
shanqing shuixiu 山青水秀
shasheng 殺生
Shen Congwen 沈從文
Shen Dan 沈剡
Shendiao xia lü 神雕俠女
shengtai dianying 生態電影
shengtai piping 生態批評
Shenlu ya, shen lu 神鹿呀，神鹿
Shenmu 神木
Shennü feng 神女峰
Shenyang 瀋陽
Shi Runjiu 施潤玖

shi xingxiang fali 失形象乏力
Shijie 世界
Shijie gongyuan 世界公園
shikumen 石庫門
Shimian maifu 十面埋伏
Shi-niao-pi 屎尿屁
Shiqi sui de danche 十七歲的單車
shouhun bei 獸魂碑
Shouji 手機
sishi 私事
Sishui 死水
Song Yu 宋玉
Sun Zengtian 孫增田
Sun Zhou 孫周
suzhi 素質
Suzhou he 蘇州河

Tai hang 太行
Taixu 太虛
Taiyuan 太原
Teng Wenji 滕文驥
Tian Zhuangzhuang 田壯壯
Tianbian yi duo yun 天邊一朵雲
Tiangou 天狗
Tianxia wuzei 天下無賊
Tianyun shan chuanqi 天雲山傳奇
tiaojie 跳接
Tiexi qu 鐵西區
Tsai Mingliang 蔡明亮
Tuan, Yi-fu 段義孚
tufu 屠夫
Tuya de hunshi 圖雅的婚事

Wang Bing 王兵
Wang Quan'an 王全安
Wang Shau-di 王小棣
Wang Wenqiang 王文強
Wang Xiaoshuai 王小帥
Wangquan 旺泉
Wanma Caidan 萬瑪才旦
Weizang 衛藏
Wen Chen-hua 溫振華
Wen Yiduo 聞一多
wo gen ta shuijiaole 我跟她睡覺了
Wohu canglong 臥虎藏龍
Wu Gang 吳剛

Wu ji 無極
Wu Tianming 吳天明
Wu Zuxiang 吳祖湘
wujie 五戒
Wushan yunyu 巫山雲雨
Wutaishan 五臺山
wuwo 無我
Wuzhishan 五指山

Xia Jun 夏俊
Xian ke lai 仙客來
Xianggang youge helihuo 香港有個荷裏活
Xianghuo 香火
Xianü 俠女
Xiao caifeng 小裁縫
Xiao Shan huijia 小山回家
Xiao wu 小武
Xie Jin 謝晉
Xifeng 喜鳳
xin ganjüe 新感覺
Xin tian you 信天遊
xin tiyan 新體驗
Xingfu shiguang 幸福時光
Xinwen huiketing 新聞會客廳
Xiu Zongdi 修宗迪
Xiyouji 西遊記
Xizao 洗澡

yan 淹
Yang Liu 楊柳
Yihe yuan 頤和園
Yin Hong 尹鴻
Ying yu Bai 英與白
Yingxiong 英雄
Yinshun 印順
Youyi Shuoyi 有一說一
yuan shengtai 原生態
yuanjumin 原居民
Yuanye 原野
Yulan pen 盂蘭盆

Zai qidai zhizhong 在期待之中
zaosi zao chaosheng 早死早超生
zaotang 澡堂
Zeng Zhuangxiang 曾壯祥
Zhan Zhou 詹周

Zhang he Lao Ji jia 張和老吉家
Zhang Ming 章明
Zhang Nuanxin 張暖昕
Zhang Xianmin 張獻民
Zhang Yang 張揚
Zhang Yimou 張藝謀
Zhang Yiqing 張以慶
Zhang Yuan 張元
Zhantai 站臺
Zhao Tao 趙濤
zhaoyun 朝雲
zhe caishi zuo shanshi 這才是做善事
Zheng Yi 鄭義
zhixiashi 直轄市
Zhong Ping 鍾萍
zhongguo chengshi pipan 中國城市批判
Zhongguo dalu xinshengdai de dianying shijie
       中國大陸新生代的電影世界
zhongyuan [chungyuan] pudu 中原普渡
Zhouzhou de shijie 舟舟的世界
Zhu Wen 朱文
zhuada fangxiao 抓大放小
Zi hudie 紫蝴蝶
ziyang 自養
Zuihou de shanshen 最後的山神

Filmography

The Filmography includes the films mentioned in the essays. The listings are arranged in alphabetical order by English title and include director, country or region of origin, and year.

Anding Hospital (documentary, Anding yiyuan). Dir. Shi Runjiu. China. 2002.

Atlantis. Dir. Kent De Mond. U.S. 2007.

Ballad of the Yellow River (Huanghe yao). Dir. Teng Wenji. China. 1989.

Balzac and the Little Chinese Seamstress (Xiao caifeng). Dir. Dai Sijie. France and China. 2002.

Beautiful Mama (Piaoliang mama). Dir. Sun Zhou. China. 2001.

Before the Flood (documentary, Yanmo). Dir. Yan Yu and Li Yifan. China. 2005.

Beijing Bicycle (Shiqi sui de danche). Dir. Wang Xiaoshuai. China. 2001.

Bicycle Thieves. Dir. Vittorio De Sica. Italy. 1948.

Blade Runner. Dir. Ridley Scott. U.S. 1982.

Blind Shaft (Mang jing). Dir. Li Yang. China. 2003

Cala, My Dog (Kala shi tiao gou). Dir. Lu Xuechang. China. 2004.

Cell Phone (Shouji). Dir. Feng Xiaogang. China. 2003.

Chung-Kuo Cina. Dir. Michelangelo Antonioni. Italy. 1972.

Clouds and Rain over Wushan (Wushan yunyu). Dir. Zhang Ming. China. 1996.

Condor Hero (Shendiao xia lü). Dir. Yu Min. China. 2006.

Crazy Stone (Fengkuang de shitou). Dir. Ning Hao. China. 2006.

Crouching Tiger Hidden Dragon (Wohu canglong). Dir. Ang Lee. Taiwan. 2000.

Curse of the Golden Flower (Mancheng jindai huangjin jia). Dir. Zhang Yimou. China. 2006.

Days, The (Dongchun de rizi). Dir. Wang Xiaoshuai. China. 1993.

Delamu (documentary, Delamu). Dir. Tian Zhuangzhuang. China. 2004.

Dong (documentary, Dong). Dir. Jia Zhangke. China. 2006.

Durian Durian (Liulian piaopiao). Dir. Fruit Chan. Hong Kong. 2000.

Floating Lives (Fu sheng). Dir. Sheng Zhimin. China 2006.

Foliage, The (Meiren cao). Dir. Lü Le. China. 2004.

Forest Ranger, The (Tiangou). Dir. Qi Jian. China. 2006.

Getting Home (Luoye guigen). Dir. Zhang Yang. China. 2007

Going East to the Native Land (Donggui yingxiong zhuang). Dir. Saifu and Bailis. China. 1993.

Grandma and Her Ghosts (Mofa ama). Dir. Wang Shau-di. Taiwan. 1998.

Grassland, The (Caoyuan). Dir. Wanma Caidan. China. 2003.

Happy Times (Xingfu shiguang). Dir. Zhang Yimou. China. 2000.

Hero (Yingxiong). Dir. Zhang Yimou. China. 2002.

Hole, The (Dong). Dir. Tsai Mingliang. Taiwan. 1998.

Hollywood Hong Kong (Xianggang youge helihuo). Dir. Fruit Chan. Hong Kong. 2001.

Horse Thief (Daoma zei). Dir. Tian Zhuangzhuang. China. 1985.

House of Flying Daggers (Shimian maifu). Dir. Zhang Yimou. China. 2004.

In Expectation (Wushan yunyu). Dir. Zhang Ming. China. 1996.

In Public (Gonggong changsuo). Dir. Jia Zhangke. China. 2001.

Incense (Xianghuo). Dir. Ning Hao. China. 2003.

Inconvenient Truth, An. Dir. Davis Guggenheim. U.S. 2006.

Judou (Judou). Dir. Zhang Yimou. China. 1989.

Kekexili: Mountain Patrol (Kekexili). Dir. Lu Chuan. China and U.S. 2004.

King of the Children (Haizi wang). Dir. Chen Kaige. China. 1988.

Last Mountain God, The (documentary, Zuihou de shanshen). Dir. Sun Zengtian. China. 1992.

Legend of Tianyun Mountain, The (Tianyun shan chuanqi). Dir. Xie Jin. China. 1980.

Life on a String (*Bian zou bian chang*). Dir. Chen Kaige. China. 1990.

Lost in Beijing (Pingguo). Dir. Li Yu. China. 2007.

Lust, Caution (Se, jie). Dir. Ang Lee. Taiwan and U.S. 2007.

Manufactured Landscapes (documentary). Dir. Jennifer Baichwal. Canada. 2006.

Marriage of Tuya, The (Tuya de hunshi). Dir. Wang Quan'an. China. 2007.

Metropolis. Dir. Fritz Lang. Germany. 1927.

Mongolian Ping Pong (Menggu pingpong, a.k.a. Lü caodi). Dir. Ning Hao. China. 2004.

Nuan (Nuan). Dir. Huo Jianqi. China. 2003.

Old Well (Laojing). Dir. Wu Tianming. China. 1986.

Olympia. Dir. Leni Riefenstahl. Germany. 1938.

On the Hunting Ground (Liechang zhasa). Dir. Tian Zhuangzhuang. China. 1985.

Papa, Can You Hear Me Sing (Da cuo che). Dir. Yue Ham Ping. Hong Kong. 1983.

Platform (Zhantai). Dir. Jia Zhangke. China and France. 2000.

Postmen in the Mountains (Nashan naren nagou). Dir. Huo Jianqi. China. 1999.

Promise, The (Wu ji). Dir. Chen Kaige. China. 2006.

Public Toilet (Renmin gongci). Dir. Fruit Chan. Hong Kong. 2002.

Purple Butterfly (Zi hudie). Dir. Ye Lou. China. 2003.

Raise the Red Lantern (Da hong denglong gaogao gua). Dir. Zhang Yimou. China. 1990.

Red River Valley, The (Honghe gu). Dir. Feng Xiaoning. China. 1997.

Red Sorghum (Hong gaoliang). Dir. Zhang Yimou. China. 1988.

Reindeer, Oh Reindeer (documentary, Shenlu). Dir. Sun Zengtian. China. 1997.

River, The (Heliu). Dir. Tsai Mingliang. Taiwan. 1997.

River Elegy (documentary, Heshang). Dir. Xia Jun. China. 1988.

Roar! The Yellow River (Nuhou ba, Huanghe). Dir. Shen Dan. China. 1979.

Sacrificed Youth (Qingchun ji). Dir. Zhang Nuanxing. China. 1985.

Savage Land, The (Yuanye). Dir. Ling Zi. China. 1979.

Shower (Xizao). Dir. Zhang Yang. China. 1999.

Silent Holy Stone, The (Jingjing de manishi). Dir. Wanma Caidan. China. 2005.

Silent Nu River, The (documentary, Chenmo de Nujiang). Dir. Hu Jia. China. 2007.

Sorrow of Brook Steppe, The (Beiqing buluke). Dir. Saifu and Bailis. China. 2005.

Still Life (Sanxia haoren). Dir. Jia Zhangke. China. 2006.

Summer Palace (Yihe yuan). Dir. Lou Ye. China and France. 2006.

Suzhou River (Suzhou he). Dir. Ye Lou. China and Germany. 2000.

Tales of the Grand Canal (documentary, Huashuo Yunhe). China. 1987.

Tales of the Yangtze River (documentary, Huashuo Changjiang). China. 1983–1987.

Tales of the Yellow River (documentary, Huashuo Huanghe). China. 1986–1987.

Touch of Zen, A (Xianü). Dir. Hu Jinquan. Taiwan. 1971.

Triumph of the Will (*Triumph des Willens*). Dir. Leni Riefenstahl. Germany. 1935.

Unknown Pleasures (Ren xiaoyao). Dir. Jia Zhangke. China. 2002.

Vertigo. Dir. Alfred Hitchcock. U.S. 1958.

Wayward Cloud, The (Tianbian yi duo yun). Dir. Tsai Mingliang. Taiwan. 2005.

West of the Tracks (documentary, Tiexi qu). Dir. Wang Bing. China. 2003.

White Countess, The. Dir. James Ivory. U.S. and China. 2005.

Woman of Wrath (Shafu). Dir. Zeng Zhuangxiang. Taiwan. 1988.

World, The (Shijie). Dir. Jia Zhangke. China. 2004.

World of Zhouzhou, The (documentary, Zhouzhou de shijie). Dir. Zhang Yiqing. China. 1998.

World without Thieves, The (Tianxia wuzei). Dir. Feng Xiaogang. China. 2004.

Xiao Shan Going Home (Xiao Shan huijia). Dir. Jia Zhangke. China. 1993.

Xiao Wu (Xiao Wu). Dir. Jia Zhangke. Hong Kong/China. 1997.

Yellow Earth (Huang tudi). Dir. Chen Kaige. China. 1984.

Ying and Bai (documentary, Ying yu Bai). Dir. Zhang Yiqing. China. 1999.

Zhang's Stir-Fried Tripe and Old Ji's Family (documentary, Baodu Zhang he Lao Ji jia). Dir. Shi Runjiu. China. 2006.

Bibliography

This bibliography includes the works mentioned in this volume.

Abbas, Ackbar. *Hong Kong: Culture and the Politics of Disappearance*. Minneapolis: University of Minnesota Press, 1997.

———. "Play It Again Shanghai: Urban Preservation In the Global Era." In *Shanghai Reflections*. Ed. Mario Gandelsonas. New York: Princeton Architectural Press, 2002. 37–55.

Acker, William. *Some T'ang and Pre-T'ang Texts on Chinese Painting*. Leiden: E. J. Brill, 1954.

Adams, Carol J. Ed. *Ecofeminism and the Sacred*. New York: Continuum, 1993.

———. Ed. *Beyond Animal Rights*. New York: Continuum, 1996.

———. *The Sexual Politics of Meat: A Feminist-Vegetarian Critical Theory*. New York: Continuum, 2006.

———. Ed. with Josephine Donovan. *Animals & Women: Feminist Theoretical Explorations*. Durham and London: Duke University Press, 1995.

Adorno, Theodor W. "The Idea of Natural History" (1932). Trans. Bob Hullot-Kentor. *Telos* no. 60 (1984): 111–124.

Agamben, Giorgio. *The Open*. Trans. Kevin Attell. Stanford: Stanford University Press, 2004.

Anderson, Roger C. "Ecocinema: A Plan for Preserving Nature." *Bioscience* Vol. 25, No. 7 (July 1975): 452. Originally published in *Arboretum News of the University of Wisconsin Arboretum and Wildlife Refuge* (1966).

Appadurai, Arjun. *Modernity at Large: Cultural Dimensions of Globalization*. Minneapolis: University of Minnesota Press, 1997.

ASIAN Film Connections. "In Expectation." usc.edu. http://www.usc.edu/isd/archives/asianfilm/china/ (Accessed 2002).

Bachelard, Gaston. *The Poetics of Space: The Classic Look at How We Experience Intimate Places*. Trans. Maria Jolas. Boston: Beacon Press, 1994.

Badiou, Alain. *Ethics: An Essay on the Understanding of Evil*. Trans. Peter Hallward. London: Verso, 2001.

Bai, Xiaojun. "Xinjing, Yijing-shanshuihua Chuangzuode Zhudao Yinsu Yanjiu" (The realms of the heart and the idea-image — A study of the guiding principles in the creation of landscape painting). *Shehui kexuejia* 48.4 (1994): 48–61.

Baker, Steve. *Picturing the Beast: Animals, Identity and Representation*. Manchester: Manchester University Press, 1993.

Bakhtin, M. M. "Forms of Time and of the Chronotope in the Novel." In *The Dialogic Imagination: Four Essays by M. M. Bakhtin*. Ed. Michael Holquist. Austin: University of Texas Press, 1981. 84–258.

Balfour, Alan, and Shiling Zhen. *World Cities: Shanghai*. London: Wiley-Academy, 2002.

Banban, Duojie. "Jianlun Dushi Siyuan Yu Shanlin Siyuan Zhi Bijiao" (A comparison between city monastery and rural monastery). In *Buddhism in the Metropolis*. Ed. Jue Xing. Beijing: Zongjiao wenhua chubanshe, 2004.

Barlow, Tani E. "'Green Blade in the Act of Being Grazed': Late Capital, Flexible Bodies, Critical Intelligibility." *Differences: A Journal of Feminist Cultural Studies* 10.3 (1998): 119–115.

Barsam, Richard M. *Nonfiction Film: A Critical History*. New York: Dutton, 1973.

Beijing Film Studio & the Beijing East-Earth Cultural Development Co., Ltd. 1997. "In Expectation (Clouds and Rain in Wushan) [Advertisement & Informational Flier]."

Beller, Jonathan. "Capital/Cinema." In *Deleuze and Guattari: New Mappings in Politics, Philosophy, and Culture*. Ed. Eleanor Kaufman and Kevin J. Heller. Minneapolis: University of Minnesota Press, 1998. 77–95.

Belsey, Catherine. "What's Real?" In *Critical Zone 1: A Forum of Chinese and Western Knowledge*. Ed. Q. S. Tong, Wang Shouren, and Douglas Kerr. Hong Kong: Hong Kong University Press, 2004. 21–36.

Benjamin, Walter. "The Work of Art in the Age of Mechanical Reproduction." In *Illuminations*. Ed. Hannah Arendt. Trans. Harry Zohn. New York: Schoken Books, 1968. 217–251.

———. *Illuminations*. Ed. Hannah Arendt. New York: Schocken Books, 1969.

———. "A Small History of Photography." In *One-Way Street and Other Writings*. Trans. Edmund Jephcott and Kingsley Shorter. London: Verso, 1992. 240–257.

———. *The Arcades Project*. Trans. Howard Eiland and Kevin McLaughlin. Cambridge: Belknap-Harvard University Press, 1999.

Bennett, Tony, et al. *New Keywords: A Revised Vocabulary of Culture and Society*. Oxford: Blackwell Publishing, 2005.

Berkman, Patience. "The Three Gorges Dam: Energy, the Environment, and the New Emperors." *Education about Asia* Vol. 3, No. 1 (Spring 1998): 27–35.

Berry, Chris. "Chinese Women's Cinema." *Camera Obscura* 18 (1988): 5–19.

———. "Happy Alone? Sad Young Men in East Asian Gay Cinema." In *Queer Asian Cinema: Shadows in the Shade*. Ed. Andrew Grossman. New York: Harrington Press, 2000. 187–200.

———. "Getting Real: Chinese Documentary, Chinese Postsocialism." In *The Urban Generation: Chinese Cinema and Society at the Turn of the Twenty-First Century*. Ed. Zhang Zhen. Durham: Duke University Press, 2006. 115–134.

Berry, Chris, and Mary Farquhar. "Post-socialist Strategies: An Analysis of *Yellow Earth* and *Black Cannon Incident*." In *Cinematic Landscapes: Observations on the Visual Arts and Cinema of China and Japan*. Ed. Linda C. Ehrlich and David Desser. Austin: University of Texas Press, 1994. 85–95.

———. *China on Screen: Cinema and Nation*. New York: Columbia University Press, 2006.

Berry, Michael. "Fruit Chan: Hong Kong Independent." In *Speaking in Images: Interviews with Contemporary Chinese Filmmakers*. Ed. Michael Berry. New York: Columbia University Press, 2005. 458–483.

——. *Speaking in Images, Interviews with Contemporary Chinese Filmmakers*. New York: Columbia University Press, 2005.

Bhabha, Homi. *The Location of Culture*. London and New York: Routledge, 1994.

Bondanella, Peter. *Italian Cinema: From Neorealism to the Present*. New York: Continuum, 1999. 402–405.

"Bonus Features." In *Quentin Tarantino Presents Jet Li: Hero* (DVD). Miramax Home Entertainment, no date.

Bookchin, Murray. "Society and Ecology." In *Debating the Earth: The Environmental Politics Reader*. Ed. John S. Dryzek and David Schlosberg. Oxford: Oxford University Press, 1998. 415–428.

Bordwell, David, and Noël Carroll. *Post-Theory: Reconstructing Film Studies*. Madison: University of Wisconsin Press, 1996.

Braester, Yomi. "Tracing the City's Scars: Demolition and the Limits of the Documentary Impulse in the New Urban Cinema." In *The Urban Generation: Chinese Cinema and Society at the Turn of the Twentieth-First Century*. Ed. Zhang Zhen. Durham, NC: Duke University Press, 2007. 161–180.

Branch, Michael P., Rochelle Johnson, Daniel Patterson, and Scott Slovic. Eds. *Reading the Earth: New Directions in the Study of Literature and the Environment*. Moscow, Idaho: University of Idaho Press, 1998.

Branch, Michael P., and Scott Slovic. Eds. *The ISLE Reader: Ecocriticism, 1993–2003*. Athens and London: University of Georgia Press, 2003.

Brand, Stewart. "Photography Changes Our Relationship to Our Planet." In *Smithsonian Photography Initiative*. http://click.si.edu/Story.aspx?story=31 (Accessed May 30, 2008).

Brereton, Pat. *Hollywood Utopia: Ecology in Contemporary American Cinema*. Bristol, UK and Portland, Oregon: Intellect Books, 2005.

Browne, Nick, Paul G. Pickowicz, Vivian Sobchack, and Esther Yau. Eds. *New Chinese Cinemas: Forms, Identities, Politics*. Cambridge: Cambridge University Press, 1994.

Bruno, Giuliana. *Atlas of Emotion: Journeys in Art, Architecture, and Film*. New York: Verso, 2002.

Buck-Morss, Susan. *The Dialectics of Seeing: Walter Benjamin and the Arcades Project*. Cambridge, Mass. and London: The MIT Press, 1989.

Buell, Lawrence. *Writing for an Endangered World: Literature, Culture, and Environment in the U.S. and Beyond*. Cambridge: Harvard University Press, 2001.

——. *The Future of Environmental Criticism: Environmental Crisis and Literary Imagination*. Oxford: Blackwell Publishing, 2005.

Burkholder, Robert E. "The Song of the Earth." *Comparative Literature Studies* Vol. 39.3 (2002): 253–256.

Buttimer, A., and D. Seamon. Eds. *The Human Experience of Space and Place*. London: Croom Helm, 1979.

Campanella, Thomas. *The Concrete Dragon: China's Urban Revolution and What It Means for the World*. New York: Princeton Architectural Press, 2008.

Cao, Tianyu. Ed. *Xiandai hua, quanqiu hua yu zhongguo daolu* (Modernization, globalization and the Chinese road). Beijing: Shehui kexue wenxian chubanshe, 2003.

Ch'en, Kenneth. "Transformations in Buddhism in Tibet." *Philosophy East and West* Vol. 7, No. 3/4 (1957–1958): 117–125, 122.

Chang, Te-Chuan. "Taiwan Xin Dianying zhong de nuxing jiaose: Ershi nian yihou" (Women's roles in Taiwanese New Cinema: After twenty years). Doctoral dissertation. Kao-hsiung, Taiwan: Zhong-shan University, 2006.

Chen, Guying. *Laozi zhuyi ji pingjie*. Hong Kong: Zhonghua Shuju, 1987.

Chen, Jianlan. "Shengtai zhuyi huayu: shengtai zhexue yu wenxue piping" (Ecophilosophy and ecocriticism: Some aspects of ecologism). *Wenyi lilun qianyan* (Frontiers of Literary Theory) No. 1 (April 2004): 3–43.

Chen, Mo. *Zhongguo dianying shi daoyan, Langman yu youhuan* (Ten Chinese film directors, Romanticism and suffering). Beijing: Renmin chubanshe, 2005.

Chen, Xiaomei. *Occidentalism: A Theory of Counter-Discourse in Post-Mao China*. New York: Oxford University Press, 1995.

——. *Acting the Right Part: Political Theater and Popular Drama in Contemporary China*. Honolulu: University of Hawai'i Press, 2007.

Chen, Yü-ling. "Li Ang *Sha-fu* de yinxing shuxie." In *Taiwan Wenxue de guodu: Nuxing, bentu, fanzhiming lunshu*. Taipei County: Boy Young Wenhua, 2000.

Cheng Qingsong, and Huang Ou. Eds. *My Camera Does Not Lie* (*Wode sheying ji bu sahuang*). Beijing: Zhongguo youyi chuban gongsi, 2002.

Chetham, Deirdre. *Before the Deluge: The Vanishing World of the Yangtze's Three Gorges*. Hampshire: Palgrave Macmillan, St. Martin's Press, 2002.

Cheung, Esther M. K. "The City That Haunts: The Uncanny in Fruit Chan's *Made in Hong Kong*." In *Between Home and World: A Reader in Hong Kong Cinema*. Ed. Esther M. K. Cheung and Chu Yiu-Wai. Hong Kong: Oxford University Press, 2004. 353–368.

Chow, Rey. *Primitive Passions: Visuality, Sexuality, Ethnography, and Contemporary Chinese Cinema*. New York: Columbia University Press, 1995.

——. "The Seductions of Homecoming: Place, Authenticity, and Chen Kaige's *Temptress Moon*." In *Cross-Cultural Readings of Chineseness: Narratives, Images, and Interpretations of the 1990s*. Ed. Wen-hsin Yeh. Berkeley: Institute of East Asian Studies, 2000. 8–26.

Chow, Wai-yin. "Religious Narrative and Ritual in a Metropolis: A Study of the Taoist Ghost Festival in Hong Kong." *Inter-Religio* 41 (Summer 2002): 5–7.

Chung, Ling. "Feminism and Female Taiwan Writers." In *Chinese Literature in the Second Half of the Twentieth Century: A Critical Survey*. Ed. David Wang and Pang-yuan Chi. Bloomington and Indianapolis: Indiana University Press, 2000.

Clarke, David. *Reclaimed Land: Hong Kong in Transition*. Hong Kong: Hong Kong University Press, 2002.

Clover, Joshua. *The Matrix*. London: British Film Institute, 2004.

Cousins, Mark. "The Asian Aesthetic." http://www.prospect-magazine.co.uk/ArticleView. asp?P_Article=12875 (Accessed October 29, 2004).

Crang, Mike. *Cultural Geography*. London: Routledge, 1998.

Cronon, William. Ed. *Uncommon Ground: Rethinking the Human Place in Nature*. New York: W. W. Norton & Company, 1996.

Cutting, James E. "Perceiving Scenes in Film and in the World." In *Moving Image Theory, Ecological Considerations*. Ed. Joseph D. Anderson and Barbara Fisher Anderson. Carbondale: Southern Illinois Press, 2005. 9–27.

Dai, Jinhua. "Wuzhong fengjing: Chudu 'Diliu dai'" (Landscape in the mist: A preliminary reading of the "Sixth Generation"). *Tianya* (Sky's Edge) Vol. 1 (1996): 1–13.

———. "Liangge wutuobang zhijian" (Between the two utopias). In *Wuzhong fengjing: Zhongguo dianying wenhua 1978–1998* (Scenes in the fog: Cinematic culture in China 1978–1998). Beijing: Beijing daxue chubanshe, 2000. 70–80.

———. *Cinema and Desire: Feminist Marxism and Cultural Politics in the Work of Dai Jinhua*. Ed. Jing Wang and Tani E. Barlow. London: Verso, 2002.

Dai, Qing. *The River Dragon Has Come!: The Three Gorges Dam and the Fate of China's Yangtze River and Its People*. Ed. John G. Thibodeau and Philip B. Williams. Trans. Yi Ming. Armonk: M. E. Sharpe, 1998.

De, Lege. *Nei Menggu Lamajiao shi* (A history of Lamaism in the Inner Mongolia). Huhehot: Nei Menggu renmin chubanshe, 2004.

De Certeau, Michel. *The Practice of Everyday Life*. Berkeley: University of California Press, 1984.

Deitering, Cynthia. "The Postnatural Novel: Toxic Consciousness in Fiction of the 1980s." In *The Ecocriticism Reader*. Ed. Cheryll Glotfelty and Harold Fromm. Athens and London: University of Georgia Press, 1996. 196–203.

Deleuze, Gilles. *Cinema 1: The Movement — Image*. Trans. Hugh Tomlinson. Minneapolis: University of Minnesota Press, 1986.

Dirlik, Arif. "Place-Based Imagination: Globalism and the Politics of Place." In *Places and Politics in an Age of Globalization*. Ed. Roxann Prazniak and Arif Dirlik. Oxford: Rowman & Littlefield Publishers. 2001. 15–51.

Dissanayake, Wimal. "The Class Imaginary in Fruit Chan's Films." *Jump Cut* 49. http://ejumpcut.org/archive/jc49.2007/FruitChan-class/text.html (Accessed May 30, 2008).

Donald, Stephanie. "Landscape and Agency: *Yellow Earth* and the Demon Lover." *Theory, Culture & Society* 14:1 (1997): 97–112.

Donovan, Josephine. "Ecofeminist Literary Criticism: Reading the Orange." In *Ecofeminist Literary Criticism: Theory, Interpretation, Pedagogy*. Ed. Greta Gaard and Patrick D. Murphy. Urbana and Chicago: University of Illinois Press, 1998. 74–96.

Dreyfus, Hubert. *Being-in-the-World: A Commentary on Heidegger's Being and Time*. Cambridge, MA: The MIT Press, 1991.

Du, Jiwen. Ed. *Fojiao shi* (A history of Buddhism). Nanjing: Jiangsu renmin chubanshe, 2006.

Dunayer, Joan. "Sexist Words, Speciesist Roots." In *Animals & Women: Feminist Theoretical Explorations*. Ed. Carol Adams and Josephine Donovan. Durham: Duke University Press, 1995. 11–23.

Economy, Elizabeth. *The River Runs Black: The Environmental Challenge to China's Future*. Ithaca and London: Cornell University Press, 2004.

Eigen, Michael. *Rage*. Middletown: Wesleyan University Press, 2002.

Eiitzen, Dirk. "When Is a Documentary?: Documentary as a Mode of Reception." *Cinema Journal* Vol. 35 (Fall 1995): 81–102.

Elley, Derek. "In Expectation" (*Wushan yunyu*). *CineEast* (1997): 1–2.

Elvin, Mark. *The Retreat of the Elephants: An Environmental History of China*. New Haven and London: Yale University Press, 2004.

Eng, Robert Y. "Is *Hero* a paean to authoritarianism?" http://www.asiamedia.ucla.edu/article.asp?parentid=14371 (Accessed November 27, 2004).

Engels, Friedrich. *The Condition of the Working Class in England*. Trans. W. O. Henderson and W. H. Chaloner. Stanford, CA: Stanford University Press, 1958.

Farquhar, Mary Ann. "The 'Hidden' Gender in *Yellow Earth*." *Screen* 33:2 (Summer 1992): 154–164.

——. Interviews at Animal Logic with the *Hero* and *Daggers* visual effects teams, Sydney (April 12, 2005).

Felman, Shoshana. *Writing and Madness (Literature/Philosophy/Psychoanalysis)*. Ithaca: Cornell University Press, 1985.

"Film shooting banned in nature reserves." http://www.radio86.co.uk/china-insight/newstoday/1833/film-shooting-banned-in-nature-reserves (Accessed March 12, 2007).

Fong, Wen. "The Problem of Forgeries in Chinese Painting." *Artibus Asiae* 25.2/3 (1962): 95–140.

Forêt, Philippe. *Mapping Chengde: The Qing Landscape Enterprise*. Honolulu: University of Hawai'i Press, 2000.

Forster, John Bellamy. *Marx's Ecology: Materialism and Nature*. New York: Monthly Press, 2000.

Foucault, Michel. *Power/Knowledge: Selected Interviews and Other Writings, 1972–1977*. Ed. Colin Gordon. Pantheon: New York, 1982.

Frazer, James G. *The Golden Bough: A Study in Magic and Religion*. New York: The Macmillan, 1922.

Friedman, Thomas L. *Hot, Flat, and Crowded: Why We Need a Green Revolution — and How It Can Renew America*. New York: Farrar, Straus and Giroux, 2008.

Freud, Sigmund. "The 'Uncanny'." In *Collected Papers* Vol. 4. London: The Hogarth Press, 1957. 368–407.

Fuller, R. Buckminster. *Your Private Sky: R. Buckminster Fuller, the Art of Design Science*. Ed. Joachim Krausse and Claude Lichtenstein. Baden, Switzerland: Lars Müller Publishers, 1991.

Gaard, Greta. "Women, Water, Energy: An Ecofeminist Approach." *Organization & Environment* 14/2 (June 2001): 157–172.

——. "Vegetarian Ecofeminism: A Review Essay." *Frontiers: A Journal of Women Studies* Vol. 23, No. 3 (2002): 117–146.

Gan, Wendy. *Fruit Chan's Durian Durian*. Hong Kong: Hong Kong University Press, 2005.

Garrard, Greg. *Ecocriticism*. London and New York: Routledge, 2004.

Glotfelty, Cheryll. "Introduction: Literary Studies in an Age of Environmental Crisis." In *The Ecocriticism Reader: Landmarks in Literary Ecology*. Ed. Cheryll Glotfelty and Harold Fromm. Athens and London: University of Georgia Press, 1996. xv–xxxvii.

Glotfelty, Cheryll, and Harold Fromm. Eds. *The Ecocriticism Reader: Landmarks in Literary Ecology*. Athens and London: University of Georgia Press, 1996.

Goldblatt, Howard. Ed. and trans. *The Butcher's Wife and Other Stories*. Boston: Cheng & Tsui Company, 1995.

Griffin, Susan. *Woman and Nature: The Roaring inside Her*. New York: Harper & Row, 1978.

Hai, Mo. *Zhongguo chengshi pipan* (A critique of Chinese cities). Wuhan: Changjiang wenyi chubanshe, 2004.

Hansen, Miriam. "Benjamin, Cinema and Experience: The Blue Flower in the Land of Technology." *New German Critique* 40 (Winter 1987): 179–224.

Haraway, Donna. *When Species Meet*. Minneapolis: University of Minnesota Press, 2008.

Harvey, David. *The Condition of Postmodernity: An Enquiry into the Origins of Cultural Change*. Cambridge, Massachusetts: Blackwell, 1990.

——. *The Limits to Capital*. London: Verso 1999.

——. "The City as Body Politic." In *Wounded Cities: Destruction and Reconstruction in a Globalized World*. Ed. Jane Schneider and Ida Susser. New York: Berg, 2003.

——. *A Brief History of Neoliberalism*. Oxford: Oxford University Press, 2005.

Hay, John. "Values and History in Chinese Painting." *Res* 6 (Fall 1983): 73–111; 7 (Autumn 1984): 103–136.

——. *Kernels of Energy, Bones of Earth: The Rock in Chinese Art*. New York: China House Gallery, 1985.

Heggelund, Gorild. *Environment and Resettlement Politics in China: The Three Gorges Project*. Burlington: Ashgate Publishing Limited, 2004.

Heidegger, Martin. *Poetry, Language, Thought*. Trans. Albert Hofstader. New York: Harper & Row, 1971.

Heine, Steven, and Charles S. Prebish. Eds. *Buddhism in the Modern World: Adaptations of an Ancient Tradition*. Oxford and New York: Oxford University Press, 2003.

Heinrich, Larissa. "Souvenirs of the Organ Trade: The Diasporic Body in Contemporary Chinese Literature and Art." In *Embodied Modernities: Corporeality, Representation, and Chinese Cultures*. Ed. Fran Martin and Larissa Heinrich. Honolulu: University of Hawai'i Press, 2006. 126–145.

Hessler, Peter. "Underwater: The World's Biggest Dam Floods the Past." *New Yorker* (July 7, 2003): 28–33.

Hoberman, J. "Review of *Hero*." *The Village Voice*. http://www.villagevoice.com/issues/0434/hoberman2.php (Accessed August 27, 2004).

Hong Kong Tourism Board. http://discoverhongkong.com/eng/touring/hiking/index.jhtml (Accessed May 30, 2008).

Horkheimer, Max, and Theodor W. Adorno. *Dialectic of Enlightenment*. Ed. Gunzelin Schmid Noerr. Trans. Edmund Jephcott. Stanford: Stanford University Press, 2002.

Hu, Kanping, and Yu Xiaogang. "Bridge Over Troubled Waters: The Role of the News Media in Promoting Public Participation in River Basin Management and Environmental Protection in China." http://www.ide.go.jp/English/Publish/Spot/pdf/28_08.pdf (Accessed December 10, 2007).

Huang, Shu-ying. "The Social Construction of Female Selves in the Fiction of Li Ang, Wang Anyi, and Amy Tan." Dissertation. Athens: University of Georgia, 1999.

Huang, Xianian. "Dushi fojiao yu renjian fojiao taolunhui zongshu" (A summary of the Conference on Earthly Buddhism and Metropolitan Buddhism). In *Buddhism in the Metropolis*. Ed. Jue Xing. Beijing: Zongjiao wenhua chubanshe, 2004. 1–12.

Huber, Christoph. "Curious About Crap: Fruit Chan's Public Toilet (2002)." *Senses of Cinema* http://www.sensesofcinema.com/contents/03/24/toilet.html (Accessed May 30, 2008).

Hunt, Leon. *Kung Fu Cult Masters: From Bruce Lee to Crouching Tiger*. London: Wallflower Press, 2003.

Huo, Jianqi. *Nuan*. Beijing: Jinhai Fangzhou Cultural Development Inc., 2003.

Hutchings, Stephen. "Ghosts in the machine." *International Journal for Cultural Studies* Vol. 5.3 (2002): 291–315.

Hwang, Sung-Uk. "Ecological Panopticism; the Problematization of the Ecological Crisis." *College Literature* 26.1 (Winter 1999): 137–149. http://findarticles.com/p/articles/mi_qa3709/is_199901/ai_n8843780/pg_3 (Accessed December 15, 2007).

Irvine, Leslie. *If You Tame Me: Understanding Our Connections with Animals*. Philadelphia: Temple University Press, 2004.

Jackson, Sukhan, et al. "Resettlement for China's Three Gorges Dam: Socio-Economic Impact and Institutional Tensions." *Communist and Post-Communist Studies* 33.2 (June 2000): 223–241.

Jacques, Derrida. *Specters of Marx: The State of the Debt, the Work of Mourning, and the New International*. London and New York: Routledge, 1994.

Jameson, Fredric. *Signatures of the Visible*. New York: Routledge, 1990.

——. *Postmodernism, or, The Cultural Logic of Late Capitalism*. Durham, NC: Duke University Press, 1991.

——. *The Geopolitical Aesthetic: Cinema and Space in the World System*. Bloomington: Indiana University Press, 1992.

——. "Notes on Globalization as a Philosophical Issue." In *The Cultures of Globalization*. Ed. Fredric Jameson and Masao Miyoshi. Durham and London: Duke University Press, 1998. 54–77.

Janos, Andrew. "Paradigms Revisited: Productionism, Globality, and Postmodernity in Comparative Politics." *World Politics* 50.1 (1997): 118–149.

Jarvis, Brian. *Postmodern Cartographies: The Geographical Imagination in Contemporary American Culture*. New York: St. Martin's Press, 1998.

Ji, Dan. "Yu huoshenshen de mingyuan xiangyu" (Encounters with the fate real life). In *Zhongguo duli jilupian dang'an* (The archive of Chinese independent documentary film). Ed. Zhu Jinjiang and Mei Bing. Xi'an: Shaanxi shifan daxue chubanshe, 2004. 230–247.

Ji, Ren. "Zhao Ziyang de jieru shou he 'Heshang' de 'xin jiyuan'" (Zhao Ziyang's theory of non-interference and the "New Epoch" in *The River Eulogy*). *Guangming Ribao* (1989), 1.

Jia, Leilei. *Wu zhi wu — Zhongguo wuxia dianyingde xingtai yu shenhun* (The dance of martial arts—Form and meaning in Chinese martial arts films). Zhengzhou: Henan renmin chubanshe, 1998.

——. *Zhongguo wuxia dianying shi* (The history of Chinese martial arts film). Beijing: Wenhua yishu chubanshe, 2005.

Jia, Qinglin. "Minzu, zongjiao gongzuo yao wei gaojian hexie shehui zuo gongxian." (Ethnic and religious policy should contribute to the building of harmonious society.) http://www.xinhuanet.com (Accessed July 6, 2007).

Johnson, Philip, and Mark Wigley. *Deconstructivist Architecture*. New York: The Museum of Modern Art, 1988.

Jones, Charles B. "Transitions in the Practice and Defense of Chinese Pure Land Buddhism." In *Buddhism in the Modern World*. Ed. Heine and Prebish. 123–142.

Jue, Xing. "Dushi siyuan yu renjian fojiao jianxing" (The practice of the city monastery and earthly Buddhism). In *Buddhism in the Metropolis*. Ed. Jue Xing. Beijing: Zongjiao wenhua chubanshe, 2004. 13–21.

——. *Dushi zhong de Fojiao: Shanghai Yufo Chansi jinian jiansi 120 zhounian yantaohui lunwenji* (Buddhism in the Metropolis: Proceedings of the Symposium in Commemoration of the 120 Anniversary of the Founding of Yufo Chansi in Shanghai). Beijing: Zongjiao wenhua chubanshe, 2004.

Kaldis, Nick. "National Development and Individual Trauma in *Wushan yunyu* (In Expectation)." *The China Review* Vol. 4, No. 2 (Fall 2004): 165–191.

Kang, Liu. *Globalization and Cultural Trends in China*. Honolulu: University of Hawai'i Press, 2004.

Kao, S. Y. Karl. *Classical Chinese Tales of the Supernatural and the Fantastic*. Bloomington: Indiana University Press, 1985.

Katz, Eric. *Nature as Subject: Human Obligation and Natural Community*. London: Rowman & Littlefield Publishers, Inc., 1997.

Keown, Damien. *A Dictionary of Buddhism*. Oxford and New York: Oxford University Press, 2003.

Keyser, Anne Sytske. "PRC and Hong Kong Films at the 1997 International Rotterdam Film Festival." *China Information* Vol. 11, No. 4 (1997): 117–125.

Ki. "In Expectation." *Queer View* (1997). http://home.snafu.de/fablab/queerview/079regenwolke nuber/qw79ef.htm.

Kinkley, Jeffrey. *Corruption and Realism in Late Socialist Literature: The Return of the Political Novel*. Stanford: Stanford University Press, 2007.

Kirshner, Lewis. "Rethinking Desire: The *Object Petite A* in Lacan's Theory." *APSA*. http://www.apsa.org/Portals/1/docs/JAPA/531/Kirshner-post-p.83-102.pdf (Accessed March 19, 2007).

Kline III, T. C., and Philip J. Ivanhoe. Eds. *Virtue, Nature, and Moral Agency in the Xunzi*. Indianapolis: Hackett, 2000.

Knoblock, John. *Xunzi: A Translation and Study of the Complete Works*. 3 Vols. Stanford: Stanford University Press, 1988–1994.

Kraicer, Shelley. "Interview with Tsai Mingliang." *Positions* 8.2 (Fall 2000): 579–588.

———. "Absence as Spectacle: Zhang Yimou's *Hero*." *Cinema Scope Magazine* 5:1, Issue 14 (Spring 2003): 9. http://www.chinesecinemas.org/hero.html (Accessed March 23, 2007).

———. "Chinese Wasteland: Jia Zhangke's *Still Life*." *Cinema Scope* No. 29. http://www.cinema-scope.com/cs29/feat_kraicer_still.html (Accessed March 14, 2007).

Lacan, Jacques. *Écrits: A Selection*. Trans. Alan Sheridan. New York: Norton, 1977.

———. "The Subject and the Other: Aphanisis." In *The Four Fundamental Concepts of Psychanalysis*. Ed. Jacques-Alain Miller. Trans. Alan Sheridan. London: The Hogarth Press, 1977. 216–229.

———. *The Four Fundamental Concepts of Psychoanalysis*. Ed. Jacques Alain Miller. Trans. Alan Sheridan. New York: Norton, 1981.

———. "Seminar on 'The Purloined Letter.'" In *Écrits: The First Complete Edition in English*. Trans. Bruce Fink, Héloïse Fink, and Russell Grigg. New York: W. W. Norton & Company, 2006. 6–48.

Lai, Linda Chiu-han. "Whither the Walker Goes: Spatial Practices and Negative Poetics in 1990s Chinese Urban Cinema." In *The Urban Generation: Chinese Cinema and Society at the Turn of the Twenty-First Century*. Ed. Zhang Zhen. Durham: Duke University Press, 2007. 205–237.

Laplanche, Jean, and Serge Leclaire. "The Unconscious: A Psychoanalytic Study." In Jean Laplanche, *The Unconscious and the Id: A Volume of Laplanche's Problématiques*. Trans. Luke Thurston and Lindsay Watson. London: Rebus Press, 1972. 224–272.

Laqueur, Thomas. Ed. *Chinese Femininities/Chinese Masculinities: A Reader*. Berkeley and Los Angeles: University of California Press, 2002.

Latour, Bruno. *Politics of Nature*. Trans. Catherine Porter. Cambridge: Harvard University Press, 2004.

Lau Shing-hon. Ed. *A Study of the Hong Kong Martial Arts Film.* Hong Kong: Urban Council, 1980.

———. Ed. *A Study of the Hong Kong Swordplay Film (1945–1980).* Hong Kong: Provisional Urban Council of Hong Kong, 1981.

Laurance, Jeremy. "Extinct: The Dolphin That Could Not Live Alongside Man." http:// environment.independent.co.uk/wildlife/article2843953.ece (Accessed 2007).

Law, Kar. Ed. *Transcending the Times: King Hu and Eileen Chang.* Hong Kong: The Provisional Urban Council of Hong Kong, 1998.

Ledderose, Lothar. *Ten Thousand Things: Module and Mass Production in Chinese Art.* Princeton: Princeton University Press, 2000.

Lefebvre, Henri. *The Production of Space.* Trans. Donald Nicholson-Smith. Oxford, UK: Blackwell, 1991.

Leung, Ping-kwan. "Urban Cinema and the Cultural Identity of Hong Kong." In *The Cinema of Hong Kong: History Arts, Identity.* Ed. Poshek Fu and David Desser. Cambridge, UK: Cambridge University Press, 2000. 227–251.

Li, Ang. *Shafu.* Taipei: Lien-Ching Publishing House, 1983.

Li, Giancheng. *Fiction of Enlightenment.* Honolulu: University of Hawai'i Press, 2004.

Liao, Guoqiang. "Zhonguo shaoshu minzu shengtaiguan dui kezhixu fazhan de jiejian he qifa" (China's national minorities' ecological consciousness as a reference and inspiration for sustainable development). *Yunnan minzu xueyuan xuebao* (Journal of Yuannan Institute of Nationalities) 9 (2001): 160–163.

Lin, Xiaoping. "New Chinese Cinema of the 'Sixth Generation': A Distant Cry of Forsaken Children." *Third Text* 16/3 (September 2002): 277–306.

———. "Jia Zhangke's Cinematic Trilogy: A Journey across the Ruins of Post-Mao China." In *Chinese-Language Film: Historiography, Poetics, Politics.* Ed. Sheldon H. Lu and Emilie Yueh-yu Yeh. Honolulu: University of Hawai'i Press, 2005. 186–209.

Liu, Jianguo, and Jared Diamond. "China's Environment in a Globalizing World: How China and the Rest of the World Affect Each Other." *Nature* No. 435 (June 2005): 1179–1186.

Liu, John D. "Environmental Challenges Facing China Rehabilitation of the Loess Plateau." http://unep.org/pcmu/project_reference/docs/BB_170707Large_scale_ecosystem_ restoration_JPMorgan_Essay_2005.pdf (Accessed December 3, 2007).

Liu, Kang. *Globalization and Cultural Trends in China.* Honolulu: University of Hawai'i Press, 2004.

Liu, Yiwei. "Dangdai Zhongguoren zongjiao xinyang diaocha" (A survey of contemporary Chinese religious beliefs). *Liaowang dongfang zhoukan (Oriental Outlook Weekly)* Issue 6 (February 8, 2007).

Liu, Yong. "Wu Guanzhong's *People's Dwellings at Sanxia* shown to the Public in Chongqing." *Chongqing Shangbao.* http://cq.qq.com/a/20070209/000027.htm (Accessed April 16, 2007).

Lorentz, Todd. "Nonduality, Language, and the Buddhist Doctrine of Anatman." *Crossing Boundaries? An Interdisciplinary Journal* 1/2 (Spring 2002): 60–77.

Lu, Duanfang. *Remaking Chinese Urban Form: Modernity, Scarcity and Space, 1949–2005.* London: Routledge, 2006.

Lu, Sheldon H. *China, Transnational Visuality, Global Postmodernity.* Stanford: Stanford University Press, 2001.

———. *Chinese Modernity and Global Biopolitics: Studies in Literature and Visual Culture*. Honolulu: University of Hawai'i Press, 2007.

———. "Tear Down the City: Reconstructing Urban Space in Contemporary Chinese Popular Cinema and Avant-Garde Art." In *The Urban Generation: Chinese Cinema and Society at the Turn of the Twentieth-First Century*. Ed. Zhang Zhen. Durham, NC: Duke University Press, 2007. 137–160.

Lu, Sheldon H., and Emilie Yueh-yu Yeh. Eds. *Chinese-Language Film: Historiography, Poetics, Politics*. Honolulu: University of Hawai'i Press, 2005.

Lü, Xinyu. *Jilu Zhongguo: dangdai Zhongguo xin jilupian yundong* (Recording China: The New Documentary movement in contemporary China). Beijing: Sanlian, 2003.

———. "*West of the Tracks*: History and Class Consciousness" (*Tiexiqu: lishi yu jieji yishi*). *Dushu 1* (January 2004): 3–15.

Lukács, Georg. *Studies in European Realism*. London: Hillway Publishing Co., 1950.

Lyotard, Jean-François. "Ecology as Discourse of the Secluded." In *Green Studies Reader: From Romanticism to Ecocriticism*. Ed. Laurence Coupe. London: Routledge, 2000. 135–138.

Ma, Jun. *China's Water Crisis*. Norwalk: Eastbridge, 2004.

MacDougall, David. "Ethnographic Film: Failure and Promise." *Annual Review of Anthropology* Vol. 7 (1978): 405–425.

Machle, Edward. *Nature and Heaven in the Xunzi: A Study of the Tian Lun*. Albany: State University of New York Press, 1993.

Mao, Tse-tung (Zedong). "Xue" (Snow). In *Mao Zedong shici da cidian* (A dictionary of Mao Zedong's poems). Ed. Ding Li. Beijing: Zhongguo funu chubanshe, 1993. 148.

Marcus, Millicent. *Italian Film in the Light of Neorealism*. Princeton: Princeton University Press, 1986.

Martha, Andrew. *China's Water Warriors: Citizen Action and Policy Change*. Ithaca and London: Cornell University Press, 2008.

Martin, Frank. *Situating Sexualities: Queer Representations in Taiwanese Fiction, Film and Public Culture*. Hong Kong: Hong Kong University Press, 2003.

Marx, Karl. *Capital*. New York: Vintage, 1976.

Mathews, Gordon. Book Review of Ackbar Abbas, *Hong Kong: Culture and the Politics of Disappearance*. *Journal of Asian Studies* 57.4 (November 1998): 1112–1113.

McDougall, Bonnie S. *The Yellow Earth: A Film by Chen Kaige with a Complete Translation of the Filmscript*. Hong Kong: The Chinese University Press, 1991.

McDowell, Michael J. "The Bakhtinian Road to Ecological Insight." In *Ecocriticism Reader*. Ed. Cheryll Glotfelty and Harold Fromm. Athens and London: University of Georgia Press, 1996. 371–391.

McGowan, Todd. *The Real Gaze: Film Theory after Lacan*. Albany: SUNY Press, 2007.

McGowan, Todd, and Sheila Kunkle. "Introduction: Lacanian Psychoanalysis in Film Theory." In *Lacan and Contemporary Film*. Ed. Todd McGowan and Sheila Kunkle. New York: Other Press, 2004. xi–xxix.

McGrath, Jason. "The Independent Cinema of Jia Zhangke: From Postsocialist Realism to a Transnational Aesthetic." In *The Urban Generation: Chinese Cinema and Society at the Turn of the Twenty-First Century*. Ed. Zhang Zhen. Durham: Duke University Press, 2007. 81–114.

———. "The Cinema of Displacement: The Three Gorges Dam in Feature Film and Video." *Displacement: The Three Gorges Dam and Contemporary Chinese Art*. Ed. Wu Hung, with Jason McGrath and Stephanie Smith. Chicago: Smart Museum of Art, University of Chicago, 2008. 33–46.

Meeker, Joseph. *The Comedy of Survival*. Tucson: University of Arizona Press, 1997.

Merchant, Carolyn. *Radical Ecology: The Search for a Livable World*. New York and London: Routledge, 1992.

Mertha, Andrew. *China's Water Warriors: Citizen Action and Policy Change*. Ithaca and London: Cornell University Press, 2008.

Mi, Jiayan. "The Visual Imagined Communities: Media State, Virtual Citizenship and *TELE*vision in *River Elegy*." *The Quarterly Review of Film and Video* 22.4 (October–December 2005): 327–340.

———. "Entropic Anxiety and the Allegory of Disappearance: Toward a Hydro-Utopianism in Zheng Yi's *Old Well* and Zhang Wei's *Old Boat*." *China Information* 21 no. 1 (March 2007): 104–140.

Mian, Mian. *Candy*. Boston: Back Bay Press, 2003.

Mitchell, W. T. J. "Preface to the Second Edition of *Landscape and Power*: Space, Place, and Landscape." In *Landscape and Power*. Ed. W. T. J. Mitchell. Chicago and London: University of Chicago Press, 2002. vii–xi.

Miyoshi, Masao. "Turn to the Planet: Literature, Diversity, and Totality." In *Globalization and the Humanities*. Ed. Leilei Li. Hong Kong: Hong Kong University Press, 2004. 19–35.

Moore, Gary T., and Reginald G. Golledge. Eds. *Environmental Knowing: Theories, Research and Methods*. Stroudsburgh, PA: Dowden, Hutchinson & Ross, 1976.

Morton, Timothy. *Ecology without Nature: Rethinking Environmental Aesthetics*. Cambridge, MA: Harvard University Press, 2007.

Munakata, Kiyohiko. "Concepts of *Lei* and *Kan-lei* in Early Chinese Art Theory." In *Theories of the Arts in China*. Ed. Susan Bush and Christian Murck. Princeton: Princeton University Press, 1983. 105–131.

Murphy, Patrick. *Literature, Nature, and Other: Ecofeminist Critiques*. Albany, NY: State University of New York Press, 1995.

Ng, Ho. "Jianghu revisited: Towards a Reconstruction of the Martial Arts World." In *A Study of the Hong Kong Swordplay Film*. Ed. Lau Shing-hon, op. cit. 73–86.

Ng, Sheung-yuen Daisy. "Feminism in the Chinese Context: Li Ang's *The Butcher's Wife*." In *Gender Politics in Modern China: Writing & Feminism*. Ed. Barlow E. Tani. Durham: Duke University Press, 1993. 266–289.

Ng, Tze-Wei. "Not even HK's storied Star Ferry can face down developers." *International Herald Tribune* (November 10, 2006). http://www.iht.com/articles/2006/11/10/news/ferry.php (Accessed May 30, 2008).

Ni, Zhen. *Memories from the Beijing Film Academy: The Genesis of China's Fifth Generation*. Trans. Chris Berry. Durham: Duke University Press. 2002.

———. "Huimou <delamu> (Reflecting on *Delamu*)." *Dangdai dianying* (Contemporary Cinema) 4 (2004): 4–7.

Nichols, Bill. *Introduction to Documentary*. Bloomington & Indianapolis: Indiana University Press, 2001.

Nordhaus, Ted, and Michael Shellenberger. *Break Through: From the Death of Environmentalism to the Politics of Possibility*. Boston: Houghton Mifflin Company, 2007.

Oakes, Tim. "The Village as Theme Park: Mimesis and Authenticity in Chinese Tourism." In *Translocal China: Linkages, Identities and the Reimagining of Space*. Ed. Tim Oakes and Louisa Schein. London and New York: Routledge, 2006. 166–192.

Ong, Aihwa. *Flexible Citizenship: The Cultural Logics of Transnationality*. Durham, NC: Duke University Press, 1999.

Oon, Clarissa. "Multi-coloured Hero Soars." *The Straits Times* (January 15, 2003). http://global. factiva.com/en/arch/print_results.asp (Accessed March 11, 2003).

Phillips, Dana. *The Truth of Ecology: Nature, Culture, and Literature in America*. New York: Oxford University Press, 2003.

Pile, Steve, and Nigel Thrift. "Mapping the Subject." In *Mapping the Subject: Geographies of Cultural Transformation*. Ed. Steve Pile and Nigel Thrift. London: Routledge, 1995. 13–51.

Plant, G. W., C. S. Covil, and R. A. Hughes. *Site Preparation for the New Hong Kong International Airport: Design, Construction and Performance of the Airport Platform*. London: Thomas Telford, 1998.

Plumwood, Val. "Animals and Ecology: Towards a Better Integration (2003)." http://hdl.handle. net/1885/41767.

Pocock, Douglas C. D. *Humanistic Geography and Literature: Essays on the Experience of Place*. London: Croom Helm Ltd., 1981.

Powers, John. *A Concise Encyclopedia of Buddhism*. Oxford: Oneworld Publications, 2000.

Quandt, James. "Unknown Pleasures: The Films of Jia Zhangke." In Julia White, et al., *Mahjong: Art, Film, and Change in China*. Berkeley: Berkeley Museum of Art and Pacific Film Archive, University of California, 2008. 109–114.

Queen, Sarah A. *From Chronicle to Canon: The Hermeneutics of the Spring and Autumn Annals according to Tung Chung-shu*. Cambridge: Cambridge University Press, 1996.

Rehm, Jean-Pierre, et al. *Tsai Mingliang*. Paris: Dis Voir, 1999.

Ren, Jiyu. Ed. *Zhongguo fojiao shi* (A history of Chinese Buddhism). Beijing: Zhongguo shehui kexue chubanshe, 1981.

Robbins, Bruce. "The Sweatshop Sublime." *PMLA* 117.1 (2002): 84–97.

Rosendale, Steven. *The Greening of Literary Scholarship: Literature, Theory, and the Environment*. Iowa City: University of Iowa Press, 2002.

Ross, Andrew. *The Chicago Gangster Theory of Life: Nature's Debt to Society*. London: Verso, 1994.

Royle, Nicholas. "Déjà Vu." In *Post-Theory: New Directions in Criticism*. Ed. Martin McQuillan, et al. Edinburgh: Edinburgh University Press, 1999. 3–20.

Rycroft, Charles. *Psychoanalysis and Beyond*. Ed. Peter Fuller. Chicago: University of Chicago Press, 1985.

———. *Rycroft on Analysis and Creativity*. Washington Square: New York University Press, 1992.

Said, Edward. *Orientalism*. New York: Vintage, 1979.

Sarkar, Bhaskar. "Hong Kong Hysteria: Martial Arts Tales from a Mutating World." In *At Full Speed: Hong Kong Cinema in a Borderless World*. Ed. Esther C. M. Yau. Minneapolis: University of Minnesota Press, 2001. 159–176.

Schafer, Edward H. *The Divine Woman: Dragon Ladies and Rain Maidens in T'ang Literature*. San Francisco: Northpoint Press, 1980.

Schama, Simon. *Landscape and Memory*. London: Fontana Press, 1996.

Schell, Orville. *Virtual Tibet*. New York: Metropolitan Books, 2000.

Seremetakis, C. Nadia. *The Senses Still: Perception and Memory as Material Culture in Modernity*. Boulder: Westview, 1994.

Shabkar, Tsogdruk Rangdrol. *Food of Bodhisattvas: Buddhist Teachings on Abstaining from Meat*. Trans. The Padmakara Translation Group. Boston and London: Shambhala Publications, 2004.

The Shambhala Dictionary of Buddhism and Zen. Boston: Shambhala, 1991.

Shan, Wanli. *Zhongguo jilu dianying shi* (A history of Chinese documentary films). Beijing: Zhongguo diangying chubanshe, 2005.

Shapiro, Judith. *Mao's War against Nature: Politics and Environment in Revolutionary China*. London and New York: Cambridge University Press, 2001.

Shapiro, Kenneth, and Marion W. Copeland. "The Caring Sleuth: Portrait of an Animal Rights Activists." In *Beyond Animal Rights*. New York: Continuum, 1996. 126–146.

———. "Toward a Critical Theory of Animal Issues in Fiction." *Society & Animals* (Editors' Note) 13/4 (2005).

Shi, Yaohua. "Maintaining Law and Order: New Tales of the People's Police." In *The Urban Generation: Chinese Cinema and Society at the Turn of the Twentieth-First Century*. Ed. Zhang Zhen. Durham, NC: Duke University Press, 2007. 316–343.

Shih, Shu-mei. *Visuality and Identity: Sinophone Articulations across the Pacific*. Berkeley: University of California Press, 2008.

Short, Stephen, and Susan Jakes. "Making of a Hero." Timeasia.com. http://www.time.com/time/asia/features/hero/story.html (Accessed January 18, 2002).

Silbergeld, Jerome. *China into Film: Frames of Reference in Contemporary Chinese Cinema*. London: Reaktion Books, 1999.

———. *Hitchcock with a Chinese Face: Cinematic Doubles, Oedipal Triangles, and China's Moral Voice*. Seattle: University of Washington Press, 2004.

———, et al. *Outside In: Chinese x American x Contemporary x Art*. Princeton, New Haven and London: Princeton University Art Museum, The P. Y. and Kinmay W. Tang Center for East Asian Art, and Yale University Press, 2009.

Silverman, Kaja. *The Subject of Semiotics*. New York: Oxford University Press, 1983.

Sima, Qian. *Records of the Grand Historian*. Trans. Burton Watson. New York: Columbia University Press, 1993.

Sima, Xiangru. "Sir Fantasy." In *Chinese Rhyme-Prose: Poems in the Fu Form from the Han and Six Dynasties Periods*. Trans. Burton Watson. New York: Columbia University Press, 1971. 29–54.

Smart, Alan, and Wing-Shing Tang. "Illegal Building in China and Hong Kong." In *Restructuring the Chinese City: Changing Society, Economy and Space*. Ed. Laurence J. C. Ma and Fulong Wu. New York: Routledge, 2005.

Song, Lidao. "Dushi fojiao de xiandai yiyi" (The modern significance of metropolitan Buddhism). In *Buddhism in the Metropolis*. Ed. Jue Xing. 73–81.

Song, Lili. "Lun wenxue de 'shengtai wei'" (On the niche of literature). *Wenyi lilun qianyan* (Frontiers of Literary Theory) No. 3 (April 2006): 126–161.

Song, Yu. "The Gao Tang Rhapsody." In *Classical Chinese Literature: An Anthology of Translations: Volume I: From Antiquity to the Tang Dynasty*. Ed. John Minford and Joseph S. M. Lau. New York: Columbia University Press, 2000. 273.

Spivak, Gayatri Chakravorty. *Death of a Discipline*. New York: Columbia University Press, 2003.

Spottiswoode, Raymond. *A Grammar of the Film*. Berkeley: University of California Press, 1959.

Stein, Rolf. *The World in Miniature: Container Gardens and Dwellings in Far Eastern Religious Thought*. Stanford: Stanford University Press, 1990.

Stephenson, Neal. *The Diamond Age or a Young Lady's Illustrated Primer*. New York: Bantam Books, 1995.

Sterckx, Roel. *The Animal and the Daemon in Early China*. Albany, NY: State University of New York, 2000.

Sterling, Bruce. *Schismatrix Plus*. New York: Ace Books, 1996.

Stibbe, Arran. "Language, Power and the Social Construction of Animals." *Society and Animals* 9/2(2001): 145–161.

Stilgoe, John R. "Foreword." In *The Poetics of Space: The Classic Look at How We Experience Intimate Places*. Trans. Maria Jolas. Boston: Beacon Press, 1994. vii–x.

Strauss, Bob, "A Little 'Hero' Worship Is in Order." http://u.dailynews.com/cda/article/print/0,1 674,211%7E24684%7E2360551,00.html (Accessed December 17, 2004).

Su, Xiaokang, Wang Luxiang, and Xia Jun. Eds. *He Shang* (Deathsong of the Yellow River). Hong Kong: Zhongguo dushu kanxingshe, 1988.

Sun, Shao-yi. "In Search of the Erased Half: *Suzhou River*, *Lunar Eclipse*, and the Sixth Generation Filmmakers of China." In *One Hundred Years of Chinese Cinema: A Generational Dialogue*. Ed. Haili Kong, et al. Norwalk: Eastbridge, 2006. 183–198.

Sunshine, Linda. Ed. Crouching Tiger Hidden Dragon: *A Portrait of the Ang Lee Film*. New York: New Market Press, 2002.

Tang, Yuankai. "Action Plan, China translates its awareness of environmental protection into workable laws." *beijingreview.com*. http://www.bjreview.com.cn/ender/txt/200612/22/content_51643.htm (Accessed March 20, 2007).

Teiser, F. Stephen. *The Ghost Festival in Medieval China*. Princeton: Princeton University Press, 1988.

Teo, Stephen. "Local and Global Identity: Whither Hong Kong Cinema?" *Senses of Cinema* (April 19, 2000). http://www.sensesofcinema.com/contents/00/7/hongkong.html (Accessed May 30, 2008).

———. "Love and Swords: The Dialectics of Martial Arts Romance, A Review of *Crouching Tiger, Hidden Dragon*." *Senses of Cinema* Issue 11 (December 2000–January 2001). http://www.sensesofcinema.com/contents/00/11/crouching.html (Accessed March 26, 2007).

———. "There Is No Sixth Generation": Director Li Yang on *Blind Shaft* and His Place in Chinese Cinema." *Senses of Cinema* (June 2003), http://www.archive.sensesofcinema.com/contents/03/27/li_yang.html.

Tester, Keith. *Animals and Society: The Humanity of Animal Rights*. London: Routledge, 1991.

Thibodeau, John G., and Philip B. Williams. "Preface." In *The River Dragon Has Come!: The Three Gorges Dam and the Fate of China's Yangtze River and Its People*. Ed. John G. Thibodeau and Philip B. Williams. Trans. Yi Ming. Armonk: M. E. Sharpe. ix–xiv.

Thierez, Régine. *Barbarian Lens: Western Photographers of the Qianlong Emperor's European Palaces*. Amsterdam: Gordon and Breach, 1998.

Tian, Zhuangzhuang. Interviewed by Zhang Tongdao, Xie Yuzhang, "<Delamu>: huxi shanshui" (*Delamu*: Breathing in mountains and rivers). *Dianying yishu* (Cinematic Art) 5 (2004): 31–36.

———. "*Xuanze le yisheng zhong zuiyukuai de shiye*" (The most enjoyable project in my life). *Beijing dianying xueyuan xuebao* (The Journal of Beijing Film Academy) 6 (2004): 62–92.

Topping, Audrey Ronning. "Foreword: The River Dragon Has Come!" In *The River Dragon Has Come!: The Three Gorges Dam and the Fate of China's Yangtze River and Its People.* Ed. John G. Thibodeau and Philip B. Williams. Trans. Yi Ming. Armonk: M. E. Sharpe, 1988. xv–xxix.

Tseng, Chen-chen. "Myth as Rhetoric: The Quest of the Goddess in Six Dynasties Poetry." *Journal of National Chung Cheng University, Sec. I: Humanities* 6.1 (1995): 235–278.

Tuan, Yi-fu. "Images and Mental Maps." *Annals of the Association of American Geographers* Vol. 65, No. 2 (June 1975): 205–213.

———. *Space and Place: The Perspective of Experience.* Minneapolis: University of Minnesota, 1977.

———. *Topophilia: A Study of Environmental Perceptions, Altitudes and Values.* New York: Columbia University Press, 1989.

———. *Passing Strange and Wonderful: Aesthetics, Nature, and Culture.* Washington, D.C.: Island Press, 1993.

Tucker, Mary Evelyn, and Duncan Ryuken Williams. Eds. *Buddhism and Ecology: The Interconnections of Dharma and Deeds.* Cambridge: Harvard University Press, 1997.

UNDP, "Beyond Scarcity: Power, Poverty and the Global Water Crisis" (2006). http://hdr.undp.org/en/reports/global/hdr2006/ (Accessed March 25, 2007).

Urban, Greg. *Metaculture: How Culture Moves through the World.* Minneapolis: University of Minnesota Press, 2001.

Van Slyke, Lyman P. *Yangtze: Nature, History, and the River.* Reading: Addison Wesley, 1988.

Vidler, Anthony. *The Architectural Uncanny: Essays in the Modern Unhomely.* Cambridge, MA: The MIT Press, 1992.

Waley, Arthur. "The Gao Tang Rhapsody." In *An Anthology of Translations: From Antique to the Tang Dynasty.* Ed. John Minford and Joseph Lau. New York: Columbia University Press, 2000. 272–278.

Wang, Ban. *Illuminations from the Past: Trauma, Memory, and History in Modern China.* Stanford, CA: Stanford University Press, 2004.

Wang, Gang. "90 niandaihou Zhongguo jilupian de `zhenshigan' he fengge yanbian" (The concept of "reality" and stylistic change in Chinese documentary film in the 1990s). Master's Thesis. Beijing Film Academy, May 2007.

Wang, Tao, et al. "Sandy Desertification in Northern China." In *China's Environment and the Challenge of Sustainable Development.* Ed. Kristen A Day. New York and London: M. E. Sharpe, 2005. 233–256.

Wang, Xinyu. "Mosheng de daoyan yu mosheng de yingpian: Mantan Zhang Ming ji qi dianying 'Wushan Yunyu'" (An obscure director and an obscure film: A casual look at Zhang Ming and his movie "Wushan Clouds and Rain"). *Dianying Yishu* (Film Art) Vol. 3 (1996): 75–79.

Wang, Yiman. "The Amateur's Lightning Rod: DV Documentary in Postsocialist China." *Film Quarterly* 58.4 (Summer 2005): 16–26.

Wang, You. "Luobai Aosike *Yingxiong* weihe nanguo Meiren guan" (Why *Hero* failed to win an Oscar and enter the gateway to America). http://www.people.com.cn/GB/yule/8222/30797/30798/2230905.html (Accessed March 27, 2007).

Wang, Yuejin. "The Cinematic Other and the Cultural Self? Decentering the Cultural Identity on Cinema." *Wide Angle* 11, No. 2 (1989): 32–39.

Ward, Kevin. "From the Pens of 'Leaping' Poets: Parataxis as a 'Leap' between Robert Bly and Wallace Stevens." *Parataxis* (Spring 2003). http://writing.colostate.edu/gallery/parataxis/ward.htm (Accessed June 7, 2008).

Warren, Karen J. Ed. *Ecological Feminism*. New York: Routledge, 1997.

Waters, Malcolm. *Modern Sociological Theory*. London: Sage, 1994.

Watson, Burton. *Early Chinese Literature*. New York: Columbia University Press, 1962.

Wei, Ming. "The Three Gorges Dam Will Turn the Fast-flowing Yangtze into Stagnant, Polluted Reservoir." In *Three Gorges Probe* (November 1999). http://www.threegorgesprobe.org/probeint/threegorges/tgp/tgp12.html (Accessed June 4, 2007).

Weller, Robert. *Discovering Nature: Globalization and Environmental Culture in China and Taiwan*. Cambridge, UK: Cambridge University Press, 2006.

Wen, Yiduo. "Sishui (Dead water)." In *Zhonghua shige bainian jinghua* (*Anthology of the Best Modern Poems in One Hundred Years*). Beijing: Renmin wenxue chubanshe, 2003. 41–42.

Williams, Paul. *Mahayana Buddhism*. London and New York: Routledge, 1993.

Williams, Raymond. *Keywords: A Vocabulary of Culture and Society*. New York: Oxford University Press, 1983.

Williams, Tony. "Thatcher's Orwell: The Spectacle of Excess in Brazil." In *Crisis Cinema: The Apocalyptic Idea in Postmodern Narrative Film*. Ed. Christopher Sharrett. Washington, D.C.: Maisonneuve Press, 1993. 203–221.

Woodside, Alexander. "Reconciling the Chinese and Western Theory Worlds in an Era of Western Development Fatigue (A Comment)." *Modern China* Vol. 24, No. 2 (April 1998): 121–134.

Wu, Hung. "Ruins, Fragmentation, and the Chinese Modern/Postmodern." In *Inside Out: New Chinese Art*. Ed. Gao Minglu. Berkeley, Calif.: University of California Press, 1998. 59–66.

Wu, Hung, with Jason McGrath and Stephanie Smith. *Displacement: The Three Gorges Dam and Contemporary Chinese Art*. Chicago: Smart Museum of Art, University of Chicago, 2008.

WWAP. "Water for People, Water for Life." (2003). http://www.unesco.org/water/wwap/ (Accessed March 20, 2007).

Xiao, Tong. *Wen xuan, or Selections of Refined Literature: Volume 1, Rhapsodies on Metropolises and Capitals* and *Volume 2, Rhapsodies on Sacrifices, Hunting, Travel, Sightseeing, Palaces and Halls, Rivers and Seas*. Trans. David Knechtges. Princeton: Princeton University Press, 1982, 1987.

Xin, Hua. "Zhang Yimou criticized for damaging environment of famous scenic lake." People's Daily online (November 1, 2006). http://english.people.com.cn/200611/01/eng20061101_317255.html (Accessed March 23, 2007).

Xu, Gary G. *Sinascape: Contemporary Chinese Cinema*. Lanham: Rowman & Littlefield Publishers, 2007.

Xu, Haofeng. "Zhang Yimou de *Yingxiong* (Zhang Yimou's *Hero*)." *Dianying yishu* No. 2 (2003): 4–9.

Xu, Wenming. "Dushi fojiao de zuoyong yu yiyi" (The role and significance of metropolitan Buddhism). In *Buddhism in the Metropolis*. Ed. Jue Xing. 89–99.

Xue, Cheng. "Zongjiao—goajian hexie shehui de dutie jingshen ziyuang (Religion—the Unique Spiritual Resources for the Building of a Harmonious Society." www.Zhongguo.net (March 8, 2006). http://www.lianghui.org.cn/chinese/zhuanti/2006lh/1147512.htm (Accessed July 5, 2007).

Xunzi. *Xunzi: Basic Writings*. Trans. Burton Watson. New York: Columbia University Press, 2003.

Yang, Ming-tu. "Shengtai nuxing zhuyi pingxi." *Shengtai renwen zhuyi 3 (Ecohumanism)*. Ed. Yao-fu Lin. Taipei: Shu-lin Ltd., 2006.

Yang, Zenwen. "Renjian fojiao yu xiandai chengshi wenming jianshe" (Earthly Buddhism and the building of modern city civilization). In *Buddhism in the Metropolis*. Ed. Jue Xing.

Yao, Xiaolei. "Jingdiande jiegou yu chongjian, yishuzhongde xia, tianxia, yu yingxiong — ye you Zhang Yimou de *Yingxiong* shuoqi" (Classic constructions and reconstructions: *xia, tianxia*, and heroism in art—speaking from Zhang Yimou's *Hero*). *Zhongguo bijiao wenxue* 51, No. 2 (2003): 40–51.

Yin, Hong. "Zai jiafengzhong zhangda: Zhongguo dalu xinshengdai de dianying shijie" (Growing up in a crevice: Mainland China's "Newborn Generation" and their cinematic world). *Ershiyi Shiji Shuangyuekan* (21st Century Bimonthly) Vol. 49 (October 1998): 88–93.

Zhang, Haiyang. "Gaojian hexie shehui yu chongjian you"shen"de shequ" (The construction of harmonious society and the rebuilding of the God-fearing communities)." *Zhongguo Minzubao* (Chinese Ethnic News) (March 24, 2006): 4.

Zhang, Huijun. "Guanzhu pingjing" (Concentrating on quietude). *Beijing dianying xueyuang xueba* (Journal of Beijing Film Academy) 6 (2004): 74–83.

Zhang, Jia-xuan. "Hero." *Film Quarterly* 58, No. 4 (2005): 51–52.

Zhang, Jinghong. "Tianye hezuozhong de qidai" (Expectations for cooperation in field work). *Minzu yishu yanjiu* (Studies in Ethnic Arts) 3 (2004): 69–76.

Zhang, Yingjin. *Screening China: Critical Interventions, Cinematic Reconfigurations, and the Transnational Imaginary in Contemporary Chinese Cinema*. Ann Arbor: Center for Chinese Studies of the University of Michigan, 2002.

——. *Chinese National Cinema*. London: Routledge, 2004.

——. "My Camera Doesn't Lie? Truth, Subjectivity, and Audience in Chinese Independent Film and Video." In *From Underground to Independent: Alternative Film Culture in Contemporary China*. Ed. Paul G. Pickowicz and Yingjin Zhang. New York: Rowman & Littlefield, 2006. 23–45.

Zhang, Yiwu. Ed. *Xiandai xing zhongguo* (Modernity and China). Kaifeng: Henan daxue chubanshe, 2005.

Zhang, Zhen. "Urban Dreamscape, Phantom Sisters, and the Identity of an Emergent Art Cinema." In *The Urban Generation: Chinese Cinema and Society at the Turn of the Twenty-First Century*. Ed. Zhang Zhen. Durham: Duke University Press, 2007. 344–387.

——. Ed. *The Urban Generation: Chinese Cinema and Society at the Turn of the Twenty-First Century*. Durham: Duke University Press, 2007.

Zheng, Jian. "Narrating the Petty Bourgeoisie: Lou Ye's *Suzhou River*." In *National, Transnational, and the International: Chinese Cinema and Asian Cinema in the Context of Globalization*. Proc. of the 2005 ACSS Conference. June 6–10, 2005. Beijing/Shanghai. 104–109.

Zhonghua kongzi xuehui (China Confucius study society). Ed. *Jingji quanqiu hua yu minzu wenhua: duoyuan fazhan* (Economic globalization and ethnic cultures: multiple developments). Beijing: Shehui kexue wenxian chubanshe, 2003.

Zhou, Weihui. *Shanghai Baby: A Novel*. New York: Washington Square Press, 2002.

Zhu, Ying. *Chinese Cinema during the Era of Reform: The Ingenuity of the System*. Westport, Conn.: Praeger Publishers, 2003.

Zhuangzi. *The Complete Works of Chuang-tzu*. Trans. Burton Watson. New York: Columbia University Press, 1970.

Žižek, Slavoj. *The Sublime Object of Ideology*. London: Verso, 1989.

——. *Interrogating the Real*. London/New York: Continuum, 2005.

——. *The Parallax View*. Cambridge: The MIT Press, 2006.

Zong, Bing. "*Hua shan shui xu*" (Preface on painting mountains and water). Trans. Jerome Silbergeld. In "Re-reading Zong Bing's Fifth-Century Essay on Landscape Painting: A Few Critical Notes." In Michael Sullivan, *festschrift* volume. Ed. Li Gongming. Shanghai: Shanghai shudian and Guangzhou Academy of Fine Art, forthcoming.

Index

Breinigsville, PA USA
02 March 2010
233437BV00002B/4/P